Faith, Power and Family

Christianity and Social Change
in French Cameroon

RELIGION IN TRANSFORMING AFRICA
ISSN 2398-8673

Series Editors
Barbara Bompani, Joseph Hellweg, Ousmane Kane and **Emma Wild-Wood**

Editorial Reading Panel
Robert Baum (Dartmouth College)
Dianna Bell (University of Cape Town)
Ezra Chitando (University of Zimbabwe)
Martha Frederiks (Utrecht University)
Paul Gifford (SOAS)
David M. Gordon (Bowdoin College)
Jörg Haustein (University of Cambridge)
Paul Lubeck (Johns Hopkins University-SAIS)
Philomena Mwaura (Kenyatta University, Nairobi)
Hassan Ndzovu (Moi University)
Ebenezer Obadare (University of Kansas)
Abdulkader I. Tayob (University of Cape Town)
M. Sani Umar (Northwestern University)
Stephen Wooten (University of Oregon)

Series description
The series is open to submissions that examine local or regional realities on the complexities of religion and spirituality in Africa. Religion in Transforming Africa will showcase cutting-edge research into continent-wide issues on Christianity, Islam and other religions of Africa; Traditional beliefs and witchcraft; Religion, culture & society; History of religion, politics and power; Global networks and new missions; Religion in conflict and peace-building processes; Religion and development; Religious rituals and texts and their role in shaping religious ideologies and theologies. Innovative, and challenging current perspectives, the series provides an indispensable resource on this key area of African Studies for academics, students, international policy-makers and development practitioners.

Please contact the Series Editors with an outline or download the proposal form at www.jamescurrey.com.

Dr Barbara Bompani, Reader in Africa and International Development, University of Edinburgh: b.bompani@ed.ac.uk
Dr Joseph Hellweg, Associate Professor of Religion, Department of Religion, Florida State University: jhellweg@fsu.edu
Professor Ousmane Kane, Prince Alwaleed Bin Talal Professor of Contemporary Islamic Religion & Society, Harvard Divinity School: okane@hds.harvard.edu
Dr Emma Wild-Wood, Senior Lecturer, African Christianity and African Indigenous Religions, University of Edinburgh: emma.wildwood@ed.ac.uk

Previously published titles in the series are listed at the back of this volume.

Faith, Power and Family
Christianity and Social Change in French Cameroon

CHARLOTTE WALKER-SAID

JAMES CURREY

James Currey
is an imprint of
Boydell & Brewer Ltd
PO Box 9, Woodbridge
Suffolk IP12 3DF (GB)
www.jamescurrey.com
and of
Boydell & Brewer Inc.
668 Mt Hope Avenue
Rochester, NY 14620-2731 (US)
www.boydellandbrewer.com

© Charlotte Walker-Said 2018
First published 2018
Paperback edition 2022

All rights reserved. No part of this book may be reproduced in any form, or by electronic or mechanical means, including information storage and retrieval systems, without permission in writing from the publishers, except by a reviewer who may quote brief passages in a review

The right of Charlotte Walker-Said to be identified as the author of this work has been asserted in accordance with sections 77 and 78 of the Copyright, Designs and Patents Act 1988

British Library Cataloguing in Publication Data
A catalogue record for this book is available on request from the British Library

ISBN 978-1-84701-182-4 (James Currey cloth)
ISBN 978-1-84701-183-1 (James Currey Africa only paperback)
ISBN 978-1-84701-327-9 (James Currey world paperback)

The publisher has no responsibility for the continued existence or accuracy of URLs for external or third-party internet websites referred to in this book, and does not guarantee that any content on such websites is, or will remain, accurate or appropriate

Typeset by Double Dagger Book Production in 9.5/13pt Georgia

For Maher

Contents

	List of Illustrations	viii
	Note on the Cover Image	ix
	Acknowledgments	x
	List of Abbreviations	xiv
	Maps	xv
1	Introduction: Marriage at the Nexus of Faith, Power, and Family	1

Part I French Rule, Social Politics, and New Religious Communities, 1914–1925

2	Christian Transmission and Colonial Imposition	53
3	African Catechists and Charismatic Activities	79
4	Evaluating Marriage and Forming a Virtuous Household	101
5	Faith, Family, and the Endurance of the Lineage	141

Part II Labor, Economic Transformation, and Family Life, 1925–1939

6	African Church Institutions in Action	173
7	African Agents of the Church and State: Male Violence and Productivity	209
8	Ethical Masculinity: The Church and the Patriarchal Order	237
9	The Significance of African Christian Communities Beyond Cameroon	271
	Bibliography	285
	Index	309

Illustrations

Maps

1. The Equatorial Forest Zone — xv
   Source: Derek Bruggeman, Patrick Meyfroidt, and Eric F. Lambin, "Production Forests as a Conservation Tool: Effectiveness of Cameroon's Land Use Zoning Policy," *Land Use Policy* 42 (January 1, 2015): 151–64 (https://doi.org/10.1016/j.landusepol.2014.07.012)

2. Major roads and railroads in Cameroon, 1914–1944 — xvi
   Source: Achille Mbembe, *La Naissance Du Maquis Dans Le Sud-Cameroun, 1920–1960 : Histoire Des Usages de La Raison En Colonie* (Paris: Karthala, 1996), 63 and 75, and ANOM Série Service des Travaux Publics et Chemins de Fer, 427/4

3. Regional boundaries and administrative centers of Cameroon, 1944 — xvii
   Source: Eugène Guernier and René Briat, *Cameroun, Togo, Encyclopédie de l'Afrique Française* (Paris: Éditions de l'Union Française, 1951), 33, 36, and 41

4. Political boundaries of French Cameroon, 1922–1960 — xviii
   Source: Cameroun, État Fédéré Orientale, *Journal Officiel*, October 1, 1961 (Yaoundé: Imprimerie Nationale)

5. Primary Catholic mission stations and larger secondary mission outposts in the French-governed Cameroon territory, 1914–1939 — xix
   Source: ACSSp. 2J1.9a3, "Vie du Diocèse de Douala," "Vie du Diocèse de Yaoundé"

6. Primary and secondary Catholic missions in the Yaoundé region, 1914–1939 — xx
   Source: ACSSp. 2J1.9a3, "Vie du Diocèse de Yaoundé"

7. Presbyterian missions in the French-governed Cameroon territory, 1914–1939 — xxi
   Source: Presbyterian Church in the U.S.A., 112th Annual report of the Board of Foreign Missions of the Presbyterian Church of the United States of America, 1949 (New York: Presbyterian Church, USA, 1949), 12

Note on the Cover Image

The image on the cover of this book is of the altar mosaic in the Notre Dame des Victoires Cathedral in Yaoundé, Cameroon, which was designed by Father Engelbert Mveng, S.J. Mveng, a Cameroonian Jesuit priest, as well as a historian, anthropologist, artist, philosopher, and theologian, is credited with conceiving of the "theology of life," which extends beyond classical "liberation theology" to promote the triumph of life over all forms of death. Mveng's philosophy and theology emphasized the relevance of the "invisible world" of creativity, spirituality, and the mystical in the defense of peoples subjugated by slavery, colonialism, neo-colonialism, racism, apartheid, and derision – which cause "death" to the human essence: history, ethnic roots, language, culture, faith, and dignity. Mveng, along with the Atélier de l'Art Nègre in Cameroon, specialized in political and religious leitmotif centered on what art historian Annette Schemmel terms "pluriculturalisme," or the inclusion of iconic images from the most culturally distinct parts of Cameroon and the areas of central-west Africa. This altar mosaic is considered to represent the welcoming Virgin Mary with the child, Jesus. According to Schemmel, Mveng transculturated canonical Immaculata iconography into a dual motif of axe-symmetrically superimposed twin figures with faces split into a dark and light side. Mveng is believed to have borrowed the facial figure design from iconic Dan masks of Liberia, which typically have a high forehead. Like the decorative imagery in churches in the Catholic tradition, Dan masks are used for protection and as a channel for communication with the spirit world. In 1964, Mveng offered that the altar mosaic represented Mary and Jesus as life's victory over death, as well as the principle of fertility through the dualities of masculine–feminine, child–adult, and individual–social.

In addition to designing the altar mosaic in the Notre Dame des Victoires Cathedral, Father Mveng and the Atélier de l'Art Nègre designed the Ugandan Martyrs Altar at Libermann College in Douala and also accepted church commissions throughout Africa and beyond.

Acknowledgments

This book has been a lengthy endeavor and I owe many people and institutions a great deal of thanks for their help along the way. I began this project during my doctoral studies at Yale University, where Robert Harms, John Merriman, and James C. Scott helped me learn how to think about the lives and strategies of rural people, entrepreneurs, migrants, laborers, farmers, pilgrims, friars, nuns, and a host of other, often obscured, historical agents who made social change possible throughout history in Africa. The guidance of these scholars was essential to the writing of this book. Ute Frevert was also an inspirational thinker and believer in my abilities to craft an interesting story. Abbas Amanat taught me the beauty of studying the history of a society's religious faith and challenged me to do away with standardized categories and eras and seek out unique historical moments. Valerie Hansen was a significant source of encouragement and she placed her trust in me early on. Her very earliest encouragements have kept me going to this day. Catherine T. Dunlop, my fellow graduate student at Yale, was my smartest intellectual challenger, keenest reader and editor, and dearest friend. Her work and thoughts on history and on life made a deep impact on me in our first years in graduate school, and I continue to be impressed by her scholarship, talent, and soulful reflection. My other fellow graduate students, including Thomas (Dodie) McDow, Jacob Dlamini, Daniel Brückenhaus, Sarah Cameron, Faith Hillis, Drew Konove, Taylor Spence, George R. Trumbull IV, and Sara McDougall – who is now a cherished colleague – were great sources of inspiration and support.

Before I even began my doctoral work, Emmanuel Kreike and Robert Tignor made a great impression on me at Princeton University and encouraged me to pursue further studies in African history. I am a professional historian today because of their careful consideration of my work. Anthony Grafton, Jeremy Adelman, and Gyan Prakash were also wonderfully inspiring and strengthened my resolve to pursue this profession.

During my year at Harvard, Caroline Elkins and Emmanuel Akyeampong offered critical opportunities to improve my knowledge and sharpen my skills. I am indebted also to Gloria Whiting, who was a brilliant discussion partner on pre-colonial African history and became a colleague and friend I very much admire.

The knowledge, advice, and support of scholars at the University of Chicago cannot go without recognition. Mark Bradley, Michael Geyer, and Susan Gzesh offered me the opportunity of a lifetime to continue my research in the most intellectually stimulating environment in the United States today. I am forever grateful for their confidence in my work and their influence in the field of human rights history. Mary Anne Case invited me to countless discussions, rigorous seminars, and lively dinners at the University of Chicago School of Law where my thoughts on gender and religion were sharply challenged. This book is very much a result of those fruitful moments. I must also thank Linda Zerilli, Jennifer Pitts, Lauren Berlant, John D. Kelly, Rachel Jean-Baptiste, and Tara Zahra for shining their light during those years. I gleaned an enormous amount from their reflections. Perhaps the single most influential mentor and colleague I met at Chicago was Emily Osborn, whose persistent encouragement and exacting criticisms shaped my work in countless ways. I owe her a debt of gratitude I can never repay.

At Webster University, Warren Rosenblum's insights and research were very motivating and his friendship was even more appreciated. I am deeply grateful to Lindsey Kingston for the opportunities provided by the Institute for Human Rights and Humanitarian Studies, and to Kelly Kate Pease and Lionel Cuillé for their collegiality and collaboration during my time in St. Louis.

The knowledge, advice, and support of scholars of Cameroon, Africa, European colonialism, Christianity, and human rights contributed enormously to this book. My deepest thanks to Ralph Austen, Frederick Cooper, Elizabeth Foster, Brian Peterson, Jean-Luc Enyegue, J.P. Daughton, Kenneth Orosz, Joel Cabrita, Rachel Kantrowitz, Jessica Pearson, Intisar Rabb, Nurfadzilah Yahaya, Liz Fink, Terry Peterson, Emmanuelle Bouilly, Ophelie Rillon, Derek Peterson, Brett Shadle, Keren Weitzberg, R. Marie Griffith, Camille Robcis, Paul Landau, Paul Ocobock, Zachary Kagan-Guthrie, Alden Young, Robyn d'Avignon, Patrick Kelly, Elizabeth Borgwardt, Lauren Coyle, Samuel Moyn, Will Reno, Danny Hoffman, Mahmood Mamdani, Hlonipha Mokoena, Abosede George, Gary Wilder, Benjamin Lawrance, Otieno Kisiara, Richard Joseph, James McCann, Edouard Boustin, Daniel Magaziner, Bradley Simpson, and Gregory Mann, who, at one point or another, invited me to discuss my work, read, edited, and critiqued parts of my manuscript, or provided a key insight at a critical moment and allowed this book to move forward.

This book would not exist without the generous financial support of many institutions. I am particularly grateful to the Fulbright Program and the Institute for International Education, as well as the Social Science Research Council for allowing me to live in Cameroon from 2007 to 2009 in order to carry out the bulk of the research for this book. At Yale, my thanks to the Department of History, the MacMillan Center, International Security Studies, the Smith-Richardson Foundation, and the Gilder Lehrman Center for the Study of Slavery, Resistance, and Abolition for grants that allowed me to travel to France and New York and carry out early and late-stage research. At the University of Chicago, the Program in Human Rights (now the Pozen Family Center for Human Rights) allowed me to conduct important research in the missionary archives in Paris between 2010 and 2012, and the Center for the Study of Gender and Sexuality provided me with a grant from the John E. Sawyer Seminar to support my writing. The American Historical Association provided critical support between postdoctoral appointments to continue research in France in 2013. At John Jay College of Criminal Justice-City University of New York, the Office for the Advancement of Research has provided consistent and generous support in funding publication costs, archive visits, and conference travel, the Research Foundation of CUNY has provided essential support in the later stages of writing and research, and the Office of the Dean for Recruitment and Diversity has provided me with generous leave time and mentorship opportunities.

My research for this book has taken me to many rich archives and libraries. In Cameroon, I would especially like to thank the archivists at the Archives Nationales du Cameroun in Yaoundé and Yves Mondo at the Archives Municipales de Douala. The Cooperation Française in Yaoundé also facilitated introductions to other institutions in Cameroon, including Friedrich-Ebert-Stiftung Kamerun. I am particularly grateful to Fr. Jean-Luc Enyegue, S.J. and Fr. Dr. Abel N'Djomon, S.J. for their introductions to the Jesuit community in Yaoundé and the faculty at the Université Catholique d'Afrique Centrale. In France, I owe a great deal of thanks to Father Gérard Vieira and Father Roger Tabard at the Spiritan Archives for providing crucial assistance and introducing me to many Cameroonian clerics as well as French Spiritan former missionaries. I am also deeply indebted to Claire-Lise Lombard at the Bibliothèque du Défap-Service protestant de mission in Paris for all her tireless assistance at all hours during the spring and summer months over the past seven years.

My colleagues at John Jay College have welcomed me since my arrival in New York, and they helped this book to continue to grow until the very end. Thanks in particular to Carlton Jama Adams, Jessica Gordon-Nembhard, Crystal Endsley, Teresa Booker, Sandrine Dikambi, Susan Kang, Samantha Majic, and Itai Sneh. I am fortunate to have had the strong support of our faculty and administrative leaders, including Jane Bowers, Anne Lopes, and Allison Pease, all of whom helped bring this book to fruition. I am fortunate that this book found a home at James Currey, which has had a long legacy of extraordinary Africanist scholarship. I am especially lucky to have worked with Emma Wild-Wood and Joseph Hellweg on the editorial board and Jaqueline Mitchell my loyal editor. Thanks to two anonymous referees of the manuscript for their excellent comments.

Finally, friends from all walks of life have encouraged me to complete and refine this book: thanks to Ania Bleszynski-Jayich, Andrew Jayich, Thomas Jackson, and Berin Szoka for their rigorous inquiries and thanks to many more from over two decades of friendship in Washington, DC, Princeton, New Haven, Cambridge, St. Louis, and New York. I am unable to express how grateful I am to my family and especially my mother, and for the love I have received from my wonderful Said parents, siblings, and nephews. I am especially blessed to have had two brothers, Robert and Alexander Walker, with whom I have shared the challenges and successes of childhood and adult life. Shaida Khan is the person who has been perhaps the most instrumental to the completion of this book, as she helped me care for an infant, and later, a toddler, during its later stages. I owe her an enormous debt of gratitude. Most important of all, I give all of my love to Maher and to our daughter Dahlia, who are the light of my world.

Abbreviations

ACCSp.	Archives de la Congrégation des Pères du Saint Esprit, Cheville-Larue
AEF	Africa Équatoriale Française
AFFPOL	Affaires Politiques
AGEFOM	Agence Économique de la France d'Outre-Mer
ANC	Archives Nationales du Cameroun
ANOM	Archives Nationales d'Outre-Mer
APA	Affaires Politiques et Administrative
APM	American Presbyterian Mission
CEBEC	Council of Baptist and Evangelical Churches of Cameroon
EEC	Eglise Evangélique du Cameroun
FB	Fonds Brutsch
FEB	Fonds Erika Brucker
FM	Fonds Ministerielles
LMEF	Ligue Missionaire des Étudiants de France
LUCEM	Ligue Universitaire Catholique et Coloniale
MF	Missions Françaises
PHS	Presbyterian Historical Society
SAC	Société Africaine de Culture
SJ	Services Judiciares
SMEP/DEFAP	Société des Missions Evangéliques de Paris [Paris Evangelical Missionary Society] / Service Protestant de Missions Défap
TP	Travaux Publiques
UPC	Union des Populations du Cameroun

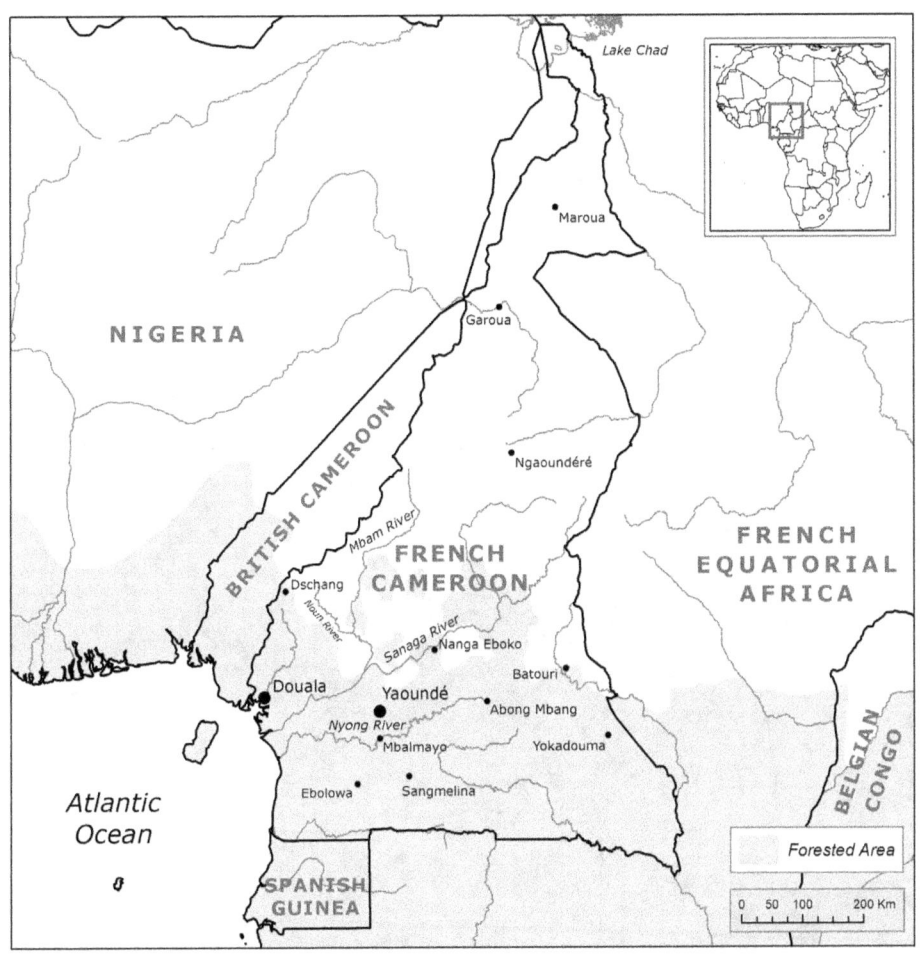

1 The Equatorial Forest Zone

2 Major roads and railroads in Cameroon, 1914–1944

3 Regional boundaries and administrative centers of Cameroon, 1944

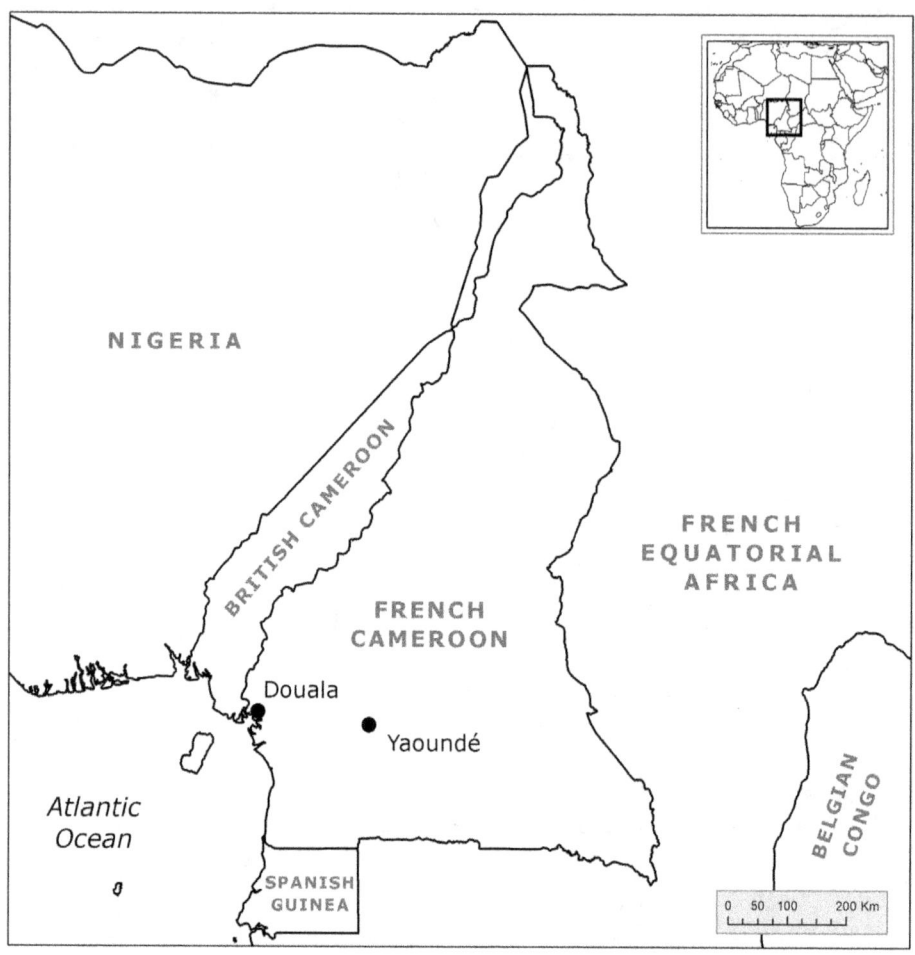

4 Political boundaries of French Cameroon, 1922–1960

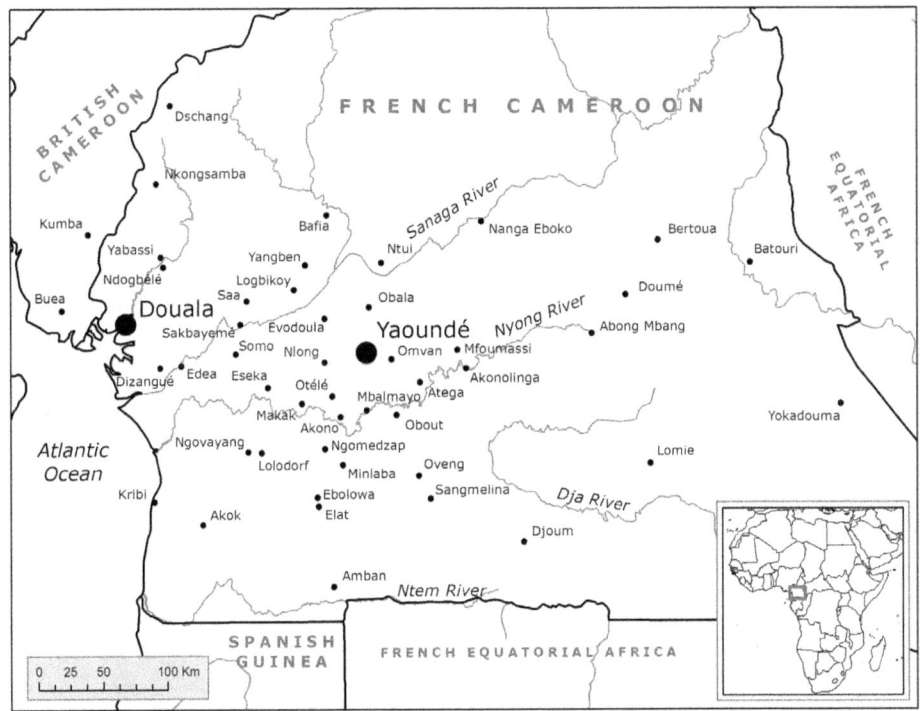

5 Primary Catholic mission stations and larger secondary mission outposts in the French-governed Cameroon territory, 1914–1939

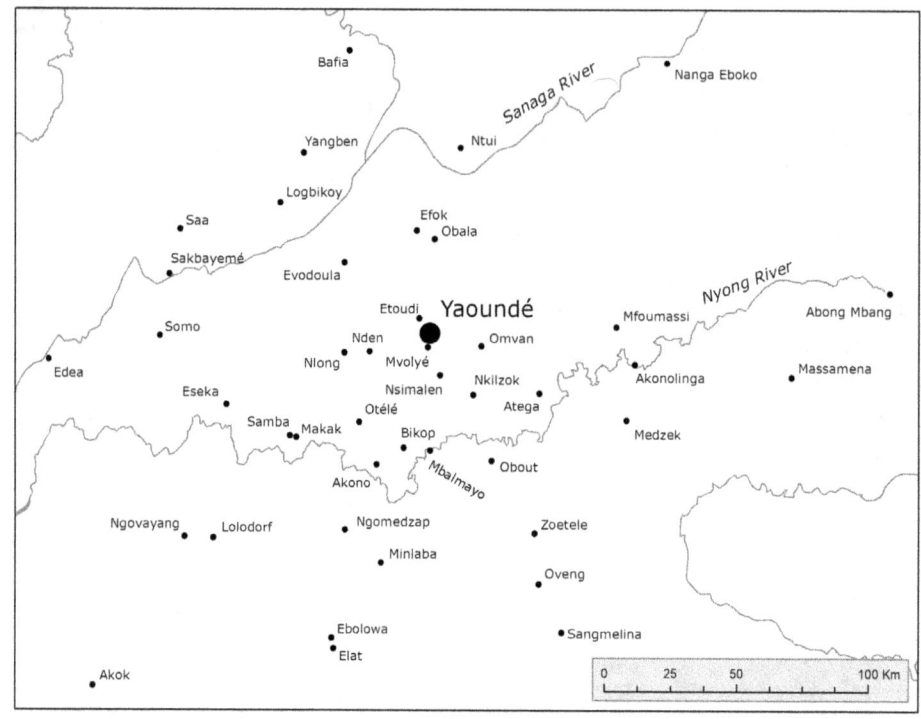

6 Primary and secondary Catholic missions in the Yaoundé region, 1914–1939

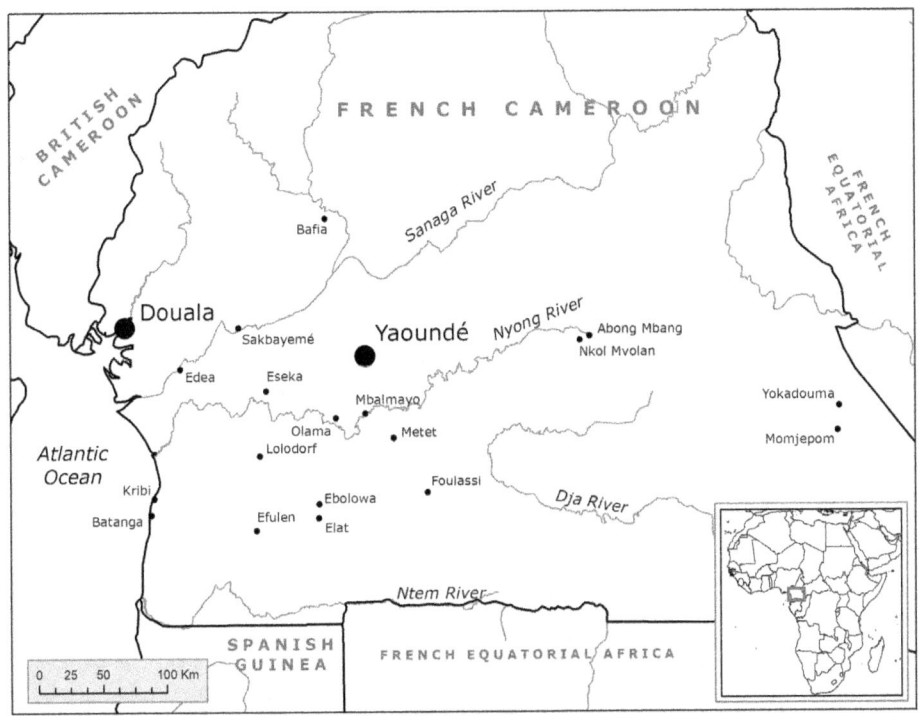

7 Presbyterian missions in the French-governed Cameroon territory, 1914–1939

CHAPTER 1

Introduction: Marriage at the Nexus of Faith, Power, and Family

On April 29, 1927, the African catechist Jean Bell whipped a local Catholic man, Matthias Bakatal, after he discovered through rumors in the village of Mangen Mandyok that Bakatal had secretly married a second wife, despite marrying his first wife according to the sacrament several years prior. Bell confronted Bakatal, saying to him, "You live like a pagan. You must come to confess." Bakatal then confessed to the French priests in the nearby Nlong Mission and received the sacrament of reconciliation, after which Bell assumed responsibility for deciding Bakatal's penance, which included divorcing his second wife, saying two rosaries per day for two weeks, and corporal punishment. Bell declared to Bakatal, "You must do public penitence because you were the subject of public scandal. I will beat you at the door of the chapel. Better to receive punishment now than in hell."[1] And so Jean Bell meted out twenty lashes to Matthais Bakatal before God and the missionaries in the Nlong chapel doorway, a liminal space that perhaps symbolically reminded the malefactor that he occupied a precarious position in the Catholic community.

African Christian men in French-administered Cameroon were both architects and targets of the strident religious rhetoric and intensive activism that characterized Christian evangelism in the southern regions of the territory between World War I and II. Over the course of the nineteenth and twentieth centuries, Christianity became a global religion and many African societies assumed a tenacious hold on the faith, using its tenets and institutions to reflect and adapt their existing worldviews.[2] French Cameroon during the

---

[1] Archives de la Congrégation des Pères du Saint-Esprit, Chevilly-Larue (hereafter ACSSp.), 2J21a Journal de la Mission Pierre Claver de Nlong, 29 avril 1927.

[2] The literature on Christianity in Africa is extensive, but those who have contributed the most to revealing the work of African societies in mobilizing evangelical forces and generating resonant rhetoric and activities necessary for organic and widespread Christian transmission include Karen Elise Fields, *Revival and Rebellion in Colonial Central Africa* (Princeton, NJ: Princeton University Press, 1985); Elizabeth Elbourne, *Blood Ground: Colonialism, Missions, and the Contest for Christianity in the Cape Colony and Britain, 1799–1853* (Montreal: McGill-Queen's University Press, 2008);

interwar decades provides a unique example of a diverse and competitive set of populations who became familiarized with Christianity through correspondingly competitive and diverse cadres of indigenous and foreign evangelists, and crafted a particularly assertive religion that provoked profound responses from those both inside and outside of African faith communities.

As the example of Matthias Bakatal shows, and as this study will reveal, Africans in Cameroon experienced the upheaval attendant with Christian conversion most frequently and poignantly in their family lives. This upheaval was concomitant with powerful economic, political, and legal changes that challenged conventional strategies for building one's family and reshaped its place in secular and religious life.[3] Between the late nineteenth century and 1960, when Cameroon was governed by successive European powers, close to 800,000 Africans converted to Catholic or Protestant Christianity and fundamentally transformed religious culture in the territory.[4] From the first appearance of foreign missionaries in Cameroon, indigenous translators and instructors evangelized alongside them, crafting accessible religious

---

J.D.Y. Peel, *Religious Encounter and the Making of the Yoruba* (Bloomington, IN: Indiana University Press, 2003); Paul Stuart Landau, *The Realm of the Word: Language, Gender, and Christianity in a Southern African Kingdom* (Portsmouth, NH: Heinemann, 1995).

[3] I am sensitive here and throughout this book to the concerns of Talal Asad regarding the recent formulations of "secular" modernity and the absolutist practices that "strip away ... myth, magic, and the sacred" from "direct reality." See Talal Asad, *Formations of the Secular: Christianity, Islam, Modernity* (Stanford: Stanford University Press, 2003), 13–14. While familiar with local southern Cameroonian societies' beliefs regarding the constantly communicative interfaces of the world of the spirit and the world of lived experience, I employ the term 'secular' to refer to experiences and processes that Cameroonians whom I interviewed described as being outside the category of the supernatural in this period and place.

[4] Statistics vary between Catholic, Protestant, and French government sources, but overall, estimates of Christians from all denominations in Cameroon between 1950 and 1960 hover between 700,000 and 800,000 souls. Philippe Laburthe-Tolra estimates that in 1943 there were 400,000 Christians in Cameroon, of which roughly 65–80,000 were Protestant. Philippe Laburthe-Tolra, *Vers La Lumiere? Ou, Le Désir d'Ariel: A Propos Des Beti Du Cameroun: Sociologie de La Conversion* (Paris: Karthala, 1999), 20. By 1960, missionary and government records point to a jump in recorded Christians to between 700,000 and 800,000. See Rapport de la 28ème Conférence des Missionaires du Cameroun, *Journal des Missions Evangéliques*, 1950, 340–60; Roger Onomo Etaba, *Histoire de l'Eglise Catholique Du Cameroun de Grégoire XVI à Jean-Paul II* (Paris: L'Harmattan, 2007); Jean Paul Messina and Jaap Van Slageren, *Histoire Du Christianisme Au Cameroun: Des Origines à Nos Jours : Approche Oecuménique* (Paris: Karthala, 2005), 67–87.

vernaculars and adapting new forms of reverence to local disciplines of spirituality.⁵ Cameroonians in the current day consider African Protestant and Catholic catechists who formed the first communities of believers in the late nineteenth century as pioneers of the Christian faith in the nation.⁶ At the onset of French and British military incursion in German Kamerun in 1914 and the flight of German and other foreign missionaries during the next two years, African proselyte agents assumed a new, privileged place in religious transmission in the territory and capitalized on their unimpaired autonomy to communicate Christianity on their own terms.⁷ Throughout the next several decades, European missionary workers were eclipsed in disseminating Christian messages by African evangelists, who shared what historian Lamin

---

⁵ For the limits and successes of Christian inculturation in the German colonial period in Cameroon, see Philippe Laburthe-Tolra, "La Mission Catholique Allemande Du Cameroun (1890–1916) et La Missologie," in *Diffusion et Acculturation Du Christianisme (XIXe–XXe s.) Vingt-Cinq Ans de Recherches Missiologiques Par Le CREDIC*, ed. Jean Comby (Paris: Karthala, 2005), 227–49. And Jean-Paul Messina, *Le Centenaire de la Conversion André Mbangue, le premier chrétien camerounais* (Yaoundé: Université de Yaoundé, 1988).

⁶ Many interviews I conducted revealed that devout Cameroonians are more likely to emphasize the role of early African evangelists like Andreas (André) Mbangue, Modi Din Jacob, Pius Ottou, and Lotin A Same, rather than foreign missionaries, in Christianizing African communities. Catholics from western Cameroon whom I interviewed referenced the catechists who returned from Fernando Po in Spanish Guinea as their community's faith founders. Common prayers and local histories also commonly refer to these figures. Oral interviews, Félix Penda, Adèle Nimboh, Nicolas Déa on July 6, 2007 in Kribi, Cameroon; oral interview, John the Baptist Zamcho Anyeh, S.J. on May 25, 2014, Maison Jesuite, Mvolyé, Cameroon. See also Séverin Alega Mbele, "Entretien Avec Le Père Olivier Paulin Awoumou, Curé de Mvolyé et Membre de La Société de l'Apostolat Catholique," *Cameroon-Info*, May 21, 2001, http://www.cameroon-info.net/stories/0,6908,@,mvolye-a-cent-ans-un-siecle-d-histoire.html [accessed January 13, 2017]. The African "roots" of Christianity has been a common theme of conferences and colloquia, both within Christian Churches and in national histories. See the analysis of the Société Africaine de Culture (SAC), at the Second Vatican Council, 1962, and Société africaine de culture, *Civilisation noire et Église catholique : colloque d'Abidjan, 12–17 septembre 1977* (Paris: Présence africaine, 1978).

⁷ While all German Protestant and Catholic missionaries and many of their auxiliaries were forced to leave in 1914, the American Presbyterian Mission was granted permission to remain in the territory during French campaigns in Kamerun and throughout the negotiations with Great Britain before and during the Treaty of Versailles. The French administration, however, remained wary of a non-French presence in Cameroon and relations remained tense, albeit courteous, between the American Presbyterian Mission and the French mandate government in the interwar period. See the orders of Governor Lucien Fourneau, Archives Nationales de Cameroun (hereafter ANC) Affaires Politiques et Administrative (hereafter APA) 10384. See also Louis-Paul Ngongo, *Histoire des forces religieuses au Cameroun* (Paris: Éditions Karthala, 1982), 17–29.

Sanneh calls the "cross-border promises" of Christianity, integrating them into the structures of everyday life.[8]

Of all the Christian sacraments (the outward signs, consisting of actions and words and symbolizing a certain grace) that moved confessional loyalties in Cameroon in the interwar years, marriage became the most exalted, coveted, and controversial.[9] Inspired by catechist instruction and pastoral preaching on Godly love, and empowered by the missions' protective interventions to "emancipate" them from polygamous marriages, African women throughout southern Cameroon challenged their existing marriages and pursued new, companionate marriages during the interwar decades.[10] Christian coupling also became rapidly popularized as it promised to extend men the power to refuse bridewealth obligations and even to guide women to "new life" in Christ with Christian men, thus granting males of common status the power to realign loyalties and obligations to elders and elites and assume guardianship over women. Concurrent with these spiritual and social dynamics, African marriages in their Christian and non-Christian forms were assailed by the profane forces of political subjugation and economic disruption inherent to

---

[8] Lamin Sanneh, *Whose Religion Is Christianity?: The Gospel Beyond the West* (Grand Rapids, MI: William B. Eerdmans Publishing, 2003), 57.

[9] The extensive historiography on Christian marriage and the transformation of indigenous marriage practices in Cameroon over the twentieth century – written largely by Cameroonian scholars – attests to centrality of marriage and the history of African marriage rites and forms in the cultures of Cameroon. See Antoine Essomba Fouda, *Le Mariage Chrétien Au Cameroun : Une Réalité Anthropologique, Civile et Sacramentelle* (Paris: L'Harmattan, 2010); Manga Bekombo, "La Femme, Le Mariage et La Compensation Matrimoniale En Pays Dwala," *L'Ethnographie* 62–3 (69 1968): 179–88; Jacques Binet, "Le Mariage et l'évolution de La Société Sud-Camerounaise," *L'Afrique Française. Bulletin Mensuel Du Comité de l'Afrique Française, Du Comité Du Maroc et Du Comité Algérie-Tunisie-Maroc* 62, no. 6 (1953): 40–2; Jean-Marie Vianney Balegamire A. Koko, *Mariage Africain et Mariage Chrétien* (Paris: L'Harmattan, 2003); Michel Legrain, *L'Eglise catholique et le mariage en Occident et en Afrique (Tome II): L'ébranlement de l'édifice matrimonial* (Paris: L'Harmattan, 2009); Luc Ndjodo, *Le Mariage Chrétien Chez Les Beti* (Douala: Yonga & Partners, 1997); Henri Ngoa, "Le Mariage chez les Ewondo: Étude sociologique" (Sorbonne, 1968); J.R. Owono Nkoudou, "Le Problème Du Mariage Dotal Au Cameroun Français," *Études Camerounaises* 39–40 (March 1953): 41–83.

[10] On the spiritual inspirations for conjugal love, see Société des Missions Evangéliques de Paris (hereafter SMEP)/Service Protestant de Missions Défap (hereafter DEFAP) Eglise Evangélique du Cameroun (hereafter EEC) divers 2/2 Culte de mariage: Mitin ma diba momene 1930; "Foyer d'Amour," Lettre d'Élie Allégret à J. Bianquis, Douala, 3 March 1921; ACSSp. 2J1.11a2 "La charité regne," Rapport sur les missions de Lobetal et Douala, 1935.

French colonialism after World War I.[11] Local proselytizers captivated considerable numbers of unmarried men by professing the shibboleth of "the right of the African man to a wife" – a message that intrigued those denied access to wives by their low status, poverty, or political or family position.[12]

Marriage is a particularly useful prism through which to examine Christian conversion in an African context because it is simultaneously a singular action and a manner of living that expresses particular beliefs.[13] Although Cameroon's diverse societies sanctioned varied and distinctive marriage practices throughout their histories, it is clear that for the individual and the community, marriage was more than a simple act; it was a worldview. In myriad forms and processes, marriage constituted a place of belonging, defined personal and group identity, and anchored all social and economic life. The transformation of matrimonial systems to reflect Christian doctrine in many of Cameroon's societies denotes broad commitments to adapt cultural systems, which, Cameroonian theologian Antoine Essomba Fouda concludes, registered the value and costs of different approaches to forging unions between individuals and alliances between collectivities.[14] Moreover, evidence of everyday people's underlying motivations for engaging and remaining in Christian marriages can reveal a conversion process that Robin Horton described as "a cognitive

---

[11] Albert Sarraut's thesis on Cameroon's *mise en valeur* and the African colonies' role in restoring French financial solvency sheds light on the administrative rationale for brutal forced labor policies. Albert Sarraut, *La Mise En Valeur Des Colonies Francaises* (Paris: Payot & Compagnie, 1923).

[12] Président Louis Marin et le Groupe parlementaire des missions, "La reglementation des marriages entre indigènes en Afrique Occidentale Francaise et Afrique Equatoriale Francaise," Session du 16 juin 1939, *Journal Officiel du Cameroun*, 1939.

[13] The literature on marriage in Africa is extensive, and is elaborated further in this chapter, but this analysis owes a particular debt to histories of marriage in nineteenth-century and early twentieth-century Africa, during the tumultuous period of early colonial encounter and the end of the slave trade, when "marriage" was frequently being interpreted along many economic, socio-cultural, and religious lines. See in particular, Richard Roberts, *Litigants and Households: African Disputes and Colonial Courts in the French Soudan, 1895–1912* (Portsmouth, NH: Heinemann, 2005); Marie Rodet, "'Under the Guise of Guardianship and Marriage': Mobilizing Juvenile and Female Labor in the Aftermath of Slavery in Kayes, French Soudan, 1900–1939," in *Trafficking in Slavery's Wake: Law and the Experience of Women and Children in Africa*, ed. Richard L. Roberts and Benjamin Lawrance (Athens, OH: Ohio University Press, 2012), 86–100.

[14] Fouda, *Le Mariage Chrétien Au Cameroun : Une Réalité Anthropologique, Civile et Sacramentelle*, 44–4.

and practical adjustment to changes in social experience"¹⁵ rather than a hegemonic exercise of colonial power.¹⁶

In the period encompassing French military incursion and German evacuation from Cameroon in 1914 to the French Third Republic's declaration of war against Germany in 1939 and the subsequent (re)departure of a large number of foreign personnel from Cameroon to serve on the European war front, roughly 400,000 Africans converted to Catholic or Protestant Christianity.¹⁷

---

[15] Robin Horton, "On the Rationality of Conversion. Part I," *Africa: Journal of the International African Institute* 45, no. 3 (1975): 219–35. See also Peel, *Religious Encounter and the Making of the Yoruba*, 3.

[16] Many histories of Christianity in Africa have attributed the reorganization of cultural patterns to unequal relations of power between foreign missionaries and colonized local populations, arguing that forms of cultural, religious, and political "hegemony" transformed African consciousness. See, in particular, Jean Comaroff and John L. Comaroff, *Of Revelation and Revolution, Volume 1: Christianity, Colonialism, and Consciousness in South Africa* (Chicago: University of Chicago Press, 1991); John L. Comaroff and Jean Comaroff, *Of Revelation and Revolution, Volume 2: The Dialectics of Modernity on a South African Frontier*, 1 edition (Chicago: University of Chicago Press, 1997). Georges Dupré, *Un Ordre et Sa Destruction* (Paris: ORSTOM, 1982).

[17] Statistics of conversion vary by denomination and missionary society, but, in aggregate, the numbers point to roughly 400,000 Africans in Cameroon becoming counted as part of Christian congregations and communities and performing Christian rituals, including the baptismal rite, between 1914 and 1939. Laburthe-Tolra estimates that in 1938, there were 300,000 recorded Catholics and between 65,000 and 80,000 Protestants in Cameroon. Laburthe-Tolra, *Vers La Lumiere? Ou, Le Désir d'Ariel: A Propos Des Beti Du Cameroun: Sociologie de La Conversion*, 20. However, newspaper reports have slightly different numbers. The 1938 issue of the Belgian newspaper, *Vers l'Avenir*, reported 325,000 Catholics in 1939. "l'Etonnante progression des catholiques au Cameroun," *Vers l'Avenir*, 9 janvier 1939, no. 9. Catholic mission logs report that between 1938 and 1939, roughly 300,000 to 350,000 Catholics participated in mass or received baptism or the Eucharist. Records of Protestants are more difficult, as each denomination was smaller and many, like the Native Baptist Church, were overseen by African principals who did not report to the Paris Evangelical Evangelical Missionary Society. But estimates range between 65,000 and 80,000 Protestants in Cameroon by the start of World War II. See ACSSp. 2J1.13b1 "Informations catholiques"; Vicaires apostoliques du Cameroun, "Le catholicisme au Cameroun," *Informations Catholiques Internationales*, 44th edition, 15 March 1957; Engelbert Mveng, *Album Du Centenaire: 1890–1990: L'Eglise Catholique Au Cameroun, 100 Ans d'évangélisation* (Yaoundé: Conférence Episcopale National du Cameroun, 1990), 46–7. André Retif, "Le Cameroun sera-t-il chrétien?" *La Croix*, 9 December 1954; SMEP/DEFAP, Papiers Jean Keller, Carton V, Fédération Evangélique du Cameroun et de l'Afrique Equatoriale, P.V. de réunion du Conseil à Ngaoundéré, 17–20 January 1953, 1–2. The number of African Christians in the territory should also be contextualized within the total population of Cameroon, which the 1924 French military census report claimed was 2,540,000. It is crucial to acknowledge that census data taken during the colonial period was not

In this brief but important era, African Christians retained their understanding of marriage as a worldview while unsettling previous spiritual and material ideas about coupling, family-building, and community coherence. This approach reassesses the presumptive "death" or "destruction" of longstanding cultural systems and rather seeks to uncover community adaptations.[18] It also works to question assumed demarcations between the political and religious realms and the public and private spheres in Africa.[19] Many previous studies on marriage in Africa have hesitated to disentangle all the human concerns – in particular, personal spirituality – that determined a marriage's endorsement or dissolution in the colonial context.[20]

In the decades between Europeans' two major departures and returns, African evangelists across the Cameroon territory translated the Bible, administered liturgical and sacramental rituals, and instructed the dogmas of Christianity while simultaneously promoting the benefits of a new sexual and social morality that attacked the claims of local patriarchs to decide marriages within their lineages and the power of administration-backed chiefs to acquire large numbers of wives and female clients. Achille Mbembe has noted that

---

highly reliable in terms of representing overall population demographics, as collection of census data was unpopular and was closely identified with tax collection and labor recruitment. Regardless, that figure is the statistic available. Archives du Service Historique de l'Armée, Vincennes, Dossier 5H6/D1, Commission Interministerielle des troupes indigènes, 2eme sous-commission rapport, "Recrutement" 1924.

[18] This book reassesses arguments made in Vansina's history of the rainforest basin in central and central–west Africa in which the "equatorial tradition" of social organization based on kinship experienced "death" as a result of colonial political integration and missionary Christianity. See Jan Vansina, *Paths in the Rainforests. Toward a History of Political Tradition in Equatorial Africa* (Madison, WI: University of Wisconsin Press, 1990), 239–48.

[19] Emily Osborn also troubles the line between "public" and "private" in her work, reminding historians that household making and statecraft are one and the same in West Africa. Emily Lynn Osborn, *Our New Husbands Are Here: Households, Gender, and Politics in a West African State from the Slave Trade to Colonial Rule* (Athens, OH: Ohio University Press, 2011), 3.

[20] Many previous works on marriage in Africa, such as Kristin Mann, *Marrying Well: Marriage, Status, and Social Change among the Educated Elite in Colonial Lagos* (Cambridge: Cambridge University Press, 1985), argue for Christian marriage as mainly an economic and social choice and do not engage with the influence of personal faith, expressions of piety, or psychological attachment. Other, more recent histories have appealed for analyses of marriage in Africa that explore more than economic and social power relations between the sexes and engage with the history of emotions. See Stephanie Newell, *The Forger's Tale: The Search for Odeziaku*, 1 edition (Athens, OH: Ohio University Press, 2006); Jennifer Cole, *Love in Africa* (Chicago: University of Chicago Press, 2009); Rachel Jean-Baptiste, *Conjugal Rights: Marriage, Sexuality, and Urban Life in Colonial Libreville, Gabon* (Athens, OH: Ohio University Press, 2014).

the "hierarchies, different roles and positions, remunerations and privileges" created by the colonial regime in Cameroon resulted in "unequal fortunes."[21] The inequitable order generated by decentralized colonial governance and a competitive market economy, worsened by the violence of forced labor and village dislocation – with attendant periodic famine and epidemic – engendered furious struggles among African men over the most productive and scarce resources: wives and children. In an entirely new way, "the problem of evil," as Cameroonian theologian Engelbert Mveng summarizes, "entered into everyday people's lives and violations of alliances, marriage, and paternity ... situated in conversations about God."[22]

Elizabeth Foster, who has explored Christian conversion in colonial Senegal, confirms that marriage "lay at the heart of missionary conversion strategy."[23] French Catholic missionaries considered monogamous unions to be essential to the creation of Christian families and future generations of African Catholics, and thus, facilitating Christian marriage became a key objective of foreign evangelizers in the empire, often in defiance of local procedures, norms, and conventional wisdom.[24] However, the history of Cameroon demonstrates that monogamous, enduring, freely chosen marriage was not only a civilizing ambition emanating from foreign powers, it was coextended by local religious principals and became a highly charged symbolic act that reconstituted the roles and relations of elders, families, and lineages.[25] While it often stood in tension with old and new practices governing the political and

---

[21] Achille Mbembe, *La Naissance Du Maquis Dans Le Sud-Cameroun, 1920–1960 : Histoire Des Usages de La Raison En Colonie* (Paris: Karthala, 1996), 8.

[22] Engelbert Mveng, *L'Art d'Afrique Noire: Liturgie Cosmique et Langage Religieux* (Paris: Mame, 1964), 122.

[23] Elizabeth Foster, *Faith in Empire: Religion, Politics, and Colonial Rule in French Senegal, 1880–1940* (Stanford: Stanford University Press, 2013), 147.

[24] There is also a considerable literature on the evolutions of marriage and the reform of polygamy in colonized spaces in Africa that was *not* the result of Christian influence, including Barbara Cooper, *Marriage in Maradi: Gender and Culture in a Hausa Society in Niger, 1900–1989* (Portsmouth, NH and Oxford: Heinemann, 1997); Emily S. Burrill, *States of Marriage: Gender, Justice, and Rights in Colonial Mali*, New African Histories (Athens, OH: Ohio University Press, 2015); Osborn, *Our New Husbands Are Here: Households, Gender, and Politics in a West African State from the Slave Trade to Colonial Rule*.

[25] Histories chronicling the importation of Christian marriage models in colonial spaces are extensive and focus heavily on the acts and beliefs of Europeans, often positioning Christian marriage doctrine as a set of imposed protocols. The most notable of these are Ann Laura Stoler, *Carnal Knowledge and Imperial Power: Race and the Intimate in Colonial Rule* (Berkeley, CA: University of California Press, 2002); Mann, *Marrying Well: Marriage, Status, and Social Change among the Educated Elite in Colonial Lagos*. See also Eileen J. Suárez Findlay, *Imposing Decency: The Politics of Sexuality*

economic worlds of African societies, Christian marriage grew in popularity as it became known as an essential rite through which to receive God's grace as well as a means of acceding to the right – derived from faith – to a matrimonial life.[26] Critically, it was African Christian leaders' refinement and reformation of matrimony and family alliance-building, and the process of crafting and circulating the vehement criticisms and enthusiastic devotional practices that allowed this to occur, that brought about a fully "local" Church, embedded in the kinship structures and relational strategies of southern Cameroon's societies, decades before the formal conferral of ecclesiastical control of the Churches to African leaders during decolonization.[27]

The Family and the World of the Spirit

In Cameroon, nascent beliefs about the sanctity of monogamous, Church-sanctioned marriage intersected with longstanding convictions regarding the numinous character of the family and its transcendence in and interface with the World of the Spirit.[28] African Christian families constituted a powerful

---

and Race in Puerto Rico, 1870–1920 (Durham, NC: Duke University Press, 2000); Sally Engle Merry, Colonizing Hawai'i (Princeton, NJ: Princeton University Press, 1999).

[26] Oral interview, Fr. Philippe Azeufack, S.J., Résidence St. François Xavier, Yaoundé, Cameroon, May 30, 2014. Fr. Azeufack stated that since the Catholic mass was said in Latin, which almost no one understood, rites and rituals in which laypersons participated, as well as songs sung in local vernaculars, held intense power and significance. Regarding the right to marriage and the juridical dispositions that the Catholic Church formulated to help people understand their claims to matrimony, see *Summa theologiae, Supplementum*, Q. 67, a. 1, ad 4th; *Catechism of Trent*, Part II, VII, §§ 13–14; as well as Catholic Church, *The Catechism of the Council of Trent*, trans. John A. McHugh and Charles J. Callan, Reprint edition (Rockford, IL: Tan Books and Publishers, 1992). And in the Christian Bible, see Hebrews 13:4; 1 Timothy 4:1–5; 1 Corinthians 7:39; 2 Corinthians 5:17.

[27] The literature on the transfer of authority within the Christian Churches to African indigenous ecclesiastical leaders at the end of empire is not vast. Some notable texts include Roger Pasquier, *La jeunesse ouvrière chrétienne en Afrique noire (1930–1950)* (Paris: Karthala, 2013) and François Constantin and Christian Coulon, *Religion et Transition Démocratique En Afrique* (Paris: Karthala, 1997). Elizabeth Foster is writing a new book on efforts to "Africanize" the Church hierarchy and movements to create an authentically "African" Church in the years just prior to and just after decolonization.

[28] This book engages most thoroughly with the societies of the southern forest zone in Cameroon, including the Beti and Bulu groups, as well the peoples of the eastern southern forests including the Maka, Gbaya, and the Mkako. Each of these linguistically and culturally distinct peoples developed singular cosmologies, but scholars of these societies' pre-Christian belief systems confirm the centrality of kinship and the relevance of the conjugal bond and its reproductive capacities to understandings of supernatural power and the "invisible world" (to borrow from the reference to the spiritual world

medium opposing the predatory powers operating in colonial Cameroon that threatened individuals and African society at large. Historians of Africa and African theologians have developed an unintentional consensus regarding what Julie Livingston refers to as "the overarching unity of the natural, cosmological, and social realms" in which Africans in history and the present have considered the health, protection, and wealth of their families to depend on spiritual forces as well as material and human resources.[29] Cameroonian theologian Fabien Eboussi-Boulaga concurs that the "unity and communion" of the family models the moral community of the faith, and that both are immortalized in "the other world where souls gather" as well as in here on earth.[30] Peter Geschiere's work – also focusing on Cameroon – has similarly called attention to the household and family as the wellsprings of supernatural belief since intimate human relations shape the landscape in which sacred or unholy forces act.[31] Geschiere's contention that, "In Africa, belief systems seem to reflect tensions within a community," is taken one step further in Derek Peterson's history of East Africa, where passionate convictions about civil order or personal salvation were anchored in the variably redeeming or confining interdependencies of family life.[32]

---

used by many societies in southern Cameroon). See in particular, Philippe Laburthe-Tolra, *Les Seigneurs de La Forêt: Essai Sur Le Passé Historique, l'organisation Sociale et Les Norms Éthiques Des Anciens Béti Du Cameroun* (Paris: Publications de la Sorbonne, 1981), 350–78; Pierre Mviena, *Univers Culturel et Religieux Du Peuple Beti* (Yaoundé: Imprimerie Saint-Paul, 1970) as well as Elisabeth Copet-Rougier, "Étude de La Transformation Du Mariage Chez Les Mkako Du Cameroun," in *Transformations of African Marriage*, ed. David Nyamwaya and David J. Parkin (Manchester and Wolfeboro, NH: Manchester University Press, for the International African Institute, 1987), 75–91; Philip Burnham, Elisabeth Copet-Rougier, and Philip Noss, "Gbaya et Mkako : Contribution Ethno-Linguistique à l'Histoire de l'Est-Cameroun," *Paideuma* 32 (1986): 87–128. For related scholarship on the centrality of the family in witchcraft practices in Cameroon, see Peter Geschiere and Cyprian Fisiy, "Domesticating Personal Violence: Witchcraft, Courts and Confessions in Cameroon," *Africa: Journal of the International African Institute* 64, no. 3 (1994): 323–41; Peter Geschiere, *Witchcraft, Intimacy, and Trust: Africa in Comparison* (Chicago and London: University of Chicago Press, 2013).

[29] Julie Livingston, *Debility and the Moral Imagination in Botswana* (Bloomington, IN: Indiana University Press, 2005). See also David L. Schoenbrun, "Conjuring the Modern in Africa: Durability and Rupture in Histories of Public Healing between the Great Lakes of East Africa," *The American Historical Review* 111, no. 5 (2006): 1403–39.

[30] F. Eboussi-Boulaga, *Christianity Without Fetishes: An African Critique and Recapture of Christianity*, 1st edition (Maryknoll, NY: Orbis Books, 1984), 59.

[31] Peter Geschiere, *The Modernity of Witchcraft: Politics and the Occult in Postcolonial Africa* (Charlottesville, VA: University of Virginia Press, 1997); Geschiere, *Witchcraft, Intimacy, and Trust*.

[32] Geschiere, *Witchcraft, Intimacy, and Trust*, 166.

Peterson provides two interrelated accounts of how African families were origin points for social criticism that evolved into broad-scale movements in East Africa. The first describes the emergence of "ethnic patriotism," where conservative beliefs about gendered, family-centered roles patterned agendas for the enforcement of political responsibilities and social duties within the ethnic *patria*. The second details the East African Revival, where Christian revivalists resisted patriots' gendered impositions and obligations for family members and renounced the liabilities of kinship.[33] Like the Luo patriots Peterson describes, Cameroonian Christian men were insecure in their rights over wives and families, and sought to reform the rules and processes that governed coupling, intimacy, and reproduction.[34] Hampered by migration, imprisonment, or labor cycles, marriages in French Cameroon – as in British Kenya – "were never fixed, stable, or finished," as Peterson states, and Christians sought to restore family unity and communitarian ethics through religious practice.[35] However, Christians in French Cameroon were very distinct from East African revivalists, who perceived the awesome obligations of family as obstructing spiritual fulfillment. Indeed, Cameroon's Christian leaders largely sought to enhance their responsibility for wives and kin as part of complete religious exercise. Because family is central to the "interpretive act" of religious conversion as well as fundamental to the architecture of African cosmologies, this study takes into account enduring and evolving conceptualizations of "family" in Africa and how this entity is consubstantial with faith in divine power.[36]

In interwar Cameroon, the marriages of young Christian couples did not simply generate a unidirectional momentum for the spiritual metamorphosis of future generations; they were also borne back into the past by inspiring their parents' baptisms and marriage sacraments. In many instances, prominent patriarchs lent their authority to the validity of Christianity following conversions by their children. Thus, the monogamous Christian conjugal household continued to play an important role in the life of the lineage. This work demonstrates that the piety and prestige attendant with Christianity greatly

---

[33] Derek R. Peterson, *Ethnic Patriotism and the East African Revival* (Cambridge: Cambridge University Press, 2012).

[34] Peterson, 138.

[35] Peterson, 130.

[36] Gauri Viswanathan describes the conversion experience as "an interpretive act, an index of material and social conflicts" that does not reject the experience of "epiphany" or metaphysical experience, but rather locates religious subjectivity more precisely in relation to the culture that produces, inhibits, or modifies it. See Gauri Viswanathan, *Outside the Fold – Conversion, Modernity, and Belief* (Princeton, NJ: Princeton University Press, 1998), 4.

appealed to both young and old men seeking to establish or reestablish positions of authority in the domestic sphere, and that these were mutually reinforcing influences. Widespread Christian conversion in French Cameroon did not dismantle the lineage structure, but rather deployed new conjugal family units to buttress lineage and community systems that were disintegrating as a result of economic and political pressures. It also argues that young Christian women and men seeking new kinds of marriages were not always resolutely repudiating the past. The incorporation of broad segments of African society into Christian congregations – usually through African catechists' proselytization of their families, lineages, and communities – illustrates that religious reform was tied to understandings of traditions that shaped the bonds of human dependence. Common preoccupations with new kinds of subjugation, companionlessness, corruption, debt, inequality, and instability inspired new systems for protection and justice but also evoked what Albert Camus referred to as a "nostalgia for ethics," or the rebel's sensibility to repudiate evil by calling forth a romantic past of unity.[37] Throughout this book, Christian marriage and family-building are explored as both individual acts and subjects of collective religious and social mobilization that contained expressions of rebellion and resistance, as well as devotion and obedience.

Land, People, and Authority

To elucidate more precisely the relationships, techniques, and disruptions that characterized colonization, this book frames its study in the tropical forest zone in southern Cameroon. Specifically, the book's evidence base is largely drawn from the area along and south of the Sanaga River to the southern boundary of Cameroon, including the littoral zone south of Douala, but also includes some evidence from the region surrounding the Douala hinterland north of the Sanaga River in proximity to the Noun and the Mbam Rivers (see Map 1). The book's analyses also occasionally refer to evidence from the plateaus of western Cameroon (west of the Noun River to the western boundary of the territory) to identify common orientations and phenomena where they exist. Cameroon's idiosyncratic linguistic and cultural diversity presents a challenge for drawing broad conclusions about societies across the entire southern forest region, and even more so if one includes analysis of coastal or western highland societies. Therefore, I borrow from Mbembe's territorial referent of *terroir* that that relies upon environmental and social geography and the positioning of colonial infrastructure projects to demonstrate prevalent or

---

[37] Albert Camus, *The Rebel: An Essay on Man in Revolt*, First Vintage Interntional Edition (New York: Random House, 1991), 53.

coincident social, political, and religious developments across the forest zone's linguistically and culturally diverse societies. Rather than relying purely on ethno-linguistic markers of space and social identity, Mbembe's approach allows the historian to identify the matrix of systems of agricultural organization, notions of property, and social dynamics, as well as the "political, symbolic, and imaginary" structures alive in African communities that came into contact with the "principal colonial events" of railroad building, road expansion, labor organization, and taxation.[38]

Throughout the period of French administration, the economic and ethno-linguistic identities of different *terroirs* were affected by the grand axes of commercial traffic, which included the North and Central railway lines as well as roads, which expanded considerably farther south and west, including a major roadway north-westward toward Abong Mbang, Doumé, and Bertoua (see Map 2). In 1924, the French administration began encouraging household cocoa cultivation along the axis that runs northward from the Wouri Valley along the line of the Chemin de Fer du Nord from Douala to Nkongsamba (see Map 2),[39] and simultaneously supported large plantations of administration-backed chiefs and elites who managed coffee, groundnut, and tobacco farms.[40] This region was home to Bamileke, Bamoun, and Tikar peoples who, in this period, negotiated with the French administration as well as each other to delimit or assert control over cultivatable lands.

Beginning in 1924, progressively interspersed populations of Banen, Bassa, Ngumba, and Bulu peoples expanded cocoa cultivation across the littoral zone near Edea, Bipindi, Ebolowa, and Kribi. The Central Railway line from Douala to Mbalmayo – which reached Yaoundé in 1927 and cemented it as the territory's capital – linked the towns along the southwestern littoral to export markets. The Ntem, Nyong-et-Sanaga, and Haut Nyong regions surrounding Yaoundé quickly developed into the territory's cocoa belt and also saw the rapid development of palm oil agriculture, as well as palm oil extraction and processing (see Map 3).[41] Here, Bulu, Ngumba, and various Beti societies, including

---

[38] Mbembe, *La Naissance Du Maquis Dans Le Sud-Cameroun, 1920–1960*, 41–4.

[39] Mbembe, 65.

[40] Archives Nationale d'Outre-Mer (hereafter ANOM) Agence Économique de la France d'Outre-Mer (hereafter AGEFOM) 799/1858 Cournarie Rapports sur le cacao, 1929–1932; Rapport de la Tournée Effectuée dans la Subdivision de Nkongsamba, M. Angelini, 1933; Jean-René Brutsch, "Région du Mungo, subdivision de Nkongsamba, Cameroun" (carte figurant les églises et les écoles catholiques et protestantes), document cartographique manuscrit, 1 sept. 1952.

[41] Local populations' lives and modes of production in Cameroon's Nyong et Sanaga, Haut Nyong, Lom et Kadei, and Ntem regions were radically affected by the commercialization of cocoa. By 1950, these regions constituted 7 percent of world cocoa production.

Eton, Ewondo, Bane, Manguissa, Etenga, and Mvele, increasingly interacted with each other at markets, trading centers, courts, and churches, as well as with peoples who were conscripted from neighboring regions or who migrated in order to reach burgeoning urban or market zones, such as Maka, Gbaya, and Kaka peoples.[42] This book's primary focus on the southern forest region along the Central Railway as well as along the roads emanating from Douala toward Edea and Eseka, the roads surrounding Yaoundé, including toward the southwestern coastal zones of Ebolowa and Kribi, the southern roads to Mbalmayo, Sangmélima, and Djoum, and the northeastern roads to Akonolinga, Abong Mbang, and Doumé, relies on a host of evidence from administration, industry, and mission sources that frequently refer to each other.

Between 1919 and 1929, the French administration vigorously executed a program of economic and social reorganization across the entire southern forest zone to rapidly expand the infrastructure that could facilitate the export of raw natural resources extracted by European concessionary companies, as well as cash crops produced by African households and African and European plantation managers.[43] This endeavor required an exacting *régime du travail* that depended on requisitioned male labor (and eventually would include women and children) organized by administration chiefs, upheld by the *indigénat*, and enforced by the powerful *force publique* – French colonial troops, and the *commandement indigène* – an indigenous auxiliary police force with

---

Estimates provided by Georges Viers, "Le cacao dans le monde," *Cahiers d'outre-mer* 6, no. 24 (1953): 297–351.

[42] The Beti comprise one ethnic grouping of the larger ethno-regional population known as the Beti-Pahouin. The background of the Beti-Pahouin (Beti) populations is one of amalgamated socio-linguistic groups whose local allegiances and common economic interests allowed for the formation of a sizable socio-political group in Cameroon throughout the nineteenth and early twentieth centuries. The Beti include among them the sub-ethnic groups of the Ewondo, Bané, Fang, Mbida-Mbane, Mvog-Nyenge, Eton, and Manguissa. The Eton are further subdivided into the Eton-Beti, Eton-Beloua, and Beloua-Eton. During the nineteenth century, the Ewondo, Eton, Bané, Bulu, and Fang peoples inhabited the region between central Cameron, northern Gabon, and western Congo. These peoples had common linguistic and cultural characteristics, and with the arrival of European imperial interests, these populations developed similar reactions to economic opportunities, notably cocoa farming. See André Amougou, Chef du département et doyen Bané (Traduction par interprète auxiliaire, André Foe Amougo, (Bané)), *La Formation de la race Bané*, no. 4 (Yaoundé: Imprimerie Coulomma, 1937); Pierre Alexandre and Jacques Binet, *Le groupe dit pahouin (Fang, Boulou, Beti)* (Paris: Presses Universitaires de France, 1958); Victor Julius Ngoh, *History of Cameroon Since 1800* (Limbé, Cameroon: Pressbook, Ltd 1996) as well as *Ethnicité, identités et citoyenneté en Afrique Centrale* (Yaoundé, Cameroun: Presses de l'UCAC, 2002).

[43] Mbembe, *La Naissance Du Maquis Dans Le Sud-Cameroun, 1920–1960*, 36.

considerable freedom to carry out their orders.[44] The capacity of African chiefs to control the means of violence in order to marshal tens of thousands of laborers across the territory for road, rail, bridge, and port construction was both stunning and unrecognizable to African societies in the southern forest zones.

Before European colonization, leaders of nearly all ethno-regional groups of the southern forest region – including, among others, the major Beti, Bassa, and Bulu groups and other Pahouin and non-Pahouin societies of the southern forests such as the Maka and Gbaya of eastern Cameroon and the Duala, Malimba, Bakweri, Banyang, and Balundu of coastal and southwest Cameroon – did not exhibit a centralized political leadership and were marked by their acephalous segmentary lineages, which lacked strong hierarchical organization.[45] Lineage heads exercised authority strictly within a family

---

[44] The French administration promulgated a number of laws organizing labor in the territory, most of which conformed to laws passed throughout French West and French Equatorial Africa. See Code du travail en A.O.F., arrêté général du 29 mars 1926; la convention sur le travail forcé de 1930; la convention sur le recrutement des travailleurs indigènes de 1936; la convention sur les contrats de travail à long terme de 1939; la convention sur les sanctions pénales de 1939. Notably, nearly every labor code passed included a chapter on the *"question de la liberté du travail"* which allowed for forced labor. Even the revised labor code passed in 1947 after World War II included the statement: "The right to requisition laborers during peacetime, notably in cases of public calamities and urgent work that concerns the health of populations, will be regulated by decrees directed by the minister of Overseas France..." chapitre 2*bis*, Code du Travail d'Outre-Mer date du 18 octobre 1947 (code Moutet). See Jacqueline Delange, "La Discussion Parlementaire Sur Le Code Du Travail En Afrique Noire," *Présence Africaine*, no. 13 (1952): 377–400. For more on the history of policing in the French colonies, see Emmanuel Blanchard and Joël Glassman, "Le Maintien de l'ordre Dans l'empire Français : Une Historiographie Émergent," in *Maintenir l'ordre Colonial. Afrique et Madagascar, XIXe-XXe Siècles*, ed. Jean-Pierre Bat and Nicolas Courtin, Histoire (Rennes: Presses Universitaires de Rennes, 2012), 11–41; Emmanuel Blanchard, Quentin Deluermoz, and Joël Glassman, "La Professionnalisation Policière En Situation Coloniale : Détour Conceptuel et Explorations Historiographiques," *Crime, Histoire & Sociétés* 15 (2011): 33–53.

[45] ANC APA 11643 Gouverneur-Général van Vollenhoven, *Journal Officiel de l'AOF*, 1917, 467 mentions this. This has also been thoroughly chronicled by Kpwang K. Robert and Samah Tondji Walters, "Invention of Tradition: Chieftaincy, Adaptation and Change in the Forest Region of Cameroon," in *La Cheffrie "Traditionnelle" Dans Les Sociétés de La Grande Zone Forestière Du Sud-Cameroun (1850–2010)*, ed. Kpwang K. Robert (Paris et Cameroun: L'Harmattan, 2011), 71–84; Paul-Gérard Pougoué, *Ethnicité, identités et citoyenneté en Afrique centrale* (Yaoundé, Cameroon: Presses Universitaires de l'Université catholique d'Afrique Centrale, 2002); Victor Julius Ngoh, *History of Cameroon since 1800* (Limbé, Cameroon: Presbook, 1996); Pierre Alexandre and Jacques Binet, *Le Groupe Dit Pahouin (Fang-Boulou-Beti)* (Paris: Presses Universitaires de France, 1958); Peter Geschiere, *Village Communities and the State: Changing*

or lineage, and worked with other lineage heads or elders to manage larger affiliated groups.[46] Bulu author Jean Louis Ndjemba Medou describes Bulu society before the European encounter as marked by a complete lack of extrafamilial authority.[47] Beti segmentary societies had no institutionalized elite or centralized chieftaincies, and family fathers or village elders ("founders") had the greatest degree of independence and autonomy relative to those of lower status.[48] Eastern Cameroon's Maka, Mkako, and Gbaya peoples were similarly patrilineal, patrilocal societies in which elders displayed varying degrees of control over youth and marriageable women.[49] Early French reports on the Maka noted, "local communities are small and they are not used to paying tribute to local authorities."[50] Other societies in this region likewise maintained relatively diffuse leadership systems, which promoted elders, groups of lineage heads, and fathers as community leaders capable of authentically expressing communal loyalties and desires.[51]

Relations among the Maka of South-Eastern Cameroon since the Colonial Conquest (London and Boston, MA: Kegan Paul International, 1982); Peter Geschiere, "Chiefs and Colonial Rule in Cameroon: Inventing Chieftaincy, French and British Style," *Africa: Journal of the International African Institute* 63, no. 2 (1993); Ralph A. Austen and Jonathan Derrick, *Middlemen of the Cameroons Rivers: The Duala and Their Hinterland, c.1600–c.1960* (Cambridge: Cambridge University Press, 1999), 40–3.

[46] Peter Geschiere provides the most thoroughly nuanced discussion of kinship-based socio-political organization in Cameroon's southern forest region and describes the Maka society before colonial conquest as based on autonomous patrilineages who formed villages of fewer than one hundred people, and were "even more segmentary" than the Beti, their western neighbors, as there was "no trace of any central authority between the villages." The Beti by contrast expressed greater cooperation between lineages and supported the authority of lineage heads over a larger scale of descendants, women, and slaves or clients. See Peter Geschiere, "Slavery and Kinship among the Maka (Cameroon, Eastern Province)," *Paideuma* 41 (1995): 207–25.

[47] Jean Louis Ndjemba Medou, *Nnanga Kon* (Yaoundé: Edition Sopecam, 1989).

[48] Laburthe-Tolra, *Les Seigneurs de La Forêt : Essai Sur Le Passé Historique, l'organisation Sociale et Les Norms Éthiques Des Anciens Béti Du Cameroun*, 356–8.

[49] Elisabeth Copet-Rougier, "Parenté et Rapports de Productions Chez Les Mkako," *L'Ethnographie* 121, no. 79 (1979): 7–39; Copet-Rougier, "Étude de La Transformation Du Mariage Chez Les Mkako Du Cameroun"; Geschiere, *Village Communities and the State*, 258–60.

[50] ANC APA 11643 *Rapport administratif, Situation politique et Justice*, May 1920.

[51] Alexandre and Binet, *Le Groupe Dit Pahouin (Fang-Boulou-Beti)*; Barnabé Bilongo, *Les Pahouins Du Sud-Cameroun : Inventaires Bibliographiques, Connaissance Des Fang, Ntoumou, Muaé, Boulou, Beti (Menguissa, Eton, Muëlë, Bënë et Ewondo) et Du Groupe Dit Sanaga* (Yaoundé, Cameroon: Imprimerie Saint-Paul, 1974); Moise Ateba Ngoa, "Histoire de La Traduction et de l'interpretation En Pays Beti: De La Période Coloniale à Nos Jours," in *Perspectives on Translation and Interpretation in Cameroon*, ed. Emmanuel Nges Chia, Joseph Che Suh, and Alexandre Ndeffo Tene

Despite the fact that indigenous organizational forms in southern Cameroon did not recognize politically dominating command structures such as chieftaincy or kingship, village leaders and elders aggressively pursued pathways to accumulation through marriage and patronage. The economic and political inequality that resulted in precolonial times – as more productive proprietors amassed large units of wives, children, and junior and dependent men – was managed through negotiations, kin relations, and generational shifts within the minor lineage (*mvog* in Beti), extended household (*boane mpanze* in Maka), or village.[52] While the lineage or village leader acquired wealth through the labor of wives, children, and low-status men, the imparity that resulted was regulated by the conditional loyalty of his kin and servants.[53] As Bertrand Lembezat summarized, "the family is a man's only valuable."[54] Diffuse leadership still supported social inequality, but, wives and dependants attained status by participation in wealth accumulation, expected redistribution, and could refuse to defend and serve the high-status elder if members of the group became unsatisfied. As Jennifer Johnson-Hanks has so carefully uncovered, women and junior men "strategically consented" to engage in a

---

(Bamenda, Cameroon: Langaa RPCIG and African Books Collective, 2009); Laburthe-Tolra, *Les Seigneurs de La Forêt: Essai Sur Le Passé Historique, l'organisation Sociale et Les Norms Éthiques Des Anciens Béti Du Cameroun*; Jacques Fulbert Owono, *Pauvreté ou paupérisation en Afrique: une étude exegético-ethique de la pauvreté chez les Beti-Fang du Cameroun* (Bamberg, Germany: University of Bamberg Press, 2011). The Muslim Fulbé tribes of the northern regions and the Chad Basin who pledged allegiance to powerful *lamidat*, as well as the close-knit political hierarchies of the Bamileke of the highland plateau region, provide alternatives to this organizational structure in Cameroon's southern forest zone. Daniel Abwa, "The French Administrative System in the Lamidate of Ngaoundéré," in *Introduction to the History of Cameroon: Nineteenth and Twentieth Centuries*, ed. Martin Njeuma (London: Macmillan, 1989), 137–69; Nicolas Argenti, *The Intestines of the State: Youth, Violence, and Belated Histories in the Cameroon Grassfields* (Chicago: University of Chicago Press, 2007).

[52] Among the Beti, who accumulated wives and clients on a much larger scale than their Maka, Gbaya, or Kaka neighbors to the east, wealthy lineage heads were known as *nukukuma*. Philippe Laburthe-Tolra, *Initiations et Sociétés Secrètes Au Cameroun: Les Mystères de La Nuit : Essai Sur La Religion Beti, Volume 1* (Paris: Karthala, 1985), 8. See also Geschiere, "Slavery and Kinship among the Maka (Cameroon, Eastern Province)."

[53] Laburthe-Tolra, *Les Seigneurs de La Forêt: Essai Sur Le Passé Historique, l'organisation Sociale et Les Norms Éthiques Des Anciens Béti Du Cameroun*, 374; Alain Leplaideur, "Vie et survie domestique en zone forestière camerounaise : la reproduction simple est-elle assurée," in *Le Risque en agriculture*, ed. Michel Eldin and Pierre Milleville (Paris: Editions de l'ORSTOM, 1989), 280–1.

[54] Bertrand Lembezat, *Le Cameroun* (Paris: Editions Maritimes et Coloniales, 1954), 54.

system of "wealth in people" in which they were subordinate so long as they understood it also contained pathways to their own personal advancement.[55]

Perceiving the need for more forceful and less transactional authority, French officials pursued a strategy of instituting a strong African chieftaincy backed by French law and police powers, which would allow for the "profound transformation" of the territory.[56] As these societies had not previously been organized through centralized polities, African government associates in the southern forest region during French administration were mostly unrecognizable principals – either elders who extended their powers, ambitious junior men who usurped authority, or men with preexisting ties to prestige but little power.[57] With the colonial bureaucracy subsidizing concessionary investments, financial interests superseded any "civilizational" initiatives or humanitarian pledges made to the League of Nations, and thus African chiefs in the southern forests were commissioned to recruit thousands of laborers to remove rock and earth, fell trees, lay stone and rails, build docks along rivers, haul mud and lumber, and perform myriad other punishing tasks under the surveillance of French guards and African police armed with *chicottes*.[58] Administration chiefs compelled men, women, and children to labor on transit lines for months or entire seasons, and often either conscripted remaining villagers to work their own agricultural enterprises or married numerous wives to manage their households and farmsteads.[59] For commoner men in the southern zone

---

[55] Jennifer Johnson-Hanks, *Uncertain Honor: Modern Motherhood in an African Crisis* (Chicago: University of Chicago Press, 2006), 30.

[56] ANOM Affaires Politiques (hereafter AFFPOL) 615/1 La Haute Conférence de la Paix au Cameroun, 18 août 1919.

[57] The history of the transformation of chieftaincy in societies in Cameroon's southern regions, from the western coasts to the eastern boundaries of Congo, typically highlights the extortive tendencies of the African agents of the administration; see Philippe Laburthe-Tolra, "Charles Atangana," in *Les Africains*, ed. Charles André Julien (Paris: Jaguar, 1977), 109–41; Philip Burnham, "'Regroupement' and Mobile Societies: Two Cameroon Cases," *Journal of African History* 15, no. 4 (1975): 577–94. Robert and Walters, "Invention of Tradition: Chieftaincy, Adaptation and Change in the Forest Region of Cameroon."

[58] A *chicotte* is a long knotted whip with a wooden handle used as a punishment in French Equatorial Africa, Belgian Congo and Portuguese Africa. The enormity (and brutality) of France's infrastructure programs in Cameroon, including roadways, railways, ports, and bridges, is captured in France's reports to the League of Nations. See ANOM Travaux Publiques (hereafter TP) Série 1 420/11, Rapport à la Société des Nations, Années 1931, 1934, and 1935.

[59] Achille Mbembe and Philippe Laburthe-Tolra have both painstakingly chronicled the extent of the use of forced labor by the French colonial government in Cameroon. Mbembe, *La Naissance Du Maquis Dans Le Sud-Cameroun, 1920–1960*, 59–88; Laburthe-Tolra, *Vers La Lumiere? Ou, Le Désir d'Ariel: A Propos Des Beti*

who were able to control landed property and capture the potential of the new market economy, a wife and any children she bore were an operational necessity, a marker of socio-economic prestige, and, increasingly, a rare and costly household component as administration-appointed chiefs often seized greater power over women and their offspring and prevented higher numbers of men from marrying.[60]

What this book will demonstrate is that southern Cameroon's forest societies' negotiable kin and lineage hierarchies that marked the precolonial era were soon captive to inflexible centralized command structures under German, and later French colonial rule. In response to this, African Christian men enacted reform strategies that rejected the rigid exclusivity and possessorship of the colonial chieftaincy system that restricted commoner men's prospects for advancement and pursued a revised patriarchal vision with privileges over a wife and children evenly distributed among baptized believers. Women's agency and desires within this remodeled patriarchy were frequently suppressed, as many of this book's later chapters will reveal. Like junior men, women had considerable negotiating power in precolonial segmentary societies, and their connections to powerful patrons could result in access to land, wealth, or advantage.[61] While Christian rhetoric emanating from foreign missionaries frequently espoused female "emancipation" through monogamous

---

  Du Cameroun: Sociologie de La Conversion, 360–91. Several works by Cameroonian scholars have also focused on the synergies between the French regime of forced labor or *prestation* and the transformation of chieftaincy systems among the Beti and Bulu societies, including Léopold-François Eze, "Le Commandement Indigène de La Région Du Nyong et Sanaga, Sud-Cameroun, de 1916 à 1945" (Université de Paris I, 1975); Essama Philippe-Roger, "Evolution de La Cheffrie Traditionnelle En Pays Bëti" (1966); Kpwang K. Robert, "La Résistance Des Ekang Du Sud-Cameroun Face Aux Chefs Supérieurs Imposés Par l'administration Coloniale Française: De l'avènement Des 'Présidents Claniques' à La Création de l'Efulameoñ (1920–1948)," in *La Cheffrie "Traditionnelle" Dans Les Sociétés de La Grande Zone Forestière Du Sud-Cameroun (1850–2010)* (Paris et Cameroun: L'Harmattan, 2011), 235–55.

[60] Jane Guyer is perhaps the most prolific writer on economic change and matrimony in Cameroonian societies. See Jane I. Guyer, "Head Tax, Social Structure and Rural Incomes in Cameroun, 1922–37," *Cahiers d'Etudes Africaines* XX, no. 3 (1980): 305–29; Jane I. Guyer and Samuel M. Eno Belinga, "Wealth in People as Wealth in Knowledge: Accumulation and Composition in Equatorial Africa," *Journal of African History* 36 (1995): 91–120; Jane I. Guyer, "Indigenous Currencies and the History of Marriage Payments: A Case Study from Cameroon," *Cahiers d'Etudes Africaines* 26, no. 104 (1986): 577–610.

[61] Laburthe-Tolra, *Les Seigneurs de La Forêt: Essai Sur Le Passé Historique, l'organisation Sociale et Les Norms Éthiques Des Anciens Bëti Du Cameroun*, 243–7. Pamela Feldman-Savelsberg discusses this phenomenon in the Grassfields area among the smaller, centralized chieftaincies of the Bamileke. See Pamela Feldman-Savelsberg,

marriage, on the ground, evangelism, catechism, and the mobilization of male believers centered on implementing new marital practices that intercepted or limited women's autonomy in marriage as part of a more deliberate strategy to check the power of acquisitive elites.[62] Women's autonomy was further limited by Christian men's collaborative dynamism in the second half of the interwar period when they regained influence and warrant over wealth and opportunity. However, there was remarkable continuity and even entrenchment of precolonial engrossment with female fertility among southern Cameroon's forest societies. Pierre Alexandre and Jacques Binet, along with Philippe Laburthe-Tolra all emphasize longstanding approaches to marriage in the southern forest zone as defined by their focus on sexuality and reproduction as a part of the male and female life course. What is unique to the period of widespread Christian conversion is how Christian men *socialized* strategies of acquiring access to females and their reproductive capacity and how they cooperated to make marriage an immutable commitment endorsed by God, rather than a system of reciprocities that accommodated changing circumstances with flexible adjustments.

Christianity and Social Change in the Equatorial Forests

During the decades between the two World Wars, Cameroon's southern forest region not only experienced some of the most dramatic political and economic discontinuities, it was also a unique space in which to observe the atmosphere of international colonialism fostered by the League of Nations, which allowed for greater exposure to Christian missions than in France's other territories.[63] After the Great War, the French territorial government in Cameroon became subordinate to the supervisory framework of the Permanent Mandates Commission, and was thus legally bound by the 1919 Treaty of Saint-Germain-

---

Plundered Kitchens, Empty Wombs (Ann Arbor, MI: University of Michigan Press, 1999).

[62] See Laburthe-Tolra, *Initiations et Sociétés Secrètes Au Cameroun: Les Mystères de La Nuit : Essai Sur La Religion Beti, Volume 1*, 134–47; Alexandre and Binet, *Le Groupe Dit Pahouin (Fang-Boulou-Beti)*, 35–78.

[63] The mandates were created as part of the Treaty of Versailles as a new category in colonial administrative law. The League of Nations envisioned three classes of mandates: Class A mandates in the Middle East were given "provisional recognition" of their political independence while Class B and C mandates in Africa and the Pacific were to be managed as colonial holdings. See René Costedoat, *L'effort Français Au Cameroun, Le Mandat Français et La Réorganisation Des Territoires Du Cameroun* (Paris: Editions Larose, 1930); Mark Mazower, *Governing the World: The History of an Idea, 1815 to the Present* (New York: Penguin, 2012), 70–80.

en-Laye to accept assistance from all religious institutions "to guide native populations towards progress and civilization."[64] As a result, a plentiful range of international missionary societies expanded their influence in the early decades of the French mandate, reopening former German mission stations in the more accessible coastal and forest areas and growing the ranks of African mission auxiliaries.

Even before the establishment of the Mandates Commission that divided the former German Kamerun into French and British mandate territories in 1922, African evangelists from Nigeria and Cameroon circulated Protestant and Catholic prayer books, hymnals, scripture passages, and newsletters during and after the European military campaigns in the Yaoundé, Douala, and Victoria regions starting in 1914.[65] The sole American mission, the Presbyterian Mission of the U.S.A., had been active in coastal and southern Cameroon since 1832, and, unlike the German Basel and Pallottine missions, was allowed to remain in the territory during the French military occupation. Following the war, the French orders of the Society of Jesus, the Congregation of the Holy Ghost, and Priests of the Sacred Heart of Saint Quentin, along with the French Protestant Mission (which included the French Evangelical Lutheran Church, the Fraternal Lutheran Church, the Union of Baptist Churches, and the Paris Society of Evangelical Missions), and the Native Baptist Church all established or extended their influence with a particularly marked presence in the coastal, western, and southern forest zones of the new mandate territory. Consequently, a vibrant association of missionary networks and their affiliated charities, hospitals, and medical organizations expanded their influence alongside the French administration to "maintain public order and morals" in the first decade of mandate rule.[66]

The religious and political influence of these sub-state agents grew considerably in the interwar period. In the forest zone and its neighboring coastal and highland plateau regions, Africans working with the Catholic Spiritan and American Presbyterian Missions had the broadest territorial ranges, operating throughout southern Cameroon between the coast and the dense eastern forests. Those who were connected with the French Society of the Sacred Heart and the Fraternal Lutheran Churches also ventured into Cameroon's northern

---

[64] See also *Acte de Londres* (1922) circumscribing France's authority over Cameroon, ANOM AFFPOL 615/1.

[65] Laburthe-Tolra, *Vers La Lumiere? Ou, Le Désir d'Ariel: A Propos Des Beti Du Cameroun: Sociologie de La Conversion*, 45–60.

[66] Article 22, Covenant of the League of Nations, Including Amendments adopted to December, 1924; Treaty of Saint-Germain-en-Laye of 1919, frequently cited in administrative reports, "Affaires religieuses," ANOM AFFPOL 3349/2; ACSSP 2J1.7a4 construction des églises et monastères.

regions where Islam was predominant. Baptist, Lutheran Evangelical, and other Protestant societies remained mostly in coastal regions as well as the western southern forest zone until the late 1950s when the independent Council of Baptist and Evangelical Churches of Cameroon (CEBEC) was formed and mission activity spread farther into the east.[67] African catechists from the Wouri river and coastal regions and those catechists from western Cameroon became the most prominent teachers of Baptist theology and coordinated with Presbyterian catechists and teachers to transmit Reformed Christianity farther south and east.[68]

African-led evangelism in the southern forest zone both shaped and was shaped by population relocation and reorganization as a result of colonial infrastructure projects and the French *régime du travail*. Jan Vansina was perhaps the first to provide a thorough analysis of the Central African forest zone, and rightly perceived that changes to the physical environment and cultural patterns considerably disturbed human relationships.[69] Vansina's insights into the "equatorial tradition," or the dynamic nature of precolonial social and legal relations, led him to believe that as African kinship, intermarriage, and decentralized authority structures mutated with incorporation into French colonial systems, they were "prevented ... from inventing new structures to cope..."[70] The "irreversible crisis" of Africans' cognitive inadaptability to "unforeseen and hitherto unimaginable events of the colonial conquest," Vansina claimed, spelled the death of the equatorial tradition in the 1920s.[71] Celebrated novelist Mongo Beti depicted societies in his Cameroonian *pays natal* experiencing this painful cultural decline in the novels, *Le Roi miraculé*, *Mission terminée*, and *Le pauvre Christ de Bomba*. In these works, only ontological insecurity, alienation, passive dependence, and confusion result from missionary Christianity and constant subordination.[72] These interpretations

---

[67] Messina and Slageren, *Histoire Du Christianisme Au Cameroun*, 65–70.

[68] The American Presbyterian Mission also received funding from the French Protestant Mission via French government funds for the operation of mission schools. SMEP/DEFAP EEC Inventaire du Fonds Brutsch (hereafter FB) 2/2, EEC Divers, vie des eglises I; PHS West Africa Mission, Mission Meeting Minutes 1952, Elat, July–August 1952.

[69] Vansina, *Paths in the Rainforests. Toward a History of Political Tradition in Equatorial Africa*.

[70] Vansina, 247.

[71] Vansina, 247.

[72] Mongo Beti, *Mission Terminée* (Paris: Buchet/Chastel, 1957); Mongo Beti, *Le Roi miraculé; chronique des Essazam, roman* (Paris: Buchet/Chastel, Correa, 1958); Mongo Beti, *Le pauvre Christ de Bomba* (Paris: Presence africaine, 1976). See also Mohamed Aït-Aarab, *Mongo Beti. Un écrivain engagé* (Paris: Karthala, 2013). While noting Beti's formidable contributions to contemporary understandings of how African

leave little room for recognizing adaptation, resistance, or accommodation among these dynamic societies.[73]

In her examination of equatorial African histories, Florence Bernault contrasted Vansina's scholarly approach with that of Jean-François Bayart, who has argued for the political and cultural continuity of equatorial peoples from the precolonial era through the late twentieth century.[74] Bayart provides evidence for the endurance of the "capacity of the lineage" in contemporary state politics, pointing to vestigal kin and family ties at work in what he terms "local popular modes of political action."[75] Likewise, Christopher Gray demonstrated that despite the ruptures of colonialism, equatorial communities in colonial Gabon retained their historic "cognitive map" of esoteric knowledge and spiritual systems to maintain community resiliency.[76] Bayart and Gray help us to more carefully perceive the continuance of the competitive and cooperative equatorial lineage structure in expressions of political power throughout history, and Gray convinces us of its strength in preserving the religious mysteries of the precolonial past.[77] Nevertheless, there remain significant distinctions

---

society experienced colonialism in Cameroon, this book challenges late twentieth-century Western academic epistemologies that have shaped what constitutes "postcolonial literature" to revisit African voices that discuss colonial experiences with Christianity in distinct and individualist terms. This book considers the insights provided in novels by Cameroonian authors Joseph Owono and Marie-Claire Matip – overlooked in postcolonial literary studies – to discern cultural change as experienced by Cameroon's devout Christians. See Joseph Owono, *Tante Bella: Roman d'aujourd'hui et de Demain* (Yaoundé: Librairie "Au Messager," 1959); Marie-Claire Matip, *Ngonda* (Paris: Bibliothèque du Jeune Africain, 1958).

[73] David Robinson provides an alternative to interpreting dramatic change as either "death" or "continuation" in Muslim West Africa and demonstrates the importance of negotiated relations wherein some autonomy is preserved while some realms of power are ceded. See David Robinson, *Paths of Accommodation: Muslim Societies and French Colonial Authorities in Senegal and Mauritania, 1880–1920*, 1 edition (Athens, OH and Oxford: Ohio University Press, 2000).

[74] Florence Bernault, *Démocraties Ambigües En Afrique Centrale, Congo-Brazzaville, Gabon: 1940–1965* (Paris: Karthala, 1996), 11–12.

[75] Jean-François Bayart, "Civil Society in Africa," in *Political Domination in Africa: Reflections on the Limits of Power*, ed. Patrick Chabal (Cambridge: Cambridge University Press, 1986), 109–25.

[76] Christopher J. Gray, *Colonial Rule and Crisis in Equatorial Africa: Southern Gabon, c. 1850–1940* (Rochester, NY: University of Rochester Press, 2002).

[77] See also Jean-François Bayart, *The State in Africa: The Politics of the Belly* (London and New York: Longman Group, 1993); Jean-François Bayart, *L'Etat Au Cameroun* (Paris: Presses de la fondation nationale de science politique, 1985). For the Church as a political agent in Cameroon, see Jean-François Bayart, "Les Rapports Entre Les Églises et l'État Du Cameroun de 1958 à 1971," *Revue Française d'Etudes Politiques Africaines* 80 (1972): 79–104; Jean-François Bayart, "Les Eglises Chrétiennes et La Politique Du

between equatorial societies "then" and "now."[78]

Incontrovertibly, increasing numbers of Africans professed Christianity throughout the interwar period in Cameroon, and the African Catholic population alone grew to more than 500,000 by the end of French rule.[79] African Protestants, largely organized by the mission schools affiliated with the Paris Evangelical Missionary Society (SMEP), the American Presbyterian Mission, and the Native Baptist Church, comprised a population of roughly 300,000 in 1960.[80] Christian commitments did not only affect marriage, sexual reproduction, the family economy, and social life, but also what Mbembe terms "symbolic coercion" – how culture produces definitions in the world and how a system of behaviors can come to reflect an understanding of truth.[81] Throughout the

---

Ventre: Le Partage Du gâteau Ecclésial in L'argent de Dieu.," *Politique Africaine*, no. 35 (1989): 3–26; Bayart, "Civil Society in Africa."

[78] This book emphasizes rupture as well as endurance in assessing the process of Christian conversion. There are many critiques of "continuity thinking" in studies of Christianity and Christianization. Joel Robbins forcefully argued that anthropologists have diminished the significance of religious and cultural change in the modern era, to the detriment of adequately explaining ruptures. Kim Bowes similarly forwards that in studies of Antiquity, historians "assume a tacit teleology" whereby longstanding customs and even worldviews endure throughout profound transformations in political, religious, or social structures such as the broad-scale conversion of inhabitants of the Roman Empire to Christianity. Peter Brown states that these kinds of assumptions "fail to do justice to the elements of novelty that ... accompanied the rise of Christianity." Joel Robbins, "Continuity Thinking and the Problem of Christian Culture: Belief, Time, and the Anthropology of Christianity," *Current Anthropology* 48, no. 1 (2007): 5–38; Kim Bowes, *Private Worship, Public Values, and Religious Change in Late Antiquity*, 1 edition (Cambridge and New York: Cambridge University Press, 2008). Peter Brown, *Through the Eye of a Needle: Wealth, the Fall of Rome, and the Making of Christianity in the West, 350–550 AD* (Princeton, NJ: Princeton University Press, 2014), 83.

[79] This number includes baptized Catholics and catechumens. In 1960, the Yaoundé diocese counted over 300,000 African Catholics and 91,000 catechumens. The Douala diocese included roughly 200,000 baptized believers. R.P. Bouchaud, "Cameroun: Eglise et Communisme," *Spiritains: Missions Des Peres Du St. Esprit* 31, no. 1 (March 1958); Bengt Sundkler & Christopher Steed, *A History of the Church in Africa* (Cambridge: Cambridge University Press, 2000), 756.

[80] Kengne Pokam, *Les eglises chrétiennes face à la montée du nationalisme camerounais* (Paris: L'Harmattan, 1987), 59–60; Roger Dussercle, *Du Kilima-Ndjaro au Cameroun, Monseigneur F.X. Vogt (1870–1943)* (Paris: Éditions du Vieux Colombier, 1954), 122; and Jean-Paul Messina, "Contribution des Camerounais à l'expansion de l'eglise catholique. Cas des populations du sud-Cameroun 1890–1961," Thèse présentée pour l'obtention du Doctorat du 3eme cycle d'histoire sous la direction du Professeur Mveng, Université de Yaoundé, 1988, pg. 194.

[81] Achille Mbembe, *Afriques Indociles : Christianisme, Pouvoir, et État en Société Postcoloniale* (Paris: Karthala, 1988), 26.

interwar years in Cameroon, there was a conversion of men and of women, conversions in villages, in cities, of the wealthy, and of the poor. Privileged church hierarchies incorporated young converts, which challenged generational cleavages of status. Through all this, the Christian Churches built a diverse set of clients, but with a similar set of strategies for reconstituting symbolic understandings, ritual life, and interpersonal responsibilities and rights.[82]

The African Catholic clergy grew more slowly than the ranks of African Protestant pastors in Cameroon, and both Churches were assisted by far more numerous and locally active cadres of catechists, evangelists, church elders, nuns, deaconesses, and friars, who often recruited their brothers, cousins, nephews, and other kin to serve alongside them. While ordained African Catholic priests could not marry and have children, they emerged in the late interwar period as a formidable influence in rural parishes and the Church hierarchy, in large part because of their continued influence in lineage and village affairs. By the later interwar period in 1937, roughly 5,000 African Catholic catechists coordinated catechism, charitable works, and mutual aid with eight African priests, nineteen African friars, and six African nuns. In that year they arranged and assisted in over 26,000 baptisms and 5,000 Catholic marriages.[83] The energy present in the religious life of close-knit lineage societies prompted hundreds of young African men to join seminaries after being inspired or encouraged by their cousins, brothers, or uncles, and by the end of World War II, Cameroon had roughly three dozen indigenous Catholic priests and nearly one hundred pastors of Protestant denominations, often assigned to multiple parishes to manage rapidly growing congregations.[84] Oral interviews with Catholic priests and friars in Cameroon revealed to me that the intimacies between siblings, uncles and nephews, grandparents and grandchildren, and other relations only strengthened as Africans molded the lineage structure to suit the Christian Churches as their new institutional homes.

Overall, African men in Cameroon had considerable success in ascending the ranks of various clerical and lay ecclesiastical hierarchies. They even forced institutions like the Catholic Church to worry about "ruptures" between

---

[82] Mbembe, 32.
[83] ACSSp. 2J1.8.a1 L'Effort Catholique Français au Cameroun, les Peres du Saint-Esprit: Vicariats apostoliques de Yaoundé et Douala, Rapport 1937.
[84] Ngongo, *Histoire des forces religieuses au Cameroun*. In conducting oral interviews, I learned that Mgr. Athanase Bala, former bishop of Bafia, is the cousin of another famous bishop, Mgr. Paul Etoga, former bishop of Mbalmayo and the first African bishop to serve in Cameroon. Many other elite clergymen also have a relative in the ranks of the ecclesiastical hierarchy. Interview with Athanase Bala, CSSp., Bishop emeritus of Bafia, Cameroon, on July 8, 2015, Seminaire des Missions, Congrégation du Saint-Esprit, Chevilly Larue, France.

the local and foreign clergies after African priests assumed greater levels of influence and popularity among the populace in the late 1930s, challenging the authority of European bishops and mission leaders.[85] African pastors in French Protestant missions also became revered and powerful authorities in their own right, and some were notorious for snubbing European clergymen who visited their churches by leaving prominent foreigners to participate in – rather than direct – rites and liturgies.[86] As African men gained legitimacy as authorities on theological and spiritual issues and made their presence known throughout the territory, they gained devoted followings and provided ideological justification for deciding actions such as baptism, betrothal, marriage, or divorce. In leading and adapting Christian agendas, African lay and ecclesiastical leaders assumed the legitimacy of foreign institutions while displacing the supremacy of their institutional leaders, becoming what the Beti termed *ntang-evindi*, a white man with black skin.[87]

African evangelists' management of Church institutions and their frequent noncompliance with colonial laws made them wildly popular among African congregations but deeply despised by French colonial officials. Having gained both eminence and a means of communication with their publics through meetings, catechism, administering sacraments, and the confessional press, Christian leaders initiated new strategies that exploited the destructive outcomes of French political decentralization in order to gain followers. Converts eagerly sought answers to the growing conflicts in families and communities that resulted from forced labor conscription and economic injustice that wrought bridewealth inflation, impoverishment, and spouselessness. Religious communities' solutions often deployed Christian social teachings and in particular, doctrinal teachings on monogramous marriage, in their efforts to restore social equilibrium and receive spiritual grace.

In every decade, indigenous authorities in the Churches inaugurated new kinds of individual and collective action, and shaped social forms and moral codes to the extent that they recreated the institution of marriage and traditions of family-building among their followers, thus enacting strategies that were arguably more transformative than those of the colonial regime.

---

[85] ACSSp. 2J1.13.b3 Lettre de Rome, Sigismondi et R.P. Murphy 2710/61, 15 juin 1960.

[86] André Privat was particularly outraged by the controlling leadership of Cameroonian Pastor Paul Jocky of the Evangelical Church. By contrast, he found the Baptist churches more welcoming of European pastors' presence and mentorship. André Privat, *Coup de coeur pour l'Afrique: 1956–1957* (Geneva: Editions du Pressoir de Montalègre, 1992), 246.

[87] Jean-Paul Messina, "Contribution Des Camerounais à l'expansion de l'Église Catholique Le Cas Des Populations Du Sud-Cameroun, 1890–1961" (Université de Yaoundé, 1988), 263.

In working to incorporate Christian marriage into the renovated traditions of Africans in the equatorial forest zone, African religious leaders mediated the cultural conflicts between social obligations, economic exigencies, political demands, and religious devotion – reconciling the population with their contemporary circumstances. Extending J.D.Y. Peel's conclusions that devout Africans determined the course of conversion in their communities by strategically preserving *and* adapting indigenous ethical codes to reflect the Commandments, this book demonstrates how African Christian leaders – and particularly catechists, priests, and pastors – acted as buffers against radical change, but also intentionally propelled it.[88]

Influenced by sermons, texts, or more intimate encounters such as confessions or prayer groups, converts became more aware of the deleterious effects of longstanding local marriage practices at the same time as they were pressured by new forces like taxation, the *indigènat*, forced labor recruitment, arbitrary rule by chiefs, and fluctuating market prices for their crops.[89] Rather than "clinging" to older cognitive systems or becoming "cultural schizophrenics" as Vansina concluded, Africans developed a dynamic series of responses with particular zeal during the period between the onset of World War I and the outbreak of World War II. In this way, new communitarian practices were produced through religious means, which gave rise to the presence of multiple lineage, transethnic, and cross-cultural confessional units, which this book will call *Christian publics*. These publics led their members toward new forms of personal piety, collective worship, and cultural expression, deriving their momentum from the desire to fully understand a new belief system that sought to alter African religious life and address the profound changes in relations between men and women in everyday life.

The Framework of French Colonial Governance: Foreign and Local Power

When the League of Nations officially recognized the French mandate territory of Cameroon's integration into the legal framework of French Equatorial Africa in 1922, French military, administration, and concessionary officials had been policing, managing, and organizing export, tax, labor systems with

---

[88] Peel, *Religious Encounter and the Making of the Yoruba*.
[89] Some of the best accounts of intimate social change in the colonial period in Cameroon include Guyer, "Head Tax, Social Structure and Rural Incomes in Cameroun, 1922–37"; Jane I Guyer, "Family and Farm in Southern Cameroon" ([Boston, MA]: Boston University, African Studies Center, 1984); Robert and Walters, "Invention of Tradition: Chieftaincy, Adaptation and Change in the Forest Region of Cameroon"; Andreas Eckert, "African Rural Entrepreneurs and Labor in the Cameroon Littoral," *Journal of African History*, no. 40 (1999): 109–26.

their indigenous intermediaries for nearly seven years.[90] Although the 1922 Original Mandate Accords' idealistic rhetoric announced a "sacred trust of civilization" that would protect the "well-being and development" of subject peoples, this study supports Alice Conklin's claim that the interwar years were "among the most coercive of the colonial period."[91] The postwar mandate was to transform Africa by increasing productivity and strengthening established hierarchies, which can be seen in 1915, when French commissioner Lorin disclosed his new vision for Cameroon after the war stating, "what is most important of all is establishing order ... mandating work ... The education of Africans now remains a question of policing them."[92]

In the first decade of French presence in Cameroon, French military and government officials were wary of disrupting productive industries or alienating potential collaborators.[93] The heavy presence of Hamburg traders for several decades had influenced labor and political organization in the coastal and southern regions, and the fledgling French colonial administration between 1915 and 1920 acted to preserve the "continuity of ideas" initiated by German

---

[90] The Treaty of Versailles granted France the greater part of the former German territory, with the smaller region bordering Nigeria granted to Great Britain (see Map 4). The League of Nations then conferred mandates to France and Great Britain to administer their respective territories in Cameroon as part of their empires. The French mandate was known as 'Cameroun' and the British territory was administered as two areas, Northern Cameroons and Southern Cameroons. See ANOM AFFPOL 615/1; Patrick Manning, *Francophone Sub-Saharan Africa 1880–1985* (Cambridge and New York: Cambridge University Press, 1988), 79–100.

[91] Alice Conklin, *A Mission to Civilize: The Republican Idea of Empire in France and West Africa, 1895–1930*, 1 edition (Stanford: Stanford University Press, 2000), 247. Convention de Saint Germain-en-Laye, 1919, see ANOM AFFPOL 3349/2. The Permanent Mandates Commission carried on day-to-day supervision under the authority of the League Council. David E. Gardinier, *Cameroon: United Nations Challenge to French Policy* (London: Oxford University Press, 1963), 9–12.

[92] ANOM AFFPOL 615/1 "Cameroun 1915–1919," Lettre du M.M. Lorin, "Les Colonies Allemandes et les Alliés en Afrique" au Délégué de Gouvernement Général de l'Afrique Equatoriale Française, Bureau d'Etudes Economiques, Décembre 1915, pg. 39.

[93] Documentary evidence suggests that French administrators hurriedly read manuals and reports on German modes of rule to swiftly gain an understanding of environmental conditions, the export potential of agricultural and forest products, and political strategy. Numerous copies of Karl Ritter's *Neu Kamerun* of 1912 and *Die Deutsch Schutzgebiete in Afrika und Der (Sudsea)* of 1913 were ordered by French officials, along with Karl von der Hedyt's *Kolonialhandbuch* and Alfred Zimmermann's *Geschichte der deutschen Kolonialpolitik*. ANOM AGEFOM 956/3199 Lettre 134 de l'administration Française au Cameroun à Monsieur le Gouverneur Général de l'AEF à Brazzaville, 3 avril 1915; ANOM AFFPOL 612/4, "Cameroun et la Politique Allemande- Liquidation des biens Allemands au Togo et Cameroun." See also ANOM AFFPOL 615/1 Rapport du Decembre 1923, "Les indigenes et la suite dans les idées."

concessionary operations.[94] Accordingly, in the years between military rule and official mandate recognition, the governance of everyday affairs was largely in the hands of private concessionary companies along with a small cadre of bureaucrats and representatives in Dakar, Brazzaville, and Paris.[95] With few regional commanders and generally scarce personnel in the early years after the war, commissioner Lorin agreed that *concessionaires* would "establish French influence" in Cameroon by managing rural labor forces.[96]

Although concessionary companies' influence was moderated in later decades, replaced by district governments, local representative bodies, and judicial systems, crude and despotic techniques of labor and population control remained in place until the Brazzaville reforms of 1944.[97] According to laws passed in 1924 and 1927, "every adult of masculine sex" was obligated to furnish 10 days per annum of *prestation* (service) for "the accomplishment of works in the public interest."[98] While the 1924 law established a salary of 1 franc per day, its revision was more vague and mentioned women could be paid

[94] ANOM AGEFOM 799/1857 Lettre de M.M. Lorin, Délégué de Gouvernement Général de l'Afrique Equatoriale Francaise Bureau d'Etudes Economiques, décembre 1915; See also ANOM AGEFOM 799/1857 Commerce Forestiere, 1917–1918.

[95] ANOM AGEFOM 799/1857 lettre de Dakar à M. le secretaire à Brazzaville, 31 août 1918. Representatives from the Compagnie Forestière de Sangha-Oubangui formed a close relationship with the transitional government and continued to lobby for lower tax and export levies and greater control of forest concessions throughout the mandate era. The Concessionary Oversight Board of French Equatorial Africa also worked alongside the French administration in Cameroon to oversee export development, and in 1919, the Board sent directives demanding the commissioner "organize labor" and "control the male population." ANOM AGEFOM 956/3199 télégramme du Dakar, 31 août 1918 de Robinneau et Angoulvant des Compagnies Forestières de Sangha-Oubangui, à M. le Gov. Sec. Général à Brazzaville; ANOM AGEFOM 956/3199 lettres du M. Weber, Directeur des Forêts à Brazzaville, 1920; ANOM AGEFOM 956/3199 lettre de P. Boisson, AEF Contrôle des Concessions, à M. le Ministre des Colonies, "Etendue des concessions territoriales au Cameroun," 13 déc. 1919.

[96] This proved to be a flawed assumption, as *concessionaries* invested little in economic development and were principally interested in short-term financial gain. Historians such as Catherine Coquery-Vidrovitch, Victor T. LeVine, Daniel N. Posner, and Jean-François Bayart argue that this behavior in the early decades of the twentieth century established a pattern of economic behavior that continues in present-day Africa. See Catherine Coquery-Vidrovitch, *Le Congo au Temps des Grands Compagnies Concessionnaires, 1898–1930* (Paris and the Hague: Mouton and Co., 1972); Victor T. Le Vine, *Poltiics in Francophone Africa*, (London: Lynne Rienner Publishers, 2004); Daniel N. Posner, *Institutions and Ethnic Politics in Africa* (Cambridge: Cambridge University Press, 2004); Bayart, *The State in Africa: The Politics of the Belly*.

[97] Léon Kaptue, *Cameroun: Travail et Main-d'Oeuvre Sous Le Régime Français, 1916–1952* (Paris: L'Harmattan, 1986), 30–44.

[98] ANOM TP Série 1 420/11, Arrêté du 1 juillet 1924; Arrêté du 9 mars 1927.

less than men, presumably because they only carried food and water for the laborers.[99] As volunteers for *prestation* were rare, forced recruitments began in 1916 to complete sanitation work in towns, roadwork on forest paths, brush clearing for railroads and highways, waterway maintenance, and building construction. While the law technically excluded the elderly, women, children under sixteen, the sick, notables, chiefs, and police from forced labor, reports throughout the 1920s and 1930s (most frequently from missionary observers) detail the extensive use of women, children, and the elderly in manual labor and the general neglect of the 10-day service limit. In 1935, the Cameroon Public Works Commission recorded 1,795,750 days of forced labor by African workers.[100]

Another notable contribution of concessionary partnerships to the long-term governance of the mandate was the use of the *indigénat* code as a central element of the authority structure. Formally established in Cameroon in 1917, the *indigénat* provided disciplinary authority for district officers but was often broadly interpreted as administrative police powers and powers to impose fines, corporal punishment, and prison sentences on Africans and all colonized peoples without a legal or judicial appeal.[101] The *indigénat* enumerated penalties for crimes including theft, assault, and refusal to pay taxes, as well as refusing to work in a labor camp, disobedience to a chief in the employment of the administration, or "disrespect" towards colonial representatives.[102] Although French ministers in Paris and in French West Africa claimed the *indigénat*

---

[99] The Annual Report of 1925 mentions that women performing work along the roads as "food porters and cooks" could be paid 0.30 francs per day. AFFPOL 2190/1 Rapport annuel du gouvernement français sur l'administration sous mandat des territoires du Cameroun pour l'année 1925.

[100] For reference, the total estimated population of all of Cameroon in 1931 was 2,223,802. ANOM TP Série 1 420/11, Rapport à la Société des Nations Année 1935, Services des Travaux Publics Chemins de Fer, Portes et Rades, 75. The 1931 census was reported in Rapport annuel adressée par le gouvernement français au conseil de la Société Des Nations sur l'administration sous mandat du territoire du Cameroun pour l'année 1931, 45.

[101] Decret du 14 mars 1917. A typical punishment was a period of fifteen days in jail or one hundred francs' fine. Eckert, "African Rural Entrepreneurs and Labor in the Cameroon Littoral."

[102] Monga and Eckert have written on the *indigénat* as a means of labor recruitment among coastal populations. Yvette Monga, "The Emergence of Duala Cocoa Planters under German Rule in Cameroon: A Case Study of Entrepreneurship," in *Cocoa Pioneer Fronts Since 1800: The Role of Smallholders, Planters, and Merchants*, ed. William Gervase Clarence-Smith (Basingstoke: Palgrave Macmillan, 1996), 119–36.; Andreas Eckert, "Cocoa Farming in Cameroon, c.1914–1960," in *Cocoa Pioneer Fronts since 1800: The Role of Planters, Smallholders, and Merchants*, ed. W. Gervase Clarence-Smith (New York: St. Martin's Press, 1996), 137–53.

was only an "early stage" system of legal authority necessary for "initiating" Africans to French law, calls for its repeal in 1924 were rejected, with officials stating that Africa was "still in an era of transition."[103] As a recently acquired territory, Cameroon embodied the "transitioning" colony until after World War II.[104] Many studies have demonstrated that colonial administrations worked through a simulacra of customary regulation, but unlike previous narratives of the "invention of tradition" in colonial Africa, the history of interwar Cameroon illustrates that punishing colonial legal systems and improvised chiefdoms, were not, as Mamdani describes, "a world...from which there was no escape."[105] Precisely, new kinds of peer restraint and popular constraint emerged—distinct from any previous counterforces—in the form of African Christian principals and publics, whose most serious challenges included new religious agendas for cultural coherence and social reform that prioritized Christian marriage and family building, mutual aid and cooperative assistance, and individualized, household-based, masculine authority.

Religious and Political Fluidity in Colonial Cameroon

The efficacy of African Christians in circulating religious tenets that criticized the behaviors of both foreign and local potentates and their success in leading reform-minded activism was evident to a great many African and white observers of early-twentieth-century Cameroon.[106] Most French officials saw African catechists as purely politically motivated, however, and routinely expressed

---

[103] ANOM Fonds AEF, 1 H 74, 540/3, Rapport au President de la Republique Francaise, suivi d'un décret portant réglementation des sanctions de police administrative indigène en Afrique Occidentale, en Afrique Equatoriale, à Madagascar, et à la Cote des Somalis, Jean Fabry, 19 nov. 1924, No. 382.

[104] ANC APA 10634/A Décret de 13 avril 1921, Article 3 de Jules Carde. The Decrees of 30 November 1926 and 27 February 1929 expanded terms of the *indigénat* to protect various district officials, police officers, and security officials in their use of the *indigénat* disciplinary functions. ANOM Fonds AEF 1 H 74, 540/2, Décret du 30 novembre 1926, article 8; Décret du 27 février 1929.

[105] Mahmood Mamdani, *Citizen and Subject: Contemporary Africa and the Legacy of Late Colonialism* (Princeton: Princeton University Press, 1996), 21. See also Martin Chanock, *Law, Custom and Social Order: The Colonial Experience in Malawi and Zambia* (Cambridge and New York: Cambridge University Press, 1985).

[106] SMEP/DEFAP Fonds Allégret: Cameroun 1920, Rapports d'Elie Allégret, Mission Protestant de Duala, 1921–1930; ANC APA 11016/G, Lettres de Mgr. Vogt, Père le Hunsec. See also Aggée Célestin Lomo Myazhiom, *Sociétés et Rivalités religieuses au Cameroun sous domination Française (1916–1958)* (Paris: L'Harmattan, 2001).

their doubts regarding Africans' religious convictions.[107] John Peel offers a rich example of how to carefully untangle the motives, inspirations, and transformations that animated African evangelists and converts but ultimately reminds us that religious change is often attendant with the emergence of both intense conflict and uneven or unjust power structures. As such, religion serves as a cosmology but also a means of shaping authority, community, and power relations between them.[108] Although spiritual inspiration in southern Cameroon likely stemmed from or merged with social, economic, and cultural influences, French officials were convinced Africans could only mobilize for worldly concerns.[109] Karen Fields, in her study of the Watchtower movement in Central Africa, offers an illuminating insight into how Christian revival can simultaneously emerge from a society's reception of revealed wisdom about God and from resistance to political subordination. Inspired by interpretations of a salvation event, Watchtower adherents launched a millenarian movement that engaged in civil disobedience against chiefs, but also colonial authorities and missionaries, freeing themselves from both neo-traditional and modern controls to prepare for an entirely new existence.[110] Fields rejects the "political view" of religious conversion that perceives "the cause of extraordinary belief lies in real social discontent" as well as the "cultural view" that assumes conversion was imposed by "stress occasioned by cultural change."[111] Fields recognizes that religion and politics were rarely separate realms in African societies. For the Watchtower followers, since the hope of salvation guided responsible action in everyday life, and spiritual belief was routine common sense, the supernatural was embedded in mundane social relations. Fields adds that

[107] ACSSp. 2J1.10.12 Lucien Fourneau, Circulaire no. 26, Douala 5 juin 1917; ACSSp. 2J1.10.12, Père Pichon, "Une escroquerie administrative, 1927"; ANOM AFFPOL 2192/9 Lettre de Delavignette à M. le Ministre des Colonies à Paris, 5 septembre 1946; AFFPOL 2192/6 Les Missions religieuses au Cameroun, 1949–1954.

[108] Peel, *Religious Encounter and the Making of the Yoruba*.

[109] Curiously, French officials' bias toward the secular was echoed decades later in historians' analyses of African value-based mobilizations, in particular in the historiography of the interactions between (anti) colonial politics, identity politics, and Christian engagement. Terence Ranger has deconstructed debates on the Watchtower movement in Central Africa, where interpretations of the Christian revival movement as variously "anti-colonialist," "nationalist," "proto-nationalist," "class-based," or "proto-proletarian" occupied scholars for decades. Ranger credits Karen Fields with being the first to assess the Watchtower movement "in its own terms and within its own context rather than as a more or less distorted and unsatisfactory forerunner of nationalism or of class consciousness." Terence O. Ranger, "Religious Movements and Politics in Sub-Saharan Africa," *African Studies Review* 29, no. 2 (1986): 1–69.

[110] Fields, *Revival and Rebellion in Colonial Central Africa*.

[111] Fields, 19–20.

this recognition would be equally necessary when studying sixteenth-century Anabaptists or seventeenth-century Puritans – dovetailing Talal Asad's argument that prior to Enlightenment methods of intellectual and political control, religion in Europe was similarly embodied in politics, economics, and social relations and was not considered "an otherworldly belief system."[112]

Similar to Fields's revivalists, African Protestant and Catholic catechists in Cameroon believed that their religious faith produced knowledge and judgments about the world of lived experience and that piety could sanction insurrection. However, they were not anti-colonial radicals. Despite being accused of such, catechists and other African Christian leaders in Cameroon typically sought to educate their lineages and societies about Christ's revelation and then worked to displace or discipline those among them whose behaviors contradicted its realization. These forms of dissent were the result of both devotional and defiant feelings inspired by scripture and theological interpretation circulating in their local environment. African catechists', priests', and pastors' criticisms of chiefs, fathers, and French officials, combined with their superior ability to recruit faithful, obedient supporters who evaded labor conscription on railroads but volunteered to build churches and paid tithes but not taxes appeared to French officials as clear indications of "political hostility, under cover of religious conviction," but the record bears little evidence of organized anti-colonial resistance.[113]

Nevertheless, African Christians' mobilizations for religious and social reform prompted the French mandate administration to pass legislation that explicitly sought to contain their influence beginning in the late 1920s. Measures in the colonial judiciary had begun over a decade earlier as indigenous evangelists were prosecuted and harshly sentenced in the colonial courts for acts of insubordination and wielding undue influence.[114] French governors interpreted Africans' religious zeal as political defiance, as popular African clergymen and catechists provoked a full-scale "diminishment of native authority" and "imperiled the natural guardians of African races."[115] African communities

---

[112] Asad, *Formations of the Secular: Christianity, Islam, Modernity*. Derek Peterson has also detailed the intellectual history of the Enlightenment formation of "otherworldly" belief systems distinct from politics and economics. See Derek Peterson, "Gambling with God: Rethinking Religion in Colonial Central Kenya," in *The Invention of Religion: Rethinking Belief in Politics and History*, ed. Derek Peterson and Darren Walhof (New Brunswick, NJ: Rutgers University Press, 2002), 37–58.

[113] ANOM AFFPOL 2192/9 Lettre de Delavignette à M. le Ministre des Colonies à Paris, 5 septembre 1946.

[114] ANC APA 11016/G réglementation sur les cultes, Bonnecarrère 1933.

[115] ANC APA 11016/G Circulaire no. 78 application de la réglementation sur les cultes, du 16 sept. 1933; Louis-Paul Ngongo, *Histoire des forces religieuses au Cameroun* (Paris: Éditions Karthala, 1982), 60–1.

innovated novel forms of authority, which French officials believed was a dangerous divergence from the pathway toward advancement projected by colonial rule.[116] As is apparent from the first edicts of Lucien Fourneau, the first civilian French governor of Cameroon, the mandate administration was never fully convinced of the possibility of real Christian conversion or of Africans' ability to direct their own cultural adaptation.

African catechists enhanced their power and multiplied their numbers considerably during the French mandate. By 1935, the Vicariate of Yaoundé counted 2,500 African catechists and the Vicariate of Douala estimated 2,000 in service in its jurisdiction, including non-salaried teachers.[117] French officials' complaints regarding catechists' propensities to disrupt work on chiefs' farms and evade concessionary and infrastructure projects were soon eclipsed by frantic objections to catechists' conversions of women in polygamous marriages, who they then delivered to missions to be given new spouses.[118] Administrators accused catechists of "scandal" and "disorder," blaming them for "new currents and factors that have transformed the region sociologically and culturally."[119] Simultaneously, however, foreign officials expressed alarm at African chiefs' "incontestably gruesome" polygamy, describing them as "a patriarchal regime in decadence."[120] Although African catechists and French officials may have been in agreement about chiefs' abuses, high-level authorities worried that Christians' criticisms and direct actions were "a dramatic upset, a premature reform ... that would provoke action in the *mileu social* where instability is already too real a threat."[121]

The furtherance of imposed chieftaincy in southern Cameroon despite officials' misgivings demonstrates that disciplining black bodies was a jealously guarded function of the colonial state. Evidence that peer-organized reform was condemned also points to the fact that in interwar Cameroon, masculine authority was a subjectivity in the making. African evangelists instructed catechesis and promoted mutual cooperation and charitable assistance to

---

[116] ACSSp. 2J1.2b2 Lettre de l'administration à Yaoundé à Mgr. Vogt, 12 Mai 1923.

[117] ACSSp. 2J1.13b1, statistiques Catholiques; ACSSp. 2J1.7a2, Abbé Michel Hardy, Cooperation missionnaire du Diocese de Séez, "Sur la Terre d'Afrique: Relation d'un voyage d'étude au Cameroun," 8–27 Janvier 1968.

[118] ANOM AGEFOM 989/3419 Cameroun 1930–1931, Les Missions 1931; ANOM AGEFOM 989/3424 Justice 1927–1933.

[119] ANOM AGEFOM 989/3424 lettre de Guibert à le chef de circonscription d'Ebolowa, 7 jul 1932.

[120] ANOM AGEFOM 989/3424 Rapport du chef de subdivision de Sangmélima, Chefs superieurs M'Boutou Abeng et Mvondo Ekoa, 1932.

[121] ANOM AGEFOM 989/3424 Rapport du chef de subdivision de Sangmélima, Chefs superieurs M'Boutou Abeng et Mvondo Ekoa, 1932.

men and women in their villages and churches, but they also abducted chiefs' wives, policed immoral behavior, and harshly reproached family fathers and other patriarchs for upholding commonplace practices like polygamy and bridewealth.[122] In the late 1920s and 1930s, they continued to build their influence by coalescing into pious collectives, raising funds, and recruiting volunteers for their respective churches and denominations. For their part, chiefs innovated their commands and invented new taxes, married absent laborers' wives, manipulated both customary and civil law to their advantage, and allied themselves with regional officials, plantation managers, and fellow chiefs to control laborers. Although imperial authorities worked to maintain their dominance, subordination and discipline were also techniques of African self-command.

The Catechist as Catalyst: Innovating Masculinity and Moral Authority

The dimensions of this book that examine Christian transmission, Christian marriage, and the invention of new forms of masculine power are in discussion with an evolving and exciting field of inquiry: the literature on African men and masculinities and how they shape organized resistance, intervention, and community defense. While colonial Cameroon was not a war zone during the mandate era, as scholars of organized male dissent like Danny Hoffman, William Minter, or Liisa Malkki discuss, this study, like that of Janet Roitman, looks at the "regimes of regulation" established by African Christian men to establish legitimacy in a period of violence and disruption.[123] Hoffman's analysis of the "resonant, even identical" activities of male violence and male productivity is particularly salient in this context as both African chiefs and African Christian principals innovated new modes of supervision, constraint,

---

[122] This book employs the term "polygamy" rather than the more precise term, "polygyny," because "polygamy" was the central referent of the local and foreign Christian agents of the time and place this book examines. Christian mobilizations centered on "polygamy," and the term was deployed in nearly every religious missive, sermon, and catechism on marriage and the family. While the anthropological term "polygyny" more accurately refers to the phenomenon of plural wives and not simply "marriage with many spouses" (gender neutral), this book uses the term "polygamy" because when the historical agents of this work referred to "polygamy," they assumed it to mean "plural wives."

[123] William Minter, *Apartheid's Contras: An Inquiry Into the Roots of War in Angola and Mozambique* (William Minter, 1994); Liisa Malkki, *Purity and Exile: Violence, Memory, and National Cosmology Mong Hutu Refugees in Tanzania* (Chicago: University of Chicago Press, 1995); Janet Roitman, *Fiscal Disobedience: An Anthropology of Economic Regulation in Central Africa* (Princeton, NJ: Princeton University Press, 2004); Danny Hoffman, *The War Machines: Young Men and Violence in Sierra Leone and Liberia* (Durham, NC: Duke University Press, 2011).

and punishment for their respective subjects or followers within the arenas of marriage, labor management, and social control.[124]

African catechists expressed gendered identities through rhetorical ability, charismatism (manifestations of spiritual gifts), and ritual performance – all public demonstrations of authority typically reserved for men in the southern forest zone – as well as through exceptional acts such as confronting chiefs, police, and colonial officials.[125] As forceful warriors for a social and spiritual cause, catechists provide an important example of masculine performance and the reconstitution of male identity outside of the structures of wage labor and war—more typical sites of historical analysis of evolving masculinity.[126] In Cameroon, African catechists were quick to perceive chiefs' abilities to control both concrete and abstract forms of power – the labor power of wives and clients, the power to deploy violence, and the powers of prestige. However, catechists soon established their own regulatory regime, which formally organized through lineages and villages in proximity to Christian missions, calling together kin and joining them with the resources of the mission, which included education, salaried employment, the press organs, and inclusion in corporate worship. These activities reinforced Christian leaders' power to influence, organize, entrall, and, critically, compel their fellow men and women to obey commandments or challenge authorities.[127] As in Roitman's

---

[124] Hoffman, *The War Machines*, 111. Foucault's theory on the production of the political subject through contingent relations of dominance and resistance is also relevant here. See Michel Foucault, *Discipline and Punish: The Birth of the Prison* (London: Vintage Books, 1977), 29–30.

[125] I am indebted to the analysis of Luise White, who remarked that among Mau Mau fighters, gender roles were "an integral part of their political struggle." Luise White, "Separating the Men from the Boys: Constructions of Gender, Sexuality, and Terrorism in Central Kenya, 1939–1959," *International Journal of African Historical Studies* 23, no. 1 (1990): 3.

[126] For histories of African wage labor, see Charles Van Onselen, *Chibaro: African Mine Labour in Southern Rhodesia, 1900–1933* (London: Pluto Press, 1976); Jeanne Penvenne, *African Workers & Colonial Racism: Mozambican Strategies & Struggles in Lourenco Marques, 1877–1962* (Portsmouth, NH: Heinemann, 1994); Lisa A. Lindsay, "'No Need... to Think of Home'? Masculinity and Domestic Life on the Nigerian Railway, c. 1940–61," *The Journal of African History* 39, no. 3 (1998): 439–66; Lisa A. Lindsay, *Working with Gender: Wage Labor and Social Change in Southwestern Nigeria* (Portsmouth, NH: Heinemann, 2003); Clive Glaser, "Managing the Sexuality of Urban Youth: Johannesburg, 1920s–1960s," *The International Journal of African Historical Studies* 38, no. 2 (2005): 301–27; Molly McCullers, "'We Do It so That We Will Be Men': Masculinity Politics in Colonial Namibia, 1915–49," *The Journal of African History* 52, no. 1 (2011): 43–62.

[127] In his study of Christian Tswana men, Paul Landau refers to this cadre as the "conspiratory male core." Landau, *The Realm of the Word: Language, Gender, and Christianity in a Southern African Kingdom*, 82.

study of the garrison-entrepôt in the Cameroon–Chad Basin, in which men operate outside of state control, African catechists engaged in regulation, accumulation, redistribution, and sociability while remaining largely exterior to governmental authority.[128]

Controlling the marriages, labor contributions, and even sexual relations of black bodies – using their own techniques and without the governmental approval granted to chiefs – were African Christians' most subversive actions. These acts were not primarily (or not exclusively) about resistance, however. African Christian leaders and publics sought to constitute an alternative order to that of the colonial state and its associated chiefs, "responding," as Father Jean-Luc Enyegue, a Cameroonian Jesuit, explained in an interview, "to a call to membership in a new sacramental structure with a new sacred identity."[129] Constructing an alternative membership structure bound by Christian conjugal and family alliances also demonstrates far more than a desire to rebel against fabricated facsimiles of African political community. It demonstrates that African believers in southern Cameroon in the interwar period constructed the symbolic systems, communities, and institutions of Christianity, thereby embedding the faith into the structures of everyday life and defining and extending the reach of their Church.

Christianity in Cameroon's History

The history of Christianity in Cameroon has been memorialized in a considerable body of literature, much of which forwards that the profound and widespread influence of the Christian missions in the late nineteenth and early twentieth centuries transformed African societies and their politics in a way that shaped – and continues to shape – modern national culture. Ecumenical histories such as those of Jean-Paul Messina and Jaap van Slageren, Louis-Paul Ngongo, Jean-Marc Ela, Engelbert Mveng, and Aggée Célestin Lomo Myazhiom have offered an expansive view of how myriad foreign Churches made Cameroon the locus of missionary interest throughout the nineteenth and twentieth centuries and how confessional communities formed around these missions, who both opposed and emulated one another to heighten their own ecclesiastical and cultural prestige.[130] Histories addressing the evolutions

---

[128] Roitman, *Fiscal Disobedience: An Anthropology of Economic Regulation in Central Africa*, 299.

[129] Oral interview with Jean-Luc Enyegue, S.J., New York, February 25, 2016.

[130] Messina and Slageren, *Histoire Du Christianisme Au Cameroun*; Myazhiom, *Sociétés et Rivalités religieuses au Cameroun sous domination Française (1916–1958)*. Ngongo, *Histoire des forces religieuses au Cameroun*. Jean-Marc Ela, "Le Droit à La Différence Ou l'enjeu Des Églises Locales En Afrique Noire," in *Civilisation Noire et Eglise*

of particular Christian denominations are far more numerous and chronicle how simple missions became powerful cultural and institutional structures whose leadership systems and administrative networks arose from local sociocultural frameworks that compelled recognition of Church authority.[131]

A diverse range of historians, including many Cameroonian clergy-scholars, have made substantive contributions in analyzing the dynamics of how Christian rites and beliefs, as well as sacred music, art, and ornamentation replaced or fused with the preexisting spiritual modes of expression of particular ethno-regional groups. Jean-Pierre Ombolo, Isidore Tabi, and Pierre Mviena, among others, have meticulously reconstructed the Beti cultural universe's encounter with Catholicism and how Beti people inscribed the faith in ceremonies and commemorations of joy, pain, birth, death, and marriage.[132] Célestine Colette Fouellefak Kana-Dongmo, Abraham Tetouom,

---

Catholique, ed. Société africaine de Culture (Paris: Editions Présence africaine, 1978), 204–17. See also Kengne Pokam, *Les Églises Chrétiennes Face à La Montée Du Nationalisme Camerounais* (Paris: L'Harmattan, 1987); Engelbert Mveng, *Histoire Des Églises Chrétiennes Au Cameroun: Les Origines* (Yaoundé, Cameroon: Saint-Paul Mvolyé, 1990); Soeur Thérèse-Michèle Essomba Akamse, "Hommes et Femmes Pour Construire Ensemble l'Église En Afrique," in *Spiritualité et Libération En Afrique*, ed. Engelbert Mveng (Paris: L'Harmattan, 1987), 79–83; Engelbert Mveng, *Histoire du Cameroun* (Paris: Présence africaine, 1963).

[131] Jaap Van Slageren, *Les Origines de l'eglise Évangélique Du Cameroun: Missions Européennes et Christianisme Autochtone* (Leiden: Brill, 1972); Messina, "Contribution Des Camerounais à l'expansion de l'Église Catholique Le Cas Des Populations Du Sud-Cameroun, 1890–1961"; Jean-François Médard, "Les Eglises Protestantes Au Cameroun, Entre Tradition Authoritaire et Ethnicité," in *Religion et Transition Démocratique En Afrique*, ed. François Constantin and Christian Coulon (Paris: Karthala, 1997), 189–220; Frédéric Fabre, *Protestantisme et colonisation: l'évolution du discours de la mission protestante française au XXe siècle* (Paris: Karthala, 2011); Laburthe-Tolra, "La Mission Catholique Allemande Du Cameroun (1890–1916) et La Missologie"; Etaba, *Histoire de l'Eglise Catholique Du Cameroun de Grégoire XVI à Jean-Paul II*; F. Owono Ada, *De La Mission de l'Église Catholique Camerounaise: Origine, Formation et Rôle Des Prêtres Noirs* (Yaoundé: ENS, 1981). See also Eugene Wonyu, *Le Chrétien, Les Dons et La Mission Dans l'Eglise Africaine Independente: Réflexions d'un Laïc* (Douala: Eglise Protestante Camerounaise (BP 5421), 1979).

[132] Mviena, *Univers Culturel et Religieux Du Peuple Beti*; Jean-Pierre Ombolo, *Etre Beti, Un Art Africain d'etre Un Homme et de Vivre En Societe?: Essai d'analyse de l'esprit d'une Population : Une Etude Ethno-Historique (Collection Societes)* (Yaoundé: Presses Universitaires de Yaoundé, 2000); Isidore Tabi, *La Theologie Des Rites Beti: Essai d'explication Religieuse Des Rites Beti et Ses Implications Socio-Culturelles* (Yaoundé, Cameroon: Éditions St. Paul, 1991); Isidore Tabi, *Les Rites Beti Au Christ. Essai de Pastorale Liturgique Sur Quelques Rites de Nos Ancêtres* (Yaoundé: Imprimerie Saint-Paul, 1991); Isidore Tabi, "Cameroun Terre Mariale: Les Sanctuaires et Centres de Pélerinage Marial du Cameroun" (Ndonko, Cameroun, 1995).

and Odette Djoumessi Dongmo and Antoine Nguimzang have paid particular attention to the work of Bamileke authority figures and powerful agents among African societies in western Cameroon, who incorporated Christian texts and sacraments into local allegiance rituals.[133] Other researchers who have studied Presbyterianism among the Bulu and Baptist, Lutheran, and Catholic Christianity among the Bamoun, Bassa, and Duala societies have similarly chronicled the coordinated and interdependent processes of forging a denominational and an ethnic identity.[134] Copious biographies and autobiographies of Cameroonian pastors, priests, nuns, and catechists have also uncovered the expansive autonomy wielded by African Christian principals in their respective Churches as well as within their societies of origin, demonstrating the seamless congruence that evolved over a century of Christian exposure between spiritual and worldly leadership.[135]

---

[133] Odette Djoumessi Dongmo and Antoine Nguimzang, *Djoumessi Mathias, 1900–1966: Un Exemple de Chef Traditionnel Chrétien* (Yaoundé, Cameroon: Éditions SOPECAM, 1991); Célestine Colette Fouellefak Kana-Dongmo, "Acteurs locaux de l'implantation du catholicisme dans le pays Bamiléké au Cameroun," *Chrétiens et sociétés. XVIe–XXIe siècles*, no. 13 (December 31, 2006); Abraham Tetouom, "La polygamie et le Christianisme au pays Bamiléké" (Faculté libre de théologie protestante, 1966).

[134] Paul Richard Dekar, "Crossing Religious Frontiers: Christianity and the Transformation of Bulu Society, 1892–1925" (University of Chicago, 1978); Jean-Pierre Yetna, "Les Bassa et Mpoo Du Cameroun à La Recherche de l'unité Perdue," *Anthropos* 97, no. 2 (January 1, 2002): 551–2; Judith Njele, "Les Débuts Du Christianisme et Son Évolution En Pays Bamoun Au Cameroun" (Université Panthéon-Sorbonne, 2005); Austen and Derrick, *Middlemen of the Cameroons Rivers*; René Bureau, "Ethno-Sociologie Religieuse Des Duala et Apparentés," *Recherches et Etudes Camerounaises* 1&2, no. 8 (1962): 1–369.

[135] Francis Grob, *Témoins Camerounais de l'Evangile (Les Origines de L'Eglise Evangélique)* (Yaoundé, Cameroon: Editions CLE, 1967); François Akoa-Mongo, *Le Pasteur François Akoa Abômô: l'homme et l'oeuvre* (Bloomington, IN: Xlibris Corp, 2011); Jean-Paul Messina, *Des témoins camerounais de l'evangile: Andre Kwa Mbange* (Yaoundé, Cameroun: Presses de l'UCAC, 2001); Jean Zoa, "La Dot Dans Les Territoires d'Afrique," in *Femmes Africaines; Témoignages de Femmes Du Cameroun, Du Congo Belge, Du Congo Français, de La Côte-d'Ivoire, Du Dahomey, Du Ghana, de La Guinéa, de La Haute-Voita, Du Nigéria, Du Togo, Réunies à Lome Par l'Union Mondiale Des Organisations Féminines Catholiques, 1958*, ed. l'Union mondiale des organisations feminines catholiques (Paris: Editions du Centurion, 1959), 53–71; Jean-Henri Tiandong, *L'autobiographie Du Pasteur Jean-Henri Tiandong de l'E.E.C.* (Douala: Douala, S.N., 1973); Soeur Gertude Thérèse Kibénél Ngo Billong, *Noces de Grâce de La Congrégation Des Soeurs Servantes de Marie de Douala: 70 Ans d'existence* (Douala: Congrégation des Soeurs Servantes de Marie de Douala, 2009); Joseph Kuate, S.C.J., *Théologie de Deux Pasteurs de l'Eglise Camerounaise: Mgr. Jean Zoa et Mgr. Albert Ndongmo* (Yaoundé: Presses de l'Université Catholique d'Afrique Centrale, 2012).

These scholars and others effectively demonstrate that African Christians appropriated the empowering discourses and goals of the Churches in the nineteenth and twentieth centuries. However, while they rightly acknowledge that foreign missionaries relied heavily on local contributions, they rarely detail the mechanisms and pressures African Christian leaders asserted to convene a broad mass of followers or how they inspired reverence for the faith. Further, many histories tend to highlight the cultural and political nature of the consequences of building new religious boundaries and forms of social differentiation.[136] In these, the focus largely remains on the evolution of particular ethno-linguistic identities through denominational attachments or on the development of individual Protestant or Catholic denominations in an African context, rendering the histories factionally divided and focused on forms of institutional progress. This is limiting in several ways, as the task all African believers assigned themselves – in the words of Cameroonian theologian Jean-Marc Ela – was not to solidify old identities or administer the institution of Christianity but rather "to advance the future."[137]

Even in superb works of history and philosophy by Cameroonian scholars such as Fabien Eboussi-Boulaga and Meinrad Hegba, which detail the emergence of the dialectic between African knowledge and Christian tradition – made possible through the agency of African Christians – there is little discussion of the deeply impactful actions and agendas of a wide range of opposing or correlative secular forces that determined how Christian theology would resonate from within.[138] This book seeks to uncover the spiritual and the

---

[136] Laburthe-Tolra, "La Mission Catholique Allemande Du Cameroun (1890–1916) et La Missologie"; Laburthe-Tolra, *Vers La Lumiere? Ou, Le Désir d'Ariel: A Propos Des Beti Du Cameroun: Sociologie de La Conversion*; Philippe Laburthe-Tolra, "Intentions missionnaires et perception africaine : quelques données camerounaises," *Civilisations. Revue internationale d'anthropologie et de sciences humaines* 41, no. 1/2 (1993): 239–55; Louis-Paul Ngongo, "Pouvoir Politique Occidental Dans Les Structures de l'Église En Afrique," in *Civilisation Noire et Eglise Catholique*, ed. Société africaine de Culture (Paris: Editions Présence africaine, 1978), 37–56; Ngongo, *Histoire des forces religieuses au Cameroun*.

[137] Jean-Marc Ela, *Ma Foi d'Africain* (Paris: Karthala, 1985), 63.

[138] Some of the most complex accounts of the evolutions of African Christian identity (which are analyzed as part of broader transformations in African identity in general) in Cameroon (and in Africa broadly) are found in works by Fabian Eboussi-Boulaga and Meinrad Hegba. See Fabien Eboussi-Boulaga, "Le Bantou problématique," *Présence Africaine* 66, no. 1 (1968): 5–40; Fabien Eboussi Boulaga, "Pour Une Catholicité Africaine," in *Civilisation Noire et Eglise Catholique*, ed. Société africaine de Culture (Paris: Editions Présence africaine, 1978), 331–70; Meinrad P. Hebga, *Personnalité africaine et catholicisme* (Paris: Présence africaine, 1963); Ela, "L'Eglise, Le Monde Noir et Le Concile."

secular forces in conversation with one another – how individuals' and groups' beliefs about the world of the spirit – the invisible world – influenced and engaged with their choices in the world of lived experience.[139] What remains to be revealed is how common religious vernaculars developed among the territory's diverse societies not only as a result of novel and broad-scale religious attachments but also as a response to the dramatic transformations in ethical, legal, and political norms that governed Cameroon's societies.[140]

Critically, this study examines the marital and familial relationships among African Catholics and Protestants in southern Cameroon in order to demonstrate the fundamentally intimate process of localizing the Christian Churches as well as the Christian faith itself. In the years between the onset of the First World War and the beginning of the Second, Africans experienced new pressures, opportunities, and forms of power, which led them to reconsider the roles, significance, advantages, and failings of their marriages and their relationships to their blood kin. Africans recognized that by expanding the missions' agency through schools, prayer groups, fraternities, and charities, they could more effectively gain control over the dynamics that were fracturing families and disassociating lineage members from one another. This

---

[139] Notions of (and terms for) the "invisible" and its relation to spiritual obscurity, the realm of unknown forces, and the uncertain (as opposed to the world of lived experience) are known in many societies in southern Cameroon. Laburthe-Tolra uses the term "the invisible world" extensively when discussing the religious realm of the Beti, Guimera reveals the Evuzok of the Kribi region employ the term *mgbël* to mean "the world of the invisible" or "the nocturnal world," and de Rosny shares that the Duala referred to *ndimsi* to mean "all that is beyond the vision and knowledge of common mortals" and "the hidden side of things." Laburthe-Tolra, *Vers La Lumiere? Ou, Le Désir d'Ariel: A Propos Des Beti Du Cameroun: Sociologie de La Conversion*, 16–20; L.M. Guimera, *Ni Dos Ni Ventre: Religion, Magie et Sorcellerie Evuzok* (Paris: Société d'Ethnographie, 1981); Eric de Rosny, *Les Yeux de Ma Chèvre: Sur Les Pas Des Maîtres de La Nuit En Pays Douala* (Paris: Plon, 1981).

[140] Despite the broad and varied accounts of the Christian Churches in Cameroon in the early twentieth century, more recent scholarship has been written with reference to the politicized roles of European and African Catholic and Protestant leaders during the violent conflagrations that characterized nationalist expression during the postwar years. Christians in the laity and the clergy expressed diverse political messages of the end of empire, but largely consistent European clerical condemnation of the politics and militarized action of the leftist anti-colonial political party, the Union des Populations du Cameroun (UPC), has complicated the history of Christianity's role in Cameroonian national self-determination. See Richard A. Joseph, *Radical Nationalism in Cameroon: Social Origins of the U.P.C. Rebellion* (Oxford: Oxford University Press, 1977); Bayart, "Les Rapports Entre Les Églises et l'État Du Cameroun de 1958 à 1971"; David E. Gardinier, *Cameroon: United Nations Challenge to French Policy* (Oxford: Oxford University Press, 1963).

book demonstrates that it was not in the conferral of ecclesiastical leadership positions such as bishoprics or synod directorships in the late 1950s that marked the emergence of fully "African" Christian Churches; rather, African Christianity and its institutions grew from the more subtle forms of church organizing, entrepreneurial leadership, and interrelational evangelism of the interwar years. This analysis owes much to Philippe Laburthe-Tolra, who has contributed the most to illuminating the interior lives of Africans as they experienced Christianity as an embodied physical and intellectual process –not simply as a foreign and otherworldly set of beliefs.[141]

The Organization of the Text

Part I of this book focuses on the first decade of French presence between 1914 and 1925, and the social politics and religious feelings emergent in an era of scarcity and disrupted foreign imperial and missionary authority. In this period, French rule advanced from a transitional phase of military occupation to a fully-fledged colonial administration overseen by the League of Nations, in which governance strategy emphasized *mise en valeur* and a clear sense of authority vis-à-vis local rulers and African subjects, per governors Théodore Paul Marchand and Paul Bonnecarrère's visions. In this decade, African chiefs claimed a steadily increasing share of power and income by wielding administrative and police powers and impressing local populations into coercive labor systems. At the same time, Africans joined into new religious communities in which they were considered equal members, but also subject to the authority of the local church. Africans' willingness to enter into domains of discipline managed by new spiritual authorities and their emergent activism in the realms

---

[141] Philippe Laburthe-Tolra, *Minlaaba: Histoire et Société Traditionnelle Chez Les Bëti Du Sud-Cameroun*, 3 vols (Paris: Librairie Honoré Champion, 1977); Laburthe-Tolra, *Les Seigneurs de La Forêt: Essai Sur Le Passé Historique, l'organisation Sociale et Les Norms Éthiques Des Anciens Béti Du Cameroun*; Laburthe-Tolra, "Intentions missionnaires et perception africaine : quelques données camerounaises," 239; Laburthe-Tolra, *Initiations et Sociétés Secrètes Au Cameroun: Les Mystères de La Nuit : Essai Sur La Religion Beti, Volume 1*; Curt Von Morgen, *A Travers Le Cameroun Du Sud Au Nord: Voyages et Explorations Dans l'Arrière Pays de 1889 à 1891*, trans. Philippe Laburthe-Tolra, Publications de la Sorbonne, Série: Afrique 7 (Paris: Serge Fleury, 1982); Georg Zenker and Philippe Laburthe-Tolra, *Yaoundé, d'après Zenker (1895): le plan de 1892*, Extrait des Annales de la Faculté des Lettres et Sciences Humaines de Yaoundé, 2 (Yaoundé, Cameroon, 1970). Laburthe-Tolra's skills as an ethnologist and anthropologist allowed him to know the intimate history of the Beti society in Cameroon and the transformation of their religious knowledge systems during an era when new pressures and incentives forced divisions that widened further with each new arrival of a European colonizer.

of marriage and the family demonstrates their autonomy within Christian communities and the degree to which they shaped the process by which they became converts and devout members. At the time, it also demonstrated to the French administration that the colonial objective of constructing African political consciousness around chiefs and strong patriarchs was floundering in the face of tens of thousands of Africans who were developing alternative and self-directed forms of communal association.

Chapters 2 and 3 provide evidence that rather than subduing the tumult of colonial transition, Africans who engaged with Christianity maneuvered through its disruptions and found openings to lead. These early chapters demonstrate how African Catholics and Protestants became mission leaders and overseers by default, and then used their position to forge new collective loyalties to Christian institutions such as schools or congregations, which they then merged with preexisting lineage, clan, or ethno-linguistic affiliations. Religious routines structured by the mass or weekly service and participation in the sacraments and catechism were solidified by the associationalism of language and local identity, and allowed for formally organized action to emerge.

Chapters 4 and 5 reveal that in this insecure time in which traditions were challenged, modified, or abandoned, Christian families consciously sought to renew patterns of communal reciprocity, family cohesion, and social trust. Religious messaging on sexual and conjugal ethics resonated with many who lived in the orbit of the missions as they recognized the confluence of factors that transformed social relations and marriage practices into unrecognizable forms of exchange or competition. Africans expressed feelings of social havoc in confession, catechism, and church meetings, and criticized local potentates' exploitation of local marital customs. African Catholic and Protestant catechists thus mobilized collective spiritual attachments to Christian marriage and shaped local populations' receptivity to evangelical messages on marriage and the family by offering a solution to the consequences of colonialism. By focusing on couples and families, African evangelists also strengthened village, community, and linguistic solidarities, localized Christian identities, and created regional attachments to elements of the family reform agenda that resonated most strongly with particular communities.[142] This process was

---

[142] ACSSp. 2J1.7b4 L'Action Sociale des Missions Catholiques au Cameroun 1925" conférence avec la Société de Géographie; "Missions Catholiques Au Cameroun," *L'Eveil Du Cameroun*, no. 374 (août 1939). Weekly mission journals and magazines during the interwar period included *Jumele la bana ba Kamerun* (The Awakening of the Children of Cameroon), a journal published in the Duala language in 1934 by the French Protestant Mission, as well as *Kaso*, a Protestant youth magazine, *Mefoe* (News), the Bulu Presbyterian newsletter, *The Drum Call*, a Presbyterian newsletter, and *L'Effort Camerounais, Le Cameroun Catholique, Vie Nouvelle*, and *Nleb Bekristen*, some of the

undoubtedly forceful, but it was also incorporative and influenced not only Africans' understandings of how to unite bodies and souls, but also how to produce new cultures.

Part II of the book examines the years between 1925 and 1939, when African small farmers, traders, merchants, transporters, and other agents in the Nyong-et-Sanaga and Abong Mbang territories in central southern Cameroon, as well as the Nyong Valley and Ebolowa regions further south, and Yabassi and Dschang in the west, shared a greater proportion of agricultural wealth.[143] Economic possibilities and more fluid communication between city and countryside meant that the cultural horizons of rural life broadened, and men and women took advantage of opportunities to transmit their grievances, aspirations, and ideas to each other and form support networks through the clergy, school, church, or pious confraternity. Catechists in Ebolowa and regions with similarly prosperous agriculture remarked that young men had difficulty fulfilling the bridewealth demands of wealthy cocoa planters, who demanded large sums and modern luxuries like bicycles. Even when these men found work in towns, they were often unable to amass the required demands.[144] Many young Africans in Catholic associations confessed to being "shackled" to the demands of their elders and frustrated in their

---

Catholic newspapers. See also Philippe Nken Ndjeng, *L'idée nationale dans le Cameroun francophone: 1920–1960* (Paris: L'Harmattan, 2012).

[143] The territorial administration estimated that 4 million coffee plants had been planted in the Mungo region in 1939 by African planters. By 1947, there were 6 million coffee plants cultivated by African farmers in Mungo, Dschang, and Foumban. Eugène Guernier and René Briat, *Cameroun, Togo, Encyclopédie de l'Afrique Française* (Paris: Éditions de l'Union Française, 1951), 202–3. See also W. Gervase Clarence-Smith, "Plantation versus Smallholder Production of Cocoa: The Legacy of the German period in Cameroon," in Peter Geschiere and Piet Konings, eds, *Pathways to Accumulation in Cameroon* (Paris: Karthala, 1993), 187–216; Eckert, "African Rural Entrepreneurs and Labor in the Cameroon Littoral," 115–17; Monga, "The Emergence of Duala Cocoa Planters under German Rule in Cameroon: A Case Study of Entrepreneurship," Rapport Annuel adressé par le gouvernement français pour l'année 1927, APA 11016/K, ANC. See also Schwarz, *Cocoa in the Cameroons under French Mandate and in Fernando Po.*

[144] ACSSp. 2J1.15.b2, lettre 24 juin 1941; Robert Kpwang also has extensively documented the wife-hoarding that occurred among Bulu chiefs in Ebolowa. Kpwang K. Robert, "Les Bulu de La Subdivision de Kribi Face Aux Méthodes Musclées Des Chefs Des Groupements Bulu-Centre (Ebemvok) et Bulu-Sud (Zingui) (1920–1944)," in *La Cheffrie "Traditionnelle" Dans Les Sociétés de La Grande Zone Forestière Du Sud-Cameroun (1850–2010)*, ed. Kpwang K. Robert (Paris et Cameroun: L'Harmattan, 2011), 139–69. Clement Egerton noted in 1939 that 40 percent of men in Ebolowa were unmarried "because they do not have the money to get wives." F. Clement C. Egerton, *African Majesty: A Record of Refuge at the Court of the King of Bangangté in the French Cameroons* (New York: Charles Scribners Sons, 1939), 46.

attempts to build a Christian life centered on *"autonomie familiale."*¹⁴⁵ As they were unable to renounce marriage *prestation*, these men typically entered into complex debt arrangements in order to establish some form of family status in an ever-more competitive economic environment.

Thus, in the second decade of French rule, the ruptures and privation of the early post-World War I years gave way to greater sufficiency, but with it came inequality and corruption. Economic growth was destabilizing to African family life in a different way than economic hardship had been. Greater circulations of wealth gave rise to more competition for laborers as well as speculation and extortion of bridewealth, which created new risks and debt burdens for young grooms. Additionally, by 1930, *indigénat* regulations fully governed forced labor in Cameroon, and the Decree of 21 August 1930 updated and expanded the powers of French officials and African chiefs and their guards to recruit labor in the provinces.¹⁴⁶ This triggered new expressions of social activism in African Christian communities led by increasingly organized and influential collectives known as *confréries* (pious confraternities). This, in turn, caused colonial officials to relentlessly prosecute indigenous evangelists for insubordination and rebellion.¹⁴⁷ African Christian men not only expressed their outrage at these kinds of administrative reactions, they vigorously recruited men and women to their congregations to serve, worship, and defend communities of believers, which the administration found "hostile" to systems of law and order.¹⁴⁸

---

[145] ACSSp. 2J1.7a7, Union Missionnaire du Clergé, juillet 1948; Direction Diocésaine des Oeuvres, Yaoundé, Les Prêtres de l'Archdiocese de Yaoundé S'Interrogent, 1959.

[146] ANOM Fonds AEF, 1 H 74, 540/2, Décret instituant le travail obligatoire au Cameroun, Titre I, Chapitre I, Article 4, 21 août 1930. According to Article 2 of the Décret du 21 August 1930 regulating the open recruitment of forced labor in Cameroon, the term "travail obligatoire" or "forced labor" applied to all services rendered by an individual for the execution of public construction. Those who were exempt from forced labor included: African members of the police force, those Africans who were part of an organization under contract or engaged with the colonial administration in some way in which they received a salary, Sultans, Lamibés, Head Chiefs of a region, canton, or village, members of the Council of Notables, agricultural commissions, or other consulting commissions organized in a specific territory, members of indigenous tribunals (*tribunaux indigènes*), those who had received medals from the French government, or those who had earned the *Ordre du Mérite Indigène,* owners of important plantations or profitable farms who "contributed to the *mise en valeur* of the colony," or anyone who was "successfully and profitably exploiting an area of more than ten hectares," as well as stipulations for "those Africans who have been previously recruited for long periods, and fathers of large families."

[147] APA 11016/G réglementation sur les cultes, Bonnecarrère 1933.

[148] ACSSp. 2J1.10.7 Père Van Bulck, S.J., avec Mr. de Calbiac, commissaire de police à Yaoundé, 17 mai 1932.

Reminded on every side of their relatively peripheral status in evangelical work vis-à-vis African religious principals in the second decade of French rule, foreign missionaries turned to challenging the administration's restrictions on religious activity, which became increasingly severe during the 1930s. By and large, Catholic and Protestant missionary societies supported African catechists, evangelists, and eventually priests and pastors' strategies for forming confessional communities through families, kin networks, and ethno-regional societies. Religious denominations were ethnically and linguistically diverse, which deepened foreign missionaries' dependency on local interlocutors. As Brother Philippe Azeufack related to me during an interview, "the mission was everyone's affair."[149] Priests, pastors, laymen, catechists, catechumens, curious villagers, volunteers, French bishops, African nuns, and all those who engaged with evangelism and social work in southern Cameroon in the second half of the interwar period developed the Christian missions into autonomous, African-led congregations with localized identities.

Chapters 6 and 7 demonstrate that in the second decade of the interwar period, the primary architects of migration, labor organization, and social loyalties – African catechists and chiefs – intensified their struggle with each other, resulting in hundreds of catechists' and Christians' arrests, as well as the murder of a French priest.[150] Shared experiences of rebuke and punishment also shaped African Christian principals' ability to influence their followers' perceptions of who was deserving of sympathy, compassion, and assistance. Developing the impetus to remedy and assist as part of Christian morality allowed young African Christians to recognize themselves as self-determining individuals as well as sustainers of righteous acts. The means by which African communities extended their religious solidarities became critical foundations for rural mobilizations against constraints on labor, marriage, and family-building, which often took the form of radical intrusions in the domestic sphere. As new interdependencies fostered growing senses of reciprocity and mutuality among Christian cohorts they also catalyzed bold and entrepreneurial forms of resistance to local enemies of Christian marriage and family-building.

The final chapters of the book demonstrate how indigenous Christian men in the laity as well as the clergy channeled the power of ecclesiastical discipline to reform the domestic sphere through developing women's personal piety

---

[149] Oral interview, Fr. Philippe Azeufack, S.J., Résidence St. François Xavier, Yaoundé Cameroon, May 30, 2014.

[150] See Alexandre Le Roy, *Un Martyr de La Morale Chrétienne, Le Père Henri de Maupeou de La Congrégation Du Saint-Esprit, Missionnaire Au Cameroun* (Paris: Editions Dillen/Maison Mère des Pères du Saint-Esprit, 1936).

and loyalty to the monogamous, paternally centralized home. As indigenous catechists and congregational leaders became the most visible and influential messengers of the benefits inherent to monogamous coupling and the perils of polygamy, they conceptually intertwined redemption with male sovereignty. African women in Christian marriages often experienced greater restrictions on their personal behavior and freedom of movement, as well as judgments about their moral character as a result of the growing influence of the church in intimate life. Although missions funded and operated women's schools, clinics, and noviciates, women also typically had fewer institutional resources from which to draw than men to coordinate their own activities. While, in the 1930s, a highly networked indigenous Christian charitable complex emerged among Christian publics, which provided more opportunities for women to advance in the realms of social work, health care, and education, married women still found themselves at odds with the new patriarchal and disciplinary order enforced and managed by African Christian men. This section as a whole demonstrates the while the Christian Churches espoused radical agendas for justice that clashed with the French mandate administration's ultimately conservative vision of colonial order, Christian radicalism remained firmly rooted in gendered conceptions of morality and equality. These last chapters also demonstrate how much African Christians modulated precolonial models of male political authority and family management while appropriating and adapting paradigmatic Christian patriarchal ideals.

Conclusion

Important studies have recently emerged that focus on marriage and the household as significant and contested categories of historical production in Africa.[151] Investigating marriage's implication in wider social and political relationships allows for better understandings of how marriages and families create formal communities with rules for membership and techniques of constituting belonging. Extending this thrust of investigation into the public role of "private" life, this book focuses on marriage and the family as critical sites of *religious* production.

Scholars have struggled to define "religion," but this book conceives of Christianity and religion in general as both a way of experiencing reality and

---

[151] Osborn, *Our New Husbands Are Here: Households, Gender, and Politics in a West African State from the Slave Trade to Colonial Rule*; Jean-Baptiste, *Conjugal Rights*; Burrill, *States of Marriage: Gender, Justice, and Rights in Colonial Mali*. For an excellent review of how these works are in conversation with each other, see Insa Nolte, "New Histories of Marriage and Politics in Africa," *Gender & History* 29, no. 3 (2017): 742–8.

a set of doctrinal formulations.[152] Recognizing the importance of the affective dimension of religion as well as the disciplinary dimension required by religious teachings, doctrines, and creeds allows the historian to perceive the social hierarchies *and* the emotional bonds, the desires and agonies of relationships *and* the rules of sociability that make marriage and family powerful engines for spiritual experience and institution building.

Before the arrival of Christianity, there was no precise word for "religion" among many societies in southern Cameroon. In the case of the Beti, Laburthe-Tolra explains it is likely because there is no single word that captures the Beti people's "profound feelings concerning the invisible world," nor one that identifies their "intensity and frequency of relations with the invisible."[153] Among the coastal Duala, who embodied spirituality in everyday words and deeds, the normal salutation historically was (and remains today), *nj'e tuse é?* (Who gives you life?), to which the response is, *Njambé* (God, or the supreme ancestor and creator).[154] In these communities, as in many others, the preexisting conceptual order was one in which all knowledge and habits of living creatures were made possible through spiritual power. As relations with the invisible were the framework of daily life for many of southern Cameroon's diverse societies, one must study the organization of daily life –moments of sociability, repeated behaviors, representations of identity – in order to understand changes in religious belief.[155]

Religious practices appear to have changed rather quickly among the indigenous societies living in French Cameroon, but then, so did political and economic behaviors. By the end of the first decade of French rule, a veritable Christian-led family reform movement had emerged among the territory's estimated 130,000 Catholics and 60,000 Protestants that gained full force in the decade leading up to World War II.[156] This movement emphasized con-

---

[152] For more on framing "religion," see Victoria S. Harrison, "The Pragmatics of Defining Religion in a Multi-Cultural World," *International Journal for Philosophy of Religion* 59, no. 3 (2006): 133–52.

[153] Laburthe-Tolra, *Les Seigneurs de La Forêt: Essai Sur Le Passé Historique, l'organisation Sociale et Les Norms Éthiques Des Anciens Béti Du Cameroun*, 17.

[154] René Bureau, *Anthropologie, Religions Africaines et Christianisme* (Paris: Karthala, 2002), 192.

[155] Laburthe-Tolra, *Les Seigneurs de La Forêt: Essai Sur Le Passé Historique, l'organisation Sociale et Les Norms Éthiques Des Anciens Béti Du Cameroun*, 17–18.

[156] Vicaires apostoliques du Cameroun, "Le Catholicisme Au Cameroun," *Informations Catholiques Internationales*, March 15, 1957, 44 edition; Bengt Sundkler and Christopher Steed, *A History of the Church in Africa* (Cambridge: Cambridge University Press, 2000), 756; Engelbert Mveng, *Album Du Centenaire: 1890–1990: L'Eglise Catholique Au Cameroun, 100 Ans d'évangélisation* (Yaoundé: Conférence Episcopale National du Cameroun, 1990), 45–50.

sented, costless, and companionate monogamous coupling as a practice and as a worldview that verified their humanity and enabled spiritual catharsis. Over time, Christian marriages in Cameroon became a means of reproducing the culture of the religious community to which spouses belonged, signifying adherence to the values espoused by the Church, or attaining status or strengthening partnerships that were corollaries of one's association with the faith. Christian marriage was perceived, in the words of Terence Ranger, "in terms of its ability to meet the religious, and social and political, needs of individuals."[157] However, it was often not merely an individualistic symbolic or pragmatic act. African Christian leaders embedded Christian marriage in the social pedagogy of Christian evangelism that supported the restructuring of family and community life around more dutiful, stable, and complementary relations between the sexes, which extended to parents, kin, and the entire lineage. What this work as a whole will reveal is how, in this period of dramatic change, African Christians enfranchised themselves to determine the renovation of their spiritual and cultural forms in a period when foreign agents competed with each other to confer such measures on them.[158]

---

[157] Terence Ranger, "Missionary Adaptation of African Religious Institutions: The Masasi Case," in *The Historical Study of African Religion*, ed. Terence Ranger and I.N. Kimambo (Berkeley, CA: University of California Press, 1972), 221.

[158] In this way, this book extends Foster's analysis of the "Catholic civilizing mission" that she demonstrates was clarified and transformed by French missionaries in Africa during the late nineteenth and early twentieth centuries, and highlights the ways in which civilizing projects based on Christian doctrine emerged within African societies and connected or competed with foreign initiatives. See Foster, *Faith in Empire: Religion, Politics, and Colonial Rule in French Senegal, 1880–1940*.

PART I

French Rule, Social Politics, and New Religious Communities, 1914–1925

CHAPTER 2

Christian Transmission and Colonial Imposition

Keeping the Flame

Between 1918 and 1919, an estimated 40,000 African men returned home to Cameroon after being released from internment in Spanish Guinea and Fernando Po.[1] Many had been imprisoned as a result of their service in the German colonial army on the fronts in Chad and Nigeria.[2] Others had been

[1] Precise numbers of Africans interned in Spanish Guinea and Fernando Po are difficult to ascertain. French general Joseph Aymerich described that in 1915, 6,000 troops fighting under the German flag (which included African troops) and 14,000 German and African civilians were interned in Rio Muni in coastal Spanish Guinea. Aymerich also recorded that in 1916, 6,000 African troops and 10,000 African civilians were transferred from coastal Spanish Guinea to the island of Fernando Po. This suggests that more African troops and civilians continued to be added to the internment camps throughout 1915 and 1916. Wilhelm Kemner's 1937 book cited a Spanish Internment Report from 1917 that recorded 16,000 African military porters interned with 11,000 German troops and civilians, and another 25,000 African civilians – including chiefs from western Cameroon and their entourages, missionaries and catechists, translators, assistants, and other adjuncts. See Wilhelm Kemner, *Kamerun* (Berlin: Freiheits-Verlag, 1937), 77–8. Philippe Laburthe-Tolra refers to Spanish sources when he claims that "at least sixty thousand Cameroonians passed the border at Rio Muni" into Spanish Guinea along with German troops between 1914 and 1916, and "40,000 Africans went back across the frontier to return home." See Laburthe-Tolra, *Vers La Lumiere? Ou, Le Désir d'Ariel: A Propos Des Beti Du Cameroun: Sociologie de La Conversion*, 252.

[2] The military campaigns against Germany in West Africa in World War I are described in detail in primary and secondary accounts, and include details on African recruits and porters drafted into the war effort on the African front. Published first-hand accounts include Fernand de Chauvenet, *Tchad, 1916–1918: Carnets de Route d'un Officier de Cavalerie*, Collection Racines Du Présent (Paris: L'Harmattan, 1999); *Through Swamp and Forest: The British Campaigns in Africa* (London: Harrison, Jehring, 1917); Joseph G. Aymerich, *La Conquête Du Cameroun* (Paris: Payot, 1931); and F.J. Moberly, *Togoland and the Cameroons 1914–1916* (London: Imperial War Museum, 1931). See also "Germans Interned in Spanish Guinea," *The Sacred Heart Review* 55, no. 9 (February 12, 1916): 3. Secondary literature has also noted the history of the role of African military recruits from Cameroon specifically: see Uwe Schulte-Varendorff,

detained because they were employed by German missionary societies or because they were porters, translators, or chiefs in the service of the German colonial government. Between 1914 and 1918, African prisoners of war were housed in close quarters with 30,000 German troops and civilians, and formed close relationships with interned German Catholic and Protestant missionaries.[3] As the war continued on various fronts in West and East Africa, missionaries heard confessions, recited the liturgy and daily prayers, and performed the sacraments for their fellow African prisoners.[4] When Spanish, French, and British forces began releasing Africans from Cameroon in staggered cohorts in 1917, many detainees rejoined their families and embarked upon new undertakings as Christian evangelists.[5]

Christian conversion and spiritual practice led by former African prisoners of war continued in Cameroon throughout the years of European military occupation before the arrival of significant French missionary cohorts.[6] In 1916, African Catholics had nearly twelve months without any interaction with a foreign missionary inside the Cameroon territory as the few remaining German mission personnel had been evacuated and Père Jules Douvry had not yet received new French mission leaders.[7] African catechists nonetheless performed and recorded 5505 baptisms, 471 marriages, 64,147 confessions, 71,506 communions, and 3023 first communions, as well as instructed 12,825 catechumens.[8] Baptisms were often improvised and confessions were frequently lengthy processes, as African evangelists collected confessions from the faithful in Cameroon and brought them to Spanish Guinea to be heard by a

---

    Krieg in Kamerun: Die Deutsche Kolonie Im Ersten Weltkrieg, 1. Aufl, Schlaglichter Der Kolonialgeschichte, Band 13 (Berlin: Ch. Links Verlag, 2011); Victor T. Le Vine, *The Cameroons from Mandate to Independence* (Berkeley, CA: University of California Press, 1964), 10–27.

[3] The African Baptist pastor Modi din Jacob was imprisoned in Fernando Po with German missionaries from July 1914 to February 1916 along with several hundred congregants from the Duala Baptist Church. SMEP/DEFAP Fonds Allégret: Cameroun 1921, "Modi Din Jacob de New Bell, 11 dec. 1921."

[4] Hermann Skolaster, *Die Pallottiner in Kamerun; 25 Jahre Missionsarbeit* (Limburg/Lahn: Kongregation der Pallottiner, 1924), 290–311.

[5] Accounts of African imprisonment on Fernando Po were told to me by Father John the Baptist Zamcho Anyeh, S.J. on May 25, 2014, Maison Jesuite, Mvolyé, Cameroon. Zamcho's paternal grandfather had been instructed by catechists returning to his village in Kumbo in western Cameroon from Spanish Guinea.

[6] ANC APA 10384 Lettre de Père Hoegn, Pieuse Société des Missions, Pallotins à Fernando Po, 1916; ACSSp. 2J1.2b2 Lettre du Père Malessard, Mission de Yaoundé, 1 octobre 1919.

[7] ACSSp. 2J1.2b2 Rapport sur la Mission Catholique de Ngowayang, Avril 1920.

[8] ACSSp. 2J1.2b2 lettre de Père Jules Douvry, Douala, 14 octobre 1917.

priest, whose absolutions and recommendations for penance would be transmitted back to believers.⁹ In 1918, the French Commissioner in Cameroon Lucien Fourneau grew suspicious of the hundreds of African men regularly crossing the border and demanded that the Spanish authority in Fernando Po supervise and disclose all the names of catechists who had regular sojourns in the territory.¹⁰

The war years were not the first time that Cameroon's villages had received a wave of devout Christians arriving from neighboring Spanish Guinea. In 1841, missionaries from the London-based Baptist Missionary Society, along with the Jamaican Baptist Missionary Society established a mission outpost on Fernando Po to convert recently freed African slaves. Within a few years, missionaries had ventured into the Cameroon territory and were baptizing souls in the Wouri estuary.¹¹ In 1866 the London Baptist mission ordained their first African pastor from the Duala society, George Nkwe, and by the official date of German colonization in 1884, there was an organized community of Duala Baptists.¹² After the London Baptist Mission was obligated to hand its work over to the German Basel Mission, some Duala Baptists rejected German Evangelical doctrines, and, led by Reverend Joshua Dibundu and a breakaway cohort of catechists, formed the independent Native Baptist Church in 1897, which grew to 10,000 adherents by the time France assumed control over the territory in 1914.¹³ The Basel Mission found greater regard among members of the Bassa, Bamileke, and Bamoun societies of western Cameroon, and founded the Bamoun Protestant Church and the Evangelical Church of Cameroon in that region, which also counted several thousand members by

---

⁹ Oral interview with Father John the Baptist Zamcho Anyeh, S.J. on May 25, 2014, Maison Jesuite, Mvolyé, Cameroon. Father John the Baptist was originally from Kumbo, a region in western Cameroon where a great number of Catholics were converted by Africans who had returned from imprisonment in Spanish Guinea. These ex-prisoners became evangelists and returned to the Spanish territory to seek out Catholic priests for continued guidance and to relate confessions as told to them by their community members.

¹⁰ ANC 2AC 9286 lettre de Fernando Poo, Lucien Fourneau, 1918.

¹¹ John Clarke, *Memoir of Joseph Merrick, Missionary to Africa* (London: Benjamin L. Green, 1850); Paul R. Dekar, "Alfred Saker and the Baptists in Cameroon," *Foundations* 14, no. 4 (1971): 325–43; Dalvan M. Coger, "An Early Missionary Enterprise: The Baptists at Fernando Po, 1840–1860," *American Baptist Quarterly* 9, no. 3 (1990): 158–66.

¹² Jean-Rene Brutsch, "A Glance at Missions in Cameroon," *International Review of Missions* 39, no. 155 (July 1950): 303; Messina and Slageren, *Histoire Du Christianisme Au Cameroun*, 37–8.

¹³ Brutsch, "A Glance at Missions in Cameroon," 303.

World War I.[14] In the last decades of the nineteenth and the early twentieth centuries, African Baptist communities expanded principally in the western regions around coastal Douala and the highlands north and west of it.[15]

The Basel Mission had been the first to open a school to train catechists (*Gehilfenschule*) in Douala in 1889 and also trained African pastors, some of whom were absorbed into the French Protestant Mission after 1920.[16] Catechists like Douala Itondo and Modi din Jacob were paid regular salaries to proselytize in the Duala language, compose Duala–German dictionaries, and translate the Bible into Duala, Bassa, Bamoun, and Bamiléké.[17] The Basel Mission also trained other auxiliaries, including Church Elders, evangelists, and pastors, to implement Christian practice among large numbers of men and women. Together they formed a leadership network that created regional channels for maintaining religious routines. When the Basel Mission was expelled from the Cameroon territory following the French invasion, African pastors and evangelists at the eleven Basler stations in eastern and coastal Cameroon maintained religious constancy among their 6,000 African Baptist believers and 11,000 students.[18] After being imprisoned along with his European religious superiors from the Basel Mission between 1914 and 1916, African Baptist Pastor Modi din Jacob declared upon his release to Cameroon his intention to embody the message of John 21:15–19, in which Jesus hands authority to Peter and tells him, "Feed my lambs and take care of my sheep."[19]

Modi din Jacob, along with his fellow pastors Thomas Ekollo and Joseph Kuo believed that coastal African Baptist communities would only be preserved through strict discipline. In their weekly travels by canoe through the estuarine villages in Sanaga, Malimba, Bakoko, Edea, and Sakbayémé, these men

---

[14] Jaap Van Slageren, *Origines de l'Eglise Evangélique du Caméroun* (Leiden: Brill Archive, 1972), 166–70.

[15] *Nwa'ni nescane Nwa'ni neji'te nescan ntsub bamileke (livre de lecture en langue bamileke à l'usage des écoles de la Mission Protestante Francaise au Cameroun)* (Paris: Societe des Missions Evangeliques, 1930).

[16] Henri Nicod, *Une École de Catéchistes Au Cameroun* (Paris: Société des Missions Evangeliques, 1930), 17–21.

[17] ANOM AGEFOM 799/1856 Question des transfuges, lettres sur Pastor Itondo, 11 mai 1932, 7 septembre 1932; oral interview, Martine Yomba (Douala, 10 July 2007). See also Grob, *Témoins Camerounais de l'Evangile (Les Origines de L'Eglise Evangélique)*.

[18] Mainline Baptist Protestantism maintained a significant presence in coastal Cameroon, as did its major religious rival in the early 1920s, the Native Baptist Church, led by the charismatic Reverend Lotin A Same, who had taken over leadership from Joshua Dibundu. Catechists affiliated with these Churches continued to be paid, although rarely in currency and mostly in assortments of fish, harvested produce, and favors. SMEP/DEFAP Fonds Allégret: Cameroun 1920–1923, Lettres de Elie Allégret, 1921.

[19] SMEP/DEFAP Fonds Allégret, Cameroon 1921, lettre de Modi Din Jacob. New Bell, 11 décembre 1921.

demanded that the baptized openly pronounce their confessions and perform public penance in addition to attending prayers and services.[20] Preserving the Church both ecclesiastically and financially in the years before 1917, when Elie Allégret and the Paris Society of Evangelical Missions reclaimed the Protestant Church in Cameroon, required that pastors, catechists, and evangelists also display their own spiritual fortitude to their Baptist publics.[21] Modi din Jacob boasted to arriving French Protestants that he "liberated the slaves of Bonaku, preached the Gospel among dangerous people, and made evangelists out of the pagans Esome King and Mbongo à Bedi," among other feats.[22] Similarly, the catechist Iasak Tutu glorified his work in reuniting the Bonadivoto Protestant assembly after they scattered into the hinterland following the *bila I mpungu* (war and troubles) of 20 October 1914, when regiments of *Tirailleurs Sénégalais* and the West Africa regiment captured Edea.[23] The catechist Mose Yeyap maintained the mission in Bali after 1914 and extended catechist posts in Bagam, Bana, and Bandjoum in part by receiving Chief Mfomenjing in the mission school.[24] The Elder Samuel Mpanjo and the catechist Timothée Penda flaunted their own victories, exulting that they directed the remaining twenty-three catechists of the Baptist community of Pongo beginning in 1915, and "ensured that the number of stations since the start of the war did not diminish."[25] The religious optimism felt by the Pongo Baptist congregation after the war was expressed in a 1920 letter to French pastor Elie Allégret, in which Mpanjo and Penda shared, "Our church could one day give birth to its own Jesus who would live and work among us."[26] Overall, between 1914 and 1916, the Basel Mission and German Protestant mission stations in coastal and western Cameroon were nearly entirely without European personnel.[27] Nevertheless, mission stations remained open and the

---

[20] Carl Jacob Bender, *Der Weltkrieg Und Die Christlichen Missionen in Kamerun* (Cassel: Oncken, 1921). See also Grob, *Témoins Camerounais de l'Evangile (Les Origines de L'Eglise Evangélique)*, 29–31.
[21] Edward A. Ford, "Reconstruction in West Africa," *Missionary Review of the World* 43 (February 1920): 122–4.
[22] SMEP/DEFAP Fonds Allégret: Cameroun 1921, Modi din Jacob.
[23] SMEP/DEFAP Fonds Allégret: Cameroun 1921, Lettre de Isaak Tutu, de Mbombo, 25 août 1921 à Douala.
[24] SMEP/DEFAP Fonds Allégret: Cameroun 1920, lettre de Anna Wuhrmann 1920.
[25] SMEP/DEFAP Fonds Allégret: Cameroun 1920, lettre de Timothée Penda et Samuel Mpanjo, 10 decembre 1920, annexes de station de Pongo.
[26] SMEP/DEFAP Fonds Allégret: Cameroun 1920, lettre de Timothée Penda et Samuel Mpanjo, 10 decembre 1920, annexes de station de Pongo.
[27] René Gouellain, *Douala: Ville et Histoire*, Enquête réalisée dans le cadre de l'ORSTOM. Publié avec le concours du CNRS (Paris: Institut d'ethnologie, Musée de l'Homme, 1975), 235.

first official counting by arriving French missionaries in 1922 revealed 18,519 African protestants in the Douala station, 2661 in Yabassi, 3998 in Foumban, and 2702 in Ndoungué, for an estimated total of nearly 30,000 believers.[28] Retelling catechists' accounts of the war years, French observer Josette Debarge revealed that those in Dschang and Foumban "assumed an enormous responsibility when they were still very young. They had been Christians only a few years, but they were called to instruct catechumens, judge their conflicts, and direct the parish. They sensed their responsibility."[29]

The German Catholic Pallottine mission had also trained African catechists in western Cameroon in the region around Dschang and in coastal Kribi and Douala in the late nineteenth century, but cultivated the greatest number of evangelists in the dense southern forest zone, where missionaries did not venture far from major outposts or transit lines.[30] In his first tour of southwestern Cameroon in 1919, Père Louis Malessard remarked on the "great numbers of those who are fully formed Christians, converted by Africans taken prisoner in Fernando Po."[31] His visit to the "Bertoua and Batouri Christians of Yokadouma and Molambo" and the "Maka and Mvan Christians of Akonolinga, Aboue Mban, and Doumé" was made possible only by a guided canoe along the Sanaga and the Njon rivers, demonstrating the inaccessibility of eastern Cameroon's villages to most Europeans.[32] Andreas (later, André) Kwa Mbangue was a translator, guide, and former Pallottine catechist in the mission at Edea, and arguably the most highly trained catechist, as he had been educated at the St. Ottilien Abbey in Bavaria after accompanying a colonial functionary home to Germany.[33] African Catholic catechists in the southern forests developed the practice of hearing and translating confessions and using intimate knowledge to pair converts with spouses.[34] Mbangue, who was not deported in 1914, maintained the hearing of confessions throughout the war and believed the ritual strengthened community solidarity as well as

---

[28] SMEP/DEFAP Fonds Allégret: Cameroun 1921, Rapport de Modi din Jacob, New Bell, 11 décembre 1921.

[29] SMEP/DEFAP Mission Médicale de Foumban, Josette Debarge, Dschang, 28 sept. 1926.

[30] Mgr. Heinrich Vieter opened a school for African catechists in 1907 in western Cameroon near Buea in the village of Einsiedeln (now called Sasse).

[31] ACSSp. 2J1.2b2 Pere. L.M. Malessard, Mission de Yaoundé, 1 oct. 1919.

[32] Père Malessard died in Cameroon of exhaustion just a few years later in 1922. See Messina and Slageren, *Histoire Du Christianisme Au Cameroun*, 156.

[33] André Mbangué, *Annales Spiritaines,* décembre 1933; see also Laburthe-Tolra, *Vers La Lumiere? Ou, Le Désir d'Ariel: A Propos Des Beti Du Cameroun: Sociologie de La Conversion*, 280.

[34] Messina, *Des temoins camerounais de l'evangile*, 27–8.

fidelity between couples.³⁵ In the year between 1914 and 1915, the Pallottines counted ten large mission stations with schools, the most prominent of which were in Douala, Edea, Mvolyé, Minlaba, and Ngowayang. The Pallottines recorded that the major posts managed a total of roughly three hundred registered catechists and were preparing roughly ten to twenty thousand Africans for baptism and marriage before they were forced to depart by French military, but believed there were many more who had grown familiar with the Catholic faith.³⁶

Following the Pallottine Mission's expulsion, many catechists not deported were imprisoned in the territory for being German "accomplices." Pius Ottou and Joseph Ayissi were arrested by British soldiers in 1916 at the mission at Mvolyé and held in Yaoundé until a Belgian Catholic priest worked for their release.³⁷ With depressed ranks, those in catechist school and receiving religious instruction assumed the responsibilities of fully trained catechists, and head catechists eagerly embraced their roles as mission leaders.³⁸ Père Jules Douvry, the French missionary to first restore control over the Catholic missions at Yaoundé-Mvolyé, Douala, and Ngowayang, noted that despite the lack of authority, 184 catechist posts remained open between 1914 and 1916, and their stewards baptized 5425 Africans during that time.³⁹ In 1919, with the war's end and the arrival of the first eight French missionaries, a new census estimated that the number of Catholics during the war had increased from 37,592 (the last German census of all Catholic believers in the Cameroon territory in 1913) to more than 50,000.⁴⁰

African catechists did not lessen their efforts after French priests began reopening missions, especially since clergymen were both slow in arriving and scarce in number. Following his release from prison at the end of 1916, Ottou founded a new mission at Doumé in eastern Cameroon, and his colleagues Pierre Mebe and Pierre Assiga became missionaries in Ngaoundéré and Mbam.⁴¹ Catechists Luc-Remi, Lucas Atangana, and Kosmas Amougou expanded their

---

35 Messina, 30–3.
36 Sources vary somewhat on the number of African Catholic catechumens at the end of German rule in Cameroon, but a good rough estimate is between 10,000 and 20,000. Hermann Skolaster, *Die Pallotiner in Kamerun* (Limburg: Lahn, 1924). Hermann Nekes, "Vierzig Jahre Im Dienste Der Kamerunmission. Zum Tode Des Schwarzen Lehrers Andreas Mbange," *Stern Der Heiden* 39, no. 12 (1932): 320. ACSSp. 2J1.2b2 F.X. Vogt, Rapport sur le vicariat apostolique du Cameroun, 1924, Yaoundé, 1 oct. 1924.
37 Samuel Efoua Mbozo'o, "La Naissance Du Clergé et Des Congrégations Religieuses Autochtones Au Cameroun 1919–1939" (Lyon III, 1978), 56–62.
38 ACSSp. 2J1.2b2 lettre de Jules Douvry, 1917 Rapport à la S.C. de la Propagande.
39 ACSSp. 2J1.2b2 lettre de Jules Douvry, 1917 Rapport à la S.C. de la Propagande.
40 ACSSp. 2J1.2b2 Jules Douvry, Rapport de 1919.
41 Messina and Slageren, *Histoire Du Christianisme Au Cameroun*, 151–3.

evangelism to Obout, and François Manga worked in Ossoessam.[42] Ayissi, who had worked with the German Father Nekes to create an Ewondo Catholic catechism, *Katekismus vikariat – apostolis ya Kamerun ayegele bekristen ye ewondo*, continued distributing this text after his release.[43] Nearly all these men, as well as other prominent evangelists such as Henri Tsala, Joseph Bala, Henri Otou, Max Owona, Nicodeme Onana, and Jean Essomba joined missions reopened by the French Congregation of the Holy Ghost (also known as the Spiritans) after 1920 and served as teachers in Spiritan schools.[44] Today, these men are regarded by many African Catholics in southern Cameroon as more prominent and prolific evangelists than the German or French missionaries.[45] Paul Etoga, who would become the first indigenous bishop in Francophone Africa, listened to Ottou's sermons in Ewondo when he was a child in the early 1910s and regularly reminded Africans that his own ministry was inspired by Ottou's pioneering evangelism.[46]

While the American Presbyterian mission trained similarly high numbers of catechists, its foreign personnel were more substantial and rather more intrepid, and thus catechists were trained and regarded more as partners rather than semi-autonomous auxiliaries.[47] The American mission and its schools, hospitals, and seminaries also remained intact during the war – having received permission to remain in the Cameroon territory by the French government – and their evangelism did not suffer serious ruptures. Thus, Presbyterian catechists became neither as disunified nor as entrepreneurial as those formerly in the service of German and Swiss missions.[48] African Presbyterians' fierce loyalty to the American mission did not go unremarked by French occupying forces and later, the Mandate government. But while suspicion about the national allegiance of Africans trained by non-French citizens marked nearly all administrative missives regarding the American mission,

---

[42] Laburthe-Tolra, *Initiations et Sociétés Secrètes Au Cameroun: Les Mystères de La Nuit : Essai Sur La Religion Beti, Volume 1*, 392.

[43] Ngoa, "Histoire de La Traduction et de l'interpretation En Pays Beti: De La Période Coloniale à Nos Jours," 38.

[44] R.P. Perraud, *L'Église Catholique En Afrique Occidentale et Équatoriale* (La Paquelais: Imprimerie Vanden Brugge, 1986), 433; Etaba, *Histoire de l'Eglise Catholique Du Cameroun de Grégoire XVI à Jean-Paul II*, 65.

[45] Oral interview, Paul Nando (Yaoundé central market, 11 June 2007).

[46] Paul Etoga and Edmond Dillinger, *Paul Etoga: Mon Autogiobraphie* (Friedrichsthal: CV-Afrika-Hilfe, 1995), 8. See also Laburthe-Tolra, *Vers La Lumiere? Ou, Le Désir d'Ariel: A Propos Des Beti Du Cameroun: Sociologie de La Conversion*, 287.

[47] Abram Woodruff Halsey, *A Visit to the West Africa Mission of the Presbyterian Church in the U.S.A.* (Philadelphia: Board of foreign missions of the Presbyterian church in the U.S.A., 1912).

[48] ANC 1AC 3523 Mission Presbyterienne Américaine.

French officials demonstrated no greater regard for devout African men who demonstrated fidelity to French missions.[49]

Extending Christianity's Gains

Before the war's end in 1918, Christianity was rapidly continuing its spread across coastal, western, and southern Cameroon despite violent disruptions to daily life. Across the southern forest zone, troop movements as well as forced military recruitments induced villagers to flee deep into the forests away from paths and roads. Around Akonolinga, villages split into smaller factions, with some moving closer to the Lobo River to allow for rapid escape while others moved into more densely forested areas for protection.[50] Along the banks of the Nyong River and at road junctions between major towns like Yaoundé, Akonolinga, Ebolowa, and Sangmélima, where German economic activity had been most pronounced, fleeing German merchants and soldiers burned homes, factories, fields, and machinery, causing nearby villages to resettle far away.[51] Relocated villages typically nominated new leaders or followed visionary guides to safer areas, as was the case when Bulu villages split between Presbyterian and Catholic factions after the war.[52]

Remote and dislocated villages posed a challenge to French officials, who wished to consolidate African populations, particularly in zones where postwar reconstruction was necessary. French Minister of the Colonies Albert Sarraut proposed in 1923 that French "penetration and concentration" commence near Yaoundé and Ebolowa and later move west along the Nyong River to "expand economic action."[53] However, African chiefs assigned to particular regions and collectivities by French officials often found themselves without villagers to recruit, as those in outlying areas had no desire to make themselves accessible.[54] African catechists were skilled at establishing deeply isolated settlements, which caused the administration to immediately identify them as potential threats to village incorporation.[55] When administration

---

[49] ANC APA 11016/A Mission Presbyterienne Americaine 1930–1944; ANC APA 11016/D Mission Protestante Française, 1944; Vicariat de Yaoundé, 1943.
[50] ANOM AGEFOM 989/3430 Cameroun administration 1927–1933. See also Moberly, *Togoland and the Cameroons 1914–1916*, 27–8; Schulte-Varendorff, *Krieg in Kamerun*, 78–80.
[51] ANOM TP 420/4 Compte rendu de Tournée 1918 de Lucien Fourneau.
[52] ACSSp. 2J1.2b2 lettre de Minlaba, 14 mai 1922, Rapport sur l'evangelisation d'Ebolowa.
[53] Sarraut, *La Mise En Valeur Des Colonies Francaises*, 443.
[54] ANOM AGEFOM 989/3430 Cameroun administration 1927–1933; ACSSp. 2J1.2b2 lettre de Minlaba, 14 mai 1922, Rapport sur l'evangelisation d'Ebolowa.
[55] ACSSp. 2J1.10.12 lettre de Lucien Fourneau, 1917.

officials tried to investigate the new village founders, both French Catholic and American Presbyterian missionary leaders admitted they did not know where all the catechists' villages were, nor exactly how many residents they had attracted.[56] In the early 1920s, the administration ordered the surveillance of Catholic and Presbyterian communities in the forests near Akonolinga, Yaoundé, Sangmélima, Elat, Lolodorf, Metet, and Ebolowa, believing that the enclosed, self-reliant, and autonomous villages promoted by the missions were an implicit criticism of the French colonial project in the territory.[57] Both foreign missionaries and local catechists believed self-sufficient villages inspired moral resilience and family cohesion and preserved spiritual routines by managing their exposure to negative influences beyond the mission and its churches, schools, and clinics.[58]

The *ad hoc* political transitions of the war and early postwar years presented other opportunities for catechists to take advantage of the relative lack of formal restrictions. As early as 1916, reports surfaced that African Baptist, Catholic, and even Presbyterian catechists were flagrantly disregarding the old Bismarkian laws that had divided German Kamerun into designated "religious zones" to limit confessional rivalries.[59] Catechists disputed previous religious boundaries and occasionally became violent over the territorial boundaries of preaching and prosleytism.[60] American Presbyterian missionaries were most vigilantly on guard against roving Catholic catechists, and reported incidents of evangelical trespassing to local police and Commissioner Fourneau.[61] Overall, African catechists' zealousness for confrontation deeply unsettled French military officials. Resulting arrests did little to subdue their ventures, and the government conceded to their defiance in the fall of 1917 by

---

[56] ANC APA 10384 lettre de Mathieu chef de circonscription d'Ebolowa, 9 décrembre 1920.

[57] ANC APA 11016/A Mission Presbyterienne Americaine; William M. Dager, "A Great Frontier Church," *Assembly Herald* 20 (September 1914): 514. See also PHS, 88th Annual Report to the Board of Foreign Missions of the Presbyterian Church in the USA, 1925.

[58] "Mrs. Patterson's Day School," Report from the Olama Mission, 1921, *Report of the Missionary and Benevolent Boards and Committees to the General Assembly of the Presbyterian Church of the United States of America 1921*, 73; Report of the Frank James Industrial School, 1919, *Report of the Missionary and Benevolent Boards and Committees to the General Assembly of the Presbyterian Church of the United States of America 1919*, 93.

[59] ANC 2AC 9286 Contrôle des catéchistes; ANC APA 10384 Intrusion de catéchistes catholiques dans la zone d'influence protestante, Lucien Fourneau, 1916, 1917.

[60] ANC APA 10384 trouble des catéchumènes à Sangmélima.

[61] ANC APA 10384 Lettres de Rev. Beanland, Mission Presbytérienne Américaine, 1916–1917; lettres de Père Guillet, Père Bioret, Adm. Penent, Adm. Chazelas, 1916–1917.

repealing the laws demarcating religious influence, as the German boundaries were hardly restricting expansive proselytism and only inviting conflict.[62] Invigorated by the revocation of laws limiting religious competition, Catholic missionaries encouraged even bolder catechist initiatives. In a letter to the Sacred Congregation of the Propaganda Fide, the arm of the Vatican dedicated to evangelization, Père Malessard wrote in 1920, "In our struggle against the messengers of error, whatever their denomination may be, our 600 catechists help us raise high the flag of Catholicism and wave the palms of victory."[63]

Restoring Order, Encountering Resistance

Frustrated by the difficulty of recruiting labor and assembling populations near major thoroughfares under the authority of a single chief, the administration enabled a large force of *tirailleurs,* or soldiers, to round up able-bodied Africans to perform repair work on damaged roads and rail lines and clear the forest for new pathways between roughly 1918 and 1925.[64] Collectively referred to as the *commandement indigène,* these enforcers were first recruited from among the African population in closest proximity to French administrative centers and were often rivals of leaders who had founded new villages in the distant forests.[65] In a meeting with French officials, Chief Ndilli Nsom recounted that members of the *commandement indigène* in the years after the war were "opportunists," and "renegades ... without many scruples" who "wanted to do harm ... to rival villages and forest refugees."[66] The *commandement*'s duties were to relocate villages, displace chosen or elected leaders,

---

[62] Circulaire no. 639 portant abrogation des anciennes zones de limitation d'influence, 9 septembre 1917.

[63] ACSSp. 2J1.2b2 lettre de P. Malessard à la Prop. Fide, Mission Cathlique de Douala, 24 novembre 1920. The Sacred Congregation of the Propaganda Fide (sacra congregatio christiano nomini propaganda) is the department of the pontifical administration charged with the spread of Catholicism and with the regulation of ecclesiastical affairs in non-Catholic countries. For a good history of its origins see Peter Guilday, "The Sacred Congregation de Propaganda Fide (1622–1922)," *The Catholic Historical Review* 6, no. 4 (January 1, 1921): 478–94.

[64] ANC 2AC/552 2 Abong-Mbang Rapport semestriel 22 février 1922.

[65] ANOM AFFPOL 2190/1 Rapport annuel du gouvernement français sur l'administration sous mandat des territoires du Cameroun pour l'année 1929, 97. See also Eze, "Le Commandement Indigène de La Région Du Nyong et Sanaga, Sud-Cameroun, de 1916 à 1945."

[66] ANOM AFFPOL 2190/1 Conseil de Notables de la Circonscription d'Ebolowa, 18 novembre 1929.

impose the authority of the new chief, and assist the chief chosen by the government with collecting taxes and mobilizing labor contingents.[67]

Chiefs quickly mobilized alongside the *commandement indigène* to exert pressure on their subject populations. In the 1920s, Chief Eyinga Bindjeme subdued a chief of a remote village and reconstituted the people along the intersection of the Biyébé–Akonolinga and Ngoassé–Akonolinga roads.[68] The work of imposing obligatory labor was fully decentralized throughout the territory by 1920, including along the Douala–Nkongsamba and Douala–Mbalmayo routes (see Map 2). However, by 1930, African chiefs controlled their own *commandements* from their own districts who spoke their languages and no longer needed to rely on the administration for *tirailleurs*.[69]

Even with the violence of forced resettlement, African catechists continued to recruit villagers to settle in new spaces. A government report from 1923 declared, "We see spiritual migrants who chose missions outside their districts … we do not want to give the impression that there are choices."[70] In 1924, Père François Pichon boasted that in the regions south of Yaoundé, there were "over 200 independent Catholic villages" and gave the example of the settlement of Mvog Mbi, which had 600 Catholics spread across four villages, who had all avoided being reconstituted.[71] The French pastor Paul Dieterlé forged ahead with plans to maintain the Protestant village at Bayangam in the Dschang circonscription of western Cameroon, and tried to keep villagers from being recruited for road work to "preserve their energy" for the erection of a new church in 1922.[72] The region surrounding Ebolowa experienced considerable tensions as Catholic as well as Protestant catechists continued to cluster followers in new settlements against the orders of the administration. Père Guillet and several catechists even built a church in the "unauthorized" village of Nkoleyop, provoking strong condemnations from the head of the Ebolowa circonscription. Strong words were often just the beginning of administrative retaliation, however. Some African village leaders who preserved independent

---

[67] ANOM AGEFOM 799/1855 Rapport: Travaux ruraux 1931; ANOM AFFPOL 2190/1 Rapport annuel du gouvernement français sur l'administration sous mandat des territoires du Cameroun pour l'année 1929; Kaptue, *Cameroun: Travail et Main-d'Oeuvre Sous Le Régime Français, 1916–1952*, 32–5.

[68] ANOM AGEFOM 989/3430 Cameroun administration 1927–1933.

[69] Kaptue, *Cameroun: Travail et Main-d'Oeuvre Sous Le Régime Français, 1916–1952*, 32–3. And ANOM AGEFOM 799/1855 "Cameroun 1935"; Rapport: Mission 1948–1949 Organisation de la Justice Repressive.

[70] ANOM AFFPOL 2190/1 Rapport annuel du gouvernement français sur l'administration sous mandat des territoires du Cameroun pour l'année 1923.

[71] ACSSp. 2J1.2b2 lettre de Francois Pichon, Yaoundé, 12 mai 1924.

[72] ANC APA 10965/A Mission Protestante Française à Bafoussam, 1922.

settlements and refused to recruit labor in coastal Cameroon were hanged or shot, which Pastor Elie Allégret vociferously protested.[73] Presbyterian pastor Frank Emerson defended his mission's catechists, stating that their desire to stay away from *"les grandes chemins"* was to "escape this fight over their domination."[74]

Wartime evacuation and French occupation also disrupted the power of African chiefs who had established vast plantations during the German colonial era. Chiefs Joseph Atamengue and Vitus Atangana expressed to French military officials that because so many of their men were requisitioned to Fernando Po after 1914, they were forced to broker deals with neighboring chiefs to acquire laborers. Saving their vast farms required that they forcibly transfer hundreds of men from their villages and reorganize labor pools, interrupting local agricultural cycles and family cohesion in communities. French military officers noted that depleted villages often suffered from hunger and were vulnerable to disease.[75] African catechists working in the Catholic Mission at Ngovayang were the first to be recorded openly criticizing Atamengue's plantation expansions in the areas around Minkan, Koum, and Adjap in 1917.[76] Africans working in the Protestant missions at Olama and Metet soon echoed and intensified public condemnations of Atamengue and his subordinate chiefs, and those with the American Presbyterian Mission urged Reverend Albert Good to write to French officials about "alarming" and "abusive" labor *prestation*.[77] As village populations suffered from having their men extracted first by the German expulsion and then further drained by powerful chiefs' labor recruitments, catechists easily "built a clientele" by denouncing those responsible and giving spiritual sustenance to the distressed.[78]

Countering mounting criticism emerging from the missions, French officials defended Atamengue, Atangana, and other chiefs' labor schemes despite evidence of considerable human suffering. Administrator Ripert, who oversaw the Yaoundé region in 1918 and 1919 wrote, "the chiefs try to hide their abuses ... but they cannot be expected to lose their farms!" and "One does not leave to rot that which should flourish!"[79] The administration soon turned to retaliatory action, however, when catechists and missions took direct aim at

---

[73] ACSSp. 2J1.2b2 Rapport sur l'evangelisation d'Ebolowa, 1922.
[74] ANC 2AC 9286 lettre de Frank O. Emerson, Batanga, 24 mai 1917 à Gov. Lucien Fourneau.
[75] ANC 2AC 9286 lettre de 4 octobre 1919 de l'Administrator Ripert à Yaoundé.
[76] ANC 2AC 9286 lettre de 4 octobre 1919 de l'Administrator Ripert à Yaoundé.
[77] ANC 2AC 9286 lettre de Pastor Good, 1918.
[78] ANC 2AC 9286 Gouverneur Carde, 1919; Mission Presbyterienne Américaine 1919; missions catholiques 1918–1919.
[79] ANC 2AC 9286 Administrateur Ripert, 1919.

chiefs by helping workers escape from chiefs' farms and reclaimed them to build mission stations and clear land for catechist posts. Evangelism in worksites and along road and railways also provoked conflict when priests and catechists defended their recruitment of laborers to weekly mass with claims that Sunday rest was a "religious freedom ... guaranteed by France according to the Treaty of Versailles."[80]

Administration observations from the late 1910s through the 1920s corroborate Africans' resistance to working on chiefs' farms at the same time as there was widespread volunteer work in mission sites and in Christian villages by African catechumens. Chef de Région Mathieu wrote to the commissariat in Douala in 1920: "The natives are more obedient to the catechist than to our chiefs!"[81] In 1922 administration officials worried that a new Protestant mission in Bafoussam would "draw many faithful volunteers" away from Chief Kom, and in 1923 Governor Théodore Paul Marchand deplored that catechumens willingly performed duties that were "not exclusively confessional."[82]

Denominational leaders like Pastor Allégret and American Pastor Cavin Beanland approvingly noted that the high number of unregulated Catholic catechists was "perturbing native chiefs and sorcerers" and "stripping the power of the secret societies of leopard men."[83] The Catholic Minlaba mission defended catechists who delivered workers from their indenture to a chief only to have them obey different leaders and serve anew, declaring to the administration that these men were "examples of spiritual liberty ... fighting against chiefs who are paid."[84] Reverend Frank Emerson defended Presbyterian catechists when Commissioner Fourneau accused them of "hiding workers in the bush, where they build huts together," pointing out that he could not be blamed if Africans worked with their "religious advisors" in areas that the mission did

---

[80] ACSSp. 2J1.10.7 1935/1936, Alexandre le Roy: "La Liberté religieuse au Cameroun et dans les colonies françaises."

[81] ANC 2AC 9286 Lettre de Chef de Region Ch. Mathieu, 4 février 1920 à le Commissaire à Douala.

[82] ANC APA 10965/A Mission Protestant de Bafoussam; ACSSp. 2J1.2b2 Lettre de Gov. Marchand, 4 novembre 1923.

[83] ANC 2AC 9286 lettres de Pasteur Allégret et Rev. Beanland, 1916. For more on secret societies and "leopard men," see Laburthe-Tolra, *Initiations et Sociétés Secrètes Au Cameroun: Les Mystères de La Nuit : Essai Sur La Religion Beti, Volume 1*; Cyprian Fisiy, *Palm Tree Justice in the Bertoua Court of Appeal: The Witchcraft Cases*, in *African Studies* Centre Leiden, Working Paper No. 12 (Leiden, Netherlands, 1990); Zenker and Laburthe-Tolra, *Yaoundé, d'après Zenker (1895)*; Laburthe-Tolra, *Les Seigneurs de La Forêt: Essai Sur Le Passé Historique, l'organisation Sociale et Les Norms Éthiques Des Anciens Béti Du Cameroun*, 187–209.

[84] ACSSp. 2J1.2b2 lettre de Minlaba, 14 mai 1922.

not oversee.[85] Another French missionary maintained that the work performed by escapees in mission stations was purely voluntary or penitent.[86] In a 2014 interview, Father John the Baptist Zamcho Anyeh, a Cameroonian Jesuit, related that his paternal grandfather had been baptized by a catechist who had returned to his village in Kumba after being released from Fernando Po. As part of his religious preparation, his grandfather worked as a carpenter for the mission in Bamenda and remained in service there nearly all his life.[87] Overall, Catholic as well as Protestant catechists were quite adept at transforming formerly captured laborers into devoted partners in mission expansion.

In light of administrative backing for continued cash crop production, catechists and their foreign missionary backers were perceived as a terrible nuisance and a political and economic threat. In addition to disrupting labor recruitment, catechists refused to pay taxes, an act of defiance supported by the missions, who petitioned that catechists be exempt because they were auxiliaries of foreign personnel.[88] As early as 1917, Lucien Fourneau decried the "excessive number of catechists" who "evade and reject the authority of chiefs and avoid porterage and road construction."[89] French officials warned missionaries as soon as they arrived in the territory to establish new missions that the catechists were an "uncontrolled force," and demanded that each mission station register a limited number of catechists with the local police so that they would be placed under surveillance and given special travel permits.[90] Fourneau wrote to his regional officers: "When they come to your offices for their papers, it is an opportunity to remind them of their loyalty to the chiefs and their duty to obey."[91] Between 1923 and 1925, administration officials arrested dozens of catechists affiliated with the American Presbyterian Mission in Sakbayeme, Metet, and Doumé who were "provoking unrest in the railroad worksites" and "helping workers escape ... causing injuries to those

---

[85] ANC 2AC 9286 lettre de la Mission Presbytérienne Américaine à Batanga à Gov. Fourneau, 24 mai 1917.
[86] ACSSp. 2J1.2b2 lettre de Minlaba, 14 mai 1922.
[87] Oral interview John the Baptist Zamcho Anyeh, S.J., May 25, 2014, Maison Jesuite, Mvolyé, Cameroon.
[88] The American Presbyterian Mission even argued that all the students, teachers, and farm workers affiliated with their missions, as well as their catechists, be exempt from taxes. 2AC 9286 lettre de Pasteur Johnson, Elat, 21 mars 1918; lettre de Frank O. Emerson, Batanga, 24 août 1918; lettre de Lucien Fourneau à le Secretaire Général de la MPA, Batanga, Douala, 1917; lettre de Capitaine Bourcart à le Commissaire à Douala, 1918.
[89] ACSSp. 2J1.10.12 lettre de Lucien Fourneau, Douala, 5 juin 1917.
[90] ANC 2AC 9286 catéchiste Elangmweng, 23 janvier 1925.
[91] ACSSp. 2J1.10.12 lettre de Lucien Fourneau, Douala, 5 juin 1917.

who are caught."[92] Under the *indigénat*, regional officials could even suppress liberties granted to Africans by *arrêté*, as well as fine, displace, and imprison local populations.[93] Almost without exception, however, foreign mission leaders not only defended their affiliated catechists against the administration's accusations, arrests, and persecutions by paying their fines, working to release them from jails and detention, and openly encouraging their disregard of local chiefs.[94]

Documentation of official investigations into mission volunteerism in the region surrounding Yaoundé during the 1920s and 1930s reveals that when administration officials interrogated local volunteers, they professed that they were performing *ekas*, a longstanding form of neighborly assistance practiced by Ewondo, Bané, Eton, Mvele, and other Beti societies.[95] In this practice, *ekas* laborers who cleared fields and built huts and lodges freely offered their labor in rotation and were remunerated with feasts.[96] Catechumens explained to investigators that daily masses, confessions, and catechism were their

[92] ANC 2AC 9286 lettre de Gov. Marchand à Pasteur Johnson, 17 nov. 1923; lettre de Mission Presbytérienne Américaine à Metet, 12 jan. 1925; lettre à Mission Presbytérienne Américaine à Sakbayeme, mai 1924; lettre de chef de circonscripton à Doumé, 12 jan. 1925; liste de catéchistes à Doumé, Subdivision de Batouri, Capitaine Foulet, 1924.

[93] Each region had a distinct set of codes within the *indigénat*, with French Soudan listing twenty-four acts as subject to the *indigénat*, and Côte d'Ivoire listing fifty-four. Rather than a modern law system with allowances for recourse and judicial arbitration of facts and arguments, the *indigénat* embodied control by coercion. ANOM Fonds Ministeriels (hereafter FM) Services Judiciaires (hereafter SJ) 1, Rapport "Organization judiciaire en Afrique Equatoriale Française et Cameroun et echelle des emplois de la magistrature outre-mer, 1950, de Mr. Rolland, en AEF et Cameroun; Richard Roberts, *Litigants and Households: African Disputes and the Colonial Courts in the French Soudan, 1895–1912* (Portsmouth, NH: Heinemann, 2005), 70–2; Tony Asiwaju, "Control Through Coercion: A Study of the Indigenat Regime in French West African Administration, 1887–1946," *Bull IFAN*, Series B, 41, 1 (1979); Raymond L. Buell, *The Native Problem in Africa* (New York: Macmillan, 1928), Vol. I, pp. 1016–20; Conklin, *Mission to Civilize*, 202.

[94] 2AC 9286 lettres de la Mission Presbytérienne Américaine, 1923–1925; see also ACSSp. 2J1.10.12 Père Pichon, 1927–1931.

[95] Mviena, *Univers Culturel et Religieux Du Peuple Beti*, 42–5; Laburthe-Tolra, *Les Seigneurs de La Forêt: Essai Sur Le Passé Historique, l'organisation Sociale et Les Norms Éthiques Des Anciens Béti Du Cameroun*, 363–4.

[96] *Ekas* refers to a voluntary work group, a rotation work group, a common initiative group, or a parochial association of workers with a common interest among the Beti societies of southern Cameroon; similar terms were used by other regional societies. See ACSSp. Dossier personnel du P. Etienne Nkodo, undated, uncataloged; Etoga and Dillinger, *Paul Etoga: Mon Autogiobraphie*, 22–4; William Armand Mala, "Knowledge Systems and Adaptive Collaborative Management of Natural Resources in Southern Cameroon" (Stellenbosch University, 2009), 220.

compensation.⁹⁷ Troublingly, these investigations led officials to ascertain that *ekas*, or solidarity labor on a voluntary basis, was equivalent to forcibly recruited work on a chief's farm, railroad, or concessionary worksite, and thus *prestation* was not coercive, exploitive, or wrong.⁹⁸ Feigning that conscriptions by the *commandement indigène* were cooperative, voluntary work also justified the administration's restriction of Africans' devotional or penitential work in missions or Christian villages. Officials claimed that Africans deliberately refused to perform legally mandated *prestation* while continuing to work on village churches and chapels, which was tantamount to rebellion.⁹⁹

Whether European missionary leaders could not regulate their affiliated catechists or did not care to, African catechists continued to refuse to pay taxes, insult chiefs and police, build chapels and temples without government permission, and encourage laborers to flee chiefs' fields and hide in the missions. For these acts of insubordination, many were arrested and beaten, which outraged missionary leaders. When the Presbyterian catechist Elangmweng and four of his colleagues were arrested and sentenced to 15 days' imprisonment for not carrying their identity papers while preaching in Doumé, Reverend Beanland paid their fines and brought them back to the Metet mission after castigating the head of circonscription.¹⁰⁰ When Ango, a Catholic catechist in Ebolowa, was stripped naked in public and imprisoned for "unregulated catechism," Père Henri Guillet, one of the first French Catholic priests to reclaim the Pallottine missions, came to his defense by scolding the administration: "Your treatment of our catechists ... will not stop Catholicism from spreading."¹⁰¹ In contradiction of administrative orders, Guillet also refused to complete the forms to register his catechists, built village churches without filing the required permits, and exasperated government officials by shielding catechists from police surveillance and promoting their "courageous" work.¹⁰²

---

⁹⁷ ANC APA 10547/M Lettre de chef de circonscription Cornarie, 16 juin 1931. See also Ngongo, *Histoire des forces religieuses au Cameroun*, 89.
⁹⁸ ANC APA 11822/B lettre de Maurice Bertaut, 7 juillet 1930.
⁹⁹ ACSSp. 2J1.10.12 Lucien Fourneau, Douala, circulaire no. 26, 1917; ANC 2AC 9286 lettre de Chef de Région Mathieu, 4 fevrier 1920; ANC APA 11822/B lettre de Maurice Bertaut, 7 juillet 1930.
¹⁰⁰ ANC 2AC 9286 plainte Mission Presbytérienne Américaine, 1925.
¹⁰¹ ANC APA 10384 Père Guillot, Minlaba, 1917≠1918.
¹⁰² ANC APA 10384 Père Guillot, Minlaba, 1917–1918; Ango 1922; see also ANC APA 10384 Lettre de Chef de circonscription Mathieu à Ebolowa, 9 décembre 1920 contre Père Guillet.

Organizing Roads and Railroads

Another palpable disruptive force during the early years of French rule in Cameroon's southern forest zone as well as in the region north of Douala was the expansion of roads and railway lines, which required tens of thousands of men to be held in virtual captivity for months in worksites. In the years immediately following the war, French officials wished to make the Douala–Bidjoka–Njock railway line usable again for concessionary export of timber and rubber and used the *commandement indigène* to locate workers for repairs.[103] Efforts in the years between 1920 and 1922 were focused on extending the Douala–Mbalmayo railroad to Yaoundé, an undertaking that required requisitioning laborers from hundreds of kilometers away.[104] Moving the site of the territorial government from Douala to Yaoundé was also challenging because there were no indigenous commercial food markets in the surrounding area. To resolve this, the administration requisitioned farmers' harvests using the *force publique*.[105]

In each year between 1922 and 1924, between 3000 and 6000 workers from Ewondo, Bakoko, and Bassa villages (as well as many other unnamed groups) were commanded in worksites along the Njock–Yaoundé rail line, the Otélé–Mbalmayo line, and the Njock–Makak road (see Map 2).[106] In 1923, Governor Marchand scolded the American Presbyterian Mission for printing in *Mefoe*, the mission newspaper, that there was "famine" in Yaoundé and Lolodorf, angrily writing in a letter, "You mention that the famine is caused by requisitioning all the food to be sent to Njock, where we are building the railroad. But others say it is just a bad growing year. You will upset the natives by announcing that the administration starves them in order to feed the workers on the railroad."[107] In his response, Pastor Johnson apologized for his "questionable paragraphs" but still added, "the lack of food in Yaoundé and Lolodorf continues."[108] Rice was then rapidly introduced into the forest zone in the mid-1920s and grown by French administrative order to feed laborers

---

[103] ANOM TP 1 420/12 Compte-rendu de Tournée du Commissaire de la République, 6 juin–11 octobre 1918; ANOM TP 1 427/6 Service des Travaux Publics, "Chemin de Fer du Centre," 10 juillet 1925.

[104] ANOM AFFPOL 2190/1 Rapport annuel du gouvernement français sur l'administration sous mandat des territoires du Cameroun pour l'année 1925, 13.

[105] Jane I. Guyer, *The Provident Societies in the Rural Economy of Yaoundé, 1945–1960*, Working Paper No. 37, African Studies Center, Boston University, 1980, 8.

[106] ANOM AFFPOL 2190/1 Rapport annuel du gouvernement français sur l'administration sous mandat des territoires du Cameroun pour l'année 1925, 14.

[107] ANC 2AC 9286 lettre de Gov. Marchand à la Mission Presbytérienne Américaine, 8 nov. 1923.

[108] ANC 2AC 9286 letter de Pastor Johnson à Gov. Marchand, 17 nov. 1923.

in construction zones.[109] Once removed from their villages for construction or new plantation work, many individuals resettled in nearby growing towns, but as they remained far from their family networks or safer, isolated villages, they were susceptible to more frequent labor impressment by chiefs' concessionary overseers.[110] Overall, as the administration built a more capable *commandement indigène* and chiefs cultivated their own allies and guards, *prestation* became considerably more difficult to escape.

The *livret du travail* or work permit was the French administration in Cameroon's first documentation system to monitor and police African laborers in the most heavily populated districts. Conceived by Minister Foury, inspector for the Ministry of Water and Forests, the Decree of 10 November 1923, sought to "place a permit in every hand" to "limit desertions and locate those who rupture their agreements with the administration. Deserters will be prosecuted for their breach of contract."[111] In 1927, Governor Marchand extended the identity card program to all of the Cameroon territory and required the inclusion of information on a person's employment history, civil status, travel allowances, tax payments, and "tattoos, scars, deformities, and amputations ... and particular marks or coloring."[112] The *Plantations de la Sanaga* concessionary company used the work permit to control male laborers' wages by enforcing work contracts and requiring laborers to acquire a "visa of administrative authority," which guaranteed their consent to punishing work schedules in the cocoa, sugarcane, tobacco, and palm oil plantations in the coastal Sanaga region.[113]

Although labor laws and local means of controlling African workers were already quite stringent, the *arrêté* of 1 July 1924 fixing the "*regime de prestation*" intensified labor demands and required 10 days of work per annum from "all adults of masculine sex," with exceptions for the old, the infirm, and the military and regional guards, and the *arrêté* of 4 October 1924 instituted

---

[109] Guyer, *The Provident Societies in the Rural Economy of Yaoundé, 1945–1960*, 11.

[110] ANOM TP 1 420/11 Rapport annuel adressée par le gouvernement français au conseil de la Société des Nations sur l'administration sous mandat du territoire du Cameroun pour l'année 1931, section on "Vagabondage."

[111] ANOM AGEFOM 151/5 Lettre de Foury, l'inspecteur-adjoint des Eaux et Forets à le commissaire à Yaounde, 10 jan. 1927; Décret du 10 Novembre 1923, *Journal Officiel du Cameroun*, 1924, 20.

[112] "Lettre du Chef de circonscription de Doumé à Monsieur le Commissaire de la République, 17 Septembre 1927 sur le carnet d'identité des indigènes." ANC APA 11326 / B.

[113] ANOM AGEFOM 799/1858 lettre du Jules Repiquet, Chef de la Région de la Sanaga Inférieure à Edea à Mr. le Directeur des Plantations de la Sanaga, 14 dec. 1935, le travail et la main d'oeuvre au Cameroun, 1935; see also Ngoh, *History of Cameroon since 1800*, 146.

special penalties for escaping construction work.[114] Justifying the laws' brutality, Governor Marchand contended, "There is a humanitarian objective to the railways: assuring the disappearance of porterage on men's heads ... Work on the railways constitutes an obligation that is to be shared by all collectivities and it is in the name of justice that no one is exempt."[115] The 1925 report to the League of Nations pointed out: "A man present for 270 days on a worksite only works 210 days because of Sundays, Saturday afternoons, and holidays, which are rest days."[116] This apparent defense of the administration's policy of confining a laborer to a worksite for 270 days away from his home was not even consistently true, as missions reported having to plead with officials and guards to allow their workers to attend church services on Sunday instead of continue their work.[117]

Long-term confinement was a lesser concern than death and disease along the transit lines. The Central Railway Line and the Otélé–Mbalmayo Railway were both grim circuits where thousands of Africans died between 1922 and 1926.[118] The annual death rate in 1923 was one hundred workers per thousand.[119] Along these major rail lines, as well as newer roads leading east toward Moyen Congo, such as the Nyong–Lomié road, the Vimili–Sangmélima road, and the Nanga–Eboko–Batouri road, high death rates were attributed to pneumococcal disease and diarrhea.[120] Acute pulmonary infections as well as diseases like sleeping sickness, syphilis, and typhoid, which were common among recruited men and women, led to high infant mortality and often left women

[114] ANOM AFFPOL 2190/1 Rapport annuel du gouvernement français sur l'administration sous mandat des territoires du Cameroun pour l'année 1926, 8.
[115] ANOM AFFPOL 2190/1 Rapport annuel du gouvernement français sur l'administration sous mandat des territoires du Cameroun pour l'année 1925, 5.
[116] ANOM AFFPOL 2190/1 Rapport annuel du gouvernement français sur l'administration sous mandat des territoires du Cameroun pour l'année 1925, 11.
[117] ACSSp. 2J1.10.12, Journal du Père François Pichon, Doumé, 1930–31; ANOM AFFPOL 2190/2 Fédération des Missions Protestantes du Cameroun et de l'Afrique Equatoriale, Voeux présentés au gouverneur du Cameroun M. Caras, 19 août 1943; ANOM AFFPOL 2190/2 "Questions d'enseignement, Mission Française au Cameroun," Pasteur Marcel Brun, 1944.
[118] This included the mission of Eseka, which had a central catechist post. ACSSp. 2J1.3, Lettre de Mgr Vogt, Yaoundé, 5 novembre 1927; ANOM AGEFOM 799/1856 exodes 1922–1933, incidents locaux. For more on village removal and resettlement, see Blaise Alfred Ngando, *La France Au Cameroun: 1916–1939: Colonialisme Ou Mission Civilisatrice?* (Paris: L'Harmattan, 2002); Gardinier, *Cameroon*.
[119] By 1927, death rates dropped to 35 per thousand but conditions were still brutal. ANC APA 11201/D rapports avec les indigènes: Violences, 1916–1936.
[120] ANOM AFFPOL 2190/1 Rapport annuel du gouvernement français sur l'administration sous mandat des territoires du Cameroun pour l'année 1926, 8; ANOM AFFPOL 2190/1 jours de porterage dans les circonscriptions, 1921–1926.

sterile.[121] Marcel Robineau recorded "extremely high" rates of syphilis, sleeping sickness, and leprosy in 1923 among Africans traders and wealthy planters in the region of Ebolowa.[122] Along the railway leading from Douala to Dschang in the west, Protestant missionaries also noted in 1926 that "pneumonia, pleurisy, lung infections, tuberculosis, and bronchitis" affected local workers.[123] The American Presbyterian Mission pointed out that the lack of food provisions and forcing laborers to forage in the forests contributed to contagious infections in surrounding areas. It was given a subvention of $50,000 in 1920 to build clinics to help combat disease in and around the worksites.[124] In 1926, over 200,000 medical consultations were recorded for recruited laborers in the Cameroon territory (the majority in the southern forest zone), who suffered from lung infections, sleeping sickness, syphilis, yaws, ulcers, dysentery, parasites, and leprosy, among other ailments.[125]

The Costs of Productivity

Not surprisingly, the status of marriage and reproduction in African societies appeared bleak to government and missionary observers alike during the early years of French rule. In 1917, a Catholic catechist preaching in the village of Issalaangué in the Sangmélima region observed that of the few villagers remaining after recruitments, nearly all were infertile women.[126] Administrator Ripert noted that the chiefs' refusal to pay wages and the reluctance of wealthy

---

[121] A report from the Mungo region in western Cameroon included medical documentation of examinations performed there, whereby female and male sterility was found in high rates, attributable to the spread and virulence of venereal disease locally. See ANOM AGEFOM 888/2538, Maladie du Sommeil Cameroun 1920–1931; ANC APA 11658-B, Circonscription de Bafia (Mbam), la maladie du sommeil, Rapports de tournées 1943–1945; ANOM AGEFOM 799/1855 Lettre du Commissaire de la République No. 403, 23 novembre 1920; ANOM AGEFOM 799/1855 Lettre de Myré Bleu sur les conditions de travail 1931, as well as Marcel Robineau, "Quelques Remarques Cliniques Sur La Lèpre Observées à Ebolowa (Cameroun)," *Bulletins de La Société de Pathologie Exotique et de Sa Filiale de l'Ouest Africain* 16 (1923); Marcel Robineau, "La Lèpre Dans La Circonscription d'Ebolowa," *Bulletins de La Société de Pathologie Exotique et de Sa Filiale de l'Ouest Africain* 16 (1923); and Edwin Ardener, *Divorce and Fertility: An African Study* (Oxford: Published for the Nigerian Institute of Social and Economic Research by Oxford University Press, 1962).

[122] Robineau, "Quelques Remarques Cliniques Sur La Lèpre Observées à Ebolowa (Cameroun)"; Robineau, "La Lèpre Dans La Circonscription d'Ebolowa."

[123] SMEP/DEFAP NM Cameroun 1925–1926 Mlle Debarge, 12 oct. 1926.

[124] ANC 2AC 9268 Gov. Carde, hôpital à la Mission Presbyterienne Américane, 1920.

[125] ANOM AFFPOL 2190/1 Rapport annuel du gouvernement français sur l'administration sous mandat des territoires du Cameroun pour l'année 1926, 31.

[126] ANC APA 10384 lettre du capitaine à Ebolowa à le Gouverneur, 18 avril 1917.

producers to share their harvest meant that laboring men could not afford to pay bridewealth and therefore did not return to their villages to form families, even if they escaped the plantations or worksites.[127] Such observations continued in the late 1920s, such as in a 1927 report from Yokadouma that noted, "But the entire population is visibly tired; women above all and everywhere young children are in a state of very marked inferior physical wellness." The report later remarked that it was Chief Djougoulong, along with his men, who prevented food planting and gathering by

> halting movements of the population between the circonscription of Yokadouma and the subdivision of Batouri ... and made it possible to lay stone for the road to AEF. He has succeeded in "fixing" the natives in the regions according to our desire to put an end to this nomadism which appears to be the result of their desire to remove themselves from all work in the general interest.[128]

Chiefs proved invaluable to the administration in systemizing productivity, but also served as French officials' scapegoats for a wide variety of afflictions plaguing the territory, from illness to famine to dislocated populations to infertility. Missionaries provide critical records of chiefs' masterful and exploitive alliances with the administration and French officials' rationalization of their partnership. In 1925 Pastor Johnson write to Allégret:

> The Yaoundé district is the most misgoverned district that I have seen in Africa. The people are practically slaves of the headmen. After the people have paid their taxes and should be free to take care of their villages and little farms, it is very common to see lines of them with strings on their necks, tied man to man or woman to woman, marched with loads on their heads toward Yaoundé. Many of them never reach Yaoundé but are turned aside to work the farms of the *grand chefs*. I think the time is coming when I will take this matter up with the governor, but I have not yet reached that point. I do not think the governor, himself, actually knows what is being done yet he countenances a policy which naturally leads to that sort of thing. After the people have paid their taxes, pressure is put on them to furnish food for the native market, to build and improve roads, to furnish rice which of course is supposed to be paid for but the people who raise the rice seldom see the money, and are also compelled to carry it a long distance to Yaoundé or Eseka; in fact, all sorts of extras are required

---

[127] ANC 2AC 9286 Administrateur Ripert, 1918–1919.
[128] ANOM AGEFOM 989/3424 Rapport trimestriel du chef de circonscription de Yokadouma, 1927.

of the people which give them little time or liberty to settle down and lead a quiet life.[129]

Other letters in 1925 between Pastors Johnson and Allégret describe chiefs' abuses in the area around Metet and a growing sense that catechists should counteract them more forcefully.[130] Priests at the Minlaba Mission noted that the Yaoundé–Ebolowa road and the Nkok railway line passed through some of the highest-density Beti villages, which turned healthy regions into "a hell and a tomb for hundreds of blacks."[131] Writing in the Minlaba journal, Père Stoll revealed that he hoped workers could find refuge "in the bush" and encouraged congregants to "hide themselves."[132]

Foreign missionaries' support of catechists' prerogatives grew decisively in the mid-1920s and continued throughout the mandate. In July 1925, catechists in Metet were censured for protesting roadwork abuses, and officials complained they had the greatest trouble "cantoning" catechists.[133] In that same month, catechists disrupted work schedules at the Eseka railroad station worksite.[134] The French Baptist missionary Maurice Farelly referred to African catechists as "an army" who could "overturn the noxious tranquility of the villages" and "awaken their congregations' consciences." [135] During the decades between the two wars, the French administration in southern Cameroon reinvented and reinforced chieftaincy as part of the belief that these intermediaries would create a framework of horizontal, interethnic linkages that would consolidate power structures to economically and politically advance the Cameroon territory.[136] However, the swift and unparalleled rise to influence of African catechists, priests, pastors, and other evangelists counteracted French colonial fantasies of the tribal chief as the intrinsic structural authority

---

[129] SMEP/DEFAP Fonds Allégret letter from Pastor Johnson, Director of the American Presbyterian Mission to Rev. E. Allégret, April 7, 1925.
[130] SMEP/DEFAP Fonds Allégret letters of Pastor Johnson.
[131] ANC APsA 11954 journal de Minlaba, 31 mai 1923.
[132] Père Stoll was also rumored to hide runaway laborers from the Nkok railway in the town of Ebolowa. See Laburthe-Tolra, *Vers La Lumiere? Ou, Le Désir d'Ariel: A Propos Des Beti Du Cameroun: Sociologie de La Conversion*, 324.
[133] L.F. Eze, "Le Commandement Indigène de La Région Du Nyong et Sanaga (Sud-Cameroun) Du 1916 à 1945" (Université de Paris I, 1974), 251.
[134] ANOM TP 1 427/6 Service des Travaux Publics et des Chemins de Fer: Avant projet d'alimentation en eau de la Gare d'Eséka, 10 juillet 1925.
[135] Maurice Farelly, *Chronique Du Pays Banen (Au Cameroun)* (Paris: Société des missions évangéliques, 1948), 76–86.
[136] Etienne Smith, "Merging Ethnic Histories in Senegal: Whose Moral Community?," in *Recasting the Past: History Writing and Political Work in Modern Africa*, ed. Derek Peterson and Giacomo Macola (Athens, OH: Ohio University Press, 2009), 222.

of African society and of a dominated population with no means of fashioning alternatives.[137]

Conclusion

During the early years of French presence in Cameroon, lay auxiliary movements brought tens of thousands of believers into the fold. African soldiers returning home, and remaining catechists, pastors, and catechumens – all freed from missionary supervision – coordinated large-scale religious activities that generated new behaviors and new ways of making meaning.[138] In 1927 – more than a decade after the French Congregations of the Holy Ghost and Sacred Heart had begun their work in Cameroon – the Catholic missions still only counted a total of thirty-four European priests and ten friars, which was an increase from 1921, when they operated with twelve priests and three friars, four of whom were persistently ill and could not perform their duties.[139] Monsignor François-Xavier Vogt, the newly appointed apostolic vicar of Cameroon, often complained of the paltry number of French missionaries, stating that Cameroon had "twice the number of Christians as Gabon and ten times fewer personnel."[140] During the first decade of French rule, African catechists served in much greater numbers, with the missions north of the Nyong River counting 1248 catechists and the southern missions 843 catechists in 1927, for a total of over 2000, of which only two hundred were formally salaried.[141] By 1935, the Vicariate of Yaoundé counted 2500 African catechists and estimated over 1000 to be operating in the Vicariate of Douala.[142]

While Africans studying to be priests would have to undergo five years of primary school, then enter a *petit séminaire* for two years before entering the *grand séminaire* at Otélé for another six, a catechist could follow two years of

---

[137] Smith, 222.

[138] It is useful here to compare the narratives recounted by Gregory Mann, who describes demobilization (the years after 1919) as a contentious and chaotic time in French West Africa. See Gregory Mann, *Native Sons: West African Veterans and France in the Twentieth Century* (Durham, NC: Duke University Press, 2006), 72–107.

[139] ACSSp. 2J1.2b2 Rapport Annuel-Vicariat Apostolique du Cameroun, 1921, P. Malessard.

[140] Jean Criaud, *La Geste des Spiritains* (Yaoundé: Imprimerie Saint Paul, 1990), 61.

[141] ACSSp, 2J.1.3 partage du Vicariat du Cameroun, Yaoundé, 24 avril 1927; 2J1.1a.10 Mgr. Vogt 1930; ACSSp. 2J1.10.7. Le Roy, "La Liberté religieuse au Cameroun et dans les colonies françaises" 1935–1936. See also Pere Louis Barde, *Au Cameroun Avec M. Wilbois, Les Graves Problèmes de La Polygamie et de l'instruction* (Paris: Maison Mère des Peres du Saint-Esprit, 1934), 11–12.

[142] ACSSp. 2J1.13b1, statistiques Catholiques; ACSSp. 2J1.7a2, Abbé Michel Hardy, Cooperation missionnaire du Diocese de Séez, "Sur la Terre d'Afrique: Relation d'un voyage d'étude au Cameroun," 8–27 Janvier 1968.

training at the local mission and begin his work as a mentor, teacher, and community leader forthwith. Other mission auxiliaries worked as interpreters or translators and also contributed to implanting theology.[143] All of these assets helped make African evangelists leaders, confidantes, and comrades of their faith communities. Writing in 1932, Monsignor Alexandre Le Roy candidly admitted, "the catechists are their brothers' teachers."[144]

By 1930, the French Protestant Mission claimed to have over 700 catechists and evangelists working in Evangelical and Baptist missions but only 32 foreign mission workers, a number that included missionary wives.[145] A diverse team of indigenous instructors, church elders, choristers, and pastors also served. Protestant missions fostered strong interdependency between the missions and their surrounding communities. Because there were more Baptist and Evangelical Lutheran missions in Cameroon's larger cities in the west such as Douala, Kribi, and Nkongsamba, African Protestant leaders learned to manage the faithful within growing and diverse urban centers.[146] The Protestant Missions also integrated more Africans into the clergy and at a much faster pace than the Catholic Church. The American Presbyterian Mission had seven African pastors and the Baptist Church had six pastors working in coastal Cameroon by 1920.[147] In comparison, the first eight African Catholic priests were ordained only in 1935, although by 1960, their numbers would rise to 151. By 1952, Pastor Jean Keller recorded that the French Protestant Mission instructed and salaried 3500 pastors, evangelists, and catechists who managed 3200 annex missions (smaller missions in rural zones).[148]

---

[143] Nicod, *Une École de Catéchistes Au Cameroun*. By 1960, the Catholic missions counted over 6000 catechists worked among over 600,000 African Catholics and catechumens.

[144] Alexandre le Roy, *Un Martyr de La Morale Chrétienne: Le Père Henri de Maupeou de La Congrégation Du Saint-Esprit, Missionnaire Au Cameroun* (Paris: Editions Dillen / Maison Mère des Pères du Saint-Esprit, 1936), 39.

[145] SMEP/DEFAP EEC FB 2/2 Liste des catéchistes de la Mission Protestant Française Region de Wouri, 1937–1938; Fonds Allégret 1930, Idellette Allier discours, 1930.

[146] Médard, "Les Eglises Protestantes Au Cameroun, Entre Tradition Authoritaire et Ethnicité," 195.

[147] Myazhiom, *Sociétés et Rivalités religieuses au Cameroun sous domination Française (1916–1958)*, 138–9.

[148] SMEP/DEFAP EEC FB 2/2 Commission Executive, Jean Keller, 1953.

CHAPTER 3

African Catechists and Charismatic Activities

Speaking the Word of God

Catechists occupied critical positions in their respective societies during the years between the start of the war in 1914, the return of European religious officials between 1919 and 1921, and the reestablishment of a fully-fledged colonial government in 1922. They vigorously demanded adherence to the doctrines of the faith and challenged African men's claims of being powerlessness over obstacles. Catechists often attained significant notoriety in local villages, as they were performers, messengers, leaders, teachers, and disciplinarians. Their prayers, proverbs, songs and other communicative devices were often their own compositions or derivations of Holy Scripture, rather than products of local tradition. Indeed, some catechists did not even evangelize among their own societies or language groups, choosing to use their position as radical newcomers to provoke reassessments of convention. Joseph Nga and Jacob Nkodo, two catechists from central-southern Cameroon, spoke Beti dialects but worked in Bafoussam and Eseka, respectively, and believed their extralocal ventures proved their "fastidiousness" to their catechumens.[1] Bulu catechists traveled to Ewondo territory in Abong Mbang, exhorted by American mission leaders who marveled, "Our native Christian leaders in true New Testament fashion are giving of themselves in this area, in fields other than their own, to make Christ known."[2] Baptist catechists Alfred Ejengele and David Nkumndab had origins in the region surrounding Nkongsamba but traveled north to the Grassfields plateau to convert new peoples. In the

---

[1] Roger Onomo Etaba, "Maximum Illud, de Benoît XV, et l'œuvre Missionnaire Au Cameroun (1890–1935) : Entre Anticipations, Applications et Contradictions," *Présence Africaine* 2, no. 172 (2005): 136.

[2] W.R. Wheeler, *The Tribe of God in Africa* (New York: Board of Foreign Missions of the Presbyterian Church in the U.S.A., 1929), 12.

Grassfields, they competed with Catholic catechists from the south who they accused of trying to "take mission stations by force."[3]

Thus, many catechists were not *griots* or repositories of longstanding practices and local knowledge. Rather, they were messengers of Good News coming from a foreign place.[4] Pastor Modi Din Jacob affirmed he was a "vagabond for God...visiting all the churches of Bonaku, Lobetal, Edea, Eseka, Badjob, and Sakbayeme in order to feed and tend God's sheep." Others also highlighted their identities as travelers and messengers, like the catechist Daniel Penjuna, who claimed he was "an assistant to our Savior Jesus Christ ... in a difficult field,"[5] and Pastor Paul Jocky, who described himself as a "traveling apostle."[6] More often, however, African Christian leaders guided familiar groups and villages in incorporating knowledge from foreign sources into their own epistemologies, demonstrating congruity with modernity while seeking the endurance of culturally relevant systems receptive to Christian dogma on the sacred nature of the family. Together, these men struggled to work intercessory prayer, gather listeners and volunteers, and attain influence over individuals' personal conduct, since, as Laburthe-Tolra recognized, all authority in the southern forests, was, in the end, a function of personality.[7]

During an interview, Cameroonian Jesuit Frère Philippe Azeufack emphasized that the Catholic missions "did not really form the catechists," and that it was only after 1935, when the first African seminarians were consecrated as priests that a more organized religious education structure emerged. He clarified: "The fact of the matter is, the mass was in Latin and people did not really understand all the doctrine or the rules or the parables. But the catechist could explain who the Good Lord was and how they could learn to receive His grace."[8] Frère Azeufack also revealed that in the vicinity of the Sacred Heart

---

[3] SMEP/DEFAP Fonds Allégret: Cameroun 1920 lettre Alfred Ejengele, 2 août 1920; lettre Alfred Ejengele, 9 août 1920; lettre Alfred Ejengele, 20 sept. 1920; notes de Samuel Kuur, Daniel Penguma, Filipe Puepere, Manfred Mulede, David Nkumndab, 1920.

[4] Paul Berliner, *The Soul of Mbira: Music and Traditions of the Shona People of Zimbabwe* (Chiacgo: University of Chicago Press, 1993), 170.

[5] SMEP/DEFAP Fonds Allégret: Cameroun 1920 lettre de Daniel Penjuna, Bangangté, 30 août 1920.

[6] SMEP/DEFAP NM Cameroun 1925–1926 Paul Jocky Allocution lors de sa consécration, 18 avril 1926.

[7] Laburthe-Tolra, *Les Seigneurs de La Forêt: Essai Sur Le Passé Historique, l'organisation Sociale et Les Norms Éthiques Des Anciens Béti Du Cameroun*, 204.

[8] Oral interview, Fr. Philippe Azeufack, S.J., Résidence St. François Xavier, Yaoundé, Cameroon, May 30, 2014. While the Catholic mass was said in Latin and Protestant services were often said in either German or French (among other languages), depending on which colonial power was present in Cameroon, there were significant efforts to

Mission in Dschang where he was raised, it was not primarily missionaries, but rather those who "felt the spirit" who educated others about Christianity. He summarized: "The catechism of the era was 'question and response,' and after mysteries were explained, the group arrived at the answer to 'Who is God?'"[9] Another Cameroonian Jesuit priest, Father John the Baptist Zamcho Anyeh encapsulated the principal significance of the catechists in another way, recounting, "Catechists became *responsible*. They felt responsible for the faith and responsible for others' understanding of that faith. Other than that, their role was never that defined, but they were considered essential and they were taken seriously."[10]

Mission records express an astonished awe at the effectiveness of catechist-led evangelism. In 1923, Mgr. Vogt calculated 79,000 Catholics in the territory and acknowledged that with only twelve French priests, credit was due to the 1227 African catechists, whose number had grown, rather than diminished, since the departure of the German Catholic missions.[11] In 1923, French-controlled Protestant mission stations reported a total of 27,880 Christians who were attended by African catechists in and around the stations in Douala, Yabassi, Ndoungué, Foumban, and Bafoussam.[12] In 1926, the Paris Evangelical Mission estimated that in the 300 Protestant chapels and temples, 30,000 worshippers from various Evangelical and Baptist cohorts gathered to "instruct third and fourth generation Protestants and newer converts

---

publish the Bible, as well as prayer books, hymns, and devotional literature in local African languages, notably Duala, Ewondo, and Bassa. In the early twentieth century, French and German were still unknown to most Africans in Cameroon, and thus indigenous-language texts were critical to forming more comprehensive understandings of the faith. Text-based learning, however, took many years to reach the majority of the African population in the territory. See Laburthe-Tolra, "La Mission Catholique Allemande Du Cameroun (1890–1916) et La Missologie"; Richard Bjornson, *The African Quest for Freedom and Identity: Cameroonian Writing and the National Experience* (Bloomington, IN: Indiana University Press, 1991); Hamidou Komidor Njimoluh, *Les Fonctions Politiques de l'école Au Cameroun: 1916–1976* (Paris: L'Harmattan, 2010); Mission Protestante Française, *Nwa'ni Nescane Nwa'ni Neji'te Nescan Ntsub Bamileke (Livre de Lecture En Langue Bamileke à l'usage Des Écoles de La Mission Protestante Francaise Au Cameroun*, third edition (Paris: Société des Missions Evangéliques, 1952).

[9] Oral interview, Fr. Philippe Azeufack, S.J., Résidence St. François Xavier, Yaoundé, Cameroon, May 30, 2014.

[10] Oral interview with Father John the Baptist Zamcho Anyeh, S.J., May 25, 2014, Maison Jesuite, Mvolyé, Cameroon.

[11] Etaba, *Histoire de l'Eglise Catholique Du Cameroun de Grégoire XVI à Jean-Paul II*, 88–90.

[12] DEFAP microfiche 3619 conférence SMEP de 1923.

from the Grassfields and Somo regions."[13] Between 1925 and 1935, Africans who affiliated with the American Presbyterian Mission grew from a population of 40,000 baptized adherents and 40,000 catechumens to an average of 100,000 worshippers in western and southern Cameroon among Bulu, Banen, Duala, Batanga, and Bassa societies.[14] During this period, virtually the entire Bulu society of southern Cameroon embraced Christianity in the form of American Presbyterianism.[15] The Presbyterian Mission also heavily relied on their African personnel, which in 1919 included seven pastors, 829 evangelists, and 225 catechists working in the Elat, Lolodorf, Metet, Sakbayémé, and Yaoundé stations, to carry on what American missionary Rowland Hill Evans termed, "a more plodding kind of missionary work."[16] In compelling people to reorient themselves towards God, the mission, and its leaders, rather than their chiefs, catechists secured a hold on their followers' consciences as well as their labor.

The intimate connection between piety and prestige among societies in the southern forest zone had serious implications for the organization of male labor as well as the organization of marriages, families, and social composition broadly. Among the Beti, the *ndzó* (orator) and the *nló dzaal* (heads of village) wielded authority by virtue of their command of language, which translated into personal dynamism in compelling diligence, heedfulness, and obedience.[17] German missionary Mgr. Franz Hennemann described the Beti state of spirituality as "comprised of magic, religion, superstition, science, and the healing arts," all of which were imbricated in communion with invisible power.[18] Laburthe-Tolra found that oratory aptitude constituted a "magico-religious dimension" in Beti society, and the Beti valorized "a man capable of uniting in himself all the abilities to influence and to orient others in common

---

[13] Nicod, *Une École de Catéchistes Au Cameroun*, 23–4; Maurice Farelly, "Les Eglises Indigènes Au Cameroun," *Journal Des Missions Évangéliques* 1946 (1946): 7–16.

[14] See Annual Reports of Board of foreign Missions of the Presbyterian Church in the USA 64th to the 88th: 1901–1925.

[15] Hyman L. Weber, *Do Missions Pay?: The Story of Dr. J. Bulla Mfum*, 1956, 11. See also Dekar, "Crossing Religious Frontiers: Christianity and the Transformation of Bulu Society, 1892–1925."

[16] SMEP/DEFAP D.13/VI-b2 Note sur la Mission Presbytérienne Américaine; Ebenezer Edwin Jones, *The Life of Rowland Hill Evans of Cameroun: A Narrative of Service in the West Africa Mission, Presbyterian Church, U.S.A., 1909–1932* (Columbus, OH: F.J. Heer Print. Co., 1932), 140.

[17] Laburthe-Tolra, *Les Seigneurs de La Forêt: Essai Sur Le Passé Historique, l'organisation Sociale et Les Norms Éthiques Des Anciens Béti Du Cameroun*, 356–61.

[18] Laburthe-Tolra, *Initiations et Sociétés Secrètes Au Cameroun: Les Mystères de La Nuit : Essai Sur La Religion Beti, Volume 1*, 18.

objectives."[19] Men of oratory influence, whatever their official political or social role, were referred to as *mfan mot,* "real men," *ntómba,* "distinguished men," or *nkúkúma,* "very rich men," and attracted *mintobo,* or voluntary clients, who offered their labor and services in exchange for protection.[20] Laburthe-Tolra emphasizes that the segmentary and competitive social order among the Beti was differentiated by the dominant force of individual male charisma, defined in large part by talent in speech – the "substance of life."[21]

The connection between speech and religious or "magical" authority in Beti society as well as in other segmentary societies in southern Cameroon was further explored by Abbé Frédéric Njougla, who compared Cameroon's diverse pre-Christian religions and cosmologies with Catholic Christianity, and contended that the human soul had a precise name and meaning in the Beti-Pahouin, Banen, Duala, Bamiléké, Bassa, Bakoko, Yambassa, and Bafia languages, which most often meant "the breath," or "the warmth," and was synonymous with the words for "heart," and, occasionally, "shadow."[22] As a vital force animating all human life, the "breath" was perceived as the source of human will, love, and emotion, and was animated to communicate with God and the realm of the invisible through spoken prayer and narrated ritual.[23] Another German missionary, Father Johannes Ittman recorded prayers and spiritual precepts of the peoples of coastal and southwestern Cameroon and also Duala people's synthesis of corporal and immaterial properties in divine communication. Ittman mentions the centrality of the "voice of the spirit" in Duala addresses for protection and defense of the community.[24] Those Duala with communicative powers that served in divination and healing were referred to as *balondedi,* or "full men."[25] Pastor Wheeler was struck that among the Bulu, "A skillful speaker or interpreter plays upon an audience so that it hums like a living instrument."[26] It is worth noting that recitation,

---

[19] Laburthe-Tolra, *Les Seigneurs de La Forêt: Essai Sur Le Passé Historique, l'organisation Sociale et Les Norms Éthiques Des Anciens Béti Du Cameroun,* 362.

[20] Laburthe-Tolra, 361.

[21] Laburthe-Tolra, 38; Laburthe-Tolra, *Vers La Lumiere? Ou, Le Désir d'Ariel: A Propos Des Beti Du Cameroun: Sociologie de La Conversion,* 286–7.

[22] Frédéric Njougla, "Dieu Dans La Pensée Originale Des Camerounais: Première Partie," *L'Effort Camerounais,* October 25, 1959.

[23] Njougla.

[24] Johannes Ittmann, *Krokodil und Löffel die Geschichte zweier Kameruner Missionsschüler* (Stuttgart: Evang. Missionsverlag, 1928). See also Johannes Ittmann and Friedrich Edbing, "Religiöse Gesänge Aus Dem Nördlichen Waldland von Kamerun," in *Afrika Und Übersee, Sprachen Und Kulturen,* ed. Seminar für Afrikanische Sprachen der Universität Hamburg (Berlin: Reimer, 1954), 169–77.

[25] Bureau, *Anthropologie, Religions Africaines et Christianisme,* 192.

[26] Wheeler, *The Tribe of God in Africa,* 6.

singing, poetic homilies, and chant – all forms of voiced prayer – were also enshrined as fundamental components of clerical masculinity in Byzantine- and Gregorian-era Christian societies.[27] Believing it essential to "fill the ears with Scripture," the Quinisext Council in 692 ordered heads of churches to preach every day and embellished religious services with increasingly diverse forms of mesmerizing vocalization.[28] Correspondingly, Duala catechist André Mbangue recounted being inspired to receive baptism after hearing the *cantus planus* in a German abbey.[29]

Engelbert Mveng, a priest, theologian, and ethnographer local to southern Cameroon, discloses that among the Bulu and the Beti, the soul was considered the source of expressive power and was disciplined through mastery of the spoken word. Mveng reminds us to place ourselves "in the grand currents of piety" that defined popular faith in precolonial Cameroon to understand prayer as a form of speech, as "words addressed to God" that carried with them the power of the individual speaker.[30] Longstanding prayer traditions in southern Cameroon were not based on "therapeutic devotions," Mveng claims, but rather had "their own structure, with an understanding of limits, to bring about advantage in life's drama through the aid of cosmic intermediaries."[31] Therefore, the Christian catechist's ability to fulfill longstanding requirements for embodying charisma in order to possess authority was rooted in the understanding that the most critical function of the spiritual orator was to deliver prayers that captured, revealed, and explained "the relationships between man, God, and their adversaries ... as all drama was the result of adversarial forces against God and man – loyal allies through eternity.[32] As Laburthe-Tolra concludes, as Beti peoples gave priority to men who had com-

[27] Svetlana Kujumdzieva, "The Byzantine–Slavic Sanctus: Its Liturgical Context through the Centuries," *Studia Musicologica Academiae Scientiarum Hungaricae* 39, no. 2/4 (1998): 223–32. Maureen C. Miller, "Masculinity, Reform, and Clerical Culture: Narratives of Episcopal Holiness in the Gregorian Era," *Church History* 72, no. 1 (2003): 25–52.

[28] *Cantus planus* or plain chant (plainsong) is a monophonic, unaccompanied melodic line. Unaccompanied chant was imported into the liturgies in southern Cameroon and became very popular. Oral interview, Fr. Philippe Azeufack, S.J., Résidence St. François Xavier, Yaoundé, Cameroon, May 30, 2014. For reference on *cantus planus*, see Egon Wellesz, "Words and Music in Byzantine Liturgy," *The Musical Quarterly* 33, no. 3 (1947): 297–310.

[29] Jean Paul Messina, *Le Centenaire de La Conversion Andre Mbangue: Le Premier Chrétien Catholique Camerounais* (Yaoundé: publisher not known, 1988); Messina, *Des temoins camerounais de l'evangile*.

[30] Mveng, *L'Art d'Afrique Noire*, 16–17.

[31] Mveng, 16–17.

[32] Mveng, 18–19.

mand of mystical and charismatic power, the catechist was emboldened to impose himself expressively or else face irrelevance.[33]

Forming Christian Publics

In addition to audible forms of charisma, catechists from all denominations seized considerable authority as charismatics by mastering literacy – the power of the book – and leading new rituals of public life, which included reading scripture aloud at public gatherings, singing psalms and canticles, and organizing the construction of sacred spaces for catechism, literary instruction, and prayer, known as the *case-chapelle* or *chapelle de brousse* (hut chapel), or the *case-temple* (hut temple).[34] Some catechists even developed a reputation for performing miracles.[35] In precolonial Cameroon, the *djana*, a Beti reference to a form of mutual aid society or lending and labor cooperative, was the principal mechanism for pooling resources in the forest zone to be dispensed for a common purpose at a given moment, such as building a house or raising the capital needed to open a market stall.[36] As catechists began organizing through the mission, they depended on their lineages' cooperation to help pool congregants' resources to plan for church and chapel expansion. Work teams and female labor were critical, and Beti catechists also coordinated their *ndébot* (extended families) and neighbors in the vicinity to gather lumber, stone, water, and palm.[37] In the Dschang Protestant mission, Christians organized to purchase a Ford truck to transport goods to market to raise funds for church

---

[33] Laburthe-Tolra, *Vers La Lumiere? Ou, Le Désir d'Ariel: A Propos Des Beti Du Cameroun: Sociologie de La Conversion*, 286.

[34] ACSSp. 2J1.2b2 Plan d'évangelisation, 3 janvier 1925. On the role of sacred music in early Christian catechism in Cameroon, see Robert Akamba, *One mvom: psaumes cantiques et autres chants liturgiques pour la prière du peuple chrétien du groupe linguistique Fang, Bulu, Beti (Cameroun, Gabon et Guinée equatoriale)* (Yaoundé: Imprimé au Centre d'edition et de production de manuels et d'auxiliaires de l'enseignement, 1971); Église Evangeliste du Cameroun, *Mjuopshe Po-Kristo: Cantiques Bamilekes* (Nkongsamba: Église Evangeliste du Cameroun, 1976); Wolfgang Laade, "Reviewed Work: Psalmodie Bassa and Missa Bassa. Directed by Abbé Aloys Lihan, Duala, Camerouns" *Ethnomusicology* 12, no. 2 (May 1968): 307–8; *Psalmodies camerounaises psalmes Ewmondo, Bassa, Bamileke*, Radiodiffusion du Cameroun (Paris: Unidisc, 1958).

[35] Apocryphal accounts of the catechist Joseph Zoa surviving an attempt to poison him as the result of a miraculous intervention still circulate today. See Messina, *Des temoins camerounais de l'evangile*, 64.

[36] J.C. Pauvert and J.L. Lancrey-Javal, *Le Groupement d'Evodoula (Cameroun): Étude Socio-Économique*, Rapports Du Conseil Supérieur Des Recherches Sociologiques Outre-Mer (ORSTOM, 1957), 32.

[37] ACSSp. 2J2.1a, Journal de la Mission Catholique de Bikop, Juillet 1933, Aôut 1933.

construction. Mission leaders and catechists also rented out the truck to local workers to source additional income.[38]

Catechists' distinct drumming performances called new and existing members to these new forms of communion, which began in the late nineteenth century with the earliest catechist peregrinations and became ritualized with the expansion of localized confessional communities.[39] Anthropologist Paul Neeley describes catechist drumming as "a mass medium surrogate language of African evangelism," which sought to modify behavior, assemble believers, and craft proverbial phrases.[40] Ewondo and Bulu catechists used drum codes to signal the start of prayer assemblies and convey joyous or ominous news to the faithful.[41] Duala Christians rapidly incorporated drums into baptismal, death, and funeral announcements.[42] As with Alain Corbin's description of village bells in the nineteenth-century French countryside, a catechist's drum strokes created a territorial identity and anchored localism, as well as communicated reminders and responsibilities.[43]

Catechists attached novel spiritual ideas to well-grounded patterns and structures of contemplation to create wellsprings for faithful, sustainable, vibrant worship and assembly. Christian collectives, or publics, embraced the old and the new principally in corporate worship and ritual performance and collaborative volunteerism in mission, church, and chapel construction in the early years of French rule. Communal worship and ritual ceremonies were known in southern Cameroonian societies long before Christianity.[44] But

[38] SMEP/DEFAP NM Cameroun 1925–1926 lettre de Madamoiselle Debarge, 1926.

[39] Paul Neeley, "Drummed Transactions: Calling the Church in Cameroon," *Anthropological Linguistics* 38, no. 4 (December 1, 1996): 683–717; Berliner, *The Soul of Mbira*; Andrew Tracey and Gei Zantzinger, *Mbira: Njari, Simon Mashoko's Traditional and Church Music*, documentary (International Library of African Music and University Museum, University of Pennsylvania, 1975).

[40] Neeley, "Drummed Transactions." See also Farelly, *Chronique Du Pays Banen (Au Cameroun)*, 80–5.

[41] Frederick Quinn, *In Search of Salt: Changes in Beti (Cameroon) Society, 1880–1960* (New York: Berghahn Books, 2006), 142; Shirley Deane, *Talking Drums: From a Village in Cameroon* (London: John Murray, 1985). Wheeler, *The Tribe of God in Africa*, 6.

[42] Rudolf Betz, "Die Trommelsprache Der Duala," in *Mitteilungen von Forschungsreisenden Und Gelehrten Aus Den Deutschen Schutzgebieten*, ed. Alexander Danckelmann, vol. 11 (Berlin: Mittler, 1898), 1–86.

[43] Alain Corbin, *Village Bells: Sound & Meaning in the 19th-Century French Countryside* (New York: Columbia University Press, 1998).

[44] The literature on communal worship as part of the *So* ritual in southern Cameroon's Beti and Bulu societies is extensive. See Alexandre and Binet, *Le Groupe Dit Pahouin (Fang-Boulou-Beti)*, 97–100; Laburthe-Tolra, *Initiations et Sociétés Secrètes Au Cameroun: Les Mystères de La Nuit : Essai Sur La Religion Beti, Volume 1*; Soter Azombo,

corporate worship in the liturgical form – adoration, confession, assurance, thanksgiving, petition, instruction, charge, and blessing – was novel. Prayer, scripture recitations, and hymnody, with an accent on sin and forgiveness and anchored in the creeds and confessions of Christianity sustained theological reflection and sponsored the rise of new *mfan mot* ("real men") and *balondedi* ("full men.")

These new "real men" assembled followers and forged people's attachments to the Latin Rite Mass or the Divine Service for Protestants (the Eucharistic liturgy), the confessional rite, and consecrated objects – particularly the Blessed Sacrament or Eucharist – which all became symbols of identity and community cohesion. Confession and penance were some of the most common religious rites in which African Christians engaged throughout the interwar period. The numbers of recorded Catholic confessions in the Cameroon territory are startling. Between 1916 and 1917, African-led mission stations reported hearing 65,000 confessions.[45] In 1921, the Spiritan Père Bioret wrote in the Mbalmayo mission journal: "Confession is heard less frequently than the faithful demand. Some men wait for days without food to confess and perform penance and are still not heard. They return with an empty belly and a disappointed soul to their villages."[46] The Mission in Nlong recorded an average of fifty confessions per day in 1925 and heard roughly 3200 confessions every month in 1927.[47] In 1928, a single catechist near Yaoundé performed 3575 deathbed confessions (*in articulo mortis*), along with last rites and funerals, which was common as there were not nearly enough priests to attend to every village's penitent, sick, and dying.[48] A 1929 Catholic mission inspection report read, "Christians confess easily and often ... It is difficult to manage confessions. Confession has to be at fixed times, not all the time, or the flow is unmanageable."[49] Confessional

---

"Séquence et Signification Des Cérémonies d'initiation So" (Université de Paris I, 1970). For the literature on communal prayer and devotion as part of healing, funeral rites, or general protection, see Nicolas Argenti, "Things of the Ground: Children's Medicine, Motherhood and Memory in the Cameroon Grassfields," *Africa: Journal of the International African Institute* 81, no. 2 (2011): 269–94; Peter Geschiere, "Funerals and Belonging: Different Patterns in South Cameroon," *African Studies Review* 48, no. 2 (2005): 45–64; Henri Koch, *Magie et Chasse Dans La Forêt Camerounaise* (Paris: Berger-Levrault, 1968).

[45] ACSSp. 2J1.2b2 lettre Jules Douvry à S.C. de le Propagande, 22 oct. 1918. This is also discussed in Jean Criaud, *La Geste Des Spiritains: Histoire de l'Eglise Au Cameroun 1916–1990* (Yaoundé: Imprimerie Saint-Paul, 1990), 51.

[46] ACSSp. 2J1.7a2 Père Bioret, 1921–1958.

[47] ACSSp. 2J2.1a Mission de Nlong, 1925–1938.

[48] ACSSp. 2J1.10.12 Rapport: l'oeuvre des Catéchistes indigènes au Vicariat apostolique du Cameroun, 1929.

[49] ACSSp. 2J1.11a2 Report: "Cameroun Visite du R.P. Soul," Janvier–Juillet 1929

congestion continued unabated, however. In 1935, Mgr. Vogt estimated that his priests heard fifty confessions every hour, and pleaded with the missionaries to "try and accord at least three minutes per confession."[50] The following year, the Mvolyé Mission complained about the "numerous confessions without one day of respite." The mission journal continued, "We hear confessions every day, night and day, without any control over it. They come in huge crowds to have their confessions heard. Priests cannot catch their breath."[51] The Omvan Mission was similarly overwhelmed and recorded 34,466 confessions from their congregation of 7000 in 1937 – an average of ninety-four confessions every single day.[52]

Protestant missions also remarked on Africans' devotion to confession. Although in typical European and American Baptist and Presbyterian churches, confession was more often a corporate act conducted as part of regular worship, rather than a private séance, African Protestants showed enthusiasm for both. In 1921, catechists regularly incorporated individualized confession into the *esulan,* or lower-level catechumen class, and the *nsamba,* or higher-level catechumen class in the American Presbyterian Mission.[53] In their mission at Sakbayemé, APM leaders reported that 2671 "confessors" were charged with monitoring church members, ensuring attendance at Sabbath services, and enforcing confession and penance among wrongdoers.[54] While confession as part of the Sunday service continued, in 1932 Pastor Rowland Hill Evans commented that as a result of *esulan* meetings, private confessions to catechists were growing substantially among catechists' followers, as well as public confessions to groups of the faithful.[55] In cases where the sin resulted in the exclusion of the person from the Presbyterian community – such as public drunkenness or polygamy – public confession was a prerequisite of full readmission. Presbyterian catechists kept records of those "in good standing" and oversaw the reintroduction of those who had been suspended.[56]

---

[50] ACSSp. 2J1.10.13 lettre de Vogt à tous les missions, Mvolyé, 30 juin 1935.

[51] ACSSp. 2J1.11a2 Compte-rendu de la visite de la Résidence du St. Esprit de Yaoundé, Mvolyé, février 1936.

[52] ACSSp. 2J1.11a2 Omvan mission journal, 1937; see also Jean Criaud, "Etienne Nkodo: Le Premier Spiritain Camerounais," *Mémoire Spiritaine* 8, no. deuxième semestre (1998): 50–73.

[53] Report of Mission 1921, Reports of the Mission and Benevolent Boards and Committees to the General Assembly of the Presbyterian Church in the U.S.A. See also Wheeler, *The Tribe of God in Africa*, 7.

[54] Report of Mission 1921, Reports of the Mission and Benevolent Boards and Committees to the General Assembly of the Presbyterian Church in the U.S.A.

[55] Jones, *The Life of Rowland Hill Evans of Cameroun*, 178–9.

[56] ANC 2AC 9286 Mission Presbytérienne Américaine, Mission à Sakbayeme, lettre de mai 1924.

When I asked several of my clerical informants about why there was such devotion to confession across southern Cameroon during these years, they appeared somewhat startled by the question. Mgr. Athanase Bala, who was raised in the Nlong Mission where his father was a catechist, replied, "You wash your body every day, don't you? Your spirit is no different from your body. It needs purifying. Time passes and if you do not perform your ordinary purifications and clean yourself, you become unwell."[57] Confirming that it was "ordinary in every way" for his neighbors and relatives to seek confession regularly because of longstanding (pre-Christian) commitments to spiritual purification, he underscored the consistency of ritual performance among the Ewondo people and the Beti and Bulu more broadly. "Simple, repetitive acts" of spiritual cleansing "were a part of daily life." Hence, many who became Christian in southern Cameroon desired to receive the sacraments with the same regularity as when they performed acts of spiritual devotion before being baptized.[58] The "overcrowding" that resulted in local churches necessitated more organized catechist leadership to manage the sacramental processes of consolation and discipline. Mgr. Bala also stressed that notions of "sin" were not foreign to those in the southern forests but that "Disruptions of the colonial periods ... left villagers without a routine way of cleansing their spirits. With the renewal of the missions ... thousands came to confess in order to be healed from their sins."[59]

Catechists reinforced and supplemented pressure to obey Church law by scrutinizing behavior, investigating rumors, and penetrating the hearts and consciences of their followers and catechumens. Penitential discipline regulated matters essential to the cultivation of religious publics in Cameroon, especially because in each denomination, catechists, priests, and confessors stressed that confession not only reconciled the individual with God, but also with the church membership. As Father Jean-Luc Enyegue summarized: "confession was about inclusion. And inclusion was about identity."[60] Penance, atonement, and reconciliation guided African Christian publics toward new understandings of the reality of sin in personal and common life, and devel-

---

[57] Oral interview with Mgr. Athanase Bala, CSSp., Bishop emeritus of Bafia, Cameroon, July 8, 2015, Seminaire des Missions, Congrégation du Saint-Esprit, Chevilly Larue, France.

[58] Oral interview with Mgr. Athanase Bala, CSSp., Bishop emeritus of Bafia, Cameroon, July 8, 2015, Seminaire des Missions, Congrégation du Saint-Esprit, Chevilly Larue, France.

[59] Oral interview with Mgr. Athanase Bala, CSSp., Bishop emeritus of Bafia, Cameroon, July 8, 2015, Seminaire des Missions, Congrégation du Saint-Esprit, Chevilly Larue, France.

[60] Interview with Jean-Luc Enyegue, S.J., February 25, 2016, by telephone.

oped consensus on what it meant to be a community of the faithful. As part of this, African catechists practiced pastoral care in enforcing confession, seizing the opportunity to discuss moral problems and personal conduct, as well as how these issues affected the church community, and, even more specifically, the local village or society. French priests noted that "missionaries of the interior" who visited villages to hear confessions, "often have a stronger rapport with the Africans." "Through confession," one surmised, "one can convince an African, clarify questions, and move away from ideas of 'proof' of God towards understandings of faith and fidelity."[61] The focus on confession as a form of communal reincorporation in interwar southern Cameroon is comparable to the public disclosures so common among Revivalists in Rwanda and Uganda in the 1950s, which, as Peterson describes, were "an intersubjective event, not a decision brokered privately between God and penitent. Converts needed to expose themselves and open up about their dark deeds in order to narrate their passage to new life."[62] However, what distinguishes popular confessional practices in southern Cameroon is African catechists' supervision of this process and the penitents, and their determination of the conditions under which the sinner could be restored to the company of the righteous, which establishes catechists' ability to influence individual and group *identity*. Over time, African evangelists implanted religious conduct as essential to identification and social cohesion – as much as one's language, ethnic, or regional affiliation.

In addition to confession, weekly prayer meetings and Eucharistic services were also very well attended. The Presbyterian mission recorded a weekly attendance of 6800 at their biggest church in Elat and a total of 14,550 in attendance at a number of smaller churches in the surrounding villages in 1928.[63] The church at Mvolyé, led by renowned orators Pius Ottou and Joseph Ayissi, regularly welcomed 15,000 Ewondo believers at weekly services that same year.[64] One French missionary reflected that Africans "fully live the ancient Catholic adage *sacramento propter homines*.[65] They are dignified before the Most Blessed Sacrament and their decorum at receiving it is impressive."[66] Even in 1918 Governor Fourneau was astonished to find that "In Mvolyé, the natives come in great numbers on Sunday to attend the celebration of mass."[67] Reflecting in 1929 on the previous decade of Christian

---

[61] ACSSp. 2J1.2b2 Rapport sur la Mission Catholique de Ngowayang, 27 avril 1920.
[62] Peterson, *Ethnic Patriotism and the East African Revival*, 181.
[63] Wheeler, *The Tribe of God in Africa*, 6.
[64] 2J1.10.3 Congrégations à Yaoundé, 1927–1934; Laburthe-Tolra, *Vers La Lumiere? Ou, Le Désir d'Ariel: A Propos Des Beti Du Cameroun: Sociologie de La Conversion*, 287.
[65] *sacramento propter homines*: "The sacraments are for the benefit of the people."
[66] ACSSp. 2J1.2b2 Rapport sur la Mission Catholique de Ngowayang, 27 avril 1920.
[67] ANOM TP 420/4 Compte rendu de Tournée 1918 de Lucien Fourneau.

transmission in Cameroon, Mgr. Vogt wrote: "The Sunday reunions are the catechists' real masterpiece. Reciting the rosary, saying prayers in the local language, the presentation of the Holy Eucharist, singing canticles, and the Kyrie, Gloria, and Credo are all performed by our catechists. Then the catechist reads the Gospel of the day, and, if he is knowledgeable enough, provides commentary."[68] Vogt's reflection goes on to include an analysis of the local public's reception of these incantations, stating, "We see children in the bush reciting word-for-word the catechism, the call and response. Illiterate adult men and women will recite not only the daily prayers but also the letter of Christian law. Even old negresses who wish to be baptized make the sign of the cross, say the act of contrition, and possess a certain notion of the principal mysteries of the faith."[69] A 1920 letter from a regional official in Elat indicates that these observations were perhaps not simply exaggerations, noting, "The believers are obedient to the catechist ... they execute orders and they are done."[70] The 1922 government inspection report similarly disclosed: "native teachers Etienne Nomo, Hicodeme Etoa, Appolinaire Bundzi, Louis Tabi, and Laurent Tamba ... teach and have the lessons and prayers recited back to them."[71]

Association and Mobilization

As much as catechists inspired spiritual attachments by virtue of their eloquence and erudition, they also convened followers through finely tuned techniques of regulation, documentation, and territorial management – implementing what Hoffman characterizes as the "logic of aggregation," which is unique to landscapes of disruption in Africa, where men seek new legitimate forms of autonomy, authority, and leadership with each new cycle of violent or peacetime transition.[72] Ewondo culture commonly emphasized the importance of *ngul*, roughly translated as "the force he exerts," which was the end point of charismatic authority. By possessing and deploying *ngul*, a Christian leader set up requirements for followers to fulfill, serving discipline and social control.[73] Beginning in the late 1910s, catechists used the roads and

---

[68] ACSSp. 2J1.10.12 Rapport: l'oeuvre des Catéchistes indigènes au Vicariat apostolique du Cameroun, 1929.
[69] ACSSp. 2J1.10.12 Rapport: l'oeuvre des Catéchistes indigènes au Vicariat apostolique du Cameroun, 1929.
[70] 2AC 9286 lettre de Chef de Region Mathieu, 4 fev. 1920.
[71] ANC APA 10384 Carde, Rapport Service d'inspection, 27 mai 1922.
[72] Hoffman, *The War Machines*, 15.
[73] Laburthe-Tolra, *Les Seigneurs de La Forêt: Essai Sur Le Passé Historique, l'organisation Sociale et Les Norms Éthiques Des Anciens Béti Du Cameroun*, 205–8.

railways to increase their mobility and penetrate areas where people primed to respect eloquent rhetoric were being coerced and abused, and hence open to intriguing messages and the provocative acts they endorsed. Catechist activity was recorded as being particularly aggressive along the railways between Eseka and Nkongsamba, the Ebolowa–Lolodorf road, the Douala–Edea roads.[74] A 1924 administrative report from Doumé in the subdivision of Batouri referred to catechists as "spiritual immigrants," and noted that of the catechists he interrogated, four were Presbyterian and had around forty followers each, and three were Catholic and had between thirty and ninety followers.[75] The high number of catechists in this eastern region as well as their greater numbers in the south was not only a result of recent and heightened population concentration but also reflected the linguistic diversity of recently agglomerated peoples, who required linguistically diverse catechists. In the Catholic Ngowayang mission, which opened near the Ebolowa–Lolodorf road, the three different languages spoken by local laborers made it "impossible" for French missionaries to preach or instruct.[76] Therefore, Ngumba, Bakoko, and Ewondo catechists were entirely responsible for sermons and prayer performance. By January 1920, there were 1129 Ngumba Christians, 216 Bakoko Christians, and 3552 Ewondo Christians registered with the Ngowayang mission, who celebrated 1777 baptisms, 752 confirmations, 215 marriages, 50 funerals, and 49,357 communion distributions between 1917 and 1920.[77] During those same years, congregants also built forty-five catechist posts – small chapels and instruction huts in secluded areas away from the main thoroughfares.

Throughout southern Cameroon, catechists strategically deployed *ngul* to mobilize followings and alter longstanding systems of mutual obligation, generating a new "wealth in people" that brought them power and prestige, but also served to aggrandize the institution of the Church.[78] Similar to what Hoffman characterizes as "aggregation" in the context of war, in which recruitment based on individual charisma is institutionalized and then captured by

---

[74] ACSSp. 2J1.2b2 Rapport sur la Mission Catholique de Ngowayang, 27 avril 1920.

[75] ANC 2AC 9286 liste de catéchistes à Doumé, Subdivision de Batouri, Capitaine Foulet, 1924.

[76] ACSSp. 2J1.2b2 Rapport sur la Mission Catholique de Ngowayang, 27 avril 1920. Even in the western plateaus, catechists who spoke Grassfield and Bamoun were required to translate every service for the Protestant Mission. See SMEP/DEFAP Mission Médicale de Foumban, Josette Debarge Dschang, 28 sept. 1926.

[77] ACSSp. 2J1.2b2 Rapport sur la Mission Catholique de Ngowayang, 27 avril 1920.

[78] Sara Berry is a classic Africanist scholar of "wealth in people," in which a person's status depends directly on his or her ability to mobilize a following. See Sara S. Berry, *No Condition Is Permanent: The Social Dynamics of Agrarian Change in Sub-Saharan Africa*, 1 edition (Madison, WI: University of Wisconsin Press, 1993), 15.

the state, African catechists aggregated new social groupings that upset both older authority structures and the new socio-political hierarchy supported by the French administration, and directed their followers to engage with a new institution of power that promised reciprocity and advancement.

French missionaries in Ngowayang attributed the rapid expansion of their mission station and its associated outposts entirely to devotional volunteers. Many offered their labor in return for instruction and baptism, but others were compelled to work as part of their penance. The catechist Frédéric Abega hewed confessionals for the hut chapels he visited, and impressed upon his acolytes the manifold purposes and meanings of contrition. Out of the fifty-six confessions Abega heard during his visit to the Nkol Angang village in 1925, a considerable number involved misdeeds and predicaments concerning marriage.[79] The catechists Joseph Zou and Hermann Mbono, who worked at the Nlong Mission alongside Jean Bell, attested in that same year that "many more men than women receive the sacrament of reconciliation." Ewondo and Bassa catechist reports from the Nlong region between 1925 and 1938 reflect that many *minkoe* (Ewondo for "single men"; Bassa: *minkue*) came to catechist posts and the mission to lament their lack of spouse or grieve the sins they committed to secure one, including paying or receiving bridewealth or contravening laws against child marriage.[80] The Ngowayang annual record states: "A penitent will perform one to two weeks of work at the mission. Their young friends ... and their fiancés can visit them at the mission while they are doing penitent work – they bring food and they inspire other confessors."[81] Along the Chemin de Fer du Nord, ninety Catholic churches were erected between 1918 and 1925.[82] The establishment of Catholic churches, hut chapels, catechist posts, and mission outposts along the Central Railroad was recorded in dozens of administrative reports and missionary letters written between 1916 and 1924, and though many were erected far away from the railroad, each religious structure recruited volunteers from the railway worksites.[83] The promise of reciprocation – labor in exchange for a shared meal, a public prayer, catechism instruction, and inclusion in a new social grouping – meant that recruitment grew substantially as work on the transit lines became ever more rarely remunerated. By 1924, one or two French missionaries occupied each of the Douala, Edea, Yaoundé, Minlaba, Ngowayang, Nkolayop, Akono, and

---

[79] ACSSp. 2J21a Journal de la Mission Pierre Claver de Nlong, entries of October 1925.
[80] ACSSp. 2J21a Journal de la Mission Pierre Claver de Nlong, 1925–1938.
[81] ACSSp. 2J1.2b2 Rapport sur la Mission Catholique de Ngowayang, 27 avril 1920.
[82] SMEP/DEFAP, MF 3681 rapport de la conférence de 1928.
[83] ANC APA 10384 Inspecteur des Colonies 1921; ACSSp. 2J1.2b2 F.X. Vogt, Rapport sur le vicariat apostolique du Cameroun, 1924, Yaoundé, 1 oct. 1924.

Banaga Catholic missions, but African catechists controlled all construction and secondary post expansion at the Marienberg, Kribi, Saint André, Batanga, and Deido stations, which were considerable operations.[84]

Presbyterian catechists also engaged road and railway laborers to such an extent that both Mgr. Vogt and Pasteur Allégret perceived them as an existential threat to their own efforts. Allégret complained, "There is competition with the American Mission and Dr. Good. We have catechists, evangelists, monitors and students of the catechist school. We have capillaries and organs. But in Ndoungué, Frank Christol and Robert build more schools and even a farm school."[85] Vogt noted that Presbyterians had an element of persuasion that most Catholic missions did not: hospitals. Witnessing Presbyterian clinics "curing thousands sick from overwork," Vogt understood how "the Anabaptists ... certainly can gather so many crowds."[86] Miraculous healing aside, the number of catechists affiliated with the American Presbyterian Mission also grew substantially in the first decade of French presence in Cameroon. In 1921, the APM counted 72 American missionaries and 1192 "native force," and in 1922 they had 74 missionaries and 1401 "native force," and claimed to oversee 700 "churches and groups" in their Bonito, Batanga, Efulen, Olama, Elat, Metet, Foulassi, Sakbayeme, and Yaoundé stations. In 1922, the Elat Mission alone recorded 16,311 "professing Christians," 92 Church Elders, 90 catechists and evangelists, and 111 "preaching points." "Spiritual welfare," a 1922 report from the Metet station declared, "is cared for by daily prayers by the evangelist."[87] Another 1922 report stated:

> At Sakbayémé Station, there are Bassa and they completely run the mission because the Evangelical Missionary Society of Paris was unable to take over the station in previous years until 1921 when the APM arrived ... Since the war native pastors have come and administered communion and baptism, leaving the matter of records to the Bible readers in charge. These in turn have

---

[84] In 1924, catechists counted 3000 Catholics at Marienberg, 2000 in Kribi, and 2000 in St. Andre. ACSSp. 2J1.2b2 F.X. Vogt, Rapport sur le vicariat apostolique du Cameroun, 1924, Yaoundé, 1 oct. 1924.

[85] SMEP/DEFAP Fonds Allégret: Cameroun 1920, lettre de Elie Allégret à J. Bianquis, Douala, 5 avril 1921.

[86] The Presbyterian Church (U.S.A.) does not conform to the Anabaptist position on symbolic Eucharist, and the denomination does not consider itself "Anabaptist" today, nor did it in the period in which Mgr. Vogt declared Presbyterians to be "Anabaptist." See Melva Wilson Costen, "The Lord's Feast," *The Presbyterian Survey*, May 1995, 11–12. ACSSp. 2J1.2b2 F.X. Vogt, Rapport sur le vicariat apostolique du Cameroun, 1924, Yaoundé, 1 oct. 1924.

[87] The Eighty-Fifth Annual Report of the Board of Foreign Missions of the Presbyterian Church in the United States of America, New York: Board of Foreign Missions, 1922, 88.

been content to keep a list of those baptized and of those who are candidates for baptism.[88]

Sakbayémé's Bassa catechists managed 165 evangelistic centers and oversaw 170 Bible readers, 5515 church members, and 12,184 total Christians.[89]

While the APM had founded numerous mission posts in the Bulu-speaking region in the early twentieth century and many American pastors spoke Bulu before 1914, increasing migration and labor internments brought Bassa, Makae, Njem, and Ewondo speakers close to the mission fields.[90] By 1922, American pastors in Metet and Elat, which had all previously been considered "Bulu regions," stated "it has been necessary to use the Makae speaking evangelists … among the Makae and Njem where these men have made evangelistic tours, they tell us the people are anxious for the missionaries to send new evangelists."[91]

Imposing the rigidity of devout life on their followers also demanded that catechists keep meticulous records of believers' journeys through the sacraments as well as note their infractions. By 1922, many Catholic catechists kept a *cahier de contrôle* or record book that they would give to the head missionary after their travels to "prove the assiduousness of native faith."[92] Missionaries encouraged catechists to pair "moral education" with doctrinal instruction, and enforce the commandments through "direct surveillance."[93] This work was assisted in Catholic missions by the introduction of the *liber status animarum*, a register of people living in a parish and events related to them, that would record who confessed, tithed, or "committed sins like adultery, drunkenness, smoking marijuana, or dancing."[94] Presbyterian catechists were also notorious disciplinarians and strictly enforced abstinence from alcohol among

---

[88] The Eighty-Fifth Annual Report of the Board of Foreign Missions of the Presbyterian Church in the United States of America, New York: Board of Foreign Missions, 1922, 92.

[89] The Eighty-Fifth Annual Report of the Board of Foreign Missions of the Presbyterian Church in the United States of America, New York: Board of Foreign Missions, 1922, 93.

[90] APA 11822/B American Presbyterian Mission 1922–1923; the Eighty-Fifth Annual Report of the Board of Foreign Missions of the Presbyterian Church in the United States of America, New York: Board of Foreign Missions, 1922, 87.

[91] The Eighty-Fifth Annual Report of the Board of Foreign Missions of the Presbyterian Church in the United States of America, New York: Board of Foreign Missions, 1922, 90.

[92] ACSSp. 2J1.10.12 Rapport: l'oeuvre des Catéchistes indigènes au Vicariat apostolique du Cameroun, 1929.

[93] ACSSp. 2J1.10.12 Rapport: l'oeuvre des Catéchistes indigènes au Vicariat apostolique du Cameroun, 1929.

[94] ACSSp. 2J1.10.12 Rapport: l'oeuvre des Catéchistes indigènes au Vicariat apostolique du Cameroun, 1929.

their followers.[95] They also carefully reported their territorial reach back to the mission, indicating where new catechists must be sent to cover inactive regions. One Presbyterian report read,

> While the Bible readers are scattered over a wide territory, it does not mean that this is by any means adequately manned. For 30 miles on the Yaoundé–Edea road there are but two Bible readers. From Edea to the Nlong crossing there is not one ... A communion tour of the Sakbayeme field is a journey of some two months' duration, over paths and trails ... The distance is, by the shortest routes possible, 350 miles.[96]

Building on traditional forms of neighborliness and mutual assistance and exerting force and command as sacred authorities, Christian leaders' recruitments for mission building created new kinds of cultural sociability. Moreover, these new methods of collective organizing allowed for the expansion of church communities and for more careful surveillance of their members. Penitents most commonly attained absolution by laboring to build chapels, schools, and catechists' huts, and clearing and planting fields. As part of their penance, they would also receive additional catechism and attend retreats and prayer sessions, which, as Mgr. Mathurin Le Mailloux reflected, "completed their religious instruction."[97] Mbembe has analyzed the process by which young converts entered into the privileged Church hierarchies and the clergy, and notes how markedly distinct it was from the French governance model, which was instead "an incorporation of the previously established."[98] Since catechists were often talented but previously undistinguished men, they aggressively worked to spark religious attachments among local and unfamiliar populations, which allowed them to build a heterogeneous and diverse set of clients, but with a unified set of spiritual ambitions and symbolic understandings. Eventually, they, like chiefs, would seek to remake the everyday lives of Africans, particularly in the private sphere. Their influence would also have implications for the status and daily functioning of the Christian missions, which, very quickly, became deeply "local" institutions.

---

[95] SMEP/DEFAP EEC FB 2/2, "Statut de la Société de Tempérance de la Croix-Bleue des églises chrétiennes du Cameroun à Yabassi," 1930.
[96] The Eighty-Fifth Annual Report of the Board of Foreign Missions of the Presbyterian Church in the United States of America, New York: Board of Foreign Missions, 1922, 93.
[97] ACSSP. 2J1.8.a1 Mgr. Le Mailloux, Douala, letter de 29 sept. 1945.
[98] Mbembe, *Afrique Indocile*, 32.

Equalizing Authority in the African Churches

Exhorted by white co-religionists, who declared them to be "like the Apostles of the early Church," "models," or "village founders," Christian catechists innovated techniques of masculine charismatic culture to reset and repair modes of social organization in a period of dislocation and disassociation.[99] They recruited new initiates through spiritual inspiration but they maintained allegiance, devotional volunteerism, and religious discipline over the longer term by building new relational networks, facilitated by shared language, which would become institutionalized through the church. Unlike administration-backed chiefs in southern Cameroon, who relied on the *commandement indigène* and ruled through extraction and impressment, catechists emerged as community leaders and patrons, rising to prominence using longstanding structures of rural authority and new pathways for building influence through religious knowledge.

In Cameroon's southern forests, the administration-appointed "chief" was expected to be "the head of a family"[100] and to "constitute the force of a people, a nation."[101] However, chiefs rarely formed familial bonds with their subject populations and benefitted far more as enforcers or entrepreneurs.[102] Instead, many African evangelists and clerics assumed the position of community "fathers," as is evidenced among Duala believers, who referred to priests as *Sango Pasteur* (father pastor), or even *Sango am Pasteur* (my father, pastor).[103] The political crisis provoked by African evangelists as a result of their attempts to inaugurate new leaders, establish separate, sovereign, "Christian villages," and reconstitute families through the "liberation" of chiefs' wives," (among other self-directed, religiously inspired programs) further demonstrates the threat posed by indigenous interference in colonial social configuration.[104] African men who sought leadership positions within

---

[99] Farelly, *Chronique Du Pays Banen (Au Cameroun)*, 80. ACSSp. 2J1.10.12 Rapport: l'oeuvre des Catéchistes indigènes au Vicariat apostolique du Cameroun, 1929; ACSSp. 2J1.11a2 Bikop, Mbalmayo, Obut, Oveng villages, 1933.

[100] ANC APA 10634/A circulaire numéro 61, droit legal, régional, penal, 1928.

[101] ANC APA/11618 Rapport Annuel, Région du Nord Cameroun, 8–9, 1943.

[102] ANOM AGEFOM 799/1855 Rapport: Travaux Ruraux, envoyé à l'ONU, 1931; ANOM AGEFOM 888/2540 Rapport de Tournée No. 14, 1934 de M. Bernier; ANOM AGEFOM 799/1856 l'Affaire Yevol, 1930; see also Charlotte Walker, "Legal Revolutions and Evolutions: Law, Chiefs, and Colonial Order in Cameroon, 1914–1955" (Yale University, 2009).

[103] Thomas Ekollo, *Mémoires d'un Pasteur Camerounais (1920–1996)* (Paris: Karthala, 2003), 15–23.

[104] Saada is helpful in understanding the "constitution" of colonial social categories, as well as their "dissolution" by the colonized. Emmanuelle Saada, *Empire's Children: Race,*

Christian communities in southern Cameroon explicitly communicated their distinction from chiefs, elders, and patriarchs, and promoted ideologies celebrating the free man and his equity with other free followers. However, these principals also had a definitive agenda for reconstituting the social unit that required securing authority over other believers – in particular, women – and reassigning female guardianship from fathers and non-Christian polygamist husbands to baptized monogamous spouses. Although both the Protestant and Catholic missions encouraged women to convert, offered education to girls and young women, and protected women who deserted polygamous or non-Christian marriages – drawing tens of thousands of women to occupy the pews – it was the promise of social renewal through Christian men's activism that determined the gendered agenda of religious transformation in the territory. The ecclesiastical realms provided numerous opportunities for men in southern Cameroon to perform the responsibilities of manhood, including what Philippe Laburthe-Tolra describes as "the substance of [Beti] life: speech" and "the fundamental form of power: the power to possess women."[105]

In French-mandate Cameroon, exposure to violence and exploitation mediated male self-refashioning, which built on longstanding traditions but became collectively organized through the act of moral criticism of those who fundamentally interfered with men's opportunities for status advancement. As greater numbers of Africans in Cameroon and even entire societies like the Bulu and the Beti collectively affiliated with Christianity, they not only freely criticized community members who transgressed the boundaries of religious acceptability, they reshaped family and group identities through religious adherence and new modes of inclusion and exclusion.[106] Their agendas politicized the religious domains of the missions, challenging the authority of local elites as well as the French administration. As Reinhart Koselleck has observed, work on behalf of morality inevitably leads into the political sphere.[107]

Filiation, and Citizenship in the French Colonies (Chicago: University of Chicago Press, 2012), 8–9.

[105] Laburthe-Tolra, *Les Seigneurs de La Forêt: Essai Sur Le Passé Historique, l'organisation Sociale et Les Norms Éthiques Des Anciens Béti Du Cameroun*, 38, 356.

[106] Histories of Duala, Bulu, and Ewondo conversion include Dekar, "Crossing Religious Frontiers: Christianity and the Transformation of Bulu Society, 1892–1925"; Antoine Ondoa Dzou, "Christianisation des Beti du centre Cameroun 192–1955: essai d'interprétation" (Lyon III, 1994); Laburthe-Tolra, *Vers La Lumiere? Ou, Le Désir d'Ariel: A Propos Des Beti Du Cameroun: Sociologie de La Conversion*; Bureau, "Ethno-Sociologie Religieuse Des Duala et Apparentés."

[107] Reinhart Koselleck, *Critique and Crisis: Enlightenment and the Pathogenesis of Modern Society* (Oxford: Berg Publishers, 1988), 89.

Catechists assisted catechumens in rural and urban areas in paying taxes and finding reprieve from forced labor, testified in court on behalf of Christians, arranged for schooling for children and family members, and, most controversially, assumed command over African women and guided them towards new marriages and lives of religious devotion.[108] However, it was their position as charismatics that emboldened them to coordinate and confer with their European and American missionary colleagues as equals. Christian commandments and religious law produced a vision for uniformity that rested on a premise of spiritual (if not political) equality. African Christians and particularly African members of the clergy took those claims to universality and equality very seriously. While Africans confronted racism and exploitation in their experiences with French labor and legal systems in Cameroon in a variety of ways, the candid and outspoken manner in which they confronted prejudice in Protestant and Catholic hierarchies and institutions reveals a greater expectation of redress and a trust in shared convictions between black and white coreligionists. Policies of forced labor, the *indigènat*, and capital punishment revealed French colonial claims of humanitarian regard as subterfuge, but as Aron Nang, an African catechist in coastal Cameroon reminded the French pastor at the Protestant Mission of Jandom in 1920, "Actions speak louder than words ... I carry zeal for God in my heart, but so must you."[109]

Foreign missionaries remarked on catechists' self-regard early on. In a 1921 letter, Pastor Allégret wrote,

> Our three pastors are not willing to be treated as salaried workers or inferiors. They demand not even to be employees! They have done the work of missionaries, they sense themselves powerful, and they are very demanding of respect. I can sense the "Bolshevik virus" in them. They demand to be treated and lodged like European missionaries. We don't even impose on them an exterior authority! They have abundant confidence. We try to make them understand that we work as one heart and one soul together in Christ. There is no feeling or prejudice with regard to race or color.[110]

---

[108] ACSSp. 2J1.9b3 Ad Lucem et l'Action Catholique en Pays de Mission; Les jeunes des villes, 1939.

[109] SMEP/DEFAP Fonds Allégret, Cameroun 1920, Lettres Africains, Aron Nang, catéchiste Duala à Jandom, November 9, 1920. Nang first reminds the Protestant Mission at Duala of the Duala proverb, "*Ebolo e si ma langwabe o mudumbu*", or "Work is not accomplished by the mouth," meaning "actions speak louder than words," or "work is not accomplished only by talking about it."

[110] SMEP/DEFAP Fonds Allégret: Cameroun 1921, lettre de Allégret à J. Bianquis, Douala, 3 mars 1921.

Catholic priests were also "struck by the spirit of independence of certain catechist posts" and advised that African mission delegates "be more restrained."[111] Isaac Makone, a catechist with the Douala Baptist mission, admitted that the catechists "have abundant confidence."[112] The 1921 report on that mission conceded, "catechists have much initiative and independence ... to the point where we no longer control them ... but we consider them masters of the task."[113]

Other missionaries were more consistent and ardent in their praise. Pastor Maurice Farelly's memoir of his experience among the Banen of western Cameroon between the 1920s and 1940s is in part an ode to African Protestant catechists in which he conceded, "the model of consecration and abnegation that is the catechist ... puts to shame our disdainful and pejorative attitudes towards blacks and reveals the vanity of the civilized and the pedantry of whites."[114] Mgr. Vogt was also habitually in awe of catechists and reported,

> From 1915–1928 the number of Catholics rose from 25,000 to 145,000 ... This unprecedented success in the annals of Catholic expansion are due, in large part, to the judicious use of competent native personnel, in particular, numerous catechists ... Our humble but active collaborator. From 1915–1928 we only had 40 missionaries in Cameroon! Who else would have managed all the catechumens?[115]

During the first decade of French rule in Cameroon, African catechists became ever more aware of their influence and inspired both admiration and alarm among foreigners in the territory. During the first half of the 1920s, catechists experienced conflicts and struggle with the increasingly powerful political, economic, and police forces active in the southern forest zone. The late 1920s was marked by increased administrative regulation and aggression toward catechists, which served to embolden, rather than curtail them.

---

[111] ACSSp. 2J1.11a2 Lettre de Mgr. Vogt, mars 1936; ACSSp. 2J1.11a2 Rapport de Mission de Samba 1936.
[112] SMEP/DEFAP Fonds Allégret: Cameroun 1921, lettre de Isaac Makone, Bonamikenge à la Mission Protestante de Douala, 2 sept. 1921.
[113] SMEP/DEFAP Fonds Allégret: Cameroun 1921, Rapport de 15 oct. 1921, Mission Protestante à Duala.
[114] Farelly, *Chronique Du Pays Banen (Au Cameroun)*, 80.
[115] ACSSp. 2J1.10.12 Rapport: l'oeuvre des Catéchistes indigènes au Vicariat apostolique du Cameroun, 1929.

CHAPTER 4

Evaluating Marriage and Forming a Virtuous Household

Marriage in the Church and State

The religious meaning-making of Christian marriage in southern Cameroon was directly linked to transformations in social relations between and within African families, and was also enmeshed in the rise of new local political authorities and, by extension, the passage of French colonial laws governing African family life and the use of wives and relatives as laborers. Even in the years leading up to the declaration of the French mandate in 1922, African Christian principals recognized that chiefs not only coordinated everyday men and women's village settlements and labor prerogatives, they also directly competed with laborers, commoner men, and family fathers for dominance in the family sphere and even within the realm of sexual intimacy. By the mid-to-late 1920s, conflicts between African chiefs and everyday men over women and laborers spurred religiously supported social mobilization on a broad scale.

Chiefs' increasing interference in Africans' family lives was in part a result of French administrative initiatives to reform polygamy and increase the birth rate. In the early 1920s, Governor Jules Carde and colonial minister Albert Sarraut envisioned that African chiefs would assist in increasing population rates (*faire du noir*),[1] which would develop Cameroon's *mise en valeur* and export productivity.[2] Later, Governor Robert Delavignette forwarded in his 1931 study, *Paysans Noirs*, that chiefs could remedy "injustices" in the family sphere that limited Africans' "productive possibilities."[3] Believing polygamy

---

[1] Jules Carde, Discours, Conseil de Gouvernement, 5 déc. 1927, *Journal officiel de l'Afrique occidentale française (JOAOF)*, 837; Jules Carde, "Instructions relatives au développement des services de médecine preventive, hygiene et assistance dans les Colonies," Ministre des Colonies, 29 déc. 1924, *JOAOF* 106.

[2] Sarraut, *La Mise En Valeur Des Colonies Francaises*, 87. See also Frédérick Cooper, *Decolonization and African Society: The Labor Question in French and British Africa* (Cambridge: Cambridge University Press, 1996), 32–3.

[3] Delavignette envisioned Africans as "serfs" and the chief as a potential "lord." Robert Louis Delavignette, *Les Paysans Noirs* (Paris: Éditions Stock, 1931).

to be a primary cause of syphilis and infertility, the French administration instituted new laws discouraging various ways of arranging marriage – never criminalizing polygamy outright, but rather shaping new boundaries for betrothal and espousal. The major flaw of the plan was that new marriage laws were to be enforced by chiefs, who were granted considerable powers to challenge rivals' claims to women or children. Chiefs in southern Cameroon were appointed as judges or *assesseurs* in *tribunaux indigènes* and tribunals of first degree, where they ruled in matters that affected their subject populations' intimate lives, and also wielded power through local police forces, who could take control of vulnerable local women.[4] Chiefs could also counter any resistance to their judgments or authority with jail sentences or fines of one hundred francs without due process of law, employing the *indigénat* with the full support of the French administration.[5] Anticipating that African chiefs could use tribunals and police powers to consolidate their power, Laurent Frébault, Secretary-General of the *Agence Economique des Territoires Africains Sous Mandat*, proposed adding a "prevention of corruption clause" to the law in 1926, which stated "to prevent African judges in *Tribunaux de Races* from judging things according to his own advantage: We must give to the [African] assessors the means by which to carry out a decent livelihood and relieve him of any temptation toward venality."[6] This proposal was put into law with the *Arrêté* of 19 January 1931, after which chiefs received a special state salary for their work as judges, as well as salaries for their efforts in tax collection and labor recruitment.[7] Chiefs' considerable financial resources further bolstered their ability to make large bridewealth payments and enlarge their land holdings, and precluded lower-status men from engaging in these pursuits. Regardless of the contradictions inherent to empowering and enriching chiefs, the sentiment that chiefs could render African societies more equitable remained popular for many decades, as was evident in French minister Henri Labouret's books in 1931 and 1941, *À la recherche d'une politique indigène dans l'ouest africain*, and *Paysans d'Afrique Occidentale*, which argued that

---

[4] ANC APA 11976 Gov. Fourneau, Circulaire du 30 décembre 1916 sur la justice indigène du régime français. The chief with the most formidable private police force in southern Cameroon was undoubtedly Charles Atangana, who converted to Christianity but was considered an unscrupulous despot by many Beti subjects. See Frédérick Quinn, "Charles Atangana of Yaounde," *The Journal of African History* 21, no. 04 (1980): 485–95.

[5] Quinn.

[6] ANOM AGEFOM 874/2409 Rapport de Laurent Frébault, 19 avril 1926.

[7] ANC APA 10634/A and CAOM GGAEF 1/H/74, Dossier 540/2, Décret du 22 Mars 1924. See also the *Arreté* de 19 janvier 1931 citing the salary of African judges and *assesseurs* in the tribunals.

a strong family and tribal patriarchate in Africa could allow for population regeneration and family stabilization.[8] Together, Carde, Sarraut, Labouret, and Delavignette all defended the fantasy that African chiefs would be "master of home affairs generation after generation."[9]

Foreign missionaries disagreed on the necessity of instilling chiefs as new patriarchal authorities, but did invest in the idea of reformed African family headship. At the 1914 Intermissionary Conference at Buea, the American Presbyterian Mission and leaders of the former Basel Mission instated a pledge to suppress polygamy, and as part of this, devised a strategy to complement African men's industrial and agricultural training in mission stations with a curriculum that would develop their leadership skills in the home and in society.[10] Women had to be liberated from polygamy and men had to develop moral autonomy and domestic authority so that they could contribute to civilization and social progress.[11] Between 1919 and 1922, European Catholic and Protestant mission leaders welcomed the passage of administrative laws regulating polygamy, child marriage, and other "customs" that would both "uplift the native woman" and ameliorate the "wretchedness" of African men.[12]

Although government and missionary rhetoric was largely complementary, their actual agendas were quite distinct. Governor Marchand believed that foreign missions had to be "guided towards an understanding" to serve the

---

[8] Henri Labouret, À La Recherche d'une Politique Indigène Dans l'ouest Africain (Paris: Editions du Comité de l'Afrique Française, 1931); Henri Labouret, Paysans D'Afrique Occidentale (Paris: Gallimard, 1941), 142–8.

[9] Robert Louis Delavignette, Service Africain (Paris: Gallimard, 1946), 76. Delavignette's assumptions regarding African potentates' historical roles drew on the questionable studies by Ernest Renan of peasant societies in Brittany as well as the Near East. See Ernest Renan, Souvenirs d'enfance et de Jeunesse (Paris: Calmann-Lévy, 1883); Ernest Renan, La Réforme Intellectuelle et Morale (Paris: Michel-Levy frères, 1871). Cited in Delavignette, Service Africain, 78–90. For more on imperial visions of African political hierarchies, see Raoul Girardet, L'idée Coloniale En France de 1871 à 1962 (Paris: La Table Ronde, 1972), 147–50; William B. Cohen, Robert Delavignette and the French Empire: Selected Writings (Chicago: University of Chicago Press, 1977). Gregory Mann also analyzes colonial nostalgia for chiefs' roles in an era of political disruption. See Mann, Native Sons: West African Veterans and France in the Twentieth Century, 73–80.

[10] SMEP/DEFAP EEC FB Jean Rene Brutsch, Histoire de l'Eglise au Cameroun, La Conférence intermissionnaire de Buéa, 7 et 8 juillet 1914.

[11] ANOM AFFPOL 2098/7 Lettre du Commissariat des Colonies à Mr. le Commissaire du Cameroun, 1940.

[12] Messina and Slageren, Histoire Du Christianisme Au Cameroun, 152–3. ACSSp 281-B, Le Cameroun Catholique, édition de Douala, no. 1, 1939; SMEP/DEFAP Dossier D.22/I-e, "Leçons sur les missions (pour les catécumènes)"; Myazhiom, Sociétés et Rivalités religieuses au Cameroun sous domination Française (1916–1958), 85.

political, administrative, and social interests of the Territory and worked to suppress the more intimate elements of cultural adaptation spearheaded by the missions.[13] In 1923, Governor Marchand invited all heads of missions to "instruct the African populations in the ways of civilization," but also insisted that they cooperate with the government.[14] In 1926 the delegate of the High Commissioner in Douala wrote, "I have always believed that the best means of avoiding missionary encroachment on our authority would be to bring the missions towards our domain and transform them into our collaborators."[15] Governor Théodore Paul Marchand and his predecessor Lucien Fourneau favored French missions like the Congregation of the Holy Ghost over foreign missions like the American Presbyterians and the Norwegian Lutherans, as they assumed French Catholics would be naturally more predisposed to the suggestions of the administration.[16] However, neither Catholic nor Protestant, French nor American missionary societies developed what could be considered a "cooperative" relationship with the French administration. Whether because they were far outnumbered by their African personnel, whose concerns and sufferings were impossible to neglect, or because they became earnestly convinced that the administration was a force for evil, over time, foreign missionaries became the French administration in Cameroon's most powerful adversaries.[17]

Foster's innovative study on Catholicism in French Senegal confirms that examining religion and empire in a single frame leads to a clearer understanding of the heterogeneity of French colonial rule. Her model of the French empire as a "heterogeneous patchwork of communities with unique, negotiated relationships to French authority" is particularly relevant in Cameroon, where both foreign missionary societies and particular African individuals and communities enjoyed special legal and administrative relationships with the colonial state and mitigated its power in a number of ways.[18] Evidence from

---

[13] As a result of this, American, Swiss, and Norwegian missionaries faced more difficulty than French Catholic or Protestant missions in gaining approval for new mission sites. Rapport du gouvernement français à la Société des Nations 1923; Circulare du gouverneur Fourneau, Cameroun, mars 1917.

[14] ANC APA 11894 Lettre du Gouverneur Marchand à Monseigneur Vogt, Directeur de la Mission Catholique à Yaoundé, 4 novembre 1923.

[15] Le délégué du Haut Commissaire du Douala, 18 septembre 1926, cited in Louis Ngongo, *Histoire des Forces Religieuses au Cameroun (De la Première Guerre Mondiale à l'Independence 1916–1955)* (Paris: Karthala, 1982), 73.

[16] Rapport du gouvernement français à la Société des Nations 1923.

[17] *Rapport Annuel du Gouvernement Français au Conseil de la Société des Nations sur l'administration du Cameroun sous Mandat* (1923), 142.

[18] Foster, *Faith in Empire: Religion, Politics, and Colonial Rule in French Senegal, 1880–1940*, 5.

interwar Cameroon, like that of interwar Senegal, demonstrates that there were Catholic and Protestant civilizing missions envisioned by foreign missionaries that ferociously clashed with the objectives and ideologies of French officials on the ground, very few of whom demonstrated any evidence of their belief in any civilizing mission, and rather aimed toward consolidating authority, extracting wealth, maintaining order, and, crucially, controlling the pace of social transformation.[19] Indeed, the few gestures made toward administrative "civilizing" ambitions stood completely at odds with schemes to render the colony more efficient, profitable, and obedient.[20]

The history of religious change – attendant with considerable social and familial changes – in Cameroon illustrates that the interwar period was a theater of international competition for virtuous souls and dutiful subjects, as well as a staging ground for local political and religious conflicts between a multitude of European and African leaders such as chiefs, patriarchs, district officials, pastors, and priests, as well as ordinary individuals like missionaries, widows, divorcées, brides, catechists, and junior men. In these differing strains of agency, the French administration and foreign missionaries sought to influence or control the means by which Africans forged alliances, planned their communities, expressed love, built wealth in people as well as wealth in property, and manifested their culture, power, and sexuality.[21]

Mission Ambitions

Immediately after arriving in Cameroon in 1925 to work with Elie Allégret, Pastor Maurice Farelly noted that among the Banen in western Cameroon, more than a third of all men of marriageable age remained spouseless while others maintained households of twenty-five wives.[22] Mgr. Vogt, a Spiritan who had previously served as the Apostolic Vicar in German Tanganyika,

---

[19] Echoing Foster, this book does not support J.P. Daughton's contention that French republican administrative ideology supported a civilizing mission that melded and accommodated Christian missionaries' goals. See J.P. Daughton, *An Empire Divided: Religion, Republicanism, and the Making of French Colonialism, 1880–1914* (Oxford: Oxford University Press, 2008).

[20] The uneven relationship between emancipatory discourse and actual policy making is also explored in Alice Conklin, "Colonialism and Human Rights, A Contradiction in Terms? The Case of France and West Africa, 1895–1914," *The American Historical Review* 103, no. 2 (April 1998): 419–42.

[21] Oral interviews, Douala, July 18–21, 2009; Douala, August 1–3, 2009, Yaoundé, May 23–24, 2009.

[22] Farelly, *Chronique Du Pays Banen (Au Cameroun)*, 125.

took up the issue of African marriage inequality with singular passion.[23] Vogt lamented that between 1917 and 1920, the Ngowayang mission performed 1777 baptisms and 752 confirmations, but only 215 marriages.[24] Similarly, he agonized that in Edea, where the Spiritan mission had baptized 652 men in 1923, only 80 were married, and in a rural mission in the Yaoundé, out of 1013 baptized men, only 308 were married.[25]

Vogt communicated the precise religious records that he required each mission to keep to the French administration as proof of an African marital crisis. Missionaries and catechists recorded baptisms, marriages, confessions, and the celebration of feast days, as well as the number of faithful receiving baptism versus those joined in holy matrimony, which was used as evidence to accuse the administration of abuse and to galvanize believers to remedy injustice. Forging wedlock among African congregants became a primary focus of mission work under Vogt's leadership. In 1924, Vogt communicated to the leaders of the five fully reoccupied Catholic mission stations that their 1200 registered catechists were to "teach the faithful and the catechumens that being married is like attending mass and receiving the sacraments," and that "the excellent dispositions of the populations of the vicariate mean that we must form families in a short time."[26] African catechists heard his sermons and public pronouncements, particularly his electrifying challenge: "we must reform those who have enslaved their own children in the cruel and immoral chains of polygamy!"[27] Allégret also complained about polygamist chiefs, sharing his concerns with Vogt, who agreed, "One polygamous man with 50 wives is preventing 50 families from being founded!"[28]

A paramount issue in encouraging marriage in southern Cameroon was the question of bridewealth. Local catechists empathized with bridewealth's longstanding importance as an institution that solidified inter-lineage and community bonds, but also recognized that it was becoming perverted as a source of revenue for families and a routine expenditure for wealthy men. Bridewealth among southern Cameroon's societies was not only the conferral of goods and/or services to the father of the bride over time (often over several years) in exchange for the father's recognition of a marriage alliance with his daughter, it also constituted a guarantee that all children born of the compensated union

---

[23] ACSSp. 2J1.2b2 Rapport sur le Vicariat apostolique du Cameroun 1924.
[24] ACSSp. 2J1.2b2 Rapport sur la Mission Catholique de Ngowayang, avril 1921.
[25] ACSSp. 2J1.2b2 Lettre de Mgr. Vogt à Gov. Marchand, 3 septembre 1924.
[26] ACSSp. 2J1.2b2 Rapport sur le Vicariat apostolique du Cameroun 1924.
[27] ACSSp 2J1.10.7 "La Polygamie au Cameroun: Son organisation – ses résultats – les remèdes."
[28] ACSSp. 2J1.2b2 lettre du 4 novembre 1923, Marchand.

were recognized as belonging to the husband.[29] Bridewealth was, in essence, a composite economic system on which marriage, family alliance, and claims to children were based.[30] In expanding their control over women, chiefs and wealthy men not only paid high bridewealth prices for many women, they also extended their lineages with wives' and daughters' offspring and claimed daughters' bridewealth, determining the marriage prospects of their age cohort peers as well as those of the next generation.[31]

In response, African Christian reformers channeled the power of ecclesiastical discipline and used it to position themselves as autonomous persons in charge of their own moral destinies, authorized to interrupt continuities and provide alternative leadership to that of corrupt chiefs and restrictive elders. Christian reformers urged believers to reject bridewealth as an engagement or marital practice and seek marriages with baptized families who were willing to accept no bridewealth. In their speeches and sermons, Christian men also called for the strengthening of the monogramous husband's authority over his wife and children, and emphatically rejected the authority of chiefs and patri-kin who interfered in their marriages. Father Simon Mpeke preached that bridewealth was the ultimate example of the unjust power wielded by

---

[29] Anne-Emmanuèle Calvès and Dominique Meekers, "The Advantages of Having Many Children for Women in Formal and Informal Unions in Cameroon," *Journal of Comparative Family Studies* 30, no. 4 (1999): 617–39; Copet-Rougier, "Étude de La Transformation Du Mariage Chez Les Mkako Du Cameroun"; Laburthe-Tolra, *Les Seigneurs de La Forêt: Essai Sur Le Passé Historique, l'organisation Sociale et Les Norms Éthiques Des Anciens Béti Du Cameroun*, 251–5.

[30] The French administration employed the term *"dot"* meaning "dowry," to describe the process by which African marriages were arranged, which was inaccurate because it both failed to grasp the totality of meaning in marriage alliance and limited the concept to a purely commercial transaction. Marriage and betrothal among societies in southern Cameroon was procedural and typically negotiated by several members of the two communities joined in the union who would decide terms of exchange, value, and substitution, as well as the obligations and expectations of each spouse to each other's kin network. Anthropologists have described the process as "bridewealth," "brideservice," or "marriage *prestation*," to describe the various forms of unions as well as emphasize marriage as a process that required theoretical study. Historian of Cameroon Jane Guyer has correctly summarized that the documentation and discussion of bridewealth in African historiography is probably more elaborate than for any other single facet of kinship and gender relations. See Guyer, "Indigenous Currencies and the History of Marriage Payments: A Case Study from Cameroon." See also Thérèse Locoh, "Evolution of the Family in Africa," in *The State of African Demography*, ed. Étienne Van de Walle, Patrick O. Ohadike, and Mpembele Sala-Diakanda (Paris: International Union for the Scientific Study of Population, 1988), 47–65.

[31] ANC APA 10634/A Loi du 26 décembre 1922 sur le mariage et le statut des veuves; decret du 31 juillet 1927 sur le mariage coutoumier.

fathers and the wealthy against men of modest means. Mpeke did not allow for flexibility in its use as part of Catholic marriage and claimed that bridewealth practices did not reflect ethical systems within local cultures but rather had become lodged within latter-day praxis of "monetizing social relations and exploiting the young." Any attempts to integrate bridewealth into the Catholic marriage sacrament, he argued, "prostitute the signification of the routines."[32] For Mpeke, localizing Catholic marriage doctrines meant building on common conceptions of contrition, reparation, redemption, and altruism, but did not include incorporating indigenous rites and practices into the liturgy or sacraments.[33] He shared his passionate stance with the catechists and brotherhoods he led, and asserted his authority to enforce Catholic commands among his subordinates.[34]

In working to integrate the anti-bridewealth agenda throughout their followings, missions encouraged their catechists to lead by example. A 1929 report by the Catholic vicariate boasted that their catechists were instructed to be "a baptized layman, married, and head of a family."[35] Protestant catechists in coastal and western Cameroon informed the head Baptist mission in Douala as soon as they found a wife.[36] Wanting his entire congregation to witness his marriage, the catechist Nongwarol requested a wedding on Christmas day.[37] Those catechists who struggled to marry also made sure the missionaries were aware that it was the result of chiefs' "bride avarice" as well as their own relative penury.[38] In 1921, the catechist Samuel Njueya boasted that he had finally found a wife after searching many years for a woman who would accept a "poor man" such as himself, and in that same year Manfred Mateke mourned that neither he nor his catechumens could afford food, wives, school fees, or repairs to the temples in the villages of Kolo, Abo, and Mangamba

---

[32] Simon Mpeke, "Témoignage," *Peuples du mode,* 53, juillet–aôut 1972.
[33] ACSSp. 2J1.9b3, Lettre de Mgr. Bonneau au Pape Pie XII, 15 avril 1955.
[34] Simon Mpeke, "C'est l'herbe que mange la chèvre que son petit mange aussi! Enseignement pour les catéchistes qui demandent la dot pour leur fille" (translated from the Bassa), *Cameroun Catholique,* September 1945; "Ne vendez plus vos filles, dotez-les!" *L'Effort Camerounais,* 168, 21 December 1958.
[35] ACSSp. 2J1.10.12 Rapport: L'Oeuvre des catéchistes indigènes au Vicariat apostolique du Cameroun, 1929.
[36] SMEP/DEFAP Fonds Allégret: Cameroun 1920–1923, lettres des chefs et des catéchistes, 1921.
[37] SMEP/DEFAP Fonds Allégret: Cameroun 1920–1923, lettre du catéchiste Nongwarol à Elie Allégret, Foumban, 5 oct. 1921.
[38] SMEP/DEFAP Fonds Allégret: Cameroun 1920–1923, lettres à Elie Allégret de Nseke Kotto, Isaac Tutu Mutedi, Joseph Essomba, Pastor Joseph Ekollo, Evangeliste Johannes Eyango.

because they received no payment for their work.³⁹ Lazare Ndim Ekoka received 35 francs per month for his services as a catechist with the French Protestant Mission in 1920, which he claimed was not enough to afford seeds for his wife's garden and insufficient support for his family when he was away preaching. Ekoka was indignant that although he had been molding Baptist catechumens since 1908, his wife still toiled in the fields to sustain the family "like a slave to a chief."⁴⁰ Nearly all letters from Protestant catechists working in villages in coastal and western Cameroon noted the rising cost of bridewealth as well as food.⁴¹ Hardships served catechists' interests, however. Mgr. Vogt estimated there were 24,646 baptisms between 1927 and 1928 alone, the majority of which were Beti and Bassa peoples who remained in relatively close proximity to their families while being deployed for labor in transit line worksites and chiefs' farms. Catechists opened new mission stations as well as catechist posts near the southern transit stations and along the railway lines, and succeeded in cultivating 120,000 catechumens that they were preparing for baptism by 1929.⁴² The vicar's report disclosed, "How could the priests have taken care of such a flock? Religious education of the 120,000 is done without us and outside of our walls, thanks to the catechists who retain their interest and instruct."⁴³

Spreading the Good News through the Confessional Press

In addition to giving sermons and supporting catechists' work, idioms of "a good marriage" and "predatory polygamist" circulated through a growing print culture.⁴⁴ In new and expanding rural and urban churches in the first decade of French presence, congregants increased the frequency and purpose of the periodic meeting as well as the printed word. In both Protestant and Catholic

---

[39] SMEP/DEFAP Fonds Allégret: Cameroun 1920–1923, lettre de Manfred Manteke, 9 novembre 1920; lettre de Samuel Njueya, 28 aôut 1921.
[40] SMEP/DEFAP Fonds Allégret: Cameroun 1920–1923, lettre de Lazare Ndim Ekoka, 7 décembre 1920.
[41] Missionaries from all denominations agreed that food scarcity in the 1920s was a result of low agricultural production due to widespread recruitment for infrastructure projects. ANC 2AC 9286 lettres de la Mission Presbytérienne Américaine et Gov. Marchand, 1923.
[42] ACSSp. 2J1.10.12 Rapport: L'Oeuvre des catéchistes indigènes au Vicariat apostolique du Cameroun, 1929.
[43] ACSSp. 2J1.10.12 Rapport: L'Oeuvre des catéchistes indigènes au Vicariat apostolique du Cameroun, 1929.
[44] For analysis of the full lacuna of print culture in Cameroon in the French colonial era, see Erik Essousse, *La Liberté de La Presse Écrite Au Cameroun: Ombres et Lumières* (Paris: L'Harmattan, 2008).

churches, the confessional press reinforced religious convictions among subscribers not only through the composition of texts, but also the means of distributing the message. After meetings with a head priest or pastor, networks of catechists circulated church newspapers and newsletters, and enlisted the aid of teachers, priests, and students in reading articles aloud to villagers. In rural areas, the arrival of the newspaper was a major event. Information was read, reread, and discussed publicly and privately. Announcements and stories were interpreted many times before a new issue would arrive. Catholic villagers were not at risk of reading or hearing Protestant news, or vice versa. Catechists were most often the newspapers' sole distributors and were tightly connected to specific villages – without threat that they might enter a village of another faith and read aloud the wrong news.[45]

Protestant missions were the first to launch press organs as vehicles of evangelism in Cameroon, and the Catholic missions soon followed. The confessional press expanded the impact of the visiting catechist, who not only preached his own interpretation and learning of scripture and doctrine, but also communicated news, teachings, and opinions of his co-religionists by reading aloud the recent record. The American Presbyterian Mission's most prominent newspaper, *Kalate Mefoé* (News Letter), was an eight-page Bulu-language monthly launched in 1910 and produced for an African audience by African journalists. The Presbyterian Mission at Elat housed the printing press, from where Africans wrote, edited, and distributed news copies. *The Drum Call* was an English-language Presbyterian newspaper written for the international Presbyterian public, although it was also distributed among Africans in Cameroon. The wide distribution of other Bulu-language religious literature, including *Bia di Zambé* (Songs of God), a collection of canticles in Bulu, and *Minfasan* (Meditations), further embedded textual culture into the faith. The Paris Evangelical Missionary Society printed *Ngengeti* (The Star), *Dikolo*, and *Mibia Ebasi* (Church News), monthly Duala-language newspapers that circulated throughout coastal Cameroon beginning in 1923, as well as their most popular weekly Duala-language magazine, *Jumwele la bana ba Kamerun* (The Awakening of the Children of Cameroon).[46] *Ngengeti* was also published in Bassa and Bamoun, although *Dikolo* was exclusively printed in Duala. Their content focused on advancements in hygiene, family planning, and nutrition, and also featured religious stories and some local and international news. In 1939 the Protestant community in Bonabela unveiled a booklet

---

[45] Ngongo, *Histoire des forces religieuses au Cameroun*, 140–50.

[46] Jean Calvin Bahoken and Engelbert Atangana, *Cultural Policy in the United Republic of Cameroon* (Paris: The Unesco Press, 1976), 66. See also Essousse, *La Liberté de La Presse Écrite Au Cameroun: Ombres et Lumières*, 148–60.

entitled *Mwemba ma myango ma bwam*, or the *Community History of Good*, which was a text to which pastors Martin Itondo, Johannes Deibol, Thomas Ekollo, and Paul Jocky had contributed, which had existed as a series of sermons that forwarded the notion that Christian communities pursued virtue in an atmosphere of injustice and that their segregation from corruption ensured their moral jurisdiction to criticize and reform an immoral world.[47]

In 1935, the Catholic Spiritan Mission launched the *Nleb Bekristen* (Christian Counselor), an Ewondo-language weekly, and *Le Cameroun Catholique*, a monthly newspaper in Ewondo and French. Beginning in 1938, *Le Cameroun Catholique* was also published in Duala and Bassa.[48] Between 1935 and 1939, the Spiritan Mission also launched *Miñañ* in Bassa and *Nkul Zambe* for Bulu speakers.[49] In addition to general news stories about agricultural production, politics, and references to world news, these papers printed wedding announcements with the declaration "*mariés sans dot*" or "married without bridewealth," prominently displayed.[50] They each also granted print space to African religious workers, who would discuss reforms to custom and the role of Christianity in marriage and family life.[51] Catechists had a penchant for sensationalist stories recounting vicious rivalries between wives in polygamous marriages, dreadful tales of African girls sold into marriage in early childhood, and the heinous acts of chiefs who were hostile to Christianity.[52] In the April 1935 edition of the Protestant newspaper, *Jumwele la Bana ba Kamerun*, Gabriel Meka Oyo, a Duala Christian, contributed a dramatic article on the evils of bridewealth, writing:

> Nature never and under no pretext authorized the sale of human beings, the kings of His creation! ... Why is marriage becoming rare? Because poor boys

---

[47] SMEP/DEFAP EEC FB 1/2 Programe'a Synode 28–29 Janvier 1939, Bonabela.
[48] Essousse, *La Liberté de La Presse Écrite Au Cameroun: Ombres et Lumières*, 50.
[49] The Catholic newspaper *L'Effort Camerounais* was not launched until 1955. It was established to update and improve the work of *Le Cameroun Catholique*. See Caroline Sappia and Olivier Servais, *Mission et engagement politique après 1945: Afrique, Amérique latine, Europe* (Paris: Karthala, 2010), 329.
[50] "214 Mariages Chrétiens," *Le Cameroun Catholique*, mai 1937; Père Dubourget, "Mariage sans Dot," *Le Cameroun Catholique*, November 1953; "Un Beau Mariage sans Dot," *Laiccam: Bulletin Trimestriel de Liaison Pour La Formation d'un Laicat d'Action Catholique Au Cameroun*, mai 1962; Michel Choupo, "Mariage sans Dot," *Essor Des Jeunes*, janvier 1962, no. 23 edition.
[51] Lucien Anya-Noa, *Pierre Mebe: Hymne a Hospitalite Beti* (Yaoundé, Cameroon: Abba Ekan/Centre culturel beti, 2003), 7–10.
[52] "L'education des filles," *Le Cameroun Catholique*, no. 4, avril 1953; "Le très grave problème de la jeunesse africaine," *Le Cameroun Catholique*, no. 7, juillet 1953; *Nleb Bekristen*, no. 295, 11 décembre 1958; *Nleb Bekristen*, no. 178, 25 décembre 1953.

cannot procure the 1000 francs that is demanded by even the most modest families ... and so the girl ... understands what drives her and her girlfriends and neighbors to prostitution. This is a barbarian practice![53]

The press organs managed by the French administration did not hold the same attention as those circulated by the churches. Not only was the government newspaper exclusively published in French, its articles rarely covered local issues, focusing rather on European events. Louis-Paul Ngongo forwards that during the interwar period the confessional press, though rudimentary in its means of production and simplistically approachable in its content, was the instrument with which Africans socialized and communicated critical social and political questions.[54] Even in the remotest corners, villagers learned of their neighbors' concerns, social issues, and calamities, and could compare their situations and worldviews to their own. Denominational print capital was also essential for circulating reports on the progress of religious communities, the battles being waged against chiefs and sinners, and updates on the work of Christian confraternities and pious organizations.

Overall, public meetings, corporate worship, and the confessional press all employed language emphasizing that polygamy and bridewealth were violations of "natural rights" of both women *and* men, which Christians had a moral duty to eliminate. In one statement, a Spiritan monk argued that polygamy was a "flagrant and tyrannical violation of two natural rights: the natural right of a woman to choose her husband and her religion, and the natural right of a single man to start a family and assist in the propagation of his race."[55] Criticisms of barriers to family building resonated most strongly among low-status Beti men who often could only access sexual union through negotiations with a wealthier headman, and were never allowed custody of any children born of such transacted copulation.[56] Missionary teachings on "rightful" guardianship over children and women in monogamous Christian marriages were also particularly gratifying to those men who felt they had been cheated out of their wife and child as a result of rising bridewealth costs or the new phenomenon of bride speculation.[57] Beti catechists and French missionaries echoed each others' articulations that chiefly "absolutism" was creating

---

[53] Gabriel Meka Oyo, "Onyol'a Bosangi Ba Mundi: Jenene La Kwankwan La Mundi Mi Duala / 'La Dot,'" *Jumwele La Bana Ba Kamerun*, 18 edition, 27 avril 1935.
[54] Ngongo, *Histoire des forces religieuses au Cameroun*, 23.
[55] ACSSp 2J1.10.7, Lettre à l'administration, 3 mars 1923.
[56] Essomba Fouda, *Le Mariage Chrétien Au Cameroun : Une Réalité Anthropologique, Civile et Sacramentelle*, 56–9.
[57] ACSSp. 2J1.9b3 D. Nzogang, "Sa Femme Coute 100,000 francs," undated; 2J1.2b2 Rapport du R. Père Fr. Pichon in Doumé, Oct. 1931.

a "second class of humanity" that rendered bachelors "minors" without full autonomy.[58]

Chiefs, Power, and Access

Yves Nicol appears to have been one of the few French officials committed to the ideal that French law should liberate African women from polygamy and "servility."[59] His forays into ethnography in the years preceding his appointment as the head of the regional government included living among the Bakoko of the Cameroon littoral, where he developed a pathos for African societies' "disfavored classes."[60] Nicol believed that the administration's actions in granting women legal rights within "customary" (i.e. non-Christian) marriage, such as the right to sue for divorce and seek damages in case of mistreatment, would greatly alter women's material and moral state, transforming them from "a simple piece of property into a human being."[61] He also sought to expand rights for African women by institutionalizing monogamy, a legal process that proved to be highly contentious in a political atmosphere that sought collaboration with indigenous leaders who often expressed their wealth and status through the maintenance of large, polygamous households.

Nicol intended to make good on the French Cameroon administration's overstated 1923 declaration to the Permanent Mandates Commission that all Africans in their employ were "penetrated by our ideas to the point where monogamous marriage has become the current rule and practice, and polygamous unions are today the exception."[62] He concluded that African society suffered from elite polygamy, resulting in "forced marriages" for women and "forced bachelorhood" for commoner men.[63] Nicol's agenda in the Yaoundé

---

[58] Joseph Wilbois, *L'Action Sociale en Pays de Missions* (Paris: Payot, 1938). ACSSp. 2J1.10.12 Memoire du Père Pichon, Mission de Minlaba, au sujet de l'imprisonnement du Chef Zacharie Mbida et de Gabriel Owono, 1930.

[59] Nicol also published scholarly monographs in his tenure as a colonial official, and his texts often gestured toward themes of native improvement and civilizational progress. See Yves Nicol, *La Tribu Des Bakoko: Étude Monographique d'Économie Coloniale. Un Stade d'Évolution d'une Tribu Noire Au Cameroun* (Paris: Larose, 1929); Yves Nicol, "Cameroun-1959," *Marchés Tropicaux* 21 (November 1959): 2564–5.

[60] ANOM AGEFOM 799/1855 Arrêté du 1926 concernant la loi du marriage; Conseil de Notables: Procès Verbal de la séance du 16 février 1926.

[61] ANOM AGEFOM 799/1855 Arrêté du 1926 concernant la loi du mariage; Conseil de Notables: Procès Verbal de la séance du 16 février 1926.

[62] Rapport annuel du gouvernement français sur l'administration sous mandat des territoires du Cameroun pour l'année 1923.

[63] Nicol, *La Tribu Des Bakoko: Étude Monographique d'Économie Coloniale. Un Stade d'Évolution d'une Tribu Noire Au Cameroun*, 81.

region was to convince Governor Marchand to work for the institution of monogamy among African families.[64] However, the governors-general of French West Africa and French Equatorial Africa, as well as the African chiefs to whom he entrusted the mission of carrying out legal reforms often considered his policies too disruptive to local systems of order. Following his tenure as head of the Yaoundé *circonscription*, the French administration gradually scaled back many of his legal initiatives transforming African marriage custom, a fact lamented by the Catholic missions.[65]

African chiefs at the February 16 meeting had decidedly mixed opinions regarding the effects of the 1922 decree on family and village life and forcefully argued for either amended legislation, new restrictions and exceptions, or greater legal powers for chiefs to adjudicate marital affairs. During the session, many chiefs voiced their frustration with the administration's contradictory demands to simultaneously curtail polygamy and reduce the divorce rate and complained either about their villagers' circumvention of French marriage laws or their enthusiasm for litigation in divorce courts, which strained social relations and challenged their authority. Charles Atangana, a Beti chief and a practicing Catholic, flattered administration officials, stating that the 1922 law "contributed to civilization in Cameroon," as well as "assisted in the Christianization of the Beti," but he also announced that he rejected legislation governing widow inheritance, which he claimed was a critical component of Beti tradition.[66] Other chiefs on the Council expressed their annoyance regarding conversions and interferences by missionaries, who inspired new communities of African reformers to defy African authorities and usurped chiefs' authority over marriage.[67] Chief Zogo Fouda proudly proclaimed that he had ninety wives and had no intention of divorcing any of them, regardless of their faith. He communicated that if the missions had the temerity to convince his wives to divorce him, then he would demand compensation for the bridewealth he had given to their families. African notable Joseph Atamengue also expressed concern about the gendered effects of Christian conversion, detailing how women's inclination to convert created conflicts with their husbands over the baptism and catechism of their children. Atamengue recommended

---

[64] ANOM AGEFOM 1007/3569 Circulaire du 2 décembre 1930, Le Contrôle des Collectivités Indigènes. Nicol, *La Tribu Des Bakoko: Étude Monographique d'Économie Coloniale. Un Stade d'Évolution d'une Tribu Noire Au Cameroun*; Nicol, "Cameroun-1959."

[65] ANOM AGEFOM 989/3424 Cameroun Justice legislation civile 1927–1933; ACSSp. 2J1.1a.10 "Difficultés avec l'administration."

[66] ANOM AGEFOM 799/1855 Arrêté du 1926 concernant la loi du mariage; Conseil de Notables: Procès Verbal de la séance du 16 février 1926.

[67] ANOM AGEFOM 799/1855 Charles Atangana, chef superieur des Yaoundé et les Bané, Conseil de Notables: Procès Verbal de la séance du 16 février 1926.

that new custody laws be passed in light of the "weakening of fathers' influence" and the necessity to instate fathers' and paternal uncles' privileges over children's education.[68]

The administration took chiefs' demands and suggestions for governing African families and labor organization seriously. Chiefs worked with the Mandate government to restrict rural men's mobility through the *livret de travail*, or work permit with photograph, instituted in 1923, and later, the *état civil*, or civil registration system, which identified each African as a member of a particular village, "custom," tribunal, and fixed location, and made it possible to identify and prosecute deserters for "breach of contract."[69] Once African populations were less mobile and more vulnerable to the influence of one chief, chiefs also negotiated labor contracts with local officials and concessionary companies to recruit laborers to their own plantations. While some chiefs were penalized for skimming laborers from administrative infrastructure projects, regional officials continued to allow chiefs considerable leeway in determining the fates of Africans in their villages.[70]

The scarcity of grooms in some regions as a result of railroad impressment provided chiefs nearly limitless opportunities to marry remaining women and put them to use on their own plantations.[71] Chiefs' increased wealth then allowed them to make larger bridewealth payments to fathers, driving up the cost of bridewealth across the southern territory. Even among the Gbaya, Mkako, and Maka of eastern Cameroon who retained their lineage loyalties, their precolonial egalitarian tendencies were eroded first by German colonialism and then French policies that allowed a few individuals to "capture" power in the form of social reproduction.[72] Significant ruptures in matrimonial practices among the societies of the eastern southern forest zone were

---

[68] ANOM AGEFOM 799/1855 Chef Atamengue, Chef Zogo Fouda, Conseil de Notables: Procès Verbal de la séance du 16 février 1926.

[69] Décret du 10 Novembre 1923, *Journal Officiel du Cameroun*, 1924, 20; ANOM AGEFOM 151/5 Lettre de Foury, l'inspecteur-adjoint des Eaux et Forets à Monsieur le commissaire de la Republique à Yaounde, le 10 Janvier 1927.

[70] ANC APA 11036/A Rapport sur les villages Eton de Sa'a et Obala, Centre Cameroun, 1930; ANC APA 11828/H Rapport sur les cheffries, 1933; ANOM AGEFOM 1007/3569 circulaire du 2 décembre 1930, Le Contrôle des Collectivités Indigènes.

[71] This was noted by the French administration in many Rapports de Tournée. See, for example, ANOM AGEFOM 989/3430 "Cameroun administration 1927–1933," Rapport de Tournée de 3 au 21 août 1932 dans la diffusion de Sangmélima, Circonscription d'Ebolowa; and, in the same dossier, Rapport de Administrateur-adjoint des Colonies Menard, au chef de la circonscription de Bafia, in Bafia, 10 février 1933.

[72] Elisabeth Copet-Rougier, "Du Clan a La Chefferie Dans l'est Du Cameroun," *Africa: Journal of the International African Institute* 57, no. 3 (1987): 345–63; Geschiere, *Village Communities and the State*.

thus in part a result of a new headship structure that Elisabeth Copet-Rougier aptly describes as "a newly instituted competition with mutated prestige, albeit without influence."[73] Longstanding agreements among Mkako families enforced that even among independently wealthy men, bridewealth could not be dispensed by one man to acquire another wife if one of his brothers was of marriageable age and in need of a wife.[74] Thus, among the Mkako, any "surplus" of women was more equitably proportioned, although high prices for rubber and tobacco harvests allowed for greater accumulation among certain individuals.[75] Similarly, prestigious family heads among the neighboring Maka had, in some cases, up to ten wives.[76] By contrast, some Bulu and Beti chiefs in central southern Cameroon were reputed to have more than one hundred wives.[77] In 1923, officials noted that Edjo Mvondo, a Bulu chief in Ebolowa had thirty-five wives.[78] Between 1920 and 1939, Chief Zogo Fouda Ngono of the Manguissa was reputed to have nearly one thousand wives who worked his roughly four hundred acres of cocoa farms.[79] Chief Tsanga Manga

---

[73] Copet-Rougier, "Du Clan a La Chefferie Dans l'est Du Cameroun," 357.

[74] Copet-Rougier, "Étude de La Transformation Du Mariage Chez Les Mkako Du Cameroun," 85.

[75] Copet-Rougier, "Étude," 88–9.

[76] Peter Geschiere, "Chiefs and Colonial Rule in Cameroon: Inventing Chieftaincy, French and British Style," *Africa: Journal of the International African Institute* 63, no, 2 (1993): 152.

[77] In the 1932 census, the Ewondo chief of the central Cameroonian town of Saa had 203 wives, and had accumulated 583 by 1939. Ngoa Evina, Chief of Mvele West, had 142 wives when he died in 1952. Demographic studies conducted in the 1920 and 1930s noted that in Yaoundé two out of five marriages were polygynous and one third of adult men were unmarried. See Guyer, "Beti Widow Inheritance and Marriage Law"; Guyer, "Head Tax, Social Structure and Rural Incomes in Cameroun, 1922–1937," *Cahiers d'Etudes Africaines* XX, no. 3 (1980): 305–22; Geschiere, "Chiefs and Colonial Rule in Cameroon," 152; Robert R. Kuczynski, *The Cameroons and Togoland: A Demographic Study* (London: Oxford University Press, 1939), 156–80.

[78] AFFPOL 2190/1 Rapport annuel du gouvernement français sur l'administration sous mandat des territoires du Cameroun pour l'année 1923, 75.

[79] In 1926 Zogo Fouda Ngono declared that he possessed 90 wives. By 1930 the French *chef de poste* who interacted with him reported that he had 300 wives. Local oral history claims that he possessed "somewhere between three hundred wives and thousands" of wives, and family archive sources record that near the end of his life he possessed 802 wives. Jean-Pierre Ombolo, "Les Eton Du Cameroun" (Yaoundé, Cameroon: Université de Yaoundé, 1978), 106. Chiefs are the principal figures in many Manguissa, Eton, and Ewondo peoples' retellings of the transformation of marriage custom in the Beti region of Cameroon and are most commonly remembered as having many wives – often "too many." Oral interview, Paul Nando (Yaoundé central market, 11 June 2007). See also ANOM AGEFOM 799/1855, *Conseil de Notables: Procès Verbal de la séance du 16 février 1926*; ANC APA 11036/A, *Rapport sur les village Eton de Sa'a et Obala, Centre*

of Eton Ouest grew over 23,000 square feet of cocoa and used scores of wives and female clients to maintain his properties, while also collecting taxes and recruiting laborers for the administration.[80] Although Chiefs Max Abé Fouda and Charles Atangana converted to Christianity and renounced all but one of their wives, they retained hundreds of women on their farms as clients and servants.[81] Atangana brutally impressed thousands of Ewondo men into road and railway work and conscripted their female kin and junior community members in his hundred-acre cocoa farms in the Nyong-et-Sanaga region and cocoa and rubber farms in Ngoulémakong.[82] Many of these chiefs' wives were women from Manguissa and Eton villages emptied by labor recruitments by French concessionary companies. American missionaries noted that among other non-Christian Bulu chiefs in the 1920s, some had twelve to fourteen wives while others had fifty, seventy, or more.[83]

These observations indicate that within transformations in marriage practices and kin relations in southern Cameroon, subtle differences between ethno-regional societies remained and social organizational forms retained some measure of longstanding precolonial patterns. Geschiere aptly assessed that while precolonial societies in Cameroon's southern forest zone were all segmentary, kinship-based systems of order still varied considerably. While the Maka formed autonomous patrilineal villages of fewer than one hundred people and important lineage heads could marry several wives, the Beti, their western neighbors, expressed greater cooperation between lineages and

Cameroun, 1930; oral history surrounding Zogo Fouda Ngono includes elements of mythology and exaggeration concerning his wealth, influence, and extravagance. Zogo Fouda is a frequent subject of praise in *Bikoutsi* music – a kind of music from southern Cameroon: Laburthe-Tolra, *Les Seigneurs de La Forêt: Essai Sur Le Passé Historique, l'organisation Sociale et Les Norms Éthiques Des Anciens Béti Du Cameroun.*

[80] *Rapport annuel du gouvernement français sur l'administration sous mandat des territoires du Cameroun pour l'année 1924*, 188; *Rapport annuel du gouvernement français sur l'administration sous mandat des territoires du Cameroun pour l'année 1928*, 54.

[81] ANOM AGEFOM 151/5, Cheffries, 1930. By 1925 Max Abé Fouda cultivated a cocoa plantation of thirty hectares, which produced roughly between twelve and fifteen tons of cocoa beans per annum and possessed over 3000 coffee bushes.

[82] In 1922, Atangana's salary was 6000 francs per year, and in 1938, it had risen to 24,000 francs. Atangana also received 2 percent of all taxes collected by lower chiefs, a salary for his role as a judge in the local Beti tribunal, and monetary remuneration for recruiting road labor and expanding agricultural production. ANOM AGEFOM 799/1855 Proceedings of the Conseil de Notables: Procès Verbal de la séance du 16 février 1926, Cameroun, Circonscription de Yaoundé; ANC APA Dossier 11954 "Charles Atangana."

[83] Wheeler, *The Tribe of God in Africa*, 12; Lucia Hammond Cozzens, "'Why I Left the Things of the Fathers': An Interview with Ndile Nsom, Native Judge," *The Drum Call* 3, no. 3 (October 1924): 20–4; Jones, *The Life of Rowland Hill Evans of Cameroun*, 34–7.

supported the authority of lineage heads over a larger scale of descendants, women, and slaves or clients.[84] When colonial domination, the market economy, and labor shortages strained preexisting systems in the interwar period, Maka and Beti political leaders both responded to scarcity and competition by accumulating wealth through coercion and control, but in ways roughly corresponding to the degree of disparity shown in earlier times.

Throughout the southern forests, though, men with well-established farms and local investments easily recruited African women, as they were the most capable of paying bridewealth most readily, especially as bridewealth prices rose terribly quickly during the 1920s as a result of greater demand for women from concessionary companies, roadwork overseers, plantation owners, and villages who depended on female labor.[85] In 1924, a Catholic missionary in Edea recorded:

> Polygamists have many resources – all his wives work for him and so he can more easily buy young girls. 500–800 francs is the going rate for a young girl. A man without resources or sisters cannot sell his own kin to raise cash, and thus must save it up, little by little. Often, men of 30, 40, 50 years will eventually save enough cash to purchase a girl of 14 or 15.[86]

While catechists and missionaries lamented that chiefs reserved many younger women for themselves, protracted labor commitments led to high numbers of desertions of men from road and railroad worksites and chiefs' plantations throughout southern Cameroon in the 1920s. Some worksite refugees never returned to their original villages, following new opportunities to growing towns and cities.[87] The Yabassi region had a very pronounced exodus during the French mandate period as a result of its proximity to Douala,

---

[84] Geschiere, "Slavery and Kinship among the Maka (Cameroon, Eastern Province)."

[85] The rising cost of bridewealth during the French colonial period has been particularly well chronicled by Jane I. Guyer and Christraud M. Geary. See Jane I. Guyer, "Beti Widow Inheritance and Marriage Law: A Social History," in *Widows in African Societies: Choices and Constraints*, ed. Betty Potash (Stanford: Stanford University Press, 1978), 193–219; Guyer, "Head Tax, Social Structure and Rural Incomes in Cameroun, 1922–37"; Stanley J. Tambiah et al., "Bridewealth and Dowry Revisited : The Position of Women in Sub-Saharan Africa and North India," *Current Anthropology* 30, no. 4 (1989): 413–35. Christraud M. Geary, *On Legal Change in Cameroon: Women, Marriage, and Bridewealth* (Boston, MA: African Studies Center, Boston University, 1986).

[86] ACSSp. 2J1.2b2 lettre de Mgr. Vogt à Gov. Marchand, 3 sept. 1924.

[87] Lynn Schler, *The Strangers of New Bell: Immigration, Public Space and Community in Colonial Douala, Cameroon, 1914–1960* (Pretoria: Unisa Press, University of South Africa, 2008); Lynn Schler, "Ambiguous Spaces: The Struggle Over African Identities and Urban Communities in Colonial Douala, 1914–1945," *Journal of African History* 44, no. 1 (2003): 51–72.

counting 120,000 inhabitants in 1920 but only 36,000 in 1960.[88] Even village men who were not recruited to work often fled, fearing tax collection and potential future recruitment.[89] Thus, gender imbalances within marriages and households were in many ways vicious, self-perpetuating cycles.[90]

To counter desertions, chiefs punished their subjects with jail sentences or fines of one hundred francs, but to little avail.[91] While acknowledging some chiefs' abuses, French officials nevertheless reinforced chiefs' elite status and endorsed their strategies for control, acting instead against those who threatened them.[92] This effect subsequently created a number of entry points for African Christians to lead movements criticizing chiefs, elders, and administration principals, who they denounced as slave traders, pimps, and corruptors. Catechists framed hardships produced by chiefs not as consequences of tradition, but rather of tradition's degeneration at the hands of unscrupulous African leaders. In this way, catechists positioned Christianity as a way to restore a lost equilibrium and a pathway to more meaningful, and, especially, more secure matrimonial and family-building practices that would be governed according to the will of devout men. Christian leaders became critical guides in efforts to reclaim individual authority over marriage and the family, and defend these realms from both French legislation and distorted customary law.

Shifts in Local Marriage and Reproductive Practices

While in precolonial African societies in Cameroon polygamy was a familiar practice among a few elder men who held positions of authority or status, monogamy was standard for many African commoners, junior men, or clients among the Beti, Bulu, Mkako, and Maka societies of the southern forest

---

[88] Guy Mainet, *Douala: Croissance et Servitudes* (Paris: L'Harmattan, 1985), 169.
[89] Quinn, "Charles Atangana of Yaounde."
[90] Frédérick Cooper has noted that asserting control over wives was intended to insure that the community would not lose the labor and childbearing capacity of females, even in periods of rural flight and labor instability. See Frédérick Cooper, *Africa since 1940: The Past of the Present* (Cambridge and New York: Cambridge University Press, 2002), 33.
[91] See, among others, Geschiere, "Chiefs and Colonial Rule in Cameroon: Inventing Chieftaincy, French and British Style"; Geschiere, *Village Communities and the State*; Robert and Walters, "Invention of Tradition: Chieftaincy, Adaptation and Change in the Forest Region of Cameroon."
[92] ANOM SJ2/1, "il fallait égaliser les peuples..." Rapport de l'Avocat General Nadaillat: Historique de l'organisation judiciaire en AEF et organization judiciaire actuelle, 9 nov. 1950.

zone (among many others) as well as for the coastal Malimba and Duala.[93] Thus, monogamy itself was not a foreign conjugal ideal nor was it necessarily equated with low status.[94] It was the scale of imbalance between wealthy men and smallholder farmers or laborers that was entirely new in the era of French rule.

In addition to magnifying unequal access to marriage, chiefs in southern Cameroon broadened and developed practices known in Beti and Bulu as *mvia* and *mgba*, which were forms of temporary sexual access that a man would grant to a client over his wife. *Mvia* was used to share power and sexual access, and *mgba* was a common form of sexual hospitality in which a husband could lend out a wife for the pleasure of his guest, and, in the process, possibly produce another member of the lineage.[95] Models of wealth in people in Cameroon described by Guyer and Feldman-Savelsberg highlight the relationship between sexual access, fertility, and social organization, and note that parental "authorship" or biological parenthood was not always as essential to making a claim over children as claims over sexual access to the mother.[96] Before colonialism and during the early years of French governance, this practice was not widely practiced among the Beti or Bulu except among *nkukuma*,[97] or very rich men who possessed a great number of spouses.[98]

---

[93] Laburthe-Tolra, *Les Seigneurs de La Forêt: Essai Sur Le Passé Historique, l'organisation Sociale et Les Norms Éthiques Des Anciens Béti Du Cameroun*, 73–108; Guyer, "Beti Widow Inheritance and Marriage Law: A Social History"; Alexandre and Binet, *Le Groupe Dit Pahouin (Fang-Boulou-Beti)*; Jacques Binet, *Le Mariage En Afrique Noire*, Foi Vivante: Série Vie Des Missions (Paris: Les Éditions du Cerf, 1959).

[94] Only spouselessness was an undesirable status among nearly all societies on which studies of marriage have been conducted. Jean-Pierre Ombolo, *Sexe et Société En Afrique Noire: L'Anthropologie Sexuelle Beti: Essai Analytique, Critique et Comparatif* (Paris: L'Harmattan, 1990), 22–4; Laburthe-Tolra, *Les Seigneurs de La Forêt: Essai Sur Le Passé Historique, l'organisation Sociale et Les Norms Éthiques Des Anciens Béti Du Cameroun*, 230–3.

[95] Ndjodo, *Le Mariage Chrétien Chez Les Beti*, 14–15. See also Ngoa, "Le Mariage chez les Ewondo: Étude sociologique," 228–30.

[96] Jane I. Guyer, "Wealth in People and Self-Realization in Equatorial Africa," *Man* 28 (1993): 243–65; Jane I. Guyer, "Traditions of Invention in Equatorial Africa," *African Studies Review* 39, no. 3 (1996): 1–28; Pamela Feldman-Savelsberg, "Cooking Inside: Kinship and Gender in Bangangte Idioms of Marriage and Procreation," *American Ethnologist* 22, no. 3 (1995): 483–502.

[97] Also called *nkouma kouma* and *nkunkuma*, or, most commonly in Bulu, *nkukum*.

[98] Laburthe-Tolra, *Les Seigneurs de La Forêt: Essai Sur Le Passé Historique, l'organisation Sociale et Les Norms Éthiques Des Anciens Béti Du Cameroun*, 20–45, 57–120. See also ANOM AGEFOM 989/3418 1923 Rapport sur les coutumes, Lettre A, "Adultère"; ANC APA 10634/A "La Situation Politique de la femme africaine," and 2AC 552 as well as ANOM AFFPOL 3349/8, Decrets du 1939–1951; ANC APA 10634/A,

Typically, a polygamous Beti man could share his wife with a junior client only if she was an *ontogò*, or junior wife. If a man had but one wife, he could lend out his sister or daughter or a female servant in his home. A polygamous man was never supposed to lend his *ékomba*, his first or senior wife, or his *edina*, his favorite wife. And a monogamous man was never supposed to lend his wife to his clients or allies at all.[99] Before colonial rule, Beti communities had few *nkukuma*, and thus *mvia* and related sexual lending customs were practiced only by an elite few.[100] However, with the rise in bridewealth prices due to the inflationary pressures of salaries and the export market, forced recruitments of women for road and railway work, and chiefs' expanded authority over villagers (and hence laborers and women), reports of *mvia* and *mgba* noted that this practice was growing in response to the dramatic rise in inequality between men.

Between 1919 and 1927 administrative reports from Edea describe a phenomenon in which Bulu chiefs recruited male laborers to their plantations by "lending" them one of their wives to serve as their temporary sexual companion.[101] French officials termed this practice "concubinage," "reciprocal adultery," or "wife exchange," and believed it made plantation work relatively more tolerable than roadwork. Chiefs could exempt their workers from administrative *prestation* and the laborer would receive a temporary lover, although any children born of the union would remain the chief's. The administration noted that farther west in Yabassi, where rural exodus was most marked because of its proximity to Douala, *mvia* as well as other, more coercive measures,

---

Extrait de Rapport d'Inspection de la Région du Haut-Nyong effectué du 19 juillet au 6 aôut, 1948; ANOM SJ 2, "Organisation de la Justice Repressive, 2eme Fascicule No. 69 D/S, 29 avril 1949," ANOM AGEFOM 989/3418 1923 Rapport sur les coutumes, Lettre A, "Adultère." See also Guyer, "Beti Widow Inheritance and Marriage Law: A Social History"; Jane Guyer, "Household and Community in African Studies," *African Studies Review* XXIV, no. 2/3 (1981): 87–137; Jane Guyer, "Indigenous Currencies and the History of Marriage Payments: A Case Study from Cameroon," *Cahiers d'Etudes Africaines* 26, no. 104 (1986): 577–610; as well as Père Lejeune, *Au Congo: la situation faite à la femme et la famille* (Paris: Éditions des Missions, 1900); Mbembe, *Afriques Indociles*.

[99] Ombolo, *Sexe et Société En Afrique Noire: L'Anthropologie Sexuelle Beti: Essai Analytique, Critique et Comparatif*, 233–43; Alexandre and Binet, *Le Groupe Dit Pahouin (Fang-Boulou-Beti)*, 53.

[100] Alexandre and Binet, *Le Groupe Dit Pahouin (Fang-Boulou-Beti)*, 52–3. See also ACSSp. 2J1.15.b2, lettre du chef de subdivison de Mbalmayo à Pere Muller, Mission d'Obout, 20 juillet 1938. See also ANOM AGEFOM 799/1855 Conseil de Notables: Procès Verbal de la séance du 16 février 1926.

[101] ANC APA 11846/B Circonscription d'Edéa, Rapports de Tournées, 1918–1923; ANC APA 11802 Circonscription d'Edéa, Rapports de Tournées, 1925–1944. See also Raymond Leslie Buell, *The Native Problem in Africa*, vol. II (New York: Macmillan Company, 1928), 345–6.

were employed to persuade male laborers to remain in the area.[102] Protestant missionaries also noted this practice by chiefs and overseers of large farms and palm groves in Yabassi.[103] Laburthe-Tolra documented that among the precolonial Beti, a wife in southern Cameroon could have many "sexual avatars" if her husband was politically and economically influential.[104] However, as the cash crop economy transformed wealth as well as social and marital agency in French Cameroon, *mvia* became more commonplace as senior men commoditized their wives' sexual labor and deployed their services to further expand their control over male clients.

French jurist André Raynaud noticed in 1928 that chiefs in Ebolowa who accumulated dozens of wives made use of them as more than simply agricultural laborers, which meant that "choosing women as the majority of the workforce" was doubly economically advantageous.[105] As a result, increasing numbers of single men faced diminished prospects of engaging in sexual intercourse through marriage and could only do so through lending practices.[106] As the colonial economy transformed social and sexual relations in this way, practices like *mvia* assumed a prominent place in discourses on marriage and family reform. Administration officials believed *mvia* was practiced because "old polygamous men" were "prevented from certain kinds of exercise," which compelled them to allow their younger and more virile neighbors to enjoy their wives.[107] But African Christians were far more disparaging of the practice, publicly condemning "wife hoarding" and "wife lending" at religious meetings, where they were encouraged by missionaries and priests to liberate women from these forms of "slavery."[108]

African Pastor Eugène Mallo inculcated repugnance for polygamy, *mvia*, and related forms of sexual exchange of women by associating all these practices with African societies' established understandings of taboo forms

---

[102] ANC APA 10634/A La législation du travail, 1922–1925.

[103] SMEP/DEFAP Fonds Allégret: Cameroun 1920–1923, lettre Allégret à J. Bianquis, Yabassi, 29 juillet 1921.

[104] Laburthe-Tolra, *Les Seigneurs de La Forêt: Essai Sur Le Passé Historique, l'organisation Sociale et Les Norms Éthiques Des Anciens Béti Du Cameroun*, 243.

[105] ANOM AGEFOM 989/3424 Lettre de Administrateur Raynaud à Monsieur le Gouverneur, APA, récu le 14 Novembre 1928; Arrêté du 26 Decembre 1922.

[106] Barde, *Au Cameroun Avec M. Wilbois, Les Graves Problèmes de La Polygamie et de l'instruction*; Ndjodo, *Le Mariage Chrétien Chez Les Beti*, 72–80.

[107] ANC APA 2AC 552 "Rapport sur les coutumes" 1931.

[108] French jurist Robert Blin stated in 1939, "There are numerous means to address this offense: we must make clear that marriage is not a form of legal slavery." ANC APA 10634/A, Lettre Robert Blin, procureur de la République près le Tribunal Supérieur, 1939. See also Decret du 31 juillet 1927 sur la justice indigène au Cameroun, Decret du 30 novembre 1925, Decret du 15 juin 1939 sur le mariage indigène.

of sexual intercourse such as illicit adultery and sexual betrayal.[109] Mallo preached that *mvia* was not part of local custom, but rather an exaggeration and perversion of custom. His approach was not what Mbembe criticized as "the indoctrination of 'sex sin,'" but rather appealed to Africans' changing perspectives on social and sexual justice. In the context of increasing privation and many commoner men's relative disadvantage, critiques and condemnations of *mvia* and *mgba* played into men's desire for rights to (and over) wives and children. Mallo and his contemporaries tapped into individuals' and local communities' values of fidelity and social equilibrium, and sought to connect them to values for matrimony and coupling.[110] It is worth noting that locals did not reject a new or modern practice, nor a longstanding tradition, but rather protested what they viewed as an elaboration of occasional phenomenon, whose acceptability was no longer authorized in light of changing social and economic conditions.

Jean Allman and Victoria Tashjian's phrase, "gender chaos" captures the essence of the marriage crisis in colonial Asante, which was brought on by men and women's struggles to manage land, accommodate political hierarchies, and negotiate legal obligations.[111] In their work, Allman and Tashjian examine gendered conflicts over who controlled various forms of production – cash crop production, household production, and reproduction – and whose loyalty would be inscribed in law. In Cameroon, "gender chaos" also describes the conflict of masculine authority between African chiefs and Christian leaders. As political men with newfound wealth and organizational power clashed with religious men with the charisma to influence individuals and transpose their grievances into new loyalties, marriage, and, to a certain extent, women, became their battlegrounds. Notions of male responsibility and male prerogative shaped catechists' self-identification with Jesus Christ and his apostles and spurred their desires to lead and to acquire and retain a spouse and children – both for themselves and their devout followers. These also motivated them to intervene in chiefs' domains and recapture and redi-

---

[109] Jean-Pierre Ombolo and Alexandre and Binet discuss various forms of "non-authorized" adultery or sexual relations that were considered taboo, including sexual intercourse between a woman and a man other than the man who was currently paying bridewealth to her family. See Ombolo, *Sexe et Société En Afrique Noire: L'Anthropologie Sexuelle Beti: Essai Analytique, Critique et Comparatif*, 228–41; Alexandre and Binet, *Le Groupe Dit Pahouin (Fang-Boulou-Beti)*.

[110] SMEP/DEFAP EEC FB 2/2 Eugène Mallo, "Formalités du mariage et donations nutpiales." See also Eugène Mallo, *Sermons de chez nous: sermons pour les temps de l'Eglise* (Yaoundé: Editions CLE, 1965), 16–20.

[111] Jean Marie Allman and Victoria B. Tashjian, *I Will Not Eat Stone: A Women's History of Colonial Asante* (Portsmouth, NH and Oxford: Heinemann; James Currey, 2000).

rect the polyvalent productive powers of African men, women, and children. Catechists further aggravated "gender chaos" as they assumed guardianship over women (including many whom chiefs believed to be their rightful wives or whom fathers believed to be their rightful wards) and introduced new forms of power within the realm of the family.[112]

In western and coastal Cameroon, a particular point of emphasis for both Catholic and Protestant reformers were the customs related to "marriages without love," more commonly referred to as *nkap* marriages, or "marriage by exchange" or "debt marriages" (*nkap* in Bamileke,[113] *lénà* in Duala,[114] and *eban* or *alug mvol* in Beti languages[115]) where a woman was married without her consent in order to service a debt obligation, restitute a wrong like adultery or a betrayal, or provide a match in a mutually planned exchange of females.[116] Other forms of exchanging women could be arranged between families while the daughters were still in infancy, with girls transferring households and becoming incorporated into their marital homes before puberty.[117] This form of marriage, which fell under the administration's designation of *mariage impunèbre*, was criminalized in the *arrêté* of 26 December 1922 and fortified by the Decree of 15 June 1939, which imposed a certification of marital age for all marriages registered in the *état civil*.

In western and coastal societies,[118] "exchange marriages" were considered alternative forms of marriage that required no bridewealth and frequently were negotiated between a concentrated elite of wealthy men.[119] Many African youth from Douala and the Bamoun and Bamiléké regions described exchange marriages as destructive in church meetings, not only because the spouses

---

[112] ACSSp. 2J1.9b3 Ad Lucem et l'Action Catholique en Pays de Mission; Les jeunes des villes, 1939.

[113] Bureau, "Ethno-Sociologie Religieuse Des Duala et Apparentés," 176–80.

[114] Bureau, 169.

[115] *Nkap* means money in Bamileke. See Justin Fotso, *Polygamie et Religion Chretienne Chez Les Bamileke de l'ouest-Cameroun* (Strasbourg: Université des sciences humaines de Strasbourg, Faculté théologie catholique, Institut de droit canonique, 1978), 54–67; Owono Nkoudou, "Le Problème Du Mariage Dotal Au Cameroun Français," 45.

[116] Ombolo, *Sexe et Société En Afrique Noire: L'Anthropologie Sexuelle Beti: Essai Analytique, Critique et Comparatif*, 236–7.

[117] Owono Nkoudou, "Le Problème Du Mariage Dotal Au Cameroun Français," 45.

[118] This form of marriage also existed in southern Cameroon among the forest peoples such as the Beti and their sub-groups. However, the southern region was home to other older and newer forms of marriage practice that Christian communities focused on, rather than exchange marriages, which were a focus of criticism in western and coastal Cameroon.

[119] Claude Tardits, *Contribution à l'étude Des Populations Bamiléké de l'Ouest Cameroun*, L'Homme d'Outre-Mer 4 (Paris: Berger-Levrault, 1960).

did not consent, but also because "love was unable to emerge when the marriage had been arranged simply in order to incorporate a new woman into a family regardless of her qualities."[120] In 1955, François Tchemba, a young Catholic Bamiléké, recounted the marriage practices of the interwar period during a Catholic youth group meeting in Nkongsamba, declaring his despair at the memory of when his elders went "cousin or sister hunting" to satisfy the conditions of *nkap*.[121] Pastor Eugène Mallo, an African Protestant leader in coastal Cameroon spoke out vociferously against *nkap*, relating the troubles that emerged when one of the exchanged women proved to be more fertile than the other, causing covetousness and remorse between families.[122] Yves Nicol, the head of the Yaoundé subdivision, stated that he desired more regulation of *nkap* and similar exchange marriage customs, arguing for their criminalization and increased administrative intervention in *nkap* conflicts in which one woman proved to be sterile. Nicol proposed that, in these cases, perhaps French law could allow for the sharing of the offspring by both families.[123] Intermediate solutions or complicated remedies aside, young Christian reformers sought to terminate such customs and underscore that sentiment and complementarity were paramount in marriage.

Masculine Hierarchies

In many regions, everyday people's marriage anxieties matched those of catechists and missionaries as death and hardship among male laborers became more apparent and as inequality grew for those who survived.[124] Vogt's message that polygamy was immoral not simply because it did not conform to canon law, but also that it was "ruinous to the population, as it allows the abuse of the weak and the poor by the powerful and the rich"[125] deeply resonated in many African men. As early as 1920, Ewondo catechists near Yaoundé proselytized the adages: *"Ntomba abyandigi nkoe,"* or "The rich man is contemptuous of

---

[120] ACSSp. 2J1.7b4 François Tchemba, "Journée d'Etude: Les Jeunes Face au Mariage," Nkongsamba, 5 juin 1955.

[121] ACSSp. 2J1.7b4 François Tchemba, "Journée d'Etude: Les Jeunes Face au Mariage," Nkongsamba, 5 juin 1955.

[122] SMEP/DEFAP EEC FB 2/2 Eugene Mallo, "Formalités du mariage et donations nuptials."

[123] Nicol, *La Tribu Des Bakoko: Étude Monographique d'Économie Coloniale. Un Stade d'Évolution d'une Tribu Noire Au Cameroun*, 85; Bureau, "Ethno-Sociologie Religieuse Des Duala et Apparentés," 167–70.

[124] Some of these apocryphal stories – the most colorful of which involve the Reverend Modi Din Jacob – are recounted and analyzed in Grob, *Témoins Camerounais de l'Evangile (Les Origines de L'Eglise Evangélique)*.

[125] ACSSp. 2J1.2b2 Mgr. Vogt, Formation religieuse et morale des Africains, 1924.

the poor man," "*minkoe misoe minoe engongol mvu*," or "All unmarried men have the sadness of dogs," and "*benya bod bayi na bongo beman wu minkoe*," which translates roughly to "We the important men want young people to stop dying unmarried." The Ewondo word *nkoe* (plural *minkoe*) means both "poor man" and "unmarried man," and contemplative proverbs frequently employed the term to convey that Christianity rejected both destitution and spouselessness, and promised both could be remedied through conversion.[126] At his pastoral consecration, Jean Mwambo recounted that he was inspired to join the Protestant Church because his catechist, Mongbet Esaie, spoke the prayer, "You, oh God, who chooses the weak for service so that you can demonstrate your great power through them, help me."[127] The missions' identification of unmarried men and poor laborers as both suffering victims and righteous and forceful objectors emboldened many to "accept the task of serving my brothers."[128]

Catechists readily observed that the broad mass of the rural population was becoming sharply differentiated from a thin seam of elite African men with access to government salaries, land allowances, and labor and taxation privileges. As part of their social criticism, catechists refused to pay taxes, and those who were officially exempt (by being a registered catechist with official paperwork) encouraged unregistered catechists and everyday followers to also refuse to render money to chiefs.[129] Spiritual and social discourses denouncing elite African men sharpened the sense of disunity between rural people and the higher orders of power in the Cameroon territory, and strong undertones of social antagonism began to characterize catechist engagements during the 1920s. The Sacred Heart Fathers who worked in western Cameroon noted in 1923 that a great number of Africans catechists in their prefecture "deepened their work" among men who had been dispossessed of land, and gave catechists literary, doctrinal, and moral instruction that specifically addressed cleavages between the powerful and powerless and the need for cohesive

---

[126] The word *minkoe* (or *minkue*) also means "single men" in Bassa. Proverbs and tenets referring to the rights and obligations of *minkoe/minkue* also circulated among Bassa Catholics.

[127] SMEP/DEFAP EEC FB divers 2/2 allocution du candidat Jean Mwambo à l'occasion de sa consécration pastorale, Bagem, 31 oct. 1954.

[128] SMEP/DEFAP EEC FB divers 2/2 allocution du candidat Jean Mwambo à l'occasion de sa consécration pastorale, Bagem, 31 oct. 1954.

[129] Administrative complaints about catechists and their resistance to taxation are rife in the archives. See ANC 2AC 9286, Mission Presbytérienne Américaine, 1918; 1924; ANC APA 10674/B impots sur les cases-chapelles; ANC 1AC 3523 Mission Catholique de Yaoundé Rapport 18 juin 1930.

Christian communities that were "oriented toward monogamy."[130] The French Protestant and the American Presbyterian Missions also believed that their catechists were critical defenders against the family instability wrought by chiefs' and French officials' labor policies. The American mission pleaded with French officials to not only exempt their catechists, but also all students in mission schools from government taxation, believing that tax collection inhibited the savings that were critical to servicing bride payments and tithes.[131]

Over time, catechists did accelerate social tensions by using preaching as a means to accuse chiefs of "wife hoarding" and "debasing their race."[132] Resentful of new ways of building "wealth in people" that transformed labor reciprocities between elders and juniors into persistent servitude and bridewealth payments into debt slavery, catechists gained mission approval to engage in more direct action.[133] European missionaries also resented that chiefs paid high bridewealth prices, which, they believed, priced poorer men out of the market for a wife and forced a woman to marry the highest bidder, rather than a man she loved. However, catechists understood that low bride price was also a threat to poorer men's marriage prospects, as lower expenditure allowed chiefs and wealthy men to accrue greater numbers of wives, which catechists called "injustices," "barbaric customs," and "sexual extortion."[134] What emerged as a plan of action among catechists was not organized action against bridewealth, but rather, the redistribution of wives. Regional distinctions in the scale of chiefs' households were not especially important to catechists, who simply made their opposition to "polygamy" a fundamental component of Christian recruitment. As African chiefs thwarted colonial intentions in the political realm, African Christian leaders aggressively intervened in matrimonial and family cohesion practices and outflanked missionary efforts to instruct Africans on the sanctity of marriage.

---

[130] Goustan Le Bayon, *Les prêtres du Sacre-Cœur et la naissance de l'Eglise au Cameroun: Kumbo, Foumban, Nkongsamba, Bafoussam* (Yaoundé, Cameroon: Procure des Missions S.C.J., 1986), 55.

[131] ANC 2AC 9286 lettre de la Mission Presbytérienne Américaine à la Capitaine Bourcart, Commandant la Circonscription d'Ebolowa, 29 janvier 1918.

[132] ACSSp 2J1.10.7 "La Polygamie au Cameroun: Son organisation – ses résultats – les remèdes."

[133] This reality is not unlike rural Asante in the interwar period, which Jean Allman describes as a period of "gender chaos" engendered by cash, cocoa, trade, and transformation. See Jean Allman, "Rounding up Spinsters: Gender Chaos and Unmarried Women in Colonial Asante," *The Journal of African History* 37, no. 02 (1996): 195–214.

[134] ACSSp 2J1.10.7, "Les ecoles de fiancées dans les missions du Cameroun"; "La situation légale de la femme en Afrique Equatoriale Française"; "Le mariage indigène."

Surrendering Wives, Securing Salvation

In 1920 the Catholic mission at Ngowayang noted that their thirty-five catechists had begun to inspire local chiefs, who arrived at the mission to be baptized and promised to build catechist posts in their villages.[135] Missionaries and catechists insisted that chiefs renounce polygamy and divorce their wives before accepting them catechumens, which often involved negotiating compromises over bridewealth. Not only did prevailing upon chiefs demonstrate catechists' uncommon abilities to local people, releasing their wives allowed for what one Catholic mission leader termed "evangelical renewal through the marriageable female element."[136] In other words, chiefs' wives, once divorced, were made available to the single men in the orbit of the mission where catechists traveled and encouraged new conjugal arrangements. This strategy was equally encouraged by Protestant missionaries, who admitted: "We are working to transform villages. Our work is advanced by converting chiefs who then liberate their wives and allow them to live Christian lives ... we ask them to refuse to lend their wives to clients and defend women's rights."[137]

Some mediation was almost always necessary when converting chiefs. Chief Tsanga-Manga, an appointed chief of the Eton-Ouest, was baptized as Jean-Baptiste in 1925, renounced his polygamous unions, and committed himself to his first wife.[138] The missionaries could not dissuade him from maintaining an enormous workforce on his farms, however – he managed over 3000 cocoa plants, 2500 oil palms, 100 goats, 100 sheep, 50 pigs, and 2 horses.[139] Jean-Baptiste Tsanga-Manga later converted his brother, François Mama, who assumed control over Tsanga-Manga's farms along with his 16 sons and 13 daughters (born before his conversion) after his death. A young Christian catechist and interpreter for Chief Ngayi of So-Dibanga asked permission to marry one of Ngayi's wives without paying bridewealth as part of his catechism. Ngayi consented to give the catechist a wife as long as he agreed that if he were to divorce her or die, she would revert back to being Ngayi's property.[140]

Other chiefs converted and surrendered their wives not through arbitration but through spiritual attachments formed during or after dramatic life events.

[135] ACSSp. 2J1.2b2 Rapport sur la Mission Catholique de Ngowayang, avril 1920.
[136] ACSSp. 2J1.2b2 Rapport sur la Mission Catholique de Ngowayang, avril 1920.
[137] SMEP/DEFAP Fonds Allégret: Cameroun 1920–1923, lettre Allégret au J. Bianquis, Douala, 30 avril 1921.
[138] Ombolo, "Les Eton Du Cameroun," 104.
[139] Ombolo, 105.
[140] ACSSp. 2J1.2b2 Vogt lettre à Marchand, 3 sept. 1924, "Formation religieuse et morale des Africains."

While many Bulu chiefs converted to Christianity after having been cured by the numerous hospitals run by the American Presbyterian mission, Ndilé Nsom, the chief of Ebolowa, attested that he converted because his son (his favorite child, who he attested he would "have given anything" to save) was *not* healed by the mission. The son told Nsom before his death: "My father, I want to confess Jesus as my Savior. If I live I want to be one of his followers and if I die I want you to know I shall go to God's town, for I die believing in him." Nsom recounted to the Presbyterian mission: "I said to myself, 'What is there in this world after all? This Book alone tells us about the path to God's town. It alone has a real word to say about after death.'"[141] After his son's death, Nsom agreed to divorce his seventy wives, many of whom were already baptized and were able to be matched with Christian husbands in the range of the Presbyterian mission in Ebolowa.

African catechists were critical influencers of other eminent men, including their own parents, and also persuaded them to dissolve their polygamous unions in favor of sanctified, monogamous marriages. Pius Ottou baptized his father, Johannes Mebanga, along with his two wives, Maria Ngah Nama and Maria Ngono. Several years later, Ottou convinced Mebanga to divorce Maria Ngah Nama, his first wife, and marry Maria Ngono, Ottou's mother, in a Catholic ceremony.[142] As a young seminarian, Jean Zoa convinced his father to cease relations with his numerous wives and receive the sacraments of baptism and marriage with one wife.[143] While these instances appear in mission records as relatively peaceful procedures, catechists also engaged in thorny confrontations to sever marriages and remake families. Spiritan missionaries at the Nkolayop mission admitted that baptizing Mroga Nyango, who had seventy wives, required intensive negotiations and the help of Nyango's son, Mbida Mbane, who had relinquished his wives in order to join the faith.[144] Between 1917 and 1920, Ango, a catechist with the Minlaba mission, persistently harassed a farmer named Essounou to give up his many wives. Ango eventually removed one of Essounou's wives by force in 1917, a transgression for which Essounou sued him in a French military court. Undeterred, Ango pressed his case for Essounou and his wives' conversion and renunciation of polygamy, and as a result was repeatedly arrested and interrogated by the captain commandant of Ebolowa.[145] Catechists had measured success in uniting

---

[141] Cozzens, "'Why I Left the Things of the Fathers': An Interview with Ndile Nsom, Native Judge," 23.

[142] Messina, *Des temoins camerounais de l'evangile*, 55–6.

[143] Jean-Paul Messina, Owono Mimboé, and Bernardin Gantin, *Jean Zoa, Prêtre, Archevêque de Yaoundé: 1922–1998* (Paris: Karthala, 2000), 22–6.

[144] ACSSp. 2J1.2b2 lettre de St. Michel de Nkolayop, 15 juin 1923.

[145] ANC APA 10384 Capitaine Commandant la Circonscription d'Ebolowa, 1922.

Christians in marriage and recorded their triumphs in mission registries, which were then sent to the Vatican. In 1919, Père Louis Malessard boasted that the Douala region's 250 catechists had facilitated 425 African marriages and Yaoundé's 600 catechists recorded another 844 in that year.[146] The administration was less appreciative of such feats, however. In 1922, reports of not only catechists' interference in marriages but also "rivalries between catechumens" for spouses in the Ebolowa region prompted Commissaire Carde to send an official to investigate.[147]

Accounts of civil negotiations and spiritual awakenings in the archives are often found alongside much greater piles of evidence of severe and strained confrontations between men with many wives and those without. A great many Protestant and Catholic catechists removed women from chiefs' farms and worksites so that they could receive religious instruction at the mission and then marry single men in the church. Catechists frequently cited childlessness justification for removing women from their homesteads in cases of *grande polygamie*. Catholic catechists in the district of Enéka reported that one polygamist had 42 wives but only two children, another had 23 wives but only one child, and that Nyemek, the district's grand chief, had 150 wives but just one child. Vogt especially encouraged mission work in correcting infertility, exclaiming in one letter: "Polygamists have thwarted an infinite number of productive households. If only these polygamists' wives had been united with monogamous husbands, the population would not be so diminished."[148]

While it might have been logical for catechists to exaggerate the negative health and reproductive effects of polygamy in order to justify their "emancipations," French officials also admitted, "the coefficient of natality is remarked as low."[149] Reports from the Sangmélima region in 1923 detail the scale of polygamy, divorce, and sterility among the chiefs working with the administration, noting the discrepancy between chiefs' high numbers of wives and low numbers of children as well as the high rates of syphilis.[150] A 1922 survey of 100 women in the forest zone reported 29 women with syphilis, and another survey of 233 pregnant women suffering from syphilis found that 28 stillbirths and 94 deaths in the first year resulted.[151] In aggregate, remarks and reports from French missionaries and officials point to the compound negative effects

---

[146] ACSSp. 2J1.2b2 lettre de P. Malessard à la Prop. Fide, Mission Catholique de Douala, 24 novembre 1920.

[147] ANC APA 10384 Trouble à Sangmélima 1922.

[148] ACSSp. 2J1.2b2 Vogt lettre à Marchand, 3 sept. 1924, "Formation religieuse et morale des Africains."

[149] AFFPOL 2190/1 Rapport annuel du Cameroun pour l'année 1923, 104.

[150] AFFPOL 2190/1 Rapport annuel du Cameroun pour l'année 1923, 75–6.

[151] AFFPOL 2190/1 Rapport annuel du Cameroun pour l'année 1923, 104–5.

of polygamy and syphilis transmission on the birth rate. French officials also clearly prioritized workforce productivity over female reproductivity, as is indicated in the 1923 annual report, which concluded, "We believe polygamy is to blame here ... but it is undeniable that polygamy permits the assembly of many hands and a family workforce.[152] Rather than tax women in polygamous marriages, as was proposed in 1922, officials pledged to "decentralize the *état civil*" to more efficiently oversee polygamous unions.[153]

Converting Women into Christian Wives

To further promote the work of recruiting, educating, baptizing, and remarrying women, the French Catholic missions decided to expand the institution of the *sixa* in 1919 and 1920.[154] *Sixa*, a pidgin form of the English word for "sister," referred to Christian institutions that were used to confine females who were to receive baptism and education before marriage and were also used to house women who had left (or who had been convinced to leave) undesirable marriages.[155] Mgr. Heinrich Vieter, the leader of the German Pallottine Mission, had launched the *sixa* initiative at the end of the nineteenth century as a means to promote marriage between young Africans by sequestering women away from their homes to more fully instill "Christian ethics" in them before marriage. Missionaries, catechists, and their followers built *sixa* schools throughout Cameroon in order to protect young African women against polygynous marriages and provide a space where young people's unions could be negotiated with the help of a missionary. Women studying at the *sixa* were encouraged to marry a Christian of the local church or given funds to divorce a polygamous husband in order to start a new household with a baptized man.[156] Under the leadership of Mgr. Alexandre le Roy, the Congregation of the Holy Ghost assumed control over German *sixa* schools after 1916.[157] While the *sixa*

---

[152] AFFPOL 2190/1 Rapport annuel du Cameroun pour l'année 1923, 106.
[153] AFFPOL 2190/1 Rapport annuel du Cameroun pour l'année 1923, 106.
[154] Charlotte Walker, "The Trafficking and Slavery of Women and Girls: The Criminalization of Marriage, Tradition, and Gender Norms in French Colonial Cameroon, 1914–1945," in *Sex Trafficking, Human Rights, and Social Justice*, ed. Tiantian Zheng (New York: Routledge, 2010), 150–69; Kenneth J. Orosz, "The 'Affaire Des Sixas' and Catholic Education of Women in French Colonial Cameroon, 1915–1939," *French Colonial History* 1 (2002): 33–49.
[155] Messina and Slageren, *Histoire Du Christianisme Au Cameroun*, 163.
[156] Soeur Marie-André du Sacré Coeur, "La Loi d'airain Du Mariage Dotal Au Cameroun Français," *Études* 267 (1950): 3–21; Le Roy, *Un Martyr de La Morale Chrétienne, Le Père Henri de Maupeou de La Congrégation Du Saint-Esprit, Missionnaire Au Cameroun*.
[157] ACSSp. 2J1.10.7 Les ecoles de fiancées dans les missions du Cameroun.

was a Catholic pursuit, Protestant and Evangelical missions established the *internat*, or women's boarding school, where young women would similarly receive instruction and were shielded from early marriage.[158]

African women in the *sixa* received catechism and basic schooling and also frequently performed onerous agricultural work and brickmaking for the missions.[159] The *sixa* also became infamous for providing sanctuary for women fleeing polygamous or undesirable marriages. Mgr. Le Roy defended the *sixa* as an institution that would allow women to pass on Christian teachings to their households, as well as provide asylum for women "seeking shelter from their horrid marriages," and "redeem women and men...from elders, chiefs ... and all the old polygamous men who are almost all syphilitic."[160] Le Roy and later, Mgr. Vogt, were committed to *sixa* recruitment, even when it became intensely controversial and led to catechists' and priests' arrests and violent confrontations over local women.[161] The end result of persistent rancor between local religious and administrative officials was the imprisonment of catechists for crimes like kidnapping, fraud, and corruption, and in extreme cases, slavery and forced labor and the consequent letters of complaint by the Congregation of the Holy Ghost to the League of Nations Mandates Commission.[162]

Le Roy championed the catechists' radically discretionary approach to bridewealth as part of *sixa* recruitment, which was to allow its payment to "greedy fathers" on behalf of impoverished Christian grooms, or permit its exchange to compensate polygamists in order to grant his wives a Christian union, at the same time as criticizing Christians who paid or accepted bridewealth between each other.[163] Catechists also made bridewealth payment more

---

[158] SMEP/DEFAP Fonds Erika Brucker (hereafter FEB) Idelette Allier, letter de 22 février 1930; Yvette Bergeret, *Banganté: Un Internat de Jeunes Filles Au Cameroun* (Paris, 1949). See also Ngongo, *Histoire des forces religieuses au Cameroun*, 127–31.

[159] ACSSp. 2J1.8.a1, Lettre d'Edea, 11 septembre 1945, Père Krummenacker, District de Douala; Orosz, "The 'Affaire Des Sixas' and Catholic Education of Women in French Colonial Cameroon, 1915–1939."

[160] ACSSp. 2J1.10.7 Alexandre le Roy, "La situation legale de la femme en Afrique Equatoriale Francaise."

[161] Direction Diocésaine des Oeuvres, Yaoundé, 1920–1959, 2J1.7a7, ACSSp.; Mission de Nlong, 1925–1938, 2J2.1a, ACSSp.

[162] ANC APA 10560/A Lettres de chef de circonscription d'Ebolowa à Père Pichon; ACSSp. 2J1.10.10 installations de mission, Théodore Paul Marchand, après 1930; lettre de Pere Faussier à Medzek, 27 juin 1930. See also Kenneth J. Orosz, "The 'Catechist War' in Inter-War French Cameroon," in *God's Empire: French Missionaries and the Modern World*, ed. Owen White and J.P. Daughton (Oxford: Oxford University Press, 2012).

[163] ACSSp. 2J1.10.7 Alexandre le Roy, "La situation legale de la femme en Afrique Equatoriale Francaise." See also the general Spiritan ambivalence on this issue in "La Dot et l'Eglise Au Cameroun," *Revue de L'Alliance Sainte Jeanne D'Arc*, 1934, 12–15.

onerous for husbands by preventing them from having any interaction (or sexual contact) with their wives prior to full payment.[164] These methods also at times unintentionally reinforced bridewealth exchange by officially recognizing and incorporating it into mission education and protection practices. Moreover, although many European and African Christian ministers considered the bride price abhorrent, they also entertained debates on its potential usefulness as a disciplinary measure – incentivizing African men to seek salaried labor, postponing marriage for very young women by forcing men to earn bridewealth and – as it grew more costly – even acting as a check on polygamy.[165]

The Mandate administration sharply condemned catechists' bride redemptions as well as their practice of cloistering women away from their families as a means of inhibiting "pagan" marriage. The *sixa* schools aggrieved African fathers and husbands who fought – at times physically – with French priests and African catechists for control over their brides, and such altercations frequently made their way to district courts. By 1930, the French administration was intensely outraged by the volume of letters from "rejected husbands, deprived of their runaway wives, who complain to the mission or the administration." One report stated, "Even if the bridewealth is reimbursed, some do not want to lose their wives ... but the little established camps of *sixas* prevent the administration from returning their wives."[166]

Throughout the 1920s and 1930s, the *sixa* continued to be a formidable institution that drew women from across southern Cameroon. Economic growth frequently determined the conflict points between the bonds of family and the requirements of production. A wife in a monogamous marriage seeking a divorce or who had separated from her husband without an official divorce faced a higher chance of financial pursuit from her forsaken husband because she contributed so considerably to the household's production of cash crops.[167] Widows' desires to join the *sixa*, enter a religious order, or remarry were also commonly contested in rural courts as their independence threatened the labor guarantees many male relatives believed was their right.[168]

---

[164] ACSSp. 2J1.10.7 Lettre de Mgr. Graffin, Mvolyé, 24 aôut 1937.
[165] Barde, *Au Cameroun Avec M. Wilbois, Les Graves Problèmes de La Polygamie et de l'instruction*, 7–11. See also ACSSp. 2J2 1A, Journal de la mission catholique de Bikop, mémoires de mai, juillet, aôut, octobre 1941; Jean Noddings, "L'Action Catholique des adultes" *Laiccam* 6, 1 décembre 1954.
[166] ANC APA 10384 Catéchistes condamnés, décembre 1930.
[167] ANOM FM SJ 2, Rapport du Nyong et Sanaga; Rapport II: Application des mesures relatives à la suppression de la "justice penal indigène," la période critique (1946–1947).
[168] 2J1.15.b2, Mission d'Obout, Rapport 1933, Mengha Mbili, veuve du Meyonia Nga Zamba; Rapport sur la loi du mariage 1934.

Among widows who attempted to legally appeal their late husband's kin's labor impressment or demands to marry, few met with success. Much to the chagrin of Christian missions, many widows' labor was too dear to discharge without a fight. If they attained emancipation, these women nearly always ordered to pay remuneration to their erstwhile inheritors.[169]

French Colonial Marriage Law

In the midst of dynamic and interventionist actions by African Christians, the French administration passed a series of laws that at least theoretically aimed at reducing polygamy, child marriage, and forced marriage. However, colonial laws governing African marriage and family life were so frequently revised and amended and were also contravened by administrative policy upholding chiefs' wealth and power (often expressed in marrying large numbers of women) that they provided little force behind official rhetoric that claimed to "eliminate wrongful marriages."[170] In 1922, Jules Carde passed the *arrêté* of 26 December, which formally regulated marriage and declared family reform part of the civilizing mission of the mandate. The law granted African women the right to divorce their polygamous husbands following their conversion to Christianity, and provided African widows the lawful right to marry according to their will, rather than be inherited by their husband's kin.[171] Carde also set legal monetary limits on bridewealth exchange according to region, which he claimed would reduce the "excesses of the ruling classes," prevent indebtedness by young grooms, and eliminate the "commerce" of young girls by powerful older men.[172] However, as Carde and Governor General of French West Africa Jules Brévié delegated the enforcement of these laws to chiefs, legal acts such as registering marriages, enforcing bridewealth limits, freeing young girls from their marriage contracts, and adjudicating divorce became dependent on men with oftentimes contradictory incentives to limit their subjects' interests and freedoms.[173] While no French decree fully criminalized

---

[169] ACSSp. 2J1.15.b2, Affaire du veuve Mengha Mbili, 1933; lettre du Chef de Subdivision de Mbalmayo au Père Mader à Obout, 14 october 1944.

[170] ANOM AFFPOL 615/1, La Haute Conference de la Paix au Cameroun, 18 aôut 1919; see also ANC APA 12032/A Rapport Annuel, Circonscription de Maroua, 1919.

[171] ANOM AGEFOM 799/1855 arrêté du 26 décembre 1922 instituant la loi du mariage; ANOM AGEFOM 989/3418 arrêté du 14 mars 1922; Rapport de 1923 sur les coutumes.

[172] ANC APA 10634/A Circulaire 1923, Loi du 26 décembre 1922, *Journal Officiel du Cameroun*, déc. 1922; Jules Carde, Yaoundé, 26 décembre 1923.

[173] ANOM AFFPOL 2153/1 Circulaire de Gouverneur Général Jules Brévié, sur la politique et l'administration en Afrique Occidentale Francaise, Gorée, 1932, 1935; ANC APA 10634/A Loi du 26 décembre 1922 sur le mariage et le statut des veuves; decret du 31

polygamy, a range of restrictions on African marriage practices theoretically claimed to "defend the African woman," "train young évolués," and "expand productive households."[174]

French officials believed that a judicial system, overseen by both colonial officials and "representatives of customary law," would secure victims' rights in the settlement of claims and conflicts.[175] In 1921 and 1925, respectively, Carde invited African chiefs and notables to serve within the colonial administration in the *tribunaux coutoumiers* and the Councils of Notables.[176] French officials proclaimed that new African marriage policies would become respected as "native law,"[177] and "a recognizable base of jurisprudence,"[178] and routinely overlooked chiefs' abuses, arguing that the government should "confer on our administrative assistants certain advantages" and "satisfy their taste for distinctions."[179]

The complex position of tradition and authority in Africa during colonial rule has dominated works of history as well as interdisciplinary studies of ethnicity and social identities. While there is little consensus between scholars or fields about how to historicize the complex socio-political dynamics that transformed culture in colonized societies, scholarship has generally concluded that indigenous authority figures wielded enormous influence over

---

juillet 1927 sur le mariage coutoumier; Décret du 26 juillet 1944; Jules Brévié, "Circulaire relative à la codification des coutumes indigènes," 19 mars 1931, *Journal Officiel de l'Afrique Occidentale Française*, 11 avril 1931, 315; and Jules Cardé, "Circulaire sur la réorganisation de la justice indigène," *Journal Officiel de l'Afrique Occidentale Française*, 24 mai 1924.

[174] ANC APA 11196/C Rapport sur le Decret Jacquinot 1951; 1 AC 108 ANC L'oeuvre francaise au Cameroun depuis vingt ans, 1938; 3AC 1350 ANC Rapport semestriel, région du N'Tem; Président Louis Marin et le Groupe parlementaire des missions, "La reglementation des mariages entre indigènes en Afrique Occidental Francaise et Afrique Equatoriale Francaise," Session du 16 juin 1939, *Journal Officiel du Cameroun*, 1939.

[175] ANC APA 10634/A Arrêté du 26 déc. 22 reglementant les mariages indigènes; Décret du 30 nov. 26 sur le mariage des impunèbres; Arrêté du 11 oct. 28 modifiant l'arrêté du 26 déc. 22 sur les mariages fétichistes; Arrêté du 25 avril 30 modifiant l'arrêté du 11 oct. 28; Arrêté du 15 juillet 30 réglementant l'état civil obligatoire.

[176] ANC APA 10634/A Décret de 13 avril 1921, Article 3 de Jules Carde; ANC APA 10634/A Décret de 9 oct. 1925.

[177] ANOM AGEFOM 799/1855 Lettre du Ministre Cardé à Yaoundé au Ministère des Colonies, Paris, au sujet de l'annulation du jugement du tribunal indigène à Bafia par le Chambre d'Homologation de Brazzaville, 12 Septembre 1921.

[178] ANC APA 10634/A Circulaire à tous les Chefs de Circonscription, 1923, *Journal Officiel du Cameroun*.

[179] ANOM AGEFOM 799/1855 Lettre du Théodore Paul Marchand au Ministre des Colonies, Direction des Affaires Politiques, Paris, 12 février 1924, "Creation d'un ordre pour le mérite indigène."

social behavior and ritual practice.[180] However, a number of historians have also demonstrated evidence of the endurance of precolonial egalitarian legal traditions and customary authority structures despite the considerable power of imperial rule, class stratification, and administrative decentralization.[181] In assessing what changed and what endured in practices and strategies used by chiefs in the southern forest zone in Cameroon, an apt characterization from Remi Clignet offers: "Some [Africans] took advantage of modernization to more rapidly and perfectly realize traditional ideals."[182] As chiefs sought advantage in all avenues open to them – through the physical and coercive powers granted through the *commandement indigène*, through the wealth they accumulated in the form of currency and prestige goods, and through their ability to build strong networks of allies and partners (French and African) – they often expressed their ascendancy in forms that were conven-

---

[180] Max Gluckman, *African Traditional Law in Historical Perspective* (London: British Academy, Oxford University Press, 1974); Max Gluckman, *Ideas in Barotse Jurisprudence* (New Haven, CT: Yale University Press, 1965); Martin Chanock, *Law, Custom, and Social Order: The Colonial Experience in Malawi and Zambia* (Cambridge: Cambridge University Press, 1995); Richard Roberts and Kristen Mann, *Law in Colonial Africa* (Portsmouth, NH: Heinemann, 1991); Landau, *The Realm of the Word: Language, Gender, and Christianity in a Southern African Kingdom*; Mamdani, *Citizen and Subject*; Sara Berry, *Chiefs Know Their Boundaries: Essays on Property, Power, and the Past in Asante, 1896–1996* (Portsmouth, NH and Oxford: Heinemann; James Currey, 2000). Joel Cabrita, *Text and Authority in the South African Nazaretha Church* (Cambridge: Cambridge University Press, 2014).

[181] Scholars who argue along this line of reasoning include Thomas Spear, "Neo-Traditionalism and the Limits of Invention in British Colonial Africa," *Journal of African History* 44, no. 1 (2003): 3–27; Jeffrey Herbst, *States and Power in Africa: Comparative Lessons in Authority and Control* (Princeton, NJ: Princeton University Press, 2000); Catherine Coquery-Vidrovitch, *Africa: Endurance and Change South of the Sahara* (San Francisco, CA: University of California Press, 1992); Gwyn Prins, *The Hidden Hippopotamus: Reappraisal in African History; The Early Colonial Experience in Western Zambia* (New York and Cambridge: Cambridge University Press, 1980); Jean Suret-Canale, *French Colonialism in Tropical Africa, 1900–1945*, trans. Till Gottheiner (New York, 1971); Meredith Terretta, "God of Independence, God of Peace: Village Politics and Nationalism in the *Maquis* of Cameroon, 1957–1971" *Journal of African History* 46, no. 1 (2005): 75–101; Olufemi Vaughan, *Nigerian Chiefs: Traditional Power in Modern Politics: 1890s–1990s*, (Rochester, NY: University of Rochester Press, 2000); John Iliffe, *Honour in African History* (Cambridge: Cambridge University Press, 2004); Isaac Ncube Mazonde, "The Basarwa of Botswana: Leadership, Legitimacy and Participation in Development Sites," *Cultural Survival* 56 (1996): 120–43, among others for excellent examples of this line of historical argumentation.

[182] Remi Clignet, "L'Influence Du Concept de Cohorte Sur La Démographie Des Pays En Voie de Développement: Le Cas Du Cameroun de l'Ouest," *Population*, no. 4–5 (1983): 709–10.

tional and locally acknowledged among many societies in southern Cameroon: the capability to amass servile clients and laborers and marry many wives.

Rather than penalize chiefs for taking advantage of absent husbands to recruit local women to work their own plantations, Cameroon's commissary instituted legislation that charged women who left their husband's farms with "abandonment of conjugal domicile." Both Carde and African chiefs applauded this measure, which they claimed would "preserve families."[183] Following the 1919 decree, increasing numbers of men sued women in court for incurring financial liabilities by deserting their marriages.[184] As agricultural and export productivity increasingly relied on the organization of female laborers (for whom chiefs paid bridewealth in greater numbers in order to maintain their farms and plantations), a November 1926 decree revised the 1922 marriage law to demand that women "make restitution" for debts incurred paying her bridewealth if she initiated divorce or refused to be inherited.[185] This stipulation was even applied to marriages of pre-pubescent girls, which was contradictory to other provisions of the 1926 act, which criminalized child marriage.[186] The 1928 revision to the 1922 law declared that a woman seeking divorce who had been married for ten or more years was still liable to repay half her bridewealth, and was only free to divorce her husband without any bridewealth reimbursement after fifteen years. In 1934, Governor Bonnecarrère revised the 1928 revision and proclaimed that a woman plaintiff in a divorce case must reimburse her entire bridewealth, except in cases of advanced old age.[187] Further revisions delineated privileges owed to African husbands as part of marriage, includ-

---

[183] ANC APA 12032/A Rapport Annuel, Circonscription de Maroua, 1919.

[184] "Abandon du domicile conjugal" was instituted as part of Article 85 of the Code Penal Indigène. In 1943, the Government of French West Africa commissioned Grand Marabout Seydou Nourou Tall, who had traveled throughout Haute Guinea and Soudan Français to report on the legal state of "abandon du domicile conjugal" among their West African colonies. Seydou Nourou Tall informed the administration that there was no Koranic precedent for the prosecution of abandonment of the conjugal domicile, and that legal prosecutions in the courts – whether in civil courts or customary courts – operated completely outside of local customary practice. ANOM AFFPOL 2098/7 "Quatrieme Partie: Textes sur le Code Penal Indigene," Dakar, 2 September 1943, Procureur générale Robert Attuly.

[185] ANC APA 10634/A Décret du 30 novembre 1926 sur le mariage des impubères; Arrêté du 1926 concernant la loi du mariage; Circulaire du 26 mai 1934 concernant le reglementation du mariage indigène.

[186] ANC APA Dossier 10634/A Circulaire du 26 mai 1934 concernant le reglementation du mariage indigene; ANOM AGEFOM 989/3418 1923 Rapport sur les coutumes, Lettre A, "Adultère."

[187] ANC APA 10634/A Rapport d'Inspection de la Région de Haut Nyong, du 19 Juillet au 6 Aout 1948.

ing that an African wife have a "kind comportment" and that she maintain a steady presence in her home to perform her "customary duties."[188] The 1927 and 1934 laws also stated that men had a right to divorce in the cases of "the poor attitude and unkind comportment of the wife; imprisonment of the wife for a crime; a wife's habitual bad behavior; prolonged absence of the wife from the conjugal domicile; and the refusal of the wife to perform her customary obligations."[189]

Bonnecarrère defended the laws, stating that bridewealth repayment obligations for female divorce plaintiffs would ensure a woman's "earnestness" in seeking a monogamous marriage and "uphold the sincerity of spouses for the choices they make."[190] Their actual rationale for interfering with bridewealth practices however, centered largely on the political threat posed by increasingly mobile women who traveled to churches, towns, or other farms according to their will, rather than remain indentured on large farms, as well as increasing inequality between salaried and unsalaried men, which contributed to difficulties in tax collection and low levels of subsistence in villages as greater numbers of women worked exclusively on chiefs' and wealthy men's farms, which were often dedicated to cash crop, rather than food production.[191] The administration's failure to legislate in a way that guaranteed commoner men's access to wives nor secured women's labor stability proves how officials were unable to disrupt practices that, by and large, benefitted chiefs.[192]

As chiefs in the southern regions sought to fulfill their contractual obligations to the administration, preserve their power through controlling the duties and commitments of their subjects, and amass wealth through wives and clients, they distorted the law and provoked broad resistance from the populace, which was channeled through the organizational frameworks of

---

[188] Arrêté du 11 Octobre 1928 modifiant l'Arrêté du 26 Decembre 1922 par Gouverneur Marchand; Loi du mariage de 1934, Cameroun.

[189] Arrêté du 11 Octobre 1928 modifiant l'Arrêté du 26 Decembre 1922 par Gouverneur Marchand; Loi du mariage de 1934, Cameroun.

[190] ANC APA 10634/A Circulaire du 26 May 1934 à tous les Circonscriptions, arrêté concernant le reglementation du mariage indigène, signé 26 Mai 1934.

[191] ANOM SJ 2 Xavier de Christen, Rapport no. 91. See also Guyer, "Family and Farm in Southern Cameroon"; Guyer, "Head Tax, Social Structure and Rural Incomes in Cameroun, 1922–37."

[192] ANC APA 10634/A Loi du 26 décembre 1922 sur le mariage et le statut des veuves; decret du 31 juillet 1927 sur le mariage coutoumier. Even when Marchand declared there to be a "crisis in customary marriage," he insisted that chiefs "resolve" it. ANOM AGEFOM 1007/3569 Circulaire du 2 décembre 1930, Le Contrôle des Collectivités Indigènes.

the Christian missions.[193] Over time, African Christians in Cameroon called on their followers to relinquish conventional rituals and fight against chiefs' restrictions and obligations, promising that greater opportunities would be further revealed through receiving Christian sacraments.

---

[193] Richard Roberts has delved deeply into France's contradictory policies governing African "tradition," including the their use of African "traditional authorities" to legitimate their rule. Presuppositions of African changelessness, however, did not mesh well with the changing context of colonial Africa. See Richard Roberts and William Worger, "Law, Colonialism, and Conflicts Over Property in Sub-Saharan Africa," *African Economic History* 25 (1997): 1–7; Roberts, *Litigants and Households*. ANC APA 10634/A Arrêté du 19 janvier 1931; see also Alice Conklin, "Colonialism and Human Rights, A Contradiction in Terms? The Case of France and West Africa, 1895–1914," *The American Historical Review* 103, no. 2 (1998): 419–42.

CHAPTER 5

Faith, Family, and the Endurance of the Lineage

A Sentimental Education

Many scholars have assessed the missionary curricula that strategically deployed the sentimental language of love and family, but this scholarship frequently lacks an assessment of how such ideologies and fantasies were received by local populations or how they influenced everyday behaviors.[1] The Sacred Heart Fathers in western Cameroon encouraged their students to "become godfathers and godmothers of the African race,"[2] and Spiritan missionaries demanded that catechists "assume the character of a family counselor."[3] These exhortations built around kin-centered language do not simply illustrate how foreign missionaries sought to instill Christian conceptions of familial love and unity, they also point to a specific form of persuasion that empowered male catechists, priests, pastors, and church elders to emerge as authorities who took responsibility for cultivating dutiful and moral behaviors among their co-religionists and intervened on their behalf when their souls were at risk. The development of a hegemonic masculine status, then, certainly emerged from religiously based gender ideologies, but also found enthusiastic supporters in secular, governmental colonial institutions and, most importantly, increasingly networked and organized African men, many of whom felt compelled to act shrewdly in the marital domain to counter the new forces constraining their advancement and autonomy.

---

[1] Anne McClintock, "Family Feuds: Gender, Nationalism and the Family," *Feminist Review*, no. 44 (July 1, 1993): 63. Cole, *Love in Africa*; Kathleen Wilson, "Rethinking the Colonial State: Family, Gender, and Governmentality in Eighteenth-Century British Frontiers," *The American Historical Review* 116, no. 5 (December 1, 2011): 1294–1322.
[2] Prospectus des missionaires de la Congrégation du Sacré Coeur de Jésus, cited in Myazhiom, *Sociétés et Rivalités religieuses au Cameroun sous domination Française (1916–1958)*, 14.
[3] Mgr. Alexandre le Roy, "L'Evangélisation des colonies françaises," *Bulletin des oevures de la Congrégation des Pères du Saint Esprit*, 1924, 3.

Philip Nord and Judith Surkis persuasively argue that during the Third Republic, married love and family life moved the French social and political imagination, resulting in a social policy that anchored the conjugal family as the bedrock of the socio-economic order.[4] This ideology complemented and reinforced foreign missionaries' convictions regarding the necessity of a nuclear matrimonial regime in French Cameroon, and bolstered their initiatives in the face of the local colonial government's resistance.[5] Missionary leaders in Cameroon termed their campaign to form individualized African households *"le plan individuel,"* which intended to demarcate the monogamous African family cell and encourage individualist self-determination by discouraging bridewealth exchange, distancing young women from their fathers' and elders' authority, and guarding young men from indebtedness and the labor demands

---

[4] French thinkers like Emile Durkheim, Claude Lévi-Strauss, and Jacques Lacan believed that the modern, nuclear family promoted constitutional unions and free association, which would thereby reduce authoritarianism and act as a motor of civilizational and moral progress. Emile Durkheim framed the "conjugal family" and the precise sexual and filial bonds it promoted as the primary determinant of Western modernity, which moved man away from barbaric social structures and toward modern understandings of the social contract. Philip Nord, *The Republican Moment: Struggles for Democracy in Nineteenth-Century France* (Cambridge, MA: Harvard University Press, 1998), 218–26; Judith Surkis, *Sexing the Citizen: Morality and Masculinity in France, 1870–1920* (Ithaca, NY: Cornell University Press, 2006), 1–2. See also Alfred Fouillée, *Les Éléments Sociologiques de La Morale* (Paris: Félix Alcan, 1905); Alfred Fouillée, *Tempérament et Caractère Selon Les Individus, Les Sexes, et Les Races* (Paris: Félix Alcan, 1895); Emile Durkheim, "La Famille Conjugale," in *Textes 3: Fonctions Sociales et Institutions*, ed. Victor Karady (Paris: Les Editions du Minuit, 1975); Emile Durkheim, "La Prohibition de l'inceste et Ses Origines," *L'année Sociologique* 1 (1896–1897): 1–70; Emile Acollas, *Nécessité de Refondre l'ensemble de Nos Codes et Notamment Le Code Napoléon Au Point de Vue de l'idée Démocratique* (Paris, 1866). For analysis of Levi-Strauss and Lacan's constructions of the heterosexual family as a universal trope for social and psychic integration and their promotion of the idealization of the nuclear family as the central focus of the modern French state, see Camille Robcis, *The Law of Kinship: Anthropology, Psychoanalysis, and the Family in France* (Ithaca, NY: Cornell University Press, 2013).

[5] Marriage reform in Africa was one of the highest priorities within the Christianization objective for French Catholic and Protestant missionaries. See Foster, *Faith in Empire: Religion, Politics, and Colonial Rule in French Senegal, 1880–1940*; Benezeri Kisembo, Laurenti Magesa, and Aylward Shorter, *African Christian Marriage* (London: Chapman, 1977). European missionary sentiments also reflected a Hegelian view of the family as the essential cell of social life, ethically bound by love, not subject to contracts or exchanges. Chatterjee has examined Hegel's influence on the European imperial project, most notably in British India. See Partha Chatterjee, *The Nation and Its Fragments: Colonial and Postcolonial Histories* (Princeton, NJ: Princeton University Press, 1993), 227–34.

of senior men.⁶ However, Africans who became familiarized with *le plan individuel* negotiated it to suit a collective (often lineage-based) purpose, while incorporating the belief that marriage was a freely chosen, sexually exclusive relationship, as well as a contract with God that guaranteed a man's right to govern his wife and children.⁷ Much as Ifi Amadiume confirmed that women's demonstrable political, economic, and social subordination in twentieth-century Africa was socially constructed and not innate, "traditional," or inevitable, an examination of the transformations in marriage practices and philosophies in French Cameroon reveals that African Christian men's discipline and domination of wives emerged in response to the confluence of specific economic and political stressors as well as coordinated religious activity promoting authority over women as morally and spiritually exemplary.⁸

Foster has convincingly argued that Spiritan missionaries in particular were wholeheartedly committed to an assimilative civilizing mission in Africa – far more than any political agents.⁹ Spiritan and Protestant mission records illustrate that marriage reform agendas in Cameroon also had an intensively sentimental dimension in addition to a civilizational imperative, which proved quite captivating as they conceptually twinned love and male power. Making Africans understand "the civility and sweetness of family life where the spirit of submission and harmony reigns"¹⁰ was not only about advancing the social order, it was also a utopian project aimed at making Africans' consciences and souls the judges of "progress." Although throughout Cameroon's societies Africans maintained various terminologies, rituals, and precepts regarding love – love of the divine, love of a sexual partner, and love of family and children – foreign missionaries did not believe that love was either fostered or even operative in the minds and relations of Africans. When François Pichon and René Graffin, two French priests working in Cameroon, stated, "wives are wealth," they succinctly conveyed the European interpretation that African

---

⁶ Abbé Jean Zoa, "Le problème de la dot," in Marie Du Rostu, *Femmes africaines: témoignages de femmes du Cameroun, du Congo belge, du Congo français, de la Côte-d'Ivoire, du Dahomey, du Ghana, de la Guinée, de la Haute-Volta, du Nigéria, du Togo, réunies à Lomé par l'Union mondiale des organisations féminines catholiques* (Paris: Centurion, 1959), 63.
⁷ ANC APA 11196/C "Evolution morale et religieuse."
⁸ Ifi Amadiume, *Male Daughters, Female Husbands: Gender and Sex in an African Society* (London and Atlantic Highlands, NJ: Zed Books, 1987). A very useful article on the religious construction of masculinity in Africa is Adriaan S. van Klinken, "Imitation as Transformation of the Male Self: How an Apocryphal Saint Reshapes Zambian Catholic Men," *Cahiers d'Études Africaines* 53, no. 209/210 (2013): 119–42.
⁹ Foster, *Faith in Empire: Religion, Politics, and Colonial Rule in French Senegal, 1880–1940*, 147–50.
¹⁰ "L'éducation de la femme africaine," *Le Cameroun Catholique*, novembre 1953.

marriage practices were unambiguously related to transactional relations and devoid of true love.[11] One 1925 Spiritan report concurred, "The wife is household manager, cook, an object of pleasure. But there is no unity, no emotional intimacy that the Church demands and that we encounter in European families...the husband and wife do not give of each other completely."[12] In reflecting on their interactions with couples in Cameroon, Sister Marie-Andre du Sacré Coeur and Joseph Wilbois, a French colonial official, wrote that African marriage was "merely a set of relations without real affection, mutual trust, or common interest."[13] True conjugal love, they argued, was "grand, tender, and passionate," but what African tradition dictated was "blind stimulation, jealousy, and tyranny."[14] Likewise, Pastor Bastard, a Protestant Evangelical missionary writing from Ndougué in 1929 reflected, "love and charity ... for blacks, have no precise meaning."[15] He proposed teaching "joy and the senses" along with typical school subjects like arithmetic, which would allow Africans to more fully engage with one another and the task of building a more advanced society.[16] African men and women were victims, these scholars and religious thinkers claimed, but they could not be held fully accountable. Rather, it was customary marriage practices that should be incriminated in the crime of keeping spouses distant from each other, unable to form deeper human bonds on which true Christian life and modern, ordered governance could be based.[17] For international missionary societies in Cameroon, love was an instrument, a means of building character and a more civilized world for Africans, but it was also a way to make Africans "live a life more deeply human ... than that of their ancestors."[18]

European concern with the thoughts and feelings of colonized peoples has been explored by Lynn Festa as a mentality that dominated overseas empires.

---

[11] René Graffin & François Pichon, *Grammaire Ewondo* (Paris: Didot et Cie, 1930).

[12] ACSSp. 2J1.7b4 L'Action Sociale des Missions Catholiques au Cameroun, 1925

[13] Institut catholique de Paris, Soeur Marie-Andre du Sacré Coeur, and Joseph Wilbois, *La femme noire dans la société africaine: conférences données à l'Institut Catholique de Paris 1938–1939* (Paris: Bibliothèque de l'Union Missionaire du Clergé, 1940).

[14] Institut catholique de Paris, Soeur Marie-Andre du Sacré Coeur, and Wilbois.

[15] Pasteur Bastard, "École et écoliers," letter de missionnaire, Ndougué, 26 décembre 1929, *Journal des Missions Évangéliques* (Paris: Société des Missions Évangéliques, 1930), 159.

[16] SMEP/DEFAP 61.767 lettre du Pasteur Bastard de la Mission de Ndougué à Elie Allegret, Société des Missions Évangéliques de Paris, 28 décembre 1929.

[17] "Le Droit de l'Homme et la Femme," *Bulletin de la Société des Missions Évangeliques de Paris*, Société des Missions Évangéliques de Paris, Paris: Eglise Loi de Dieu, 1928; SMEP/DEFAP D.22/I-e "Amitié réelle entre les Africains monogames," 1934.

[18] Société des Missions Évangéliques, "Cameroun et Togo: Dernières Nouvelles," *Journal des Missions Évangéliques* (Paris: Société des Missions Évangéliques, 1930), 33.

By seeking to understand and reform Africans' "interiority," Europeans invested in the notion of Africans' innate humanity while simultaneously differentiating themselves from their psychology.[19] European missionaries were particularly apt to interrogate the emotional bonds between Africans in the hopes of using Christianity as a vehicle of developing the modern psychological self. The Swiss pastor Roland de Pury taught a class on marriage at the French Protestant Mission in Ndoungué in which he urged Africans to "learn to love" in their new Christian married life. His colleagues at the Ndoungué Mission also believed that somehow African "custom" neutralized all real affection and the ability of Africans to cherish their spouse, and only in distancing themselves from their traditional conceptions of marriage could they experience real love.[20]

The love dimension of marriage reform as envisioned by Europeans in Cameroon in the interwar years also complicates Cannadine's argument that civilizing efforts were about the replication of sameness originating from the metropole. While many missionaries desired that Africans form nuclear families according to the western Christian model, the emphasis on teaching true love between man and woman was more complex than simply a domestication of the savage and the reordering of the foreign into analogous terms.[21] More accurately, this utopian project based on married love aimed to elevate Africans to a higher plane of goodness and self-knowledge than even Europeans. Love would free Africans from the bondage of tradition and superstition, and moreover, would shield them from the corruption of Western materialism, greed, and secularism. Indeed, missionaries often worried that Africans would adopt too many European habits and ambitions as a result of "brutal contact with the modern world, which weakens the values of the traditional family."[22] A report detailing missionary efforts in Cameroon quoted a French missionary who cited Rousseau's precept, *"l'homme naît bon, mais la civilisation le déprave"* (man is born good, but society makes him depraved), which revealed some French evangelists' fears of too *much* development. The report stressed that French education must ensure that Africans would be "moved by the

---

[19] Lynn Festa, *Sentimental Figures of Empire in Eighteenth-Century Britain and France* (Baltimore, MD: Johns Hopkins University Press, 2006).

[20] SMEP/DEFAP 61.745 B.192 Roland de Pury, "L'Alliance et la dot," Rapport au Synode Général de Douala, janvier 1958; Roland de Pury, *Les Eglises d'Afrique Entre l'Evangile et La Coutume* (Paris: Collection Présence de la mission, SMEP, 1958); Lettre de Roland de Pury à Jean Zoa, cited in Zoa, "La Dot Dans Les Territoires d'Afrique."

[21] David Cannadine, *Ornamentalism: How the British Saw Their Empire* (Oxford: Oxford University Press, 2001).

[22] Msgr. Jean Zoa, Msgr. Nku, témoignage des "Journées sociales," 2–3 janvier 1965, Mouvements d'Action Catholique de Yaoundé, Mbalmayo, et Sangmélima.

dearest virtues" and "understand beauty and goodness," without succumbing to modern forces of "violence, anti-clericalism, materialism, family dissolution," and other pitfalls of secular modernity.[23] Religious marriage reform in Cameroon, then, would ideally make way for an entirely new society based on Christian principles where transcendent love would form the basis of everyday life and secure the family against modern menaces.[24]

Educating Men and Boys

Missions and their schools played a vital role in the preliminary phase of mobilizing catechists to become community leaders and form faith collectives through which marriage reform and family transitions could develop through social interaction, rather than simply inculcation. Mission schools were increasingly common in both villages and cities in southern Cameroon by the mid-1930s.[25] By 1938, the American Presbyterian Mission ran 1098 primary, secondary, and theological schools, which taught 35,143 students, of which the overwhelming majority were boys.[26] In 1937, the Society of the Sacred Heart operated 327 primary schools with 11,026 students.[27] The Dominican and Spiritan Fathers continually pressed for more personnel for their 1,100 schools, which they operated in all the districts in which they had a mission, and counted fifty thousand students.[28]

---

[23] ANOM AGEFOM 888/2539 Rapport sur les morales des kirdis, undated.

[24] ACSSp. 2J1.13.b3, Notes sur les Centres d'apprentissage des missions catholiques, 24 mai 1959.

[25] Contemporary literacy rates in Cameroon are significantly higher than in other areas of equatorial Africa and sub-Saharan Africa, broadly. The World Bank estimated in 2008 that Cameroon's literacy rate was at 75.90 percent. See The World Bank, "Cameroon: Literacy Rate, adult total (% of people ages 15 and above)," SE.ADT.LITR.ZS, www.databanksearch.worldbank.org. Richard Bjornson attributes much of late twentieth-century education and literacy rates to the widespread presence of missionary education in Cameroon in the early twentieth century. See Bjornson, *The African Quest for Freedom and Identity*.

[26] *Rapport Annuel adressé par le gouvernement français au conseil de la Société des Nations, conformément à l'article 22 du Pacte sur l'administration sous mandate du territoire du Cameroun pour l'année 1938* (Paris: Larose, 1939), 104.

[27] *Rapport Annuel adressé par le gouvernement français au conseil de la Société des Nations, conformément à l'article 22 du Pacte sur l'administration sous mandate du territoire du Cameroun pour l'année 1938* (Paris: Larose, 1939), 104.

[28] ACSSp. 2J1.7b4, "L'Action Sociale des Missions Catholiques au Cameroun," 1925; André Retif, "Le Cameroun sera-t-il chrétien?" *La Croix*, 9 dec. 1954; Joseph Wilbois, *Le Cameroun: Les Indigènes-Les Colons-Les Missions-l'administration Française* (Paris: Payot, 1934), 132–3; Essomba Fouda, *Le Mariage Chrétien Au Cameroun : Une Réalité Anthropologique, Civile et Sacramentelle*, 29.

The 1914 Intermissionary Conference pledged that Protestant education and marriage reform in Cameroon would develop male morality and *"faire de lui un homme."*[29] Boys' Catholic and Protestant mission schools expanded rapidly between 1918 and 1924 in Yaoundé, Edea, Ebolowa, Bafia, Yokadouma, Batanga, Efulan, Lolodorf, Elat, Metet, Fulassi, Olama, and other towns. Boys' schools taught trades and skills like carpentry, masonry, printing, typing, and agronomy alongside catechism in order "to make real men"—translated as *benya moto* in Bulu and *nnya modo* in Beti, which were the terms for a "real man" or "older man"—in essence, a mature married man.[30] In Bulu, seminaries and bible colleges were referred to as *Sikulu be minisi,* "school of the prophets."[31] Christian schooling emphasized that education for boys and young men was crucial to achieving the intellectual and spiritual capacity to know love, as well as be the leader of a family in control of a wife, children, and household. Crucially, mission education called upon young men to be reformers. Education would civilize and then the educated would become civilizers, replacing the patriarchs of the villages with modern leaders. In their in youth ministry and liturgies, Protestant catechists and pastors repeatedly invoked Proverbs 20, verse 29, "The faith of young men is their strength" and Proverbs 31, in which young men are called to reform their communities, ("speak up for those who cannot speak for themselves"), turn away from alcohol ("it is not for kings to drink wine, nor for rulers to crave beer"), and cultivate a loving and dutiful wife ("Who can find a virtuous wife?")[32]

As one of the main controversies that dominated social life among southern Cameroon's societies was bridewealth (and its manifestations in polygamy, forced marriage, and senior men's corruption), conversion to Christianity promised not only a new set of expectations for marriage, it offered a new worldview. The promise of companionate marriage was, as Mgr. Jean Zoa, the first indigenous Catholic bishop of Yaoundé, phrased it, "necessary...in order to create a viable society where individuals—men and women—take charge

---

[29] Ministre des Colonies, *Journal Officiel de la République Française*, 1921, 431.

[30] Presbyterian Historical Society (PHS) Record Group 74: Box 2, File 15, Annual Report of the Dager Memorial Theological and Bible Training School, November 1, 1926. See also Melvin Fraser, "First Annual Report, Dager Memorial Theological and Bible Training School," November 1, 1923–October 31, 1924, RG 74, Box 2, File 15; 2AC 9286 lettre de Gov. Marchand à la Mission Presbytérienne Américane à Sakbayeme, mai 1924.

[31] PHS Record Group 74: Box 2, File 15, Annual Report of the Dager Memorial Theological and Bible Training School, November 1, 1926. See also Melvin Fraser, "First Annual Report, Dager Memorial Theological and Bible Training School," November 1, 1923–October 31, 1924, RG 74, Box 2, File 15.

[32] SMEP/DEFAP 51.915, B.128 Eskul'a Baledi (livret scolaire, école de catéchistes), Ndoungué, 1930; SMEP/DEFAP EEC FB 1/2 Synodes, Mwemba ma myango ma bwam Programe'a Synode, 28–29 Janvier 1939, Bonabela.

of themselves as fully human and fully adult."[33] African catechists' social and spiritual action related to loving companionship and the renunciation of bridewealth and polygamy appealed to a wide range of Africans, but engaged young Africans most intensively. Protestant and Catholic initiatives to promote marriage based on costlessness and amity employed the language of romance, ecstasy, and spiritual rapture, and emphasized the Christian monogamous bond as a uniquely modern and liberating step toward inclusion in the civilized world. It also critically linked monogamous Christian marriage with masculinity, authority, and individual responsibility. Rejecting the Beti proverb regarding marital engagement, *sulug ya dedan osoe tege ai eban* ("the ant cannot cross the stream without the help of a footbridge"), Catholic missionaries among the Beti warned against marriage proposal traditions that involved a family entourage, who brought gifts and nominated appointed speakers and negotiators for the groom.[34] Catechists urged instead that African Christian men speak and act on their own behalf. The prospects for an independent, unallied groom likely appeared perilous to most men in southern Cameroon, but fears over this pressure could be outweighed by the religious promise of the man as the center of domestic discipline, which dovetailed with many Beti converts' long-suppressed desires to be seen as autonomous leaders of their own families.[35] Charles Kassi, an African Protestant pastor preached that to be a Christian man was to hear Jesus' directive to Saint Paul: "Now rise and stand on your feet (Acts 26:16)."[36]

French Protestant ministers preached that bridewealth was "the fathers' and elders' beliefs, which say that money gives man rights," and, instead, young men would uphold love – of God and the woman – that would "give the man the strength to be the leader of his family."[37] "Money destroys conjugal love," one pastor preached, "And love renders man a hero. And heroes

[33] Zoa, "La Dot Dans Les Territoires d'Afrique," 68.
[34] Essomba Fouda, *Le Mariage Chrétien Au Cameroun : Une Réalité Anthropologique, Civile et Sacramentelle*, 38–40.
[35] Ombolo, *Sexe et Société En Afrique Noire: L'Anthropologie Sexuelle Beti: Essai Analytique, Critique et Comparatif*, 67–90. See also Laburthe-Tolra, *Les Seigneurs de La Forêt: Essai Sur Le Passé Historique, l'organisation Sociale et Les Norms Éthiques Des Anciens Béti Du Cameroun*, 350–63.
[36] SMEP/DEFAP EEC FB 2/2 Consécration pastorale de Charles Kassi le 17 octobre 1954. Kwame Bediako has written that many African societies that received Christianity recognized the intuition in the writings of the Apostle Paul. Paul's theology that local culture – the general human web of relationships – mediated the way in which individuals understood Jesus Christ, intuits that redemption takes place in one's own indigenous environment. Kwame Bediako, *Jesus in African Culture* (Accra: Asempa Publishers, 1990), 5–6.
[37] SMEP/DEFAP EEC FB 2/2, La Formation de l'Alliance.

do not purchase their conquest."[38] Churches also heavily emphasized the evil inherent in rising bridewealth costs in song. A common canticle recited in Protestant congregations went: "When a man gives all his riches to buy love, he reaps only scorn."[39] The absence of bridewealth liberated the woman from commodification, but more importantly, it gave the man moral privileges over his domestic partner, as he had saved the woman's dignity by not buying or selling a human person and civilized her by marrying her.

Protestant pastors, elders, and deacons conspicuously exhibited marriage liturgies in the most heavily attended Sunday Last Supper Service (*Culte de Sainte Cène*). Congregations also hosted separate marriage services with prayers in local languages sanctifying the union and heavily emphasizing compatible French and Duala idioms such as "the good news" (*myango ma bwam*) and "rules of purity" (*betiledi ba bosangi*), as well as the concept of the family father as "shepherd" (*mutatedi*).[40] Fridays were the "day of prayer to educate the African household" (*besukulu na mamboa*) with scripture readings such as Matthew 25:14–30, which teaches that servitude, productive use of talent, and faith result in prosperity and large families.[41]

Christian tenets and idealizations related to love were crucial to the project of recasting the African man as a leader of a new social unit – the Christian family – which took its place in a new community of similarly self-regarding men. During his consecration as pastor, Charles Kassi declared: "I was an instrument of Satan, not knowing my Creator or how to serve Him ... before I learned to love women and children and teach both."[42] Fellow pastor Jacques Kemajou attested that he "discovered the loving God" as a young man when he "learned to speak intimately with my wife, my companion."[43] These testimonies affirm missionary goals for deeper attachments between African husbands and wives, but also reveal that the stronger conjugal and relational bonds that drew young men to Catholic and Protestant churches and eventually, a life of ministry, took place in context of increasingly powerful chiefs, progressively more brutal labor conditions, greater numbers of men without wives, and a "perversity" of power in village life.[44] Well-known injustices by chiefs, elders, and moneyed traders and planters testified to the need

---

[38] SMEP/DEFAP EEC FB 2/2, "Mitin ma diba momene" (culte de mariage).
[39] SMEP/DEFAP 61.745 B.192, Cantique 8/7, cited in Roland de Pury, "L'Alliance et la dot," Rapport au Synode Général de Douala, janvier 1958.
[40] SMEP/DEFAP EEC FB 2/2, Mitin Ma Diba Momene (culte de mariage), Lata la Diba (Liturgie de mariage au culte de dimanche).
[41] SMEP/DEFAP EEC FB 2/2, Semaine universelle de prière, 1953.
[42] SMEP/DEFAP EEC FB 2/2 Consécration du Pasteur Charles Kassi, 1954.
[43] SMEP/DEFAP EEC FB 2/2 Allocution prononcée par le candidat Jacques Kemajou 1957.
[44] SMEP/DEFAP EEC FB 2/2 Pasteurs camerounais, 1950–1960.

for Christian men to proclaim new codes and expectations for the domestic sphere as well as society at large, and for vigilant enforcement.

Adjusting the Loving Bond: Beti and Duala Christian Publics

In Beti societies, cultivating what Paul Landau refers to as the "complex social alliance" between local communities and evangelists required altering beliefs regarding marriage and polygamy in a way that extended and reinforced local understandings of a masculine-centered order.[45] Although European missionaries believed that African societies must "learn to love," love was already a sacred concept and considered by many societies in Cameroon as a force to be controlled by mature men, particularly since – as in European societies – it could be a source of power as well as controversy.[46]

Among the Beti, from the verb *lugu*, to marry, comes *melugena*, a term that communicated reciprocity and mutual esteem between two spouses. Father Léon Messi, a Beti priest, preached to his congregations that *melugena* was analogous to the Christian idea of a love marriage based on mutual understanding and individual desire.[47] A romantic form of marriage known as *eluluga* or *mfan alug* was conducted between a free Beti man and a free Beti woman. A Beti woman in an *eluluga* marriage was married according to the *ékomba* and *mevek* customs and could therefore inherit property, control rights to land from their father's family, and even name her own inheritors.[48] Typically, a woman in an *eluluga* marriage was the first wife, and was referred to as the *ékomba*. The *ékomba* wife had significant duties in an *eluluga* marriage. Her behavior reflected on her husband and his family and she was considered an integral part of the husband's household. Divorce and remarriage were con-

---

[45] Landau, *The Realm of the Word: Language, Gender, and Christianity in a Southern African Kingdom*.

[46] Abbé Jean Zoa has detailed how love, affection, and allegiance were essential components in precolonial Beti marriages, which were integrated within marriages that were also based on pacts of neighborliness, non-aggression, and solidarity. That marriage was the apparatus of diplomacy in political and social life, Zoa argues, should not mislead us into believing that love was not a foundational concept in precolonial, pre-Christian African marriage. Jean Zoa, "Les Chrétiens et La Communauté Nationale," *Nova et Vetera* 1 (1960): 12–14.

[47] Ombolo, *Sexe et Société En Afrique Noire: L'Anthropologie Sexuelle Beti: Essai Analytique, Critique et Comparatif*, 228–9. See also Léon Messi, cited in Eugénie Abessolo, "L'épiscopat de Monseigneur Paul Etog: 1955–1987," *Mémoire de DIPES II En Histoire* ENS (2000).

[48] Ngoa, "Le Mariage chez les Ewondo: Étude sociologique"; Ndjodo, *Le Mariage Chrétien Chez Les Beti*; Ombolo, *Sexe et Société En Afrique Noire: L'Anthropologie Sexuelle Beti: Essai Analytique, Critique et Comparatif*.

siderably more difficult in an *eluluga* marriage relative to other forms of marriage, as the *ékomba* rite bound two families and passed considerable wealth between them.[49] By contrast, *alug-atud* or *alug étuga* ("marriage by chance") was a marriage between a free Beti man and a *bituga* or *metud*, a woman who was a household slave, a domestic servant, or of low status.[50] In polygamous marriages, *bituga* would often be junior wives, and their departure or divorce was typically more common and easier to negotiate. Missionaries and Beti catechists promoted *eluluga* marriage as a respectable alternative to *alug-atud*, despite the fact that bridewealth was still a critical linchpin of this bond.[51]

The distinctions made between the *ékomba*, the first wife, the *edina* (the Beti word for the favorite wife), and the *bituga* (unfree or servant wife) complicated the undoing of polygamous marriages as part of conversion processes.[52] Conflicts arose when catechists or missionaries demanded that a Beti man must divorce all his wives save the *ékomba*, or first wife, even at the risk of divorcing the *edina*, or favorite wife, ostensibly the woman with whom the man desired to share the idealized, conjugal love.[53] Manga Mbani, Abbé Jean Zoa's father, fought (and won) against Catholic missionaries who insisted that he receive the sacrament of marriage with his first wife, and instead chose to wed his favorite.[54]

The *eluluga* marriage became the idealized form of Christian marriage among the Beti, not only because it held out the promise of romantic love and reciprocal duties. Wives in *eluluga* marriages were considered an integral part of the household (not simply laborers or servants) whose options for divorce were limited. As Beti societies built considerable followings of devout Catholics, the *eluluga* wife became known as the wife who "belonged" exclusively to one

---

[49] ACSSp 2J1.10.7, Lettre de Charles Atangana Mvolyé, 23 mars 1932.

[50] In the eighteenth and nineteenth centuries, these women could be war captives or slaves. By the late nineteenth and early twentieth centuries, the *bituga* were more likely to be young daughters or household servants exchanged as part of bridewealth. While an *alug-atud* marriage was not considered a love match, over time, there was minimal distinction between women who contracted *eluluga* marriages and those in *alug-atud* marriage. If either of these women gave a child to her husband, the slave or lower-caste woman was freed of her status, and assumed the same status as a free Beti woman. ACSSp 2J1.10.7, Lettre de Charles Atangana Mvolyé, 23 mars 1932.

[51] ACSSp 2J1.10.7, Lettre de Charles Atangana à Mvolyé, 23 mars 1932. See also Nicod, *Une École de Catéchistes Au Cameroun*.

[52] Marie-Paule Bochet de Thé, "Rites et associations traditionnelles chez les femmes bëti (sud du Cameroun)," in *Femmes du Cameroun: mères pacifiques, femmes rebelles* (Paris: Karthala, 1985), 245–76.

[53] ACSSp 2J1.10.7 "La Polygamie au Cameroun: Son organisation – ses résultats – les remèdes."

[54] Messina, Mimboé, and Gantin, *Jean Zoa, Prêtre, Archevêque de Yaoundé*, 25–7.

guardian and was a definitive component of a family sphere overseen by one patriarch.[55] French missionaries often championed a chauvinist perception of monogamy, declaring: "Man does not need to lose his authority for the woman to become conscious of her dignity."[56]

Catechists underlined masculine spousal authority in this reified form of Beti marriage by preaching that the Council of Trent protected the right of men to choose their conjugal partner "without parental conditions or restrictions on the marriage choice that would satisfy the love between them."[57] Missionaries and catechists alike espoused the fundamental importance of spousal choice and uninhibited conjugal love to their male converts, and urged young Africans to eschew politically advantageous or convenient partnerships in favor of love matches that would guarantee a woman's loyalty and dutifulness.[58] Simultaneously, however, catechists had to be sensitive to locally condemned and contemptible practices such as *alug abom*, or "marriage by capture," in which couples escaped without the groom paying bridewealth to his bride's family, or *alug estig zen*, "the marriage that cuts the path," which was a marriage marked by arguments, delays, and complications.[59]

Christian publics of coastal Cameroon were tightly knit denominational communities of Baptists, Native Baptists, Presbyterians, and Catholics, who, since the mid-nineteenth century, emphasized the sacred aspects of marriage in conversion and religious rites. However, these believers did not necessarily follow strict doctrinal lines.[60] Duala society was considered for several centuries as a segmentary lineage society, organized and divided by kinship

---

[55] ACSSp. 2J1.7b4 L'Action Sociale des Missions Catholiques au Cameroun, 1925.
[56] ACSSp. 2J1.7b4 L'Action Sociale des Missions Catholiques au Cameroun, 1925.
[57] ACSSp 2J1.10.7, Lettre de Charles Atangana Mvolyé, 23 mars 1932.
[58] "L'archêveque de Yaoundé interdit aux catholiques la pratique de la dôt," *Nleb Bekristen*, 15 December 1958; Vincent Nana, J. Toguem, "Appel aux jeunes Bamiléké," *Essor des Jeunes*, no. 34, 1 December, 1962; Loi du mariage de 1934 du Gouverneur Bonnecarrère.
[59] Philippe Laburthe-Tolra, "Minlaaba" (Atelier de l'Université de Lille III, 1977), 239–40; Owono, *Pauvreté ou paupérisation en Afrique*, 82.
[60] René Bureau, "Ethno-Sociologie Religieuse Des Duala et Apparentés," *Recherches et Etudes Camerounaises* 1&2, no. 8 (1962): 317–29; Brian Stanley, *The History of the Baptist Missionary Society, 1792–1992* (Edinburgh: T&T Clark, 1992), 68–88; SMEP/DEFAP EEC FB 1/2, *Beteledi onala Dube la Mbale Nokise bato nje ye mwemba ma Dube la Mbale o Kamerun*; SMEP/DEFAP 61.992 B.0, *Dube la mbale la nolo na midi ma bato oteten ekombo*; Dager, "A Great Frontier Church"; Mission Protestante Française, *Nwa'ni Nescane Nwa'ni Neji'te Nescan Ntsub Bamileke (Livre de Lecture En Langue Bamileke à l'usage Des Écoles de La Mission Protestante Francaise Au Cameroun)*; Wonyu, *Le Chrétien, Les Dons et La Mission Dans l'Eglise Africaine Independente: Réflexions d'un Laïc*.

groups called *mboa*, which were either matrilineal or patrilineal.[61] Although the Duala often maintained large, polygamous households with wives as well as numerous household servants or slaves who could bear the children of the family father, Duala Christians still emphasized the sacred aspect of love and procreation in the sacraments of baptism and marriage. Marriage in Duala society was not an event, but rather a process by which the social order was reshuffled.[62] Each *mboa* decided the *bémà*, or bridewealth, which was the exchange that characterized the juridical recognition of the union between the man and woman.[63] Attachments to polygamy and bridewealth exchange in Duala society coexisted alongside beliefs that the conditions for a marriage rested both on the consent of both spouses as well as the consecration of the alliance between families. Christian doctrine paralleled aspects of longstanding Duala ideologies, such as the belief that sexual coupling, reproduction, or any partnership between a man and woman without a formal marriage process was taboo.

Duala Christians guaranteed the continuation of many of their marriage rituals and terms despite foreign missionary disapproval until more stringent constraints on maintaining large households emerged in the interwar years with high taxes on wives and female household members.[64] Local and foreign Baptist and Presbyterian leaders preached the values of monogamy and nuclear families, although their dependence on popular devotion forced them to make compromises about the rigidity of interdictions on polygamous and lineage-based family structures.[65] French Spiritan priests, however, refused the Eucharist to both men and women in polygamous marriages and have little to no recorded instances of flexibility on marital issues. Spiritan priests

---

[61] Manga Bekombo, "Conflits d'autorité Au Sein de La Société Familiale Chez Les Dwala Du Sud-Cameroun," *Cahiers d'études Africaines* 4, no. 14 (1963): 317–29. Albert Wirz, "La 'Rivière Du Cameroun': Commerce Précolonial et Contrôle Du Pouvoir En Société Lignagère," *Revue Française d'Histoire d'Outre-Mer*, no. 60 (1973): 172–95; Monga, "The Emergence of Duala Cocoa Planters under German Rule in Cameroon: A Case Study of Entrepreneurship."

[62] Bureau, *Anthropologie, Religions Africaines et Christianisme*, 188–95; Bureau, "Ethno-Sociologie Religieuse Des Duala et Apparentés," 134–40.

[63] Bureau, "Ethno-Sociologie Religieuse Des Duala et Apparentés," 160–3. See also Bekombo, "La Femme, Le Mariage et La Compensation Matrimoniale En Pays Dwala."

[64] *Bulletin des Missions*, Abbaye de Saint-André-lès-Bruges 16 (1937): 13–20; ANOM AGEFOM 1003/3518, rapport confidentiel au Commissaire de la République au Cameroun, 2 aôut 1929.

[65] Dager, "A Great Frontier Church"; Mission Protestante Française, *Nwa'ni Nescane Nwa'ni Neji'te Nescan Ntsub Bamileke (Livre de Lecture En Langue Bamileke à l'usage Des Écoles de La Mission Protestante Francaise Au Cameroun)*; Wonyu, *Le Chrétien, Les Dons et La Mission Dans l'Eglise Africaine Independente: Réflexions d'un Laïc*.

referred to Duala headmen as "slave traders"[66] of their wives and daughters, and accused the Baptist Church of exhibiting a "practical laxity" that was "not doctrinal" regarding their willingness to yield, albeit infrequently, in matters of the family among the Duala.[67] In response, some Protestant Duala women condemned their kinsmen who converted to Catholicism.[68]

African Kinship and the Clash of Ideologies

In general, foreign missionaries strongly condemned Africans' adherence to the lineage-based family and urged their subjects and catechumens to devote themselves to building loving, "independent" marriages. European priests, teachers, and colonial officials centered the biological father as the head of the family and sought to reduce the social and educational influence of matrilineage and matri-kin.[69] The *plan individuel* discouraged collectivity-focused and indirect kinship bonds, which mission societies believed enforced inherently burdensome responsibilities and dispossession as a result of having to maintain a lineage through copious marital unions and wealth exchanges.[70] Bridewealth ran counter to idealizations of the *plan individuel*, as it demanded protracted and exigent payments and duties from male spouses and cemented a husband's commitment to his wife's extended family, rather than centering his focus on his wife and children – his conjugal base.[71] An African Christian man would no longer be saddled to an extended family through marriage, but instead would be the master of his own unique family.[72]

[66] *Bulletin des Missions*, Abbaye de Saint-André-lès-Bruges 16 (1937): 13–20; ANOM AGEFOM 1003/3518, rapport confidentiel au Commissaire de la République au Cameroun, 2 aôut 1929.

[67] Barde, *Au Cameroun Avec M. Wilbois, Les Graves Problèmes de La Polygamie et de l'instruction*, 4.

[68] Soeur Marie Joseph Epeti, in Kibénél Ngo Billong, *Noces de Grâce de La Congrégation Des Soeurs Servantes de Marie de Douala: 70 Ans d'existence*, 82.

[69] Ardener, *Divorce and Fertility*.

[70] Abbé Jean Zoa, "Le problème de la dot," in Marie Du Rostu, *Femmes africaines: témoignages de femmes du Cameroun, du Congo belge, du Congo français, de la Côte-d'Ivoire, du Dahomey, du Ghana, de la Guinée, de la Haute-Volta, du Nigéria, du Togo, réunies à Lomé par l'Union mondiale des organisations féminines catholiques* (Paris: Centurion, 1959), 63.

[71] John and Jean Comaroff have summarized the history of the home as a site of colonial contestation in Jean Comaroff and John Comaroff, "Home-Made Hegemony: Modernity, Domesticity, and Colonialism in South Africa," in *African Encounters with Domesticity*, ed. Karen Tranberg Hansen (New Brunswick, NJ: Rutgers University Press, 1992), 37–74.

[72] Loi du mariage de 1934; ACSSp 2J1.15.b2, Groupe parlementaire des missions (President: Louis Marin) sur la reglementation des mariages entre indigenes en Afrique

This ideology ran counter to approaches to family organizational structure among Cameroon's African societies. In the southern forest zone's Beti and Bulu societies and among western and coastal societies like the Bamileke, Duala, and Bakoko, as well as societies in the eastern regions such as the Maka, long-standing processes of family constitution included episodic transfers of wives and children among various households within the family or lineage. All wives in a domestic compound possessed freedoms to move between paternal and conjugal homes in certain periods, and often had access to agricultural plots in all spaces.[73] Women circulated between houses and maintained close relationships with males throughout their patri-kin group including their father, uncles, and brothers.[74] Reciprocally, men were dependent on their relationships with maternal kin and uterine siblings, particularly sisters and their sons, in maintaining political and social alliances and negotiating marriage and inheritance arrangements.[75]

In both monogamous and polygamous marriages in societies across southern Cameroon, the mother's brother – the maternal uncle – (known as the *nyia-ndomo* in Beti and the *mulalo* in Duala) played a significant role in child-rearing in a child's early years. After giving birth, a mother would often leave her conjugal household to return to her parents' home to be near her brothers so her children could develop strong relations with her patri-kin group.[76] After a child reached puberty, the mother and child would then return to the conjugal family compound so that his father and paternal uncles could continue his education. The maternal uncle, however, remained supremely important in

---

Occidental Francaise et Afrique Equatoriale Francaise, Rapport au president de la republique francaise, 15 juin 1939 par Georges Mandel, *Journal Officiel du 16 juin 1939*.

[73] Ngoa, "Le Mariage chez les Ewondo: Étude sociologique"; Jane I. Guyer, "Female Farming and the Evolution of Food Production Patterns Amongst the Beti of South-Central Cameroon," *Africa: Journal of the International African Institute* 50, no. 4 (1980): 341–56; Jane I. Guyer, "Family and Farm in Southern Cameroon" (Boston, MA: Boston University, African Studies Center, 1984); Jan H.B. den Ouden, "In Search of Personal Mobility: Changing Interpersonal Relations in Two Bamiléké Chiefdoms," *Africa: Journal of the International African Institute* 57, no. 1 (1987): 3–27.

[74] *Journal des Missions Évangéliques*, juillet–août 1940, 259; Jean René Brutsch, "Les Relations de Parenté Chez Les Duala," *Bulletin de La Société Des Études Camerounaises* III (1950): 216–17.

[75] Edwin Ardener, *Coastal Bantu of the Cameroons: The Kpe-Mboko, Duala Limba, and Tanga-Yasa Groups of the British and French Trusteeship Territories of the Cameroons (Western Africa, Part XI)* (London: International African Institute, 1956), 56.

[76] Ardener, 51–69; Idelette Dugast, *Monographie de La Tribu Des Ndiki (Banen Du Cameroun)*, Travaux et Mémoires de l'Institut d'ethnologie 58 (Paris: Institut d'ethnologie, 1955); Jean-Pierre Ombolo, *Essai Sur l'histoire, Les Clans et Les Regroupements Claniques Des Eton Du Cameroun* (Yaoundé: Presses Universitaires de Yaoundé, 1986); Ndjodo, *Le Mariage Chrétien Chez Les Beti*.

the life and education of his nephew, and their relationship symbolized what the Beti termed *nfaàn ènyin*, "a life of dignity."[77]

The nephew, himself (the uterine sister's child) also held an important place in these societies and was also given honorific nomenclature.[78] In Duala culture, the nephew was termed *mwan'ali* and possessed rights to inheritance from his *mulalo*.[79] Among the Bulu and Beti, the *mone ka* or *man kal* referred to the nephew (or more specifically, "son of my sister") as well as the special affiliation he symbolized.[80] As a woman would marry into another lineage, thereby leaving her family of origin, the *mone ka* would bind two lineages and villages together by maintaining strong sibling and kin ties. The Presbyterian Mission took note of the precious place of the *mone ka* and adopted its meaning to refer to Jesus Christ – a reconciler, an intermediary, and unifier of mankind.[81] The Beti likewise honored the relationship between the nephew (*mán kál*) and his maternal uncle.[82] Through the *mán kál*, one Beti adage summarized, "the sister allows the brother to prosper."[83]

Close kin ties often signaled corresponding obligations. Among the Beti, the designation *nnom*, referred both to a woman's uterine brother as well as her husband. The Beti word *ngal*, or wife, referred to a man's own female spouse, as well as his brother's spouse or spouses.[84] This coextending nomenclature inferred a parallel status of reciprocity as well as duty. A man had responsibilities to his brothers' wives in case of his death. A woman was expected to perform service for her patri-kin group as well as her husband and his family. These commitments created family structures that extended far beyond the bonds of the conjugal couple.

These deep and complex allegiances shared between males, females, and children who were not conjugally bound were deemed unacceptably degenerate by missionaries, who sought a narrower vision of a *pater familias* and a family that was more centrally patriarchal – where the unity of the conjugal couple

[77] Marie-José Simone Onambélé, *Oncle Maternel–Neveu: Une Relation Privilégiée Chez Les Éwondo* (Paris: L'Harmattan, 2010).
[78] Ardener, *Coastal Bantu of the Cameroons: The Kpe-Mboko, Duala Limba, and Tanga-Yasa Groups of the British and French Trusteeship Territories of the Cameroons (Western Africa, Part XI)*, 59.
[79] Ardener, 56.
[80] Laburthe-Tolra, *Les Seigneurs de La Forêt: Essai Sur Le Passé Historique, l'organisation Sociale et Les Norms Éthiques Des Anciens Béti Du Cameroun*, 214.
[81] Albert I. Good, "A Missionary Deals with Language," *Drum Call* 28 (April 1949): 11–19.
[82] Laburthe-Tolra, *Les Seigneurs de La Forêt: Essai Sur Le Passé Historique, l'organisation Sociale et Les Norms Éthiques Des Anciens Béti Du Cameroun*, 211–14.
[83] Laburthe-Tolra, 214.
[84] Ombolo, *Essai Sur l'histoire, Les Clans et Les Regroupements Claniques Des Eton Du Cameroun*, 428–9.

would be paramount and the mother–father–child triangle privileged above all other social and familial relationships and networks.[85] Joseph Wilbois, founder of France's *Ecole d'administration et d'affaires* and a policy theorist of agendas for the domestic sphere in Cameroon, argued that the "avuncular regime" disrupted male authority in the African family.[86] He believed that social reform in Africa should concentrate on restoring male authority to the proper husband and father to prevent rivalries within the family, and allow the child to "develop sound intelligence as part of a household with less capricious relationships."[87] He was also concerned with the non-explicitly patriarchal structures of Cameroon's coastal societies, which configured marriage and inheritance arrangements through the father as well as the maternal uncle.[88]

Spiritan missionaries claimed to have mapped the "human geography" of African communities in Cameroon and wrote emotional reflections on what troubled them about African family structure. One missionary entry claimed that what caused him the greatest anxiety was that women "belonged to two households: that of her husband and that of her father," which meant that she was never truly "free to give of herself fully to her husband" and, furthermore, that her paternal kin could always interfere in her marriage.[89] Another missionary from the Protestant Mission complained that African family customs meant that a child was never raised by his own parents, but rather, by "strangers." Because of this, African children never knew true love or sound discipline.[90] Protestant and Catholic missionaries shared the opinion that the inclusion of women and children in various households and their "limited" attachment to their conjugal or parental base was "a moral plague, incompatible with progress, moral development, and economic growth."[91] While missionary criticisms of the

---

[85] ACSSp 2J1.8a6 "La Petite Femme Noire," Évêque Bonneau, 1930, Documentation sur la famille africaine; ACSSp 2J1.10.7, "Polygamie et mariage au Cameroun."

[86] Wilbois viewed the "avuncular regime" as maternal filiation and viewed the uncle as "head of the family." Joseph Wilbois, *L'Action Sociale En Pays de Missions* (Paris: Payot, 1938), 35–40. See also Bernard Kalaora, "Le Mysticisme Technique de Joseph Wilbois," in *Les chantiers de la paix sociale: 1900–1940*, ed. Yves Cohen and Rémi Baudouï (Paris: ENS Editions, 1995), 185–94.

[87] Wilbois, *L'Action Sociale En Pays de Missions*, 35–6.

[88] Wilbois, 34–6. Edwin Ardener's work has examined the responsibility of maternal uncles in arranging marriages for their nephews in Duala and Kpe societies: Ardener, *Coastal Bantu of the Cameroons: The Kpe-Mboko, Duala Limba, and Tanga-Yasa Groups of the British and French Trusteeship Territories of the Cameroons (Western Africa, Part XI)*, 50–60.

[89] ACSSp. 2J1.7b4 L'Action Sociale des Missions Catholiques au Cameroun, 1925.

[90] SMEP/DEFAP EEC Rapport de la Mission de Cameroun, Bangwa du 18 au 27 juillet 1947.

[91] ACSSp. 2J1.7b4 L'Action Sociale des Missions Catholiques au Cameroun, 1925.

lineage structure and the bonds of extended families had a somewhat limited effect, European clergymen's disapproval of women's behaviors and the various practices that limited a husband's full control over his wife resonated quite strongly with many male audiences in southern Cameroon.

Missionaries' goals for the transformation of familial, sexual, and marital traditions were much more than a campaign to instill European social norms in African society, they were also components of an idealistic movement to reconceptualize human suffering and broaden the conditions on which a man or woman could claim to be a righteous victim. According to this logic, bridewealth, arranged marriage, bachelorhood, polygamy, widow inheritance, and other practices constituted "suffering" and violations of natural rights for African women, but even more so for African men. While the French administration maintained the rhetoric that polygamy and other African marriage "customs" were crimes against rational human order, morality, hygiene, and demography, the Catholic and Protestant foreign missionaries personalized their civilizing mission to reformulate its goals to empower and invigorate the position and claims to rights of commoner men.[92]

Christian Love and the Lineage

In contrast to foreign agents, African catechists, evangelists, pastors, and priests understood that rigid Christian monogamy and an exclusively nuclear family structure was anathema to most Africans' idealizations of marriage, as they understood the expansive networks of social loyalties that organized marriages in Cameroon. As Laburthe-Tolra summarized, among the patrilineal segmentary lineages of the Beti, most matrimonial alliances were "personified political alliances."[93] Indigenous Christian guides in the southern forests supported the practical and cooperative dimensions of long-established marriage norms, but they also observed that these were not manifest in many marriages in the interwar years. The state of marriage as it appeared to them ran contrary to the spirit of longstanding beliefs about social cohesion. Rather than approaching marriage reform as outsiders, catechists and other African Christian leaders were able to influence changes to African marital processes and behaviors by forming strategic alliances between men facing similarly disadvantaged circumstances across villages and regions in the territory, which

---

[92] Decret du 15 juin 1939, Decret Georges Mandel; Arrêté de l'Afrique Equatoriale Française du 13 décembre 1940 sur le régime matrimoniale legal; Wilbois, *Le Cameroun: Les Indigènes-Les Colons-Les Missions-l'administration Française*.

[93] Laburthe-Tolra, *Vers La Lumiere? Ou, Le Désir d'Ariel: A Propos Des Beti Du Cameroun: Sociologie de La Conversion*, 47.

allowed for the expression of evangelical messages that monogamous, freely chosen spousal love sanctified by the Church secured loyalty, family growth, freedom from indebtedness and poverty, and social and moral prestige.

Missionary romanticism captured African Christians' imaginations in different ways. Among the unmarried or the unhappily wed, it appeared to endorse rebellion against conventions that excluded them from ideal, Christian love. Among catechists and Christian leaders, it spurred undisguised confrontation of elders, fathers, chiefs, and other agents who obstructed love. And in certain communities and families, it inaugurated an aesthetic of solidarity between couples and between families and kin, which embraced loyalty and affection but also refigured the rigid missionary *plan individuel* that assumed the necessity for distance from the extended family to achieve a deep spousal bond.

In contradiction to missionary idealizations, extended families and lineages were key to forming Christian publics. Couples formed a cell, but were surrounded by equally strong cells of uncle–nephew ties, grandparent ties, sibling ties, and cousin pairs. When Frère Philippe Azeufack recounted the history of his aunt, Anne Nguimeya, who, in 1926 fled her father's home in Balefeh-Bafou to avoid marrying a polygamist, he did not emphasize his grandparents' vexation or the reconciliation process negotiated by the local chief. Rather, he underscored that his aunt's determination to become a Christian eventually inspired her entire family's conversion to Christianity at the mission of the Prêtres du Sacré-Coeur de Saint Quentin in Dschang. There, Nguimeya entered the *sixa* and convinced her sister, Sophia Ayimélé, to receive baptism. She also eventually even convinced their father, Moh-Tejou Woukeng, a polygamist and nonbeliever in Christianity, to seek baptism, renounce all his wives except one, and enter into holy matrimony with his first wife, Mah Feudjo. "After converting, my grandfather built the first chapel in Balefeh-Bafou," Frère Philippe recounted, "and led a transformation of faith in the village."[94]

Frère Philippe was also proud to share that Anne later married Sylvestre Tsamo, a mason and a congregant in the Dschang mission church, and had a son, whom she named André Wouking in 1930.[95] A few years later, Sophia

---

[94] Oral interview, Fr. Philippe Azeufack, S.J., Résidence St. François Xavier, Yaoundé, Cameroon, May 30, 2014. The precise date of Anne Nguimeya's escape from her wedding night is unknown to Brother Philippe.

[95] The name Wouking, also spelled Woukeng, comes from the Bafou words "Wou" and "keng," which mean, respectively, "sparrowhawk" and "tree of peace." Together, the name "Woukeng" is meant to communicate "fierce warrior who wins the battle and restores peace." The Wouking name was given to André Wouking in memory of his grandfather, Moh-Tejou Woukeng, who was a renowned warrior whose skill in battle

Ayimélé, Anne's sister, likewise married and gave birth to a son – Philippe Azeufack – and Philippe and André were raised together in the towns of Bafou and Dschang and remained close to the catechists, choristers, and priests who organized spiritual life in the villages. In 1961, André Wouking was ordained a priest and a few years after, Philippe Azeufack joined the Jesuit Order. Wouking would later become the Archbishop of Yaoundé, and Azeufack, a Catholic youth leader in Cameroon.[96]

Thus, these founding mothers and their consecrated sons were drawn to the individualizing and self-determining promise of Christianity while remaining resolutely devoted to their extended families. The rebellious Anne Nguimeya who defied her father's arranged married also shaped her father's faith and that of her entire lineage. Frère Philippe recalled his earliest memories of his mother and aunt's religious devotion as it was expressed in daily mass attendance, fifteen-kilometer walks on Sundays to church, and teaching catechism to their grandchildren. Nguimeya's spiritual convictions began as an individual experience but were made manifest in her marriage and family life in a way that set in motion broad community adaptations.

As in the previous example, the African extended family became a nucleus of religious activity and organization in many villages in southern Cameroon. In some cases, entire families would follow religious vocations, with multiple siblings or uncle–nephew pairs entering seminary and becoming ordained. One of my sources, Mgr. Athanase Bala, entered the seminary after being inspired by his cousin, Paul Etoga, who later became bishop of Mbalmayo.[97]

---

and swiftness evoked that of the sparrowhawk. Oral interview, Fr. Philippe Azeufack, S.J., Résidence St. François Xavier, Yaoundé, Cameroon, May 30, 2014. See also Philippe Azeufack, S.J., *Mgr. André Wouking: Artisan de Paix* (Yaoundé, Cameroon: Presses Universitaires de Yaoundé, 2010), 15–18.

[96] It was noted in the Catholic press that some Cameroonians were surprised that André Wouking, who was originally from western Cameroon, was named to the country's highest ecclesiastical position because of suspicions about Westerners' true belief in Christianity (see Père Antoine de Padoue Chonang, "Mgr Dieudonné Watio et Le Culte Des Ancêtres: Notre Tradition Comporte Des Éléments Positifs Qu'il Faut Exploiter," *L'Effort Camerounais*, January 2006). Despite the western region's long history of Christian presence, those from western Cameroon are sometimes called "adorateurs des crânes," or "skull worshippers," by outsiders. This epithet references the region's ancestor cults and has been employed to describe the Bamiléké as well as other societies in the area. In particular, it is often used to impugn not only these societies' level of civilizational advancement, but also their commitment to Christianity. See Jean-Claude Shanda Tonme, *La France a-t-elle commis un génocide au Cameroun ?: Les Bamiléké accusent* (Paris: L'Harmattan, 2009), 140–4.

[97] Oral interview with Mgr. Athanase Bala, CSSp., Bishop emeritus of Bafia, Cameroon, July 8, 2015, Seminaire des Missions, Congrégation du Saint-Esprit, Chevilly Larue, France.

Etoga entered the Catholic priesthood after his brother, Albert Okala, who had been a seminarian in Mvolyé, assigned him a religious tutor.[98] Abbé Benoît Bell Bayamack's father, Jean Bayamack, along with his brothers and cousins, had been catechists among the Bikok.[99] Soeur Marie Michel Ngo Ngwe of the Soeurs Servantes de Marie religious order was the daughter of the catechist Luc Ngwe of the Log-Bagui lineage, who were fervent Catholics.[100] Like many of her contemporaries, Soeur Marie Michel Ngo Ngwe entered into a *prépostulat* in 1936 at Saint Therese d'Edea, then the noviciate in Ngovayang in 1938, and completed her education at the Collège du Saint Esprit in Douala in 1942 to become a religious instructor. During this time, she encouraged her nieces and nephews to follow ecclesiastical professions. Joh Ekollo, one of the first African Protestant pastors, entered catechist training in the Baptist Mission along with his brother; was ordained a pastor alongside his servant, Joseph Kuoh Issedou; and later prepared his son, Thomas Ekollo, to enter the ministry with the French Protestant Mission.[101] Joh Ekollo cultivated a deeply familiar relationship with his spiritual mentor, the Jamaican Baptist minister, Joseph Jackson Fuller, calling him *Sango am* Fuller (my father, Fuller).[102] The famed evangelist Eugène Ngilé opened a Bible school with the support of Frank Christol and Elie Robert at the Baptist Mission at Bafoussam to train his own son, Jean Koto, to be a pastor.[103]

Among the Bikok and Bassa peoples of the littoral, notably among the villages between Pouma, Nkonga-Bikok, and Andréasberg (later renamed Saint-André),[104] Pallottine conversions during the late nineteenth century had contributed to the development of communitarian and family-based Christian devotion as an expression of local identity.[105] Bikok lineages including the Elog-Biti, Elog-Okoo, Ndog-Bassanbèn, and Son-Magne all had multiple family members join religious orders or the clergy, and families collectively took part in Catholic evangelism and religious organization throughout the

---

[98] Etoga and Dillinger, *Paul Etoga: Mon Autobiographie*, 10.

[99] Claude Zéba, "L'Eglise Dit Adieu à l'Abbé Benoît Bell Bayamack," *L'Effort Camerounais*, November 14, 2007.

[100] Soeur Marie Michel Ngo, in Ngwe Kibénél Ngo Billong, *Noces de Grâce de La Congrégation Des Soeurs Servantes de Marie de Douala: 70 Ans d'existence*, 48.

[101] Ekollo, *Mémoires d'un Pasteur Camerounais (1920–1996)*, 15–23.

[102] Ekollo, 15.

[103] SMEP/DEFAP Fonds Allégret Cameroun 1926, Frank Christol, "Fondation de la station de Bafousam MBO 1926."

[104] Andreasberg was renamed Saint André during the French Mandate and again renamed Nkondjock after independence.

[105] Zéba, "L'Eglise Dit Adieu à l'Abbé Benoît Bell Bayamack." Kibénél Ngo Billong, *Noces de Grâce de La Congrégation Des Soeurs Servantes de Marie de Douala: 70 Ans d'existence*, 6–10.

littoral around Edea. During the 1920s, the Ndog Nem family, a Bassa lineage, expanded the parish of Maria Assumpta de Kan in the village of Bassap and became the church's guardians.[106] Masses at the parish of Saint-André were organized by local families, and often said by clergymen who had been educated at the Catholic mission in nearby Edea.

The Catholic Congregations of the Holy Ghost and Sacred Heart could not weaken young seminarians' lineage bonds, despite their exhortations to reshape family links. Mission were known to provide funds to African men during their seminary training not only for school fees and lodging, but also for the monetary support of seminarians' families. Young men could rarely forbear their duties to sustain their kin while studying and serving, particularly as entering the Catholic priesthood meant sacrificing marriage that would economically sustain their parents and dependant kin. In one instance, a mission gave an African priest's mother 30,000 francs with which to buy a house after he insisted that it was his obligation to provide for her in her old age.[107] Other records indicate priests received allotments with which they purchased tools, houses, wagons, and bicycles for their families.[108]

Catechists often openly defied orders to maintain strictly nuclear households, in part out of necessity. Although nearly always monogamously married, catechists and their families would often live in the wife's father's home so children could be raised near kin who followed less peripatetic lives.[109] Many Protestant pastors who were consecrated in the 1950s confirmed that they had been raised by their maternal grandfathers and uncles while their fathers were away proselytizing.[110] Catholic catechists like Henri Tsala, who directed the mission at Akono in the 1920s, also traveled far to reach new audiences, but proselytized mainly within his extended kin networks to recruit his relatives to the faith. Many Africans who entered religious life in the inter-

---

[106] Soeur Thérésita Ngo Nleng, in Kibénél Ngo Billong, *Noces de Grâce de La Congrégation Des Soeurs Servantes de Marie de Douala: 70 Ans d'existence*, 77–8.

[107] ACSSp. 2J1.13.b3, lettre du 12 sept. 1958 sur le Père Tana. Missionary archives went to great lengths to record the "special assistance" given to African priests (which would have been unorthodox or unheard of in Europe) as evidence against the African clergy's charges of racism and unequal treatment by the French clergy that arose during the 1950s. See ACSSp. 2J1.13.b3 as well as Paule Brasseur, "L'Église Catholique et La Décolonisation En Afrique Noire," in *Les Chemins de La Décolonisation de l'Empire Colonial Français, 1936–1956: Colloque Organisé Les 4 et 5 Octobre 1984*, ed. Charles-Robert Ageron (Paris: Editions du Centre National de la Recherche Scientifique (CNRS), 1986), 55–68.

[108] ACSSp. 2J1.13.b3 Lettres Graffin–Bazin 1952–1962.

[109] SMEP/DEFAP EEC FB divers 2/2, Allocution du candidat Moise Lamère; discours de Pastor Josué Muishé, 1943.

[110] SMEP/DEFAP EEC FB divers 2/2, Allocutions des candidates: consécration pastorale.

war period attested to having fathers or relations who worked as catechists. Jean Mbadi, Oscar Bidjeck, Fritz Aoue, and Pierre Nkot, all salaried Catholic catechists in western Cameroon between 1920 and 1930, had catechist fathers or maternal uncles, and each sent one of his daughters to join the convent in Edea.[111] Others claimed to owe their spiritual devotion to the instruction of their mothers – many of whom had been schooled at the *Sixa*, or fiancée schools run by German Pallottines.[112] African Protestants often had similar family and lineage ties to their Church. Pastor Mosé Lamère had been raised by his devout maternal uncles and maternal grandmother in Foumban, as his father worked as a traveling catechist. Lamère's grandmother, Marthe Mbouayié, began instructing him in 1928 and ensured his acceptance to the Theological School of Ndoungué in 1951.[113]

Lineage conversions and expressions of family devotion for Christianity transformed pre-existing family building practices among Cameroon's societies. The Bikok community, who throughout the nineteenth century had intermarried and paid tribute in the form of wives to the Aidè society farther west along the Sanaga, terminated this practice and compelled their community members to intermarry among each other and other similarly devout local communities.[114] Some devoutly Catholic Bassa fathers renounced the practice of giving a daughter in marriage to a political ally or a cultivated patron, and instead would choose one of their daughters to become a *bod aba Djob* or "wife of God," and enroll her in a noviciate to become a nun. Bassa catechists instructed that to marry was a high calling, but to become married to the Church was the highest calling of all.[115]

The familial nature of devotional life in many of southern Cameroon's towns and villages was simultaneously satisfying and disconcerting for many European missionaries. While Catholic missions boasted "a new Christian family equilibrium" as a result of high rates of conversion, they also worried that spiritual life remained too strongly based on "collective conscience" and that there was "not enough development of individual moral character."[116] However, too much religious individualism could also appear inappropriate.

---

[111] Soeur Madeleine Therese Ngo Nkot in Kibénél Ngo Billong, *Noces de Grâce de La Congrégation Des Soeurs Servantes de Marie de Douala: 70 Ans d'existence*, 97.

[112] Soeur Martine Ngo Bayongbog, in Kibénél Ngo Billong, 54–56.

[113] SMEP/DEFAP EEC FB 2/2, Allocution du candidat à l'occasion de sa consécration pastorale, Mosé Lamère, 15 avril 1956.

[114] Soeur Marie Michel Ngo, in Kibénél Ngo Billong, *Noces de Grâce de La Congrégation Des Soeurs Servantes de Marie de Douala: 70 Ans d'existence*, 48.

[115] Soeur Martine Ngo Bayongbog, in Kibénél Ngo Billong, 74.

[116] René Bureau, "Sociologie Religieuse," *Mission d'Aujourd'hui: Bulletin Mensuel Des Oeuvres Catholiques*, October 15, 1958.

French Catholic clergy expressed alarm when the son of a devout Catholic family converted to Protestantism and declared to his newfound parish in Edea that he preferred the closer individual relationship with Jesus promoted by the Reformed faith.[117] Josette Debarge, of the French Protestant Mission in Foumban, reflected more sanguinely on the emergence of "a Christian society," in western Cameroon, writing, "Among the Bamoun, all in the village refer to one another as 'brother' and when you compliment one, all are proud. Rather than individualists, their vivacious collectivity contributes significantly to the formation of new churches."[118]

During an interview, Father Jean-Luc Enyegue stressed the longstanding sacred dimensions of membership and belonging in southern Cameroonian societies, relating that regardless of the Catholic Church's emphasis on the *fides qua creditur*, the faith by which one believes, or, more specifically, the individual's reception of the true divine word, African communities actually arrived collectively at the *fides quae creditur*, or contents of the faith, which can be diverse and contradictory to the *fides qua creditor*, but are the organon for understanding God.[119] "Spiritual attachments and understandings of God were not arrived at individually," Father Jean-Luc shared. "Only by belonging, by being a *member* did one feel a sense of participation and inclusion in the process of *fides qua creditur* – the knowing."[120]

Father Jean-Luc's descriptions of collective identification with theological interpretations complement testimonies in the archives such as that of Chief Imacone, who wrote to a pastor in Bonaku in coastal Cameroon in 1920 that, "my worries concern the future of my people following Satan. We need a school for young people so that we do not fall into Satan's trap. We seek the Holy Spirit with water and salt. I will give because these people are my worries."[121] Spiritual conviction in southern Cameroon was often expressed as a collective concern. Distress about God or the afterlife was based not on fears of individual suffering, but rather, community peril. In many Baptist

---

[117] SMEP/DEFAP EEC FB 2/2, Les Nouvelles de l'Amicale d'Edea, La Conversion de Mr. l'Abbé Luc Bell, 27 janvier 1947; lettre de Abbé Joseph Melone, Saint André, 25 Janvier 1947.

[118] SMEP/DEFAP Mission Médicale de Foumban, Josette Debarge, Dschang, 28 September 1926.

[119] The Catholic Church also stresses the importance of the on the *sensus fidei fidelis*, or the sense of the faith of the individual believer in the theology and magisterium. See Ormond Rush, *The Eyes of Faith: The Sense of the Faithful and the Church's Reception of Revelation*, reprint edition (Washington, DC: The Catholic University of America Press, 2016), 215–16.

[120] Interview with Jean-Luc Enyegue, S.J., February 25, 2016, by telephone.

[121] SMEP/DEFAP Fonds Allégret Cameroun 1920, Chef Imacone, Bonaku, 13 dec. 1920.

and Presbyterian communities, Church Elders, or *Anciens* worked alongside catechists to maintain unified religious understandings.[122] An administrative report from 1945 noted, "In Ebolowa, at the American mission, the *anciens presbuteros* are very listened to by the population."[123] Catechists' surveillance and intensive disciplining of their followers is more understandable in light of these insights. African religious leaders were not simply asserting their dominance, they were working towards an idea of salvation in which their disciples' triumph over sin and admission to eternal life ("knowing the path to God's Town" as Ndilé Nsôm termed it) was inextricably linked to their own.

As Catholic family networks deepened their ties in the interwar period, a great many uncle-nephew bonds flourished among the African clergy, which created relational networks within the Church that threatened the integrity of a clerical hierarchy based on rank and tenure. The Swiss Benedictines ran the seminary at Otélé, which was a regional hub preparing African men from Cameroon, Moyen Congo, and other neighboring Francophone territories, and complained of the strong attachments between male relatives who entered the seminary at the same time.[124] Following their education in the seminary, uncle-nephew pairs of priests also cultivated large followings of parishioners and, according to their superiors, prioritized their personal and relational ties above their oaths of duty to the Church as an institution. In one example in the 1950s, European bishops reported that Father Emile Tana and his uncle, Father André Noa, the superior *abbé* of Oveng, worked collaboratively to undermine the authority of European priests in the parishes of Mvaa and Oveng and sought to "purge" their churches of white clergymen.[125] In their letters defending their acts, Fathers Tana and Noa challenged the Church's elites, accusing the bishops of fulminating at the African clergy and trampling their right to manage the internal affairs of their missions. What was perhaps most troublesome for the high clergy was Tana and Noa's popularity with their flocks and their ability to cultivate the support of other African priests in intra-clerical conflicts. African parishes' devotion and high esteem for their local priests eroded the ability of French men like Bishop René Graffin to control his subordinates, despite demanding an obedient and submissive African clergy.[126]

---

[122] SMEP/DEFAP Fonds Allégret Cameroun 1920 lettres des Anciens à Allégret, 1920; ANC APA 10170/F Mission Presbytérienne à Ebolowa, les Bulu, 1945.

[123] ANC APA 10170/F Mission Presbytérienne à Ebolowa, les Bulu, 1945.

[124] The Spiritan missionaries appear to have tried to mollify their Swiss colleagues' unease with this tendency by encouraging them to "develop your [own] filial bonds and cordiality with the African students." ACSSp. 2J1.13.b3 Grand Séminaire d'Otélé.

[125] ACSSp. 2J1.13.b3, l'Affaire Tana, lettres de Abbé Tana, Père Battman, Père Kapps, René Graffin, 1956–1959.

[126] ACSSp. 2J1.13.b3, Lettre de René Graffin au Vatican, 21 septembre 1959.

The African clergy were not the only targets of suspicion for their ability to deftly wield the power of the Christian religion. Although defensive of catechists' rights against government suppression, privately, French bishops in the Cameroon territory were anxious about which authorities the African faithful recognized. Bishop Graffin frequently reminded both European and African missionary workers of his supreme authority and warned popular African priests of their loyalty to the institution of the Church, and not simply their flocks.[127] Protestant missions recorded fewer anxieties regarding African leadership of faith communities overall, but concerns over segregated spheres of influence did arise. In 1946, Pastor Maurice Farelly suggested that all local ministry of the Baptist Church be left to African pastors and evangelists while European missionaries should lead political programs and engaging with the colonial government.[128]

Ecclesiastical concerns about Africans' authority over the dissemination of the faith and their power within Church institutions and communities were not always shared by all Europeans. Some foreign missionaries and friars who lived for years in African Christian communities built trust with African religious leaders and depended on their work in deepening the impact of the faith. In 1931, the African seminarian Tobie Atangana reflected that in his work with Père Henri de Maupeou "he made me feel as if I were an equal, a brother, a friend. He maintained his authority as a priest, but he seemed to forget that he was white."[129] In 1941, French missionaries at the mission in Bikop celebrated the ordination of Léon Messi with members of his Etenga lineage, dining with his family and celebrating the Catholic heritage of the Etenga people. After Messi was ordained, locals in Bikop insisted on having their confessions heard and masses said exclusively by him. Rather than expressing jealousy or anxiety about Messi's ability to authentically communicate the faith unaided, missionaries in Bikop promoted his solitary work and lauded his energy in recruiting families for baptism, women to the *sixa*, and wood choppers, stone masons, construction workers, carpenters, and bricklayers for the construction of churches and chapels.[130] Père Jean Criaud recorded that he and his colleague, Father Henri Hurstel, dutifully stepped aside when the majority of villagers from towns surrounding Yaoundé preferred that the recently ordained priest, Etienne Nkodo, baptize their children. As villages morphed

---

[127] ACSSp. 2J1.10.7 Alexandre le Roy, Note sur la Liberté religieuse au Cameroun et dans les colonies françaises, 1935–1936.

[128] Maurice Farelly, "Les Eglises Indigènes," *Journal des Missions Évangéliques*, 1946, 14.

[129] Reflections of Tobie Atangana, in Le Roy, *Un Martyr de La Morale Chrétienne, Le Père Henri de Maupeou de La Congrégation Du Saint-Esprit, Missionnaire Au Cameroun*, 71.

[130] ACSSp. 2J2 1A, Journal de la mission catholique de Bikop, 1941, 1942.

into neighborhoods of the urban center, Criaud and Hurstel were reliant on the indigenous clergy to maintain strong ties and ensure that city life did not erode spirituality.[131] Other missionaries also admired fathers and chiefs who converted their families and villages to Christianity, comparing them to Clovis I, the first Christian king to rule Gaul.[132] Père Roger Mille, a Spiritan missionary who served in southern Cameroon during the 1950s, confided to me that he felt more at home in the mission at Akonolinga than he ever did in his hometown in France:

> In Cameroon, I did not have to just carry out orders from my local bishop as I did in the village in France. I was in Cameroon to work alongside others, to build ... Building and doing manual labor together [with locals] were the best ways to prove to people that the church would remain theirs. There was no carrying off this treasure.[133]

Ethno-Linguistic Affiliations and Christian Attachment

While eager to profess affinity for the Church as a universal institution, African worshippers were also fastidiously associative within their linguistic group, demanding catechism, scripture readings, and masses said in their own language, rather than in that of their neighbors. In 1914–15, in the midst of the chaos of war, the Yekomba society founded their own Catholic mission to be set apart from that of their Bulu neighbors.[134] In 1925, the American Presbyterian Mission agreed to catechist pressure to distribute different literature and perform separate services for their Bulu and Bassa adherents.[135] They became even more sensitive to linguistic difference when one group

---

[131] Jean Criaud, "Etienne Nkodo, de 1911 à 1983: Le Premier Spiritan Camerounais," *Mémoire Spiritane* deuxième semestre, no. 8 (1998): 50–73.

[132] ACSSP.2J1.7b4, *Ad Lucem: Milieux sociaux africains,* Cameroun, fév–mars, 1946, no. 7.

[133] Oral interview with Père Roger Mille, CSSp., September 4, 2015, Seminaire des Missions, Congrégation du Saint-Esprit, Chevilly Larue, France.

[134] ACSSp. 2J1.2b2 lettre de St. Michel de Nkolayop, 15 juin 1923.

[135] In 1918 the French territorial administration granted 9440 francs to the French Catholic Missions, 4738 francs to the French Protestant Missions, and 820 francs to the American Presbyterian Mission. Between 1923 and 1935, the administration gave the most money to the American Presbyterian Mission, then the French Protestant Mission, and last, the French Catholic Missions, However, by 1952, the French Catholic Missions were once again receiving the most subventions. See Ministère des Colonies, Rapport au Ministre des Colonies sur l'administration des Territoires occupies du Cameroun de la conquête au 1 juillet 1921," *Journal Officiel de la République française,* 1921: 430; Annual Reports of Board of foreign Missions of the Presbyterian Church in the USA

of Ngumba Presbyterians led by Pastor Martin Bambba Minkio broke away from the mission to found their own denomination, the *Église Protestante Ngumba*, so that they could pray in their own tongue and incorporate their own practices.[136] In 1920, the Paris Evangelical Mission became heavily reliant on Mose Yeyap, a Bamoun head catechist, to train other Bamoun and create a new catechism and grammar when Bamoun Protestants refused to be taught in Duala any longer.[137] The Protestant mission similarly bent to the will of their Banen congregants, who requested that services be said exclusively in Banen at the Nitoukou Temple in Ndiki-Somo.[138] At the Catholic mission at Ngowayang, African catechists read the prayers and performed the rites at nearly all baptisms, confirmations, marriages, and burials in 1920 because that year the mission comprised 1129 Ngumba, 216 Bakoko, and 3552 Ewondo Christians, which made French missionary communication "nearly impossible."[139] On one Sunday in 1927, "complete disorder" broke out at the Catholic mission in Nlong when some Bassa congregants had mistakenly arrived for the Ewondo mass at six in the morning and some Ewondo had arrived for the Bassa mass at seven, resulting in "thousands of confused participants."[140] The Nlong mission also organized separate Bassa and Ewondo voluntary associations after congregants insisted.[141] In 1931, the Catholics of Doumé reported to Monsignor Vogt that they needed new mission stations and their own cadre of catechists, as the catechists from Yaoundé, Medzeck, and Efok did not effectively service their needs.[142]

Thus, although African networks and societies were increasingly converging as religious and economic affairs drew them into shared spheres, societies and communities retained strong senses of their local and linguistic identities. Unlike other histories that have highlighted the creation of Biblical vernaculars as a critical stage in the process of creating fixed linguistic and

---

64th to the 88th: 1901–1925. See also Marcel Nguini, "La Valeur Politique & Sociale de La Tutelle Française Au Cameroun" (L'Université d'Aix-Marseille, 1956), 202–3.

[136] This church, now simply called the *Église Protestante Africaine*, currently counts some 10,000 members in Cameroon in 32 congregations and retains a church synod. See Société africaine de culture, *Les religions Africaines Comme Source de Valeurs de Civilisations: Colloque du Cotonou 16–22 aôut 1970* (Paris: Présence Africaine, 1972); J. Gordon Melton and Martin Baumann, *Religions of the World, Second Edition: A Comprehensive Encyclopedia of Beliefs and Practices* (Santa Barbara, CA: ABC-CLIO, 2010).

[137] SMEP/DEFAP Fonds Allégret 1920, Dossier Felix Vernet à Foumban, 16 juillet 1920.

[138] Privat, *Coup de coeur pour l'Afrique: 1956–1957*, 246.

[139] ACSSp. 2J1.2b2 Rapport sur la Mission Catholique de Ngowayang, avril 1920.

[140] ACSSp. 2J2.1a Journal de la Mission de Nlong, 6 février 1927.

[141] ACSSp. 2J2.1a Journal de la Mission de Nlong, 1925–1938.

[142] ACSSp. 2J1.1a.10 Record of 5 September 1931, Vogt, Doumé.

ethnic identity in Africa, societies in Cameroon largely guided the translation of sacred texts toward their own vernaculars.[143] Therefore, Christian publics were comprised of linguistically unified communities within diverse congregations. While multilingual, multiethnic churches allowed for a sense of a transsocietal Christianity to emerge, local sociability and neighborly dependency remained the primary expression of religious solidarity. Village and regional networks fused their preexisting sense of identity with a new, but equally strong Christian identity, led by catechists who were often indigenous to the community and gave rise to new patterns of engagement and activism.

---

[143] Adrian Hastings, *The Construction of Nationhood: Ethnicity, Religion and Nationalism* (Cambridge: Cambridge University Press, 1997); Derek Peterson, "The Rhetoric of the Word: Bible Translation and Mau Mau in Central Kenya," in *Missions, Nationalism, and the End of Empire*, ed. Brian Stanley (Grand Rapids, MI: William B. Eerdmans, 2003), 165–79.

PART II

Labor, Economic Transformation, and Family Life, 1925–1939

CHAPTER 6

African Church Institutions in Action

Economic Transition and Resourceful Churches

Part I of this book examined the social politics and religious feelings emergent in an era of scarcity and disrupted foreign imperial and missionary authority. In the first decade of French rule, from 1914 to 1925, African chiefs in the employ of the French administration claimed a steadily increasing share of wealth from land management, agricultural production, and government salaries. By contrast, during the next decade of French rule, which is examined in the following three chapters, African small farmers, traders, merchants, transporters, and other agents in the Abong Mbang, Nyong Valley, and Ebolowa regions, as well as some eastern regions including Doumé and Batouri enjoyed increasing wealth as a result of cash crop expansion and a growth in regional and international markets for their goods.[1] Government statistics from 1927 to 1930 reported that African smallholder farmers around Yaoundé planted 80,000 cocoa plants and that "millions" of young palm oil and coffee seedlings had been distributed throughout southern and coastal Cameroon.[2] Reports from 1927 to 1933 describe "hundreds of thousands" of groundnut, cocoa, and

---

[1] In 1927, the government reported 150,000 palm seedlings planted in Ebolowa and 120,000 planted in Lomié. It also boasted of hundreds of thousands of cocoa and coffee plants and seeds distributed in the Yaoundé, Dschang, Lomié, Ebolowa, and Djoum regions. ANC APA 11016/K Rapport Annuel adressé par le gouvernement français pour l'année 1927, 97–100. By 1939, the administration estimated that 4 million coffee plants had been planted in the Mungo region by African planters and by 1940, cocoa production reached 40,000–50,000 tons per year, representing one-fourth of all exports out of the port in Douala. By 1947, there were 6 million coffee plants cultivated by African farmers in Mungo, Dschang, and Foumban. Viers, "Le cacao dans le monde," and Eugène Guernier and René Briat, *Cameroun, Togo, Encyclopédie de l'Afrique Française* (Paris: Éditions de l'Union Française, 1951), 202–3. W. Gervase Clarence-Smith, "Plantation versus Smallholder Production of Cocoa: The Legacy of the German Period in Cameroon," in *Pathways to Accumulation in Cameroon*, ed. Peter Geschiere and Piet Konings (Paris: Karthala, 1993), 187–21.; Eckert, "African Rural Entrepreneurs and Labor in the Cameroon Littoral," 115–17; Monga, "The Emergence of Duala Cocoa Planters under German Rule in Cameroon: A Case Study of Entrepreneurship."

[2] "Agriculture," *La Gazette du Cameroun*, no. 47, 15 nov. 1928.

coffee plants bearing fruit in neighboring Mbalmayo and Akonolinga, coffee and cotton crop expansion in the western highlands, and copra, coconut, and kola nut in the southwest towards Edea.[3] Cocoa exports grew from roughly 492 tons in 1910 and 2290 tons in 1920, to 10,000 tons in 1929 and 27,000 tons in 1939.[4] In 1947 and 1948, the administration announced record harvests by the estimated 150,000 cocoa-producing household farms in Cameroon.[5] Along with cocoa, harvests of coffee, palm oil, tobacco, and groundnut accounted for 75 percent of the 73 million francs worth of exports from Cameroon in 1930.[6] Reports to the League of Nations detail the proliferation of palm plantations in Akonolinga, groundnut production in Nyong-et-Sanaga, and cocoa, coffee, and tobacco harvests from southern and western regions, which were produced by African small farmers as well as large plantation owners who created a lucrative trans-regional cash crop economy that also enriched those assisting in drying, fermenting, sorting, selling, and transporting crops to the port of Kribi.[7] Government reports between 1925 and 1935 cheerfully announced southern Cameroon's burgeoning harvests and lauded Africans' "infatuation" with cocoa, which generated considerable revenues.[8] The region of Abong Mbang was also known for record rubber harvests in the 1925–1935 decade, with the surrounding regions producing palm oil in greater amounts each successive year.[9]

---

[3] ANOM AGEFOM 799/1858 Cournarie Rapports sur le cacao, 1929–1932; Rapport de la Tournée Effectuée dans les Subdivisions de M'balmayo et d'Akonolinga, M. Angelini, 1933; ANC APA 11016/K Rapport Annuel pour l'année 1927, 98.

[4] See Martin-René Atangana, *French Investment in Colonial Cameroon: The FIDES Era (1946–1957)* (New York: Peter Lang, 2009), 150–2. Daleep Singh, *Francophone Africa, 1905–2005: A Century of Economic and Social Change* (Delhi: Allied Publishers, 2008), 126.

[5] "Cacaos et Cafés," *Revue Internationale des produits coloniaux et du materiel colonial*, no. 200, mai 1950.

[6] ANOM AGEFOM 151/5 Agriculture en Cameroun, 1923–1936; Monga, "The Emergence of Duala Cocoa Planters under German Rule in Cameroon: A Case Study of Entrepreneurship." See also Leonard John Schwarz, *Cocoa in the Cameroons under French Mandate and in Fernando Po*, United States Bureau of Foreign and Domestic Commerce, Trade Promotion Series, no. 148 (Washington, DC: U.S. Govt. Printing Office, 1933).

[7] "Le Cameroun," *Marchés coloniaux du monde*, no. 361, 11 octobre 1953; Viers, "Le cacao dans le monde," 316.

[8] AFFPOL 2190/1 Rapport annuel du gouvernement français sur l'administration sous mandat des territoires du Cameroun pour l'année 1929; ANOM TP Série 1 420/12 Rapports annuel, Services de travaux publics, 1933, 1934, 1935, 1938.

[9] ANOM AGEFOM 989/3430 Cameroun administration 1927–1933, Circ. d'Abong Mbang Bulletin Agricole; Circ. d'Abong Mbang Bulletin Commercial, 1935; ANOM AGEFOM 989/3423 Circulaire no. 70 Bonnecarrère, 1932.

Economic growth fostered greater economic cooperation among Christian publics: in 1926 Presbyterian Bulu farmers and traders formed the Yevol Mutual Aid Society to pool their incomes for tax payments;[10] from 1926 to 1927 in Ebolowa and Sangmélima, several Bané-Bulu-Fang cooperatives contributed 31,000 francs to buy agricultural tools and launch a truck transport service for their harvests; in Lolodorf, the Protestant Chameleon Society purchased an automobile to travel to Eseka, Ebolowa, and Kribi to sell their goods; in Kribi, locals formed a cooperative fishery; in Nanga-Eboko, a local farmers' cooperative purchased oil extraction and rice husk removal machines; and in Yoko, a herders' cooperative bought traps to capture panthers who ate their sheep.[11] Records also testify African planters in the south commonly made collective capital investments in drying facilities for cocoa and tobacco and refineries for palm oil.[12] Quarterly and annual reports from 1925 to 1935 also attest to only a brief depression between 1929 and 1931 when exports fetched lower prices. Even with the temporary downturn, French officials professed a continued "amelioration of personal situation...of the families of the artisans of much of the agricultural production."[13]

Economic growth fostered greater inter-cooperation among African Christians as the missions became centers where marriage was negotiated and congregants developed programs of mutual aid. Expanded rural–urban road and rail lines allowed for easier transit between cities and villages, which meant that religious outreach was more fluid and frequent. Greater personal resources and freedom of movement motivated greater numbers of African men with evangelical inclinations to pursue peripatetic vocations, as they could leave their wives and families at home to nurture cash crops.[14]

---

[10] The society's tax pool was intended to guard against chiefs' arbitrary and exorbitant tax demands, which, if collected during harvest season or before a feast day, could have crippling financial effects. ANC 2AC/8992 Lettre du Monsieur André Beton à le Ministre de la Justice, 15 sept. 1930; AFFPOL 2190/1 Rapport Annuel du Cameroun, 1927, 71.

[11] AFFPOL 2190/1 Rapport Annuel du Cameroun, 71.

[12] ANC APA 11016/K Rapport Annuel adressé par le gouvernement français pour l'année 1927.

[13] ANOM TP Série 1 420/11 Rapport annuel Travaux Publics, 1931, 75; ANC APA 3AC 1350 Rapport semestriel sur la situation agricole de la région de N'Tem 1930.

[14] Many catechist accounts emphasize the role of their wives in maintaining "gardens," or "farms" that provided for their families while they were away. See SMEP/DEFAP Fonds Allégret: Cameroun 1920–1923, lettre de Lazare Ndim Ekoka, 7 décembre 1920; ACSSp. 2J1.10.12 lettre au Révérend Père Faussier, Mission Catholique de Medzek, 14 juillet 1930. Also, Pauvert and Lancrey-Javal discuss the continuing rural–urban links within consistent patterns of migration from villages from the 1930s through the 1950s. Pauvert and Lancrey-Javal, "Le Groupement d'Evodoula (Cameroun): Étude

The new and higher incomes enjoyed by those who benefitted from this new economy in the late 1920s and 1930s only aggravated local labor shortages, however. Chiefs in the second decade of French rule complained to district officials and in Councils of Notables about their inability to recruit workers as a result of men's increasing ability to pay the *ticket de rachat,* a fee which bought out their *prestation* requirement for public works.[15] This meant that only poor, young, or low-status men without access to fields or farms were left to perform forced or low-salaried labor. Chief Edjoa Mvondo confessed during a 1929 Council session that the last time the administration demanded workers, he was only able to find twenty-three who could not produce a *ticket de rachat.* The administration nevertheless scolded Mvondo, as they needed fifty workers to clear forests and repair roads and of those he found, eight were returned to their villages for being too elderly.[16] Other chiefs like Ndille Nsom proposed that the *taux de rachat* be adjusted according to salaries of the people in his district so as to raise fees for chauffeurs, clerks, artisans, and planters avoiding roadwork.[17] Nsom also suggested that the administration "grant greater authority to have individual decisions over recruitment," which President Martin rejected, stating, "Given the cupidity and venality unfortunately so exhibited by village chiefs, the task of authorizing labor should be not entirely given to chiefs without limitations or it could start a clandestine traffic in permissions and demands."[18]

In general, most chiefs agreed that the increasing scarcity of laborers made it nearly impossible to fulfill their quotas, and made suggestions as to how to adjust *prestation* requirements in their regions. One chief offered that the administration officially recognize the difference between construction and maintenance work on roads, and suggested that the latter "not be included

---

Socio-Économique. Rapports Du Conseil Supérieur Des Recherches Sociologiques Outre-Mer," 14–19.

[15] Occasionally also referred to as the *patente de colporteur*. AFFPOL 2190/1 Simon Ndille, Ebolowa, Conseil de Notables de la Circonscription d'Ebolowa, scéance de 18 nov. 1929, Rapport annuel du gouvernement français sur l'administration du Cameroun pour l'année 1929.

[16] ANOM AFFPOL 2190/1 Edjoa Mvondo, Conseil de Notables de la Circonscription d'Ebolowa, scéance de 18 nov. 1929, Rapport annuel du gouvernement français sur l'administration du Cameroun pour l'année 1929, 95.

[17] ANOM AFFPOL 2190/1 Conseil de Notables de la Circonscription d'Ebolowa, scéance de 18 nov. 1929, Rapport annuel du gouvernement français sur l'administration du Cameroun pour l'année 1929, 93.

[18] ANOM AFFPOL 2190/1 Conseil de Notables de la Circonscription d'Ebolowa, scéance de 18 nov. 1929, Rapport annuel du gouvernement français sur l'administration du Cameroun pour l'année 1929, 94.

in the annual ten days of required labor, per the *arrêté* of 9 March 1927."[19] President Martin agreed that much roadwork constituted "maybe just twenty minutes, which cannot be counted as one day and should be performed without pay and without being included as part of the ten days." Another chief concurred, "It is for the villagers' own benefit to fill the ruts left by the rains. Their sheep can drown. And the work is insignificant."[20]

Rising inequality and coercion did not appear to disturb French officials. Indeed, in the second decade of the mandate, they were more likely to celebrate increases in productivity. When the Yaoundé railway was completed, Governor Marchand toasted in champagne with Chiefs Atangana and Erdman Etéki.[21] In 1933, as government reports touted the wealth of African palm oil planters who earned 120 francs per ton and the oil refiners who earned 320 francs per ton, they also debated whether to pay forest workers who had the backbreaking task of clearing forests for modern thoroughfares in francs or simply in manioc, dried fish, bananas, and rice.[22] Travelers in southern Cameroon in 1931 and 1933 noted that "for some African planters ... certain grades of Cameroon tobacco wrapper sell for $2.50 a pound wholesale ... in the prosperous city of Yaoundé," but also that African laborers in the villages would sing "How many of us will be taken away to the railroads? How many of us will come back?"[23] Thousands of Africans also continued to be forcibly recruited into chiefs' plantations across southern Cameroon, where they received little or no pay.[24]

Although economic disparities strained social relations, the expansion of trade, migration, and commerce invigorated Christian commitment in a number of ways. Church attendance, access to catechism, and the circulation of scripture, prayers, and hymns was made possible by increasing rural–urban migration and village interconnection. Market development and expanded communication networks, including the expansion of the confessional press,

---

[19] ANOM AFFPOL 2190/1 Conseil de Notables de la Circonscription d'Ebolowa, scéance de 18 nov. 1929, Rapport annuel du gouvernement français sur l'administration du Cameroun pour l'année 1929, 90–4.

[20] ANOM AFFPOL 2190/1 Conseil de Notables de la Circonscription d'Ebolowa, scéance de 18 nov. 1929, Rapport annuel du gouvernement français sur l'administration du Cameroun pour l'année 1929, 93.

[21] *La Gazette du Cameroun*, no. 39, jan.–mars 1927.

[22] In the end, the administration chose to pay forest laborers in francs, as it was cheaper than transporting, storing, and distributing food. ANOM AGEFOM 151/5 Agriculture en Cameroun, 1923–1936.

[23] John W. Vandercook, "The French Mandate of Cameroun," *National Geographic Magazine* LIX, no. 2 (1931): 225–60; Margery Perham, "France in the Cameroons," *The Times (London)*, May 17, 1933.

[24] ANOM AGEFOM 799/1858 Cameroun 1935 Travail et main d'oeuvres.

spurred the growth of pious voluntary associations and centered the village church as a space to discuss social and spiritual goals. Finally, generous donations made possible by cash crop revenues funded the construction of churches, chapels, temples, and cathedrals throughout the territory.[25] Overall, Christian publics in the second decade of French rule overall had greater access to financial resources and appropriated the institutional resources of the missions to serve local needs.

In the Mbam region, for example, churches were built in small towns like Somo, Bafia, Ntui, Ombessa, Yangben, Yoko, Makenene, Balamba, Djole, and Ngoro for a Christian population that was estimated to be 32,000 in 1936.[26] Mgr. Vogt and his successor, René Graffin, expanded Catholic ecclesiastical subdivisions and missions stations in zones with burgeoning trade and urban linkages near transit points. The Minlaba Mission in Mbalmayo, which sat at the intersection of the Mbalmayo–Ebolowa and Mengueme–Ngomezap roadways where Ewondo, Bene, Bassa, and Bulu villagers circulated, received up to 10,000 participants at Sunday masses, prompting nervous police reports about crowding and threats to public order.[27] The Catholic missions farther southwest in Edea, Efok, and Akono, which likewise were situated at transit crossroads, all boasted between 10,000 and 16,000 Bassa, Ewondo, and Bakoko congregants in 1930. Villages like Bikop, Obut, Mbalmayo, Makak, Omvan, and Oveng in the central southern forest region, which had once been catechist posts, grew into large church communities in this period with generous and active memberships: in 1930, Omvan calculated 1500 regular attendants at Sunday mass, and Bikop calculated over 2,000.[28] Catholic missions in coastal Douala, Kribi, and Ngowayang managed the most diverse mission populations as a result of migrations from the north and the interior, and said masses in Duala, Ewondo, Grassfield, Bassa, Bakoko, and Ngumba to crowds of 2500–6000 people. In southwestern Cameroon, the village of Ndogbambi, which housed a thriving Protestant community, grew rapidly as a result of its increasing interaction with the neighboring villages of Logtol and Ndogonihibo, all of which were linked by forest paths and paved roads to the major market town of Edea. Factory work in Edea meant that men receiving

---

[25] ACSSp. 2J1.8.a1, Douala pendant la guerre, Rapport sur le District de Douala.
[26] ACSSp. 2J1.6.2 Département de Mbam, 1923–1936.
[27] ACSSp. 2J1.10.7 Père Van Bulck, S.J. avec Mr. de Calbiac, commissaire de police à Yaoundé, 17 mai 1932.
[28] Well-attended catechist posts often evolved into "annex missions," and later fully-fledged primary mission stations. Bikop, Oveng, and Makak began as catechist posts and annex missions of the Mission of Notre Dame des Sept Douleurs in Akono. ACSSp. 2J1.11a2 Compte-rendu des stations à Bikop, Balmayo, Obut, et Oveng, 13–14 fev. 1936.

salaries in town could make donations to the Ndogbambi church on Sundays when they visited their wives and children in the forest.[29] The French administration confirmed the increasing wealth and corresponding piety of rural Africans during the 1930s, when palm oil, cocoa, and groundnut producers received up to 300 francs per ton for their harvests, which "allow[ed] them to make offerings to the Virgin Mary."[30]

Men who managed to escape road work or servicing a chief could be easily convinced to labor alongside other catechumens and congregants erecting bell towers and fashioning pews, and receive spiritual graces and a shared meal at the local mission. After churches were built, they became spaces where antagonisms were channeled into movements for relief, particularly for those who resented endless roadwork conscription, paying taxes, or servicing bridewealth with the year's revenue collected at harvest. The rural and urban poor excluded from the cultivatable land or salaried labor that would allow them to marry and the ranks of women in undesirable unions who sought an ally in changing their destinies also found refuge in the missions' walls.

Developing Church Institutions with African Labor

The increasing organizational capacities of individual missions and congregations spurred the Catholic missions in Cameroon to consider dividing the vicariate of Cameroon into two jurisdictions – Yaoundé and Douala – to better manage local affairs. In 1927, Vogt proposed dividing the regions along the Nyong River, with the Yaoundé Vicariate absorbing the missions in Yaoundé, Akono, Minlaba, Nden, Efok, and Nlon, with 19 European priests and around 90,000 registered Catholics, and the Vicariate of Douala absorbing the Douala, Edea, Ngowayang, Kribi, and Somo stations with 11 priests and around 40,000 Christians.[31] In 1931, the Sacred Congregation of the Propaganda Fide approved dividing the Cameroon vicariate with Mgr. Vogt and Mgr. Mathurin le Mailloux as its two bishops.[32] The Douala vicariate included eight principal

---

[29] SMEP/DEFAP Cameroun 1925–1926 (Ségrégation) NM, Pasteur Charles Maitre, lettre de 10 sept. 1926.

[30] ANOM AGEFOM 151/5 Rapport Agricole, Subdivision de M'Balmayo et d'Akonolinga, M. Angelini, Inspecteur d'agriculture, 1933; ACSSp. 2J1.7a7, "Chez nous soyez Reine, chez nous les africains"; "Yaoundé, Cité Mariale," *La Croix*, 19 août 1954.

[31] ACSSp. 2J1.2b2 Mgr. Vogt, Division du Vicariat de Cameroun, 12 sept. 1927.

[32] By that time, the Catholic missions estimated that the whole Cameroon territory contained over 130,000 Catholics and 130,000 catechumens. ACSSp. 2J1.1 Rapport de Mgr Vogt du 5 septembre 1928. See also "Vicariat Apostolique de Yaoundé (Cameroun)," *Chronique des missions*, 1930–1931, 148. See also Salvador Eyezo'o, "La Partition Du Vicariat Apostolique Du Cameroun," in *Histoire et Missions Chrétiennes N-007. A La*

missions (three more than was proposed in 1927) at Douala, Édéa, Marienberg, Somo, Samba, Éséka, Kribi, Ngowayang, and Ebolowa, and René Graffin was made sub-prefect of the Yaoundé vicariate (and would later assume the bishopric after Vogt's death), which had more than twice the number of secondary missions attached to the eight primary mission stations (two more than were proposed in 1927) at Akono, Nlong, Efok, Minlaba, Nden, Medzek, Bafia, and Doumé. Both vicariates had much greater numbers of annex missions and village chapels, which occasionally grew as large as principal mission stations (see Maps 5 and 6).[33]

In 1932, the Paris Evangelical Mission estimated 120,000 Protestants in Cameroon.[34] The Douala circonscription alone counted a rough total of 17,000 African Baptists and over 30,000 members attending 17 Baptist and 21 Lutheran Evangelical churches. The circonscriptions of Abong-Mbang, Bafia, Ebolowa, and Edea counted 17 Presbyterian churches and an "uncounted" number of other Protestant religious structures.[35] African Protestants in Cameroon attained higher status in the ecclesiastical hierarchy more rapidly and in greater numbers than their Catholic counterparts. While the Catholic Church ordained its first African priests from Cameroon only in 1935, by 1930, African pastors in the French Protestant Mission were leading the seven regional Bamoun, Bamileke, Ndoungué, Pongo, Yabassi, Sanaga, and Douala synods.[36] By 1945, there were eleven synodal regions of the French Protestant Mission, which oversaw roughly 800 churches, chapels, and catechist posts throughout the Cameroon territory. These were administered by a growing number of indigenous pastors, as well as evangelists and catechists and counted about 80,000 total adherents in Cameroon in 1945, of which roughly 64,000 were baptized members and another 16,000 were catechumens.[37]

In 1935, Bishop Vogt ordained the first African priests, including four from southern Cameroon – Théodore Tsala, Tobie Atangana, André Manga and Jean Tabi – and four from the west – Simon Mpeke, Jean-Oscar Aoué,

---

Rencontre de l'Asie – La Société Des Missions Etrangères de Paris (1658–2008), ed. Catherine Marin (Paris: Karthala, 2008), 130–49.

[33] Salvador Eyezo'o, "La partition du vicariat apostolique du Cameroun," *Histoire, monde et cultures religieuses* n°7, no. 3 (September 1, 2008): 121–46.

[34] ACSSp. 2J1.10.12 Dannewig Commission Protestante, Commission des Mandats, 1932.

[35] ANC APA 11016/Q Réglementation des edifices.

[36] SMEP/DEFAP EEC FB 1/2, Synodes. Pastor Muishe led the regional synod in Bamoun, Pastor Mondjo in Bamileke, Pastor Dooh in Ndoungué, Pastor Gottlieb Soppo in Pongo, Pastor Nkondo in Yabassi, Pastor Bila in Sanaga, Pastor Ekombo in Douala, and Pastor Jean Kotto as general secretary, led in Douala.

[37] Maurice Farelly, "Les Eglises indigènes au Cameroun," *Journal des Missions Évangéliques* (1946): 7–16. See also Farelly, *Chronique Du Pays Banen (Au Cameroun)*.

Oscar Misoka, and Joseph Melone. By the time of his death in 1943, Vogt had ordained a total of 41 African priests from the territory.[38] Throughout the 1930s, Catholic seminaries swelled with students, although not all young men completed their training as some left to pursue the more lucrative careers opening to educated African men.[39] Encouragement to indigenize the clergy and embed the faith fully in local culture came directly from the Roman Pontiff, with Pope Pius XI insisting in a 1926 encyclical that foreign missions devote themselves to education so that receiving populations could better embrace Christianity through professionalization.[40] Long-serving catechists Martin Atangana, Joseph Essomba, and Sylvestre Otou became priests after working with graduates of the Seminary of Saint Joseph and observing the opportunities clerical life afforded learned men.[41] The *Grand Seminaire* at Otélé, run by the Swiss Benedictines of Engelberg, attracted hundreds of young African men between 1928 and 1960, many of whom came from the catechist ranks.[42]

Catechists in both the Protestant and Catholic Churches who were operative in the second interwar decade from 1925 to 1935 marshaled greater organizational resources than their predecessors. Many African catechists were now second- or third-generation Christians and had elders or kin who were catechists. They had greater power in their local communities, particularly as the missions negotiated with the territorial administration to exempt them from *corvée* labor and taxation, which allowed them significantly greater freedom and mobility than those without catechist appointments.[43] Critically,

---

[38] ACSSp. Mgr. Vogt, *Cahier ss* 19, 42–3.

[39] Etaba, *Histoire de l'Eglise Catholique Du Cameroun de Grégoire XVI à Jean-Paul II*, 88–90.

[40] For more on Maximum Illud, the Apostolic Letter of Pope Benedict XV issued on 30 November 1919 regarding Catholic missions worldwide after World War I, see Joel Cabrita, David Maxwell, and Emma Wild-Wood, *Relocating World Christianity: Interdisciplinary Studies in Universal and Local Expressions of the Christian Faith* (Boston, MA: Brill, 2017), 1–26.

[41] Etaba, "Maximum Illud, de Benoît XV, et l'œuvre Missionnaire Au Cameroun (1890–1935) : Entre Anticipations, Applications et Contradictions."

[42] ACSSp. 2J1.13.b3, Grand Seminaire d'Otélé.

[43] ANOM AGEFOM 355/170bis, Liberté de conscience, Pays Bamiléké 1930; "A Bulu Missionary," *Drum Call*, 28 (January 1949): 21; Envana Ngo'obene, "How I Chose the Ministry," *Drum Call*, 8 (October 1929): 12–13; Timothy Evina Zambô, "Pioneer Missionary: As Told By Himself," *Drum Call*, 11 (January 1932): 23–7; Albert I. Good, "Bekali, a Servant of the Lord," in *The Black Pioneer* (New York: Board of Foreign Missions of the Presbyterian Church in the U.S.A., 1924), 17–26. Others who were exempt from forced labor included African members of the police force, Africans under contract or salaried with the colonial administration, Sultans, *lamido, grand chefs*, members of the Council of Notables, judges of the *tribunaux indigènes*, those who had received medals or privileges by the French government, or those who had earned the French *Ordre du Mérite*,

catechists in the late 1920s and 1930s could also rely on longstanding family and social networks as well as the socio-religious ecosystem of Cameroon's burgeoning towns and cities to build larger followings.

Particularly in Catholic communities, catechists' ministries remained critical in shaping the faith community even while greater numbers of Africans entered the priesthood. Newly inducted African priests often began their clerical careers in rural mission stations in regions from which they did not originate. This meant that African priests often did not recognize the culture nor spoke the same language as the people they had been assigned to serve. Thus, catechists were necessary adjuncts for African priests as they had been for foreign missionaries, and worked alongside them and other mission leaders to communicate with local residents and congregations, translate the Bible, and lead sermons.[44] Empathy with victims of economic and social inequality also remained the catechists' strongest emotional connection with their publics. In his ministry in southern and northern Cameroon, Simon Mpeke continuously reiterated the teaching of Matthew 23: 8–9, "You have but one father, who lives in heaven ... and you are all brothers" – affirming that all Christians enjoyed corresponding rank and their only true ruler was Jesus Christ.[45] The Protestant catechist Mounz Diboundou not only preached against the sins committed by rapacious elders and predatory in-laws, he also invited his

---

owners of large plantations or farms who were considered to have "contributed to the *mise en valeur* of the colony," or anyone who was officially recognized as commercially exploiting an area of more than ten hectares, as well as "Africans who have been previously recruited for long periods and fathers of large families." ANOM AFFPOL 2688/3 Décret instituant le travail obligatoire au Cameroun, Titre I, Chapitre I, Article 4, le 21 Aout 1930.

[44] Spiritan records recount the full measure of catechists' work in regions where no European missionaries or African priests had command of the local language. While there were Bible translations in Bulu, Bassa, various Beti languages, Duala, and a number of other languages, there were very few catechism or prayer books in languages of smaller populations like the Banen (which comprised roughly 50,000 people in 1935), or Mwumbo or Batanga. The German Pallottines had translated one Mwumbo text, *Katekismus Katolisch na Kieli Mwumbo*, in 1913, with the assistance of a local catechist, but no other texts had been completed since their departure. The Spiritans relied on Duala or Beti-language Bibles and texts until catechists could preach and impart catechism in the local language. ACSSp. 2J1.8.a1, Lettre de Douala, 29 septembre 1945, note au sujet de l'enseignement réligieux; Lettre d'Edea, 11 septembre 1945, Abbé Hammenackschen; ACSSp. 2J1.1a.10 Cameroun: 1926–1940: Vicariat, Yaoundé, Douala. Even in 1950, the Spiritan Mission was heavily reliant on catechists to translate sermons, announcements, etc., see Vicariat de Doumé, "Lumière Vers l'Est," *Le Cameroun Catholique*, June 15, 1950.

[45] Grégoire Cador, *L'héritage de Simon Mpeke: prêtre de Jésus et frère universel* (Paris: Lethielleux: Desclée de Brouwer, 2009), 12.

catechumens to "condemn evil" and encouraged daring criticisms of social superiors.[46]

In Protestant parishes overseen by the Paris Evangelical Missionary Society, catechists worked alongside evangelists who were their institutional superiors and would have the responsibility of several dozen annex missions to manage in one evangelical district. Evangelists were in turn managed by a pastor, who would oversee several evangelist districts. Catechists were assisted by their wives, who were the only women in the Protestant community who could work in catechism.[47] The American Presbyterian Mission also hierarchized indigenous ministry, pairing evangelists with pastors in the mission field.[48] In the French Protestant Mission, pastors, evangelists, and catechists worked together with the Council of Elders (*Mboko ma Batudu* in Duala), which were formed in all synodal regions. Each *Mboko* was made up of African male and female congregants, with two elders representing fifty members of the local church and one for each twenty-five additional members. These individuals were chosen from the congregation and were expected to materially support the church by underwriting construction, receiving visitors, and paying for meals and ceremonies. Their other duties included visiting the faithful, informing catechists of congregants' troubles and illnesses, and working with pastors to promote the life of the faith.[49] The nature of mission organization in the Protestant Church in Cameroon allowed for a great deal of indigenous incorporation across the institutional hierarchy. Catechists, evangelists, and pastors all presided over services, particularly the Last Supper Service (*Culte de Sainte Cène*) and oversaw baptisms, marriages, and missionary education and assisted in council meetings of the Church Elders.[50]

Developing the *Terroirs*

Mariteuw Chimère Diaw argues that in the "forest amphitheater" of southern Cameroon, all territorial identities before the arrival of Europeans were rooted

---

[46] ANC APA 11016/G Maurice Farelly avec Mounz Diboundou et Pastor Itondo, 6 janvier 1934; Farelly, *Chronique Du Pays Banen (Au Cameroun)*, 32–3.
[47] Wives of catechists could instruct alongside their husbands, but not single women. SMEP/DEFAP EEC FB divers 2/2 Allocution du candidat à l'occasion de sa consécration pastorale, Mosé Lamère, 15 avril 1956.
[48] Jones, *The Life of Rowland Hill Evans of Cameroun*, 170.
[49] Maurice Farelly, "Les Eglises indigènes au Cameroun," *Journal des Missions Évangéliques*, 1946.
[50] Maurice Farelly, "Les Eglises indigènes au Cameroun," *Journal des Missions Évangéliques*, 1946.

in the *si*, *nda bot*, and *ayong* (land, nuclear lineage, and clan groups).[51] Achille Mbembe confirms that these elements, which shaped endogenous politics and social practices, indeed constituted the basis of a number of distinct *terroirs* in colonial Cameroon, but that the colonial encounter reshaped them through introducing market capitalism, new modes of agricultural production, and European political strategies, which brought about new ways of demarcating territorial identities.[52] Mbembe also examines the work of *terroir* in building collective aspirations and even transcendent collective memory in the late colonial and early postcolonial periods, while Ibrahim Mouiche builds on this to claim that Cameroon's *terroirs* in the current day operate as a "logic" in contestation with the authoritarian state.[53]

Looking to the late 1920s and early 1930s, one can clearly discern the transition point from land, lineage, and clan-based territorial identities to a constitution of *terroir* based on a more diverse set of cultural and linguistic affiliations. Governor Bonncarrère expressed alarm at this development, reporting in 1930 from the Nyong et Sanaga region, "Administrative heads of region and circonscription should apply themselves seriously to protecting and conserving the native communities in their collective solidarity ... there are transfusions and population transfers of all kinds."[54] A local example of this was Sangmélima, which, during the early 1920s was populated mainly by

[51] Mariteuw Chimère Diaw, *Si, nda bot et ayong: Culture itinérante sur brulis, occupation des sols et droits fonciers au Sud Cameroun*, Réseau de foresterie pour le développement rural 21e, Working Paper. See also Mariteuw Chimère Diaw and Phil René Oyono, "Dynamiques et Représentation Des Espaces Forestiers Au Sud-Cameroun: Pour Une Relecture Sociale Des Paysages," *Bulletin Arbres, Forêts et Communautés Rurales* 15, no. 16 (1998): 36–43. Diaw discusses how *ayong*, or "clan groups," also intersects with references to language and ethnicity, like its closely related word *mëyong*. *Nda bot* (from *nda*, house, and *bot*, person) refers specifically to the nuclear lineage, which is an essential constituent of the corporate lineage among the Beti-Fang and Bulu ethnic formations, and is the basic lineal unit covering three generations (parents, children and grandchildren of the male line).

[52] Mbembe, *La Naissance Du Maquis Dans Le Sud-Cameroun, 1920–1960*; Achille Mbembe, "Domaines de La Nuit et Autorité Onirique Dans Les Maquis Du Sud-Cameroun (1955–1958)," *Journal of African History* 31 (1986): 37–72.

[53] Mouiche defines *terroir* as Cameroonian societies' cultural, spiritual, and artistic heritage, and claims that local guardians of these domains demand recognition and resources from the state in exchange for a share of power. Ibrahim Mouiche, "Mutations Socio-Politiques et Replis Identitaires En Afrique: Le Cas Du Cameroun," *African Journal of Political Science / Revue Africaine de Science Politique* 1, no. 2 (December 1, 1996): 176–201; Ibrahim Mouiche, *Autorités traditionnelles et démocratisation au Cameroun: entre centralité de l'Etat et logiques de terroir* (Munster: LIT Verlag Münster, 2005).

[54] ANOM AGEFOM 1007/569 Circulaire du 2 Décembre 1930.

Bulu peoples, but by 1929, was also a place of residence for Beti and Bamileke peoples who convened for employment in production centers along the roads and railways that intersected at Sangmélima: the southwest road to Kribi and the western road to Djoum. In 1930, construction also began on two smaller roads that connected with the Douala–Yaoundé road and by 1931, *état civil* centers around Sangmélima recorded four new ethnic categories – Messock, Bengbis, Nkpwang, and Mbieleme – in addition to the Bulu, Beti, Ntumu, and Bamileke peoples who were already registered.[55] Records also note similar shifts in population and accompanying linguistic and societal diversity in Kribi and Lolodorf.[56] Population mixing was also shaped by economic and religious activities that brought distinct families, lineages, and individual African leaders into contact with one another and influenced the collective conduct of Christian publics. In this period, these distinct but increasingly interactive *terroirs* in southern Cameroon experienced relations of domination and resistance that transformed the ecology and social organization of communities.

Some examples of the formation of new ethno-religious-economic *terroirs* can be seen in contrasting reports from French regional officials and local missionaries. Between the late 1920s and mid-1930s, in the region between the Edea and Eseka railway stops, Bassa peoples presented a conundrum for local officials. Although Bassa villagers produced record amounts of palm oil and cocoa in 1931 and 1932, administrator Guibert wrote, "Tax collection is difficult. The Bassa population is individualist and manifests an independence each time the administration tries to engage. The chiefs are often contested and the Bassa are scattered in the forests in small villages."[57] While the local chief, Eone Eone, was considered "excellent" for encouraging local productivity, he failed at reversing his subjects' "disinterest regarding fiscal obligations."[58] However, while Bassa villagers resisted paying taxes to their assigned chief, they were generous with their earnings when it came to the local churches. In 1936, the Edea and Eseka Catholic missions collected some of the largest regional contributions, with Eseka bringing in 23,901 francs and Edea amassing 22,098 francs through parish tithes. By comparison, Samba only collected 12,845 francs and prosperous Ebolowa collected only 18,946 francs that same year. European mission leaders noted the "extraordinary" generosity of Edea

---

[55] Etablissment de quatre centres d'etat-civil, 18 février 1931 pour les quatre distinctions éthnographiques, Messock, Bengbis, Nkpwang, Mbieleme, *Journal Officiel du Cameroun*, no. 258, 1 mars 1931.

[56] ANOM AGEFOM 874/2409 Rapport de L. Frébault, Agence Economique des Territoires Africains sous mandat, 19 Avril 1926.

[57] ANOM AGEFOM 989/3424 Rapport Guibert, Edea, 20 août 1932.

[58] ANOM AGEFOM 989/3424 Rapport Guibert, Edea, 20 août 1932.

and Eseka's local populations, who contributed a hefty percentage of the operating budget of the Vicariate of Douala.[59]

Some mission records provide evidence that the discipline of local Bassa Catholic catechists, who organized retreats beginning in 1929, and the ordination of the African seminarian Albert Eyike and his assignment to Eseka as pastor, contributed to the expansion of Bassa pious devotion.[60] Many records point to the lack of European personnel in the Edea and Eseka mission posts, whose individual congregations of over 10,000 Bassa, Bakoko, and Ewondo believers were assigned only one French priest in the late 1920s and early 1930s.[61] In 1925, both Edea and Eseka counted roughly 3000 Catholics in each mission, but by 1936, the Edea mission had grown to 10,228 Catholics and 8000 catechumens, and Eseka recorded 11,804 Catholics and 9000 catechumens. Even the annex mission post, Saint André, which was between Edea and Eseka, counted over 4000 Christians, 48 catechists, and 601 "Christian families," in 1936, who collected over 5000 francs in tithes.[62] One missionary record concisely summarized: "We rely entirely on catechists here."[63] This area also counted 1400 Presbyterians who were served by two large mission stations and saw greater numbers of Baptist catechists, who arrived by railroad from Nkongsamba starting in 1928.[64]

Deeper investigations into the precise work of African Christian leaders and political appointees in the Eseka–Edea region reveal that there were highly competitive forces in determining the culture, governance, and discipline of each *terroir*. Much like mission stations had few European overseers and only occasional visits from ordained priests (the mission at Somo received a priest on motorbike "every few weeks"), chiefs could not occupy or supervise the entirety of their territories.[65] While Chief Eone Eone and others of his rank lived along the rivers or roads to allow for easy communication with French officials, their subject populations were often several days' journey from these nodal points.[66] Therefore, chiefs' regiments of guards and enforcers patrolled

---

[59] ACSSp. 2J1.11a2 lettre sur le Vicariat de Douala, 16 mars 1936.
[60] ACCSp. 2J2.1a Mission de Nlong, 1925–1938; ACSSp. 2J1.8b2 *Le Cameroun Catholique*, 1 May 1937.
[61] Père Krummenacker was the only assigned priest in the Edea–Eseka region for several years. CSSp. 2J1.11a2 Journal de la Résidence du Sacré-Coeur d'Edea, 1928, 1929, 1930, 1931.
[62] ACSSp. 2J1.11a2 Compte-rendu du R.P. Biechy, Résidence du Sacré Coeur d'Edea, 27 jan–3 fév. 1936.
[63] ACSSp. 2J1.11a2 Journal de la Résidence du Sacré-Coeur d'Edea, 1931.
[64] SMEP/DEFAP MF 3681, rapport de la conférence de 1928.
[65] ACSSp. 2J1.11a2 Journal de la Résidence de Saint Jean-Baptiste de Somo, 1932.
[66] ANOM AGEFOM 989/3424 Rapport Guibert, Edea, 20 août 1932.

villages, conscripted labor, and extracted fees or fines.[67] When tax collection or conscription was low, French officials would offer to supplement the muscle necessary to command the area.[68] In 1929, French officials demanded greater numbers of recruits from chiefs in Edea and Eseka, and in 1931 and 1932, administrator Guibert increased the Eseka Regional Guard in an attempt to enforce tax payments and recruitment on the Eseka, Lolodorf, and Mbalmayo rail lines.[69] The results were simultaneously financially lucrative and socially devastating. In the years after more rigorous tax enforcement, Edea built two hotels, Eseka opened its first petrol station, and neighboring Kribi, Batouri, and Sangmélima all opened government-funded hospitals.[70] However, reports from 1931 to 1934 also mention "increases in the *population flottante*," between 1.3 and 1.7 million days of forced labor collected annually, "major displacements of zones outside villages to counter sleeping sickness" and arrests of worksite deserters, catechists, and "1200 vagabonds on their way to Douala who were returned to their villages."[71]

While political and economic transformation altered human affiliations with *terroir* based on land, lineage, and language as a result of migration, forced dislocation, and financial and labor exploitation, Christian activism worked to adapt and strengthen family systems to better sustain human bonds while accommodating dramatic changes in approaches to founding a family and building a life. During the late 1920s through the 1930s, spiritual collectives known as *confréries*, or pious confraternities, energized African men and women in new ways by more directly demonstrating empathy, compassion, mutual assistance, and the benefits of monogamous, companionate marriage to individuals and families in their region of operation. Confraternal organizations operated at an even greater distance from mission overseers, which were often established and constituted entirely by devout laypersons. By 1927, confraternities were established in each of the eleven largest Catholic mission stations in the territory. With only thirty French priests, and despite 1700 registered catechists, the work of convening worship, organizing charity, advising penitents, and pairing spouses required the formation of lay brotherhoods to maintain the solidarities required to serve and continue to influence the

---

[67] ACSSp. 2J1.10.12 Arbitraire des Agents de la Force Publique, 15 juin 1930.
[68] ANOM TP Série 1 420/11 Rapport annuel à la Société des Nations 1931– Travaux publics.
[69] ANOM AGEFOM 989/3424 Rapport Guibert, Edea, 20 août 1932.
[70] ANOM TP Série 1 420/12 Rapport annuel Service des Travaux publics, Douala, Eseka, Edea, 31 mars 1938.
[71] ANOM TP Série 1 420/11 Rapports annuel Service des Travaux publics, 1931–1934.

roughly 130,000 baptized adherents in these major regions.[72] New Catholic pious collectives emphasized more disciplined modes of worship and networked through mission churches, village catechism assemblies, schools, and towns to build a muscular movement for resetting family ties.[73]

Devoted Volunteers

The journal entries of the Catholic mission at Bikop from the summer of 1933 paint a stirring scene. After having labored for several weeks to prepare the foundation site of an expansive new church, a multitude of bodies encircled the worksite preparing the structure. Scores of African laborers walked around wooden beams, trestles, and sawhorses as they approached the bays and buttresses of the ground-level construction to add concrete, brick, and stone. Others filed through the brush at the rear of the site carrying wood to fire bricks in the kiln. Still others farther in the forest searched for timber for the rafters and major columns.[74] Although some remained skeptical regarding how the project would emerge, (there plan was for a nave of 70 meters long, with a 40-meter transept and an overall height of twenty meters with two square bell towers) the "assiduousness of the workers convinced the local populace ... that the Christians had God's and the mission's interest in their hearts."[75] By 1936, Africans executed the final plans for the *Église Notre-Dame des Sept Douleurs* in Bikop, and "collected palms in the forest and then wove them into mats to lay the roof ... felled trees and cleaved wood to carve the pews and altar ... and hand-plastered the earthen walls and hardened them with lime." As Père Louis Vuachet attested in the entries describing the completion of the structure: "The Africans have harvested the forest and raised the church of their own labor."[76]

During the second decade of French rule, Catholic mission stations developed autonomous cadres of African mission workers who coordinated construction efforts and assisted in deciding the location of new annex missions. Catechists heard pleas to build new sites, such as that of Gottfried Mbala, who wrote in 1925:

---

[72] ACSSp. 2J1.2b2 Division du vicariate du Cameroun, 1927; ACSSp. 2J1.2b2 Associations chrétiennes 1919– 1920.

[73] For reports on the extensive performance of the ritual of the adoration of the Holy Eucharist, see ACSSp. 2J2.1a; ACSSp. 2J1.10.13 lettre de Mgr. Vogt à tous les missions, 30 juin 1935.

[74] ACSSp. 2J2.1a, Journal de la Mission Catholique de Bikop, Juillet 1933, Aôut 1933.

[75] CSSp. 2J2.1a, Journal de la Mission Catholique de Bikop, Aôut 1933.

[76] ANC APA 11016/K Lettre de Père L. Vuachet, Akono Ebolowa district, 6 juillet 1936.

we carry our sick all the way to Mvolyé. Sometimes they die along the way. We walk so far to attend mass. Old women fall exhausted on the path, trekking to receive graces. We request a Holy Mass for our own village. We need to see the priest and hear the Gospel ... Please do not be displeased with your children who cry out for you![77]

The expansion of church construction laid the material and social groundwork for the expansion of pious collectives who would carry out religious work in new ways. New spaces congregated larger masses of rural and urban believers, and an increasing number of laymen sought positions within the church community to assist in social causes. Religious collectives not only assisted in expanding the number of mission stations and catechist posts, they held out the prospect of erecting a church as both a motivator and a reward for religious devotion and significant acts of piety. In 1932, construction began on a mission in Omvan after the local population proved their fervor by receiving 973 baptisms, forming 1051 catechumens, distributing 94,373 communions, and performing 108 Catholic weddings during the previous year.[78]

Father Simon Mpeke, who was originally from Edea and worked in central and eastern Cameroon for much of his ministry, noted that devotional voluntarism expanded during the 1930s despite increased demands for labor in fields and roads.[79] In his reflections on his ministerial life, Paul Etoga, who would later become bishop of Mbalmayo, corroborated Mpeke's testimony of widespread and active voluntarism throughout southern Cameroon in the 1930s, stating that demands for a new church or an expanded chapel from spiritually earnest but also status-conscious Africans were joined with offers of money, labor, stones, and cement, as well as the use of trucks and equipment.[80] Eugène Wonyu, an Elder in the Protestant Church, had similar recollections of communicants' dedication, writing in his memoirs: "penury ... could not halt so magnificent and noble a work ... as building a church." Wonyu contended that even when finances were low among the leaders of the *Consistoire Sanaga* (the governing body of Protestant churches in coastal Cameroon), "there was never true penury ... as that would mean that there would be misunderstanding, unexamined scripture, a lack of total abandon to the work of our church, a refusal to commit to the tasks that reconcile us with God."[81] Across southern

---

[77] ACSSp. 2J1.2b2 lettre de Gottfried Mbala, Yaoundé, avril 1925.
[78] ACSSp. AF 6, Père Eugène Keller (1884–1955). See also Criaud, "Etienne Nkodo: Le Premier Spiritan Camerounais."
[79] Cador, *L'héritage de Simon Mpeke: prêtre de Jésus et frère universel*, 108–11.
[80] Etoga and Dillinger, *Paul Etoga: Mon Autobiographie*, 16–19.
[81] Wonyu, *Le Chrétien, Les Dons et La Mission Dans l'Eglise Africaine Independente: Réflexions d'un Laïc*, 11–15.

Cameroon, from the coast to the eastern border, charitable giving through contributions to construction and maintenance work ensured the continuation of the church community and empowered the religious denomination's mission, consistory, synod, or general assembly.

Christian Networks

Between 1925 and 1939, charitable intervention and benevolent works led by increasingly organized pious confraternities became centralizing forces in Catholic and Protestant communities, their forms sculpted according to the highly localized circumstances believers faced. Nearly all confraternities focused on the problem of unmarried men and women in polygamous marriages, but each regional or ethno-linguistic cadre also offered a specific form of charity or intervention to the needy, whether it was financially strapped grooms, widows seeking refuge from their late husband's family, or testifying against chiefs in courtrooms. Each group also had its own preferred rituals, whether it was public confession and penance, spiritual retreats, saying the Rosary, or performing the adoration of the Holy Eucharist, and each had its own banner or insignia, statutes, and coffers.[82] In some ways, membership of the *confréries* partially built on pre-Christian rural mutual aid societies (known as *djama* in Eton[83]) and networked alliances for group protection (*avusô* in Bulu) where resources were pooled for feasting, rituals, fighting battles or conflicts, or preventing crisis in times of dearth. These preexisting organizations did not dissipate, but could be absorbed into Christian confraternities and other aid societies if local Christians found it useful.[84] As in earlier forms of mutual aid, these new religious organizations also worked to pool resources to assist members with funds for weddings, housing construction, funds to start a market stall, commercial investment in a business, or to pay seasonal taxes and fines.[85]

---

[82] ACSSp. 2J1.2b2 Rapport sur la Mission Catholique de Ngowayang, Avril 1920; ACSSp. 2J2.1a Journal de la Mission de Nlong, 27 sept. 1929; ACSSp. 2J1.11.a2 Rapport sur la Mission de Nkilzok, 1939.

[83] Eton is a Beti language, which is mutually intelligible with Ewondo, spoken in central-southern Cameroon. See Mark L.O. Van de Velde, *A Grammar of Eton* (Berlin: Mouton de Gruyter, 2008). Eton notes from Victor T. Levine archive.

[84] Pauvert and Lancrey-Javal, "Le Groupement d'Evodoula (Cameroun): Étude Socio-Économique. Rapports Du Conseil Supérieur Des Recherches Sociologiques Outre-Mer."

[85] Pauvert and Lancrey-Javal; George R. Horner, "The Allocation of Power and Responsibility in Bulu Society: A Test of the Usefulness of a Methodology Developed by Marion Levy Jr. in 'The Structure of Society,'" *Cahiers d'Études Africaines* 4, no. 15 (1964): 400–34.

New and stronger religious solidarities also buttressed other community and linguistic solidarities, such as in the case of linguistically distinct catechist cadres appointing *chef catéchistes* to lead them, and African nuns from regions like Nanga Eboko, Mfoumasi, or Lomié forming their own charity organizations to serve their local areas.[86] Administration officials and African chiefs felt increasingly apprehensive at burgeoning Christian cooperation in part because Christian groups had the unparalleled ability to draw strength from economic transformation, rural–urban migration, shifting employment horizons, and growing cosmopolitanism in cities, towns, and villages. Contrary to chiefs and wealthy elders, Christian groups built loyal followings as a result of an increasingly complex political economy. Rather than building on or corrupting progressively outmoded cultural forms, young Christians faced up to the tensions and conflicts of contemporary society.[87]

In 1930, the Catholic community affiliated with the Nlong Mission was overwhelmed by demands for more services in different languages, more priests to hear confessions, and more chapel construction in neighboring villages. Despite "many volunteers from the *confréries*," construction enlistment, mass schedules, school openings, and other functions were often unsystematic and disordered.[88] African catechists argued that they were overburdened with responsibilities, and that they could not hear and organize confessions, teach, minister to the sick, visit the villages, and assist with religious services without rest.[89] After meetings with French missionaries, the Nlong catechist cohort planned to expand the ranks of Catholic volunteers by starting new Ewondo and Bassa chapters of the *Confrérie du Tres Saint Sacrement*, a pious fraternal organization that would assist in construction work and organizing Eucharistic masses, as well as establishing scheduled rotations for catechists in the villages, and putting catechumens and postulants to work making bricks and leading prayer sessions, which would free the more senior catechists to attend to higher-level mission work.[90]

Each confraternity in Cameroon cultivated a special kind of piety. The *Confrérie de l'Adoration Réparatrice*, which was particularly active near Mbalmayo and Ebolowa, built and repaired missions, churches, and chapels and was responsible for constructing the churches of Sainte Anne d'Ebolowa,

---

[86] ACSSp. 2J1.11.a2 Nanga Eboko, soeurs, 1933–1939; Lomié sixa, 20 jul. 1939.

[87] This is precisely what Jean-Marc Ela called on Cameroonians to do to renew Christian communalism in Africa during the period of market liberalization in the 1980s in Africa, when economic adjustments and hardship plagued the populace. Ela, *Ma Foi d'Africain*.

[88] ACSSp. 2J2.1a Journal de la Mission de Nlong, 28 mai 1927; 8 jul. 1928.

[89] ACSSp. 2J2.1a Journal de la Mission de Nlong, 1 jan. 1929; 22 mars 1929.

[90] ACSSp. 2J2.1a Journal de la Mission de Nlong, 1925–1938.

Saint Coeur de Marie de Minlaba, St. Therese d'Akok, Christ-Roi d'Obout, Sainte-Rosaire de Mbalmayo, Saint Michel d'Atega, and Saint-Philippe et Jacques de Ndonko during the 1930s and early 1940s in that region.[91] In the Akonolinga region, local chapters of the *Confrérie de l'Adoration Réparatrice* built the five churches of Saint Paul de Medzek, Saint Francois-Xavier de Mfumasi, Notre-Dame de Lourdes d'Akonolinga, Saint Odile de Ndele, and Notre Dame de Lourdes de Mebasa.[92] These religious groups also organized pilgrimages to the cathedrals at Sangmélima, Mvolyé, and Abang-Ebolowa.[93] Construction of the Mvolyé cathedral between 1923 and 1927 brought hundreds of Africans to work as bricklayers and carpenters from surrounding areas, greatly increasing circulation in the region and contributing to a larger number of languages written and spoken in liturgies, prayers, and song.[94] In 1930, three catechists in the *Confrérie de l'Adoration Réparatrice* in Obut, Zacharie Mbida, Gabriel Owono, and Benoit Mvog Manga, were arrested and sentenced to prison and fines by the head of the Mbalmayo subdivision for enlisting confraternal members in railway worksites.[95] Officer Cuillé retrieved the *confrérie*'s volunteers and returned them to the roads as soon as the catechists were removed from the village.[96]

The *Confrérie de la Doctrine Chrétienne* was reserved for catechists and catechists' aids, and organized retreats to develop religious curricula.[97] The *Confrérie du Très Saint Sacrement* organized young men for fervent ritual performance, including daily mass, weekly solemn adoration of the Holy Eucharist, days-long spiritual retreats, and rosary recitations.[98] The *Confrérie du Très Saint Sacrement* was famous for organizing "bachelor confessions" *en*

---

[91] ACSSp. 2J1.7a7, consecration d'Eglise de Ste. Anne d'Ebolowa; ACSSp. 2J2 1a, Journal de la mission catholique de Bikop, 1–2 mai 1941.

[92] ACSSp. 2J2 1a, Journal de la mission catholique de Bikop, 1–2 mai 1941; 2J1.7a7, consecration d'Eglise de Ste. Anne d'Ebolowa.

[93] Tabi, "Cameroun Terre Mariale: Les Sanctuaires et Centres de Pélerinage Marial du Cameroun." In 1990, the church in Mvolyé was transformed into the Marial Sanctuary of Mvolyé, which then became Mary, Queen of the Apostles Minor Basilica by order of Pope Benedict XVI in April 2006. Mirabel Azangeh Tandafor, "Marial Sanctuary in Mvolye Becomes Minor Basilica," *L'Effort Camerounais*, April 30, 2006; Emmanuel Kendemeh, "Mvolye Basilica – The Pope's Church," *Cameroon Tribune*, December 6, 2006.

[94] Mbembe, *La Naissance Du Maquis Dans Le Sud-Cameroun, 1920–1960*, 93–7.

[95] ACSSp. 2J1.10.12 Mémoire du Père Pichon, Minlaba, l'imprisonnement du Chef Zacharie Mbida et de Gabriel Owono, 1930.

[96] ACSSp. 2J1.10.12 Mémoire du Père Pichon, Zacharie Mbida et de Gabriel Owono, 1930.

[97] ACSSp. 2J1.10.13 lettre de Mgr. Vogt à tous les missions, 30 juin 1935.

[98] ACSSp. 2J1.11a2 Visite du P. Salomon, Yokadouma, 15 jul 1939; ACSSp. 2J1.2b2 Rapport, Mission Catholique de Ngowayang, avril 1920; Vogt rapport du 12 Sept. 1927.

masse, which took place after an hour of group prayer. In 1929, one particularly long night of bachelor confessions left a French missionary exhausted, declaring, "You need even more patience with them than with the old men!"[99] In 1935, The *Confrérie du Saint Sacrement* in Mbalmayo counted more than 500 members, and the *Confrérie du Christ-Roi*, which was a similar confraternity of young, unmarried men, had 200 members.[100] Confraternal members were particularly useful in newer mission stations and outposts in southeastern Cameroon, where visits from French priests were quite rare. Between 1935 and 1939 in the region of Yokadouma, laymen as well as the women they recruited to the local *sixa* taught the area's 9000 catechumens, who spoke either Yangele, Bimu, Bidjuki, Mvomvon, Ngunabembe, Essel, Bangandu, or Bakpele. By frequently performing "exercises of piety" in the local church and in conjunction with evening services, catechists and confraternal members made the faith visually apparent to their diverse audience.[101]

In addition to their particular devotional duties, all confraternities were committed to forming monogamous, loving marriages between baptized believers. In November 1926, the mission at Kribi recorded that the *Confrérie de l'Adoration Réparatrice* had "registered many Batanga and Ewondo volunteers," and that the clearest evidence of their work was "the many marriages that have resulted."[102] The *Confrérie de Sainte Marie* and the *Confrérie de Saint Joseph* (known as *Ekoan Maria* and *Ekoan Josef* in Ewondo) were two pious collectives whose primary devotional focus was forging Christian marriages and families. Originally launched under the guidance of the German leader of the Pallottine missionaries, Heinrich Vieter, in 1906, *Ekoan Maria* and *Ekoan Josef* grew more active in conversion and charitable outreach throughout southern Cameroon during the interwar period. Activities included charismatic forms of prayer and professed goals of humility (*edzòdi*, in Ewondo), piety (*nyebe*), and progress (*mebugeban*). The success of *Ekoan Maria*, which today includes 7000 members from across Cameroon,[103] launched *Ekoan Anna* for widows, *Ekoan Agnès* for unmarried women, and *Ekoan Benjamin*, also known as the *Confrérie de l'Enfant Jésus*, for unmarried men.[104] These

---

[99] ACSSp. 2J2.1a Journal de la Mission de Nlong, 22 mars 1929.
[100] ACSSp. 2J1.11a2 Confréries de Bikop, Mbalmayo, Obut, Oveng, 1936.
[101] ACSSp. 2J1.11a2 Visite du P. Salomon, Yokadouma, 15 jul 1939.
[102] ACSSp. 2J2.1a Journal de la Mission Saint Joseph de Kribi, 14 novembre 1926.
[103] "Les femmes de l'Ekoan Maria à l'honneur, *Cameroon Tribune*, 27 mars 2011; Théorine Nicole Efiri Nziou, "Ebolowa: La Confrérie de Marie, "Ekoan Maria," s'implante dans le diocèse," *L'Effort Camerounais*, 29 octobre 2009.
[104] Père Tobie Atangana, cited in Le Roy, *Un Martyr de La Morale Chrétienne, Le Père Henri de Maupeou de La Congrégation Du Saint-Esprit, Missionnaire Au Cameroun*, 68–73. Aloyse Kisito Patrice Essono, *L'annonce de l'Evangile Au Cameroun: L'oeuvre*

groups described themselves as "public associations in the service of the Catholic Church for a more human society."[105] They were committed to benevolent work in the domains of marriage and the family, such as counseling bachelors, recruiting women to catechism and service work, and urging families to reject bridewealth. Their members expressed deep consternation for the stresses and tensions that isolated youth from their villages, encouraged fierce competition between villagers, and burdened marriages with financial and political tensions.[106]

An exclusively male pious brotherhood was the *Confrérie de Saint Jean*, which was made up of unmarried and mostly unemployed males. These young Catholics were typically students, educated at mission schools and eager to enter into the professional cadres in cities and large towns but unable to secure a position for themselves. These young men were largely preoccupied with marriage concerns, primarily finding resources with which to pay bridewealth, or finding fathers who would agree to a marriage without it. Members of the *Confrérie de Saint Jean* recounted tales of "wife hoarding" and the high price of marriage where cash cropping had generously rewarded a certain cadre within the village who refused to relinquish their daughters without a payment that reflected their status.[107] This group discussed bridewealth during meetings, and its catechists and missionaries advocated that a man's labor and his salary was to be invested in the stability and the prosperity of the spousal couple, rather than used to satisfy the arbitrary demands of the bride's father.[108]

After his ordination in 1935, Father Simon Mpeke founded a new confraternity that was "both contemplative and activist," in being committed to promoting spiritual life, prayerful devotion, and social engagement among local

---

Missionnaire Des Pallottins de 1890 à 1916 et de 1964 à 2010 (Paris: Karthala, 2013), 214–15. And Criaud, "Etienne Nkodo: Le Premier Spiritan Camerounais." These groups in particular had gender-appropriate saints who had moral lessons regarding marriage for their members. The *ekoan* for married men and women were named for the couple of the Holy Family, Mary and Joseph. The *ekoan* for unmarried women, *Ekoan Agnès*, was named for Saint Agnès, a Roman beauty known for her piety and rejection of marriage in favor of Christ's love, who was eventually martyred as a result of her confirmed chastity. *Ekoan Anna* was not named for the mother of the Virgin, but rather the Prophetess Anna (Luke 2:36–38), who remained a widow for life after being married only seven years. The *Confrérie de l'Enfant Jésus* termed their adherents "*Benjamins*," as they were called to be virtuous young men, like the Old Testament figure of Benjamin, son of Jacob and brother of Joseph. The trials of these holy figures were intended to inspire model behaviors among *ekoan* members.

[105] ACCSp. 2J1.7b4, Ekoan Maria.
[106] ACSSp. 2J2 1A, Journal de la mission catholique de Bikop, 1–2 mai 1941.
[107] ACSSp. 2J1.6.2 mariage department de Mbam.
[108] ACSSp. 2J1.15.b2 Mission d'Obouti-M'balmayo.

men.[109] He also launched a chapter of the *Confrérie du Très Saint Sacrement* in Douala (called *Lekwag Lepem* in Bakoko) in which he recruited local young men to join him in corporal mortification, fasting, and barefoot proselytism, imitating the work and passion of Jesus Christ.[110] In 1930, Mpeke, along with his fellow seminarian Jean-Oscar Aoué, also launched one of the most active and interventionist Catholic brotherhoods in Cameroon: the *Confrérie des Cinq Plaies de Jésus*.[111] This group primarily raised funds to engage in bride redemption, which meant making payments to polygamous men and husbands of child brides to redeem their wives.[112] The *Confrérie des Cinq Plaies'* funds were also used to relinquish women from debt-bonded labor, which kept them indentured to chiefs or wealthy plantation managers in exchange for protection from labor recruitment for roads or railways.[113]

Catholic nun Sister Germaine Ngo Nguidjol's account of her life relates her experience of being freed by the *Confrérie des Cinq Plaies de Jésus* from debt imprisonment on a chief-judge's farm in 1930. Given in marriage by her uncle as a child, Germaine Ngo escaped from her husband during a village fishing expedition and returned to her family. However, her husband soon found her and sued her for bridewealth repayment in the court of first instance

---

[109] Cador, *L'héritage de Simon Mpeke: prêtre de Jésus et frère universel*, 41–3.

[110] Soeur Catherine-Noël Inibena, "Aspects fondamentaux de la spiritualité de Baba Simon," unpublished manuscript, 1995, cited in Cador, 108–9.

[111] Translation: the Brotherhood of the Five Wounds of Jesus (referring to the five wounds of Christ in his hands, feet, and side, according to the Gospel of John (19) and the prophesy of the Psalms (22, 16). In various texts, the *Confrérie des Cinq Plaies* is referred to alternatively as the *Confréries des Saintes Plaies*. Each reference refers back to the group's struggle against bridewealth and engaging in bride redemption and financial assistance to women in servitude. Organizations under the name of *Confrérie des Cinq Plaies* have a very old history in Europe, with brotherhoods organized in Bordeaux and in Vyt-lès-Belvoir in Franche-Comté in the fifteenth century ("Confréries des Cinq Plaies," in Heinrich Joseph Wetzer, Benedikt Welte, and Isidore Goschler, *Dictionnaire Encyclopédique de La Théologie Catholique* (Paris: Gaume Frères et J. Duprey, 1865)). It is unclear how the organization or its name came to Cameroon.

[112] Whether these unions were ones the women wished to exit or which the *Confrérie* simply believed they should renounce is not explored in documentation. Cador, *L'héritage de Simon Mpeke: prêtre de Jésus et frère universel*. See also Kibénél Ngo Billong, *Noces de Grâce de La Congrégation Des Soeurs Servantes de Marie de Douala: 70 Ans d'existence*, 5.

[113] Pere Louis Barde, *Au Cameroun Avec M. Wilbois, Les Graves Problèmes de La Polygamie et de L'instruction* (Paris: Maison Mère des Peres du Saint-Esprit, 1934); Soeur Germaine Ngo Nguidjol in Kibénél Ngo Billong, *Noces de Grâce de La Congrégation Des Soeurs Servantes de Marie de Douala: 70 Ans d'existence*, 45–8. Jane Guyer describes the phenomenon of women given by their parents to influential chiefs as wives qua laborers when families desired to protect their daughters from *corvée* labor. See Guyer, "Beti Widow Inheritance and Marriage Law: A Social History," 205.

in Edea. Without the funds to repay her bridewealth (it had been paid to her uncle), she was taken into bondage by the tribunal chief who impressed her into work on his farm to recover the debt. Père Albert Krummenacker, a priest with the nearby Catholic mission, informed the *Confrérie des Cinq Plaies* of Germaine's plight, who paid her bridewealth debt and liberated her from the judge. The *confrérie* placed her in a Christian family, baptized her, and entered her into the *pré-postulat* (pre-noviciate) in Edea in 1932, after which she entered religious life at the Convent in Ngovayang in 1939. Germaine Ngo Nguidjol's testimony illustrates that victims like her could expect little intervention from the civil administration in cases of an extortive tribunal chief. It also demonstrates how much power Christian men assumed and the bold acts they authorized in the name of religious reform.[114]

The *Confrérie's* intercessions on behalf of women in "un-Christian" marital and labor configurations exemplified the disciplinarian and aggressively reformist mentality of many socio-religious collectives in French-administered Cameroon. Catechists in the *Confrérie des Cinq Plaies* disregarded questions of female agency and pursued emancipation in gendered terms – designating themselves liberators as well as caretakers of the more vulnerable sex. Moreover, they intentionally provoked societal elders such as family fathers, chiefs, and male guardians in order to depict them as retrograde and rapacious, and more importantly, incapable of being moral leaders.[115] Acts like those of the *Confrérie des Cinq Plaies* and their near-exclusive focus on youth endorsement and marriage renovation engendered local chiefs' hostility for both Catholic and Protestant missions.

Although pious confraternities were largely the domain of men and male Christian leaders, women were also effective evangelists, and not only through escaping their own unchristian marriages or forging new companionate unions. In 1926, the women's chapter of the *Confrérie de la Sainte Vièrge* in Kribi recruited dozens of women to the *sixa* at the Kribi mission. The women of *la Sainte Vièrge* in Kribi continued their efforts through the 1930s, and often could operate without arousing the same suspicion as male catechists as they did not pay bridewealth to redeem wives or have the same propensity to engage in physical confrontations.[116] Women in confraternal organizations and

---

[114] In her account, Soeur Germaine describes Père Krummenacker and the *confrérie* as "brave" for intervening where colonial authorities "dared not interfere." Account of Soeur Germaine Ngo Nguidjol in Kibénél Ngo Billong, *Noces de Grâce de La Congrégation Des Soeurs Servantes de Marie de Douala: 70 Ans d'existence*, 45–8.

[115] Owono Nkoudou, "Le Problème Du Mariage Dotal Au Cameroun Français," 76–7. See also Soeur Germaine Ngo Nguidjol in Kibénél Ngo Billong, *Noces de Grâce de La Congrégation Des Soeurs Servantes de Marie de Douala: 70 Ans d'existence*, 45–8.

[116] ACSSp. 2J2.1a Journal de la Mission Saint Joseph de Kribi, 4 avril 1926; 30 jan. 1927.

benevolent societies in Saa –which was headed by African priest Luc Bomba, Nsimalen, Mfoumasi, Yébé, and Massamena – also "shared instruction and methods" with catechists to "fight polygamy through charity."[117] Novices preparing to be nuns were no less aggressive in convincing women to leave un-Christian marriages and recruiting widows to join women's religious orders.[118]

Reports from the early 1930s attest that male-dominated confraternities such as the *Confrérie de l'Adoration Réparatrice*, the *Confrérie de Saint Joseph*, and newer collectives such as the *Confrérie du Bienheureux Charles Lwangué*,[119] another brotherhood of unmarried men, were paying bridewealth to fathers, husbands, and chiefs to liberate women from unwanted domestic arrangements and displaying flexibility in converting polygamists who wanted to choose the spouse to whom they would be bound sacramentally, rather than marry their first wife, per mission rules.[120] Male confraternities were also known to compel obedience from and mete out discipline to their own members, and were especially strict when policing ecclesial loyalties. In 1929, an Ewondo man in the *Confrérie du Très Saint Sacrement* was caught making a "pagan sacrifice," after which the group deliberated whether to expel him from the brotherhood or have him face "exemplary public punishment."[121] Between 1946 and 1947, Père Luc Bell faced death threats from his confraternal brothers, including his kin, for leaving the priesthood to join the American Presbyterian Church.[122]

Confraternities positioned the loving, consensual, monogamous union as a spiritual ideal in which all African men should engage, but also worked to make the transformation of African society into a collective of monogamous families a realistic possibility. This demonstrated not only Christians' sympathy for those who lacked a spouse and progeny, but also created the operative structure that forged solidarities between men and communities through which they could reduce hardship. In 1935, a missionary report on the missions around Lobetal and Douala noted that among members of the *confréries*, "charity reigns" and that believers joined in marriage by the

---

[117] ACSSp. 2J1.11a2 Rapports de Missions de Saa, Nsimalen, Mfoumasi, Yébé, Massamena, 1939.
[118] ACSSp. 2J1.11a2 Soeurs missionnaires de St. Esprit, 1939; Sixa de Batouri, 16 août 1939; Doumé catéchistes et Sixa, 1939.
[119] This brotherhood was named after Charles Lwanga, a nineteenth-century Ugandan Catholic convert who was martyred by a king for enforcing Christian standards of chastity and decency among converts.
[120] ACSSp. 2J1.5b6 Mgr. Le Mailloux, "Le coutumier du vicariat apostolique de Douala," 1940.
[121] ACSSp. 2J2.1a Journal de la Mission de Nlong, Sept. 27, 1929.
[122] SMEP/DEFAP EEC FB divers 2/2, La conversion de Luc Bell.

brotherhoods "continued to live together with their parents like members of the same family."[123] Christians' emphasis on marriage, a man's right to a wife and descendants – in essence, a right to posterity – was a means of establishing the ultimate purpose of the faith as a way to cement and repair the notion of the stable family.

Embedding the Church in Africa through Confraternal Organizing

Beginning in 1930, with the vast expansion of church and chapel construction led by catechists and lay organizations and the increased territorial ranges and intercessions of Christian activists, French Catholic mission leaders were forced to admit they had little control or oversight of evangelical work in Cameroon. By the mid-1930s, Mgr. Vogt was "struck by the spirit of independence of certain catechists," and accused many missionaries of "negligence" for "not controlling the work of mission annexes," insisting that mission superiors must visit each annex "at least once per year."[124] In 1935, one missionary defended himself against such criticism, writing, "A single missionary oversees two to three thousand Christians and at least twenty catechist posts. We cannot visit all the villages."[125] Père le Dez, a missionary in Samba, simply reported back that the *confréries* were doing righteous, important work, and while they were "less restrained," more oversight was unnecessary.[126] Père Biechy, who inspected the Samba Mission in 1936, did, however, note that "access is difficult" around Samba and that the "humid climate," along with "one day's walk to the river or three days' walk to the nearest town," affected the health of the missionaries.[127] Thus, Père le Dez, who was the sole missionary there between 1927 and 1931, and Pères Perono and Kapps, who took over in 1935, generally left the organizing of apostolic life to local believers. Missionary reports from other, newer missions like Omvan and Etudi, which were annex missions of Yaoundé, or Medzek, which was farther east, or Bikop, Obut, and Oveng, which were annexes of Mbalmayo (see Map 6), likewise reported that catechists and pious confraternities were "independent" since their missions were "congested" and the French missionary was "alone with

---

[123] ACSSp. 2J1.11a2 Rapport sur les missions de Lobetal de Douala, 1935.
[124] ACSSp. 2J1.10.13 lettre de Mgr. Vogt à tous les missions, Mvolyé, 30 juin 1935; ACSSp. 2J1.11.a2 lettre de Mgr. F.X. Vogt, mars 1936.
[125] ACSSp. 2J1.10.13 lettre a Mgr. Vogt, 30 jul. 1935.
[126] ACSSp. 2J1.11.a2 Père le Dez, Journal de la Mission de Samba, nov. 1931.
[127] ACSSp. 2J1.11a2 R.P. Biechy, Résidence de Saint Thérèse de l'enfant Jésus de Samba, 1936.

thousands of Catholics."¹²⁸ In contast, confraternal members far exceeded the organizational skills of French missionaries. Between 1935 and 1938, the annex mission of Nkilzok saw eight French priests come and leave again as a result of sickness or reassignment to other, needier stations. Despite this, in 1938, the local confraternity of the Nkilzok congregation collected an astonishing 27,000 francs in tithes, and "assembled each week for prayer and services, religious instruction, and practical counsel."¹²⁹

The wealth of evidence in the Spiritan archives that reveals the unflagging efforts of catechists and confraternal members to reach deeply secluded forest communities not only speaks to the diligence of local leaders, but also to the relative quiescence of many French missionaries on the ground, who yielded to more energetic, locally acquainted evangelists. In contrast to studies of French Senegal, where Catholic missionaries possessively retained control over their fields of influence, Africans gained greater jurisdictional authority in southern Cameroon.¹³⁰ However, much like in Senegal, pathways to advancement to higher-level ecclesiastical positions such as the priesthood or bishopric were similarly restricted.

Urbanization and Protestant Fraternal Assistance

While Catholic missions organized their largest congregations and affiliated organizations in the rural southern forest zones, Protestant social organizations largely grew in influence in urban and peri-urban areas, where they connected with itinerant men and migrants who lived and worked in both rural and urban spaces in order to circulate ideas, give sermons, share the Gospel, organize retreats, distribute newspapers, and generally work to "prevent negative influences such as consumerism, alcoholism, and degeneracy."¹³¹ Through various Protestant organizations, the most common of which was the *associa-*

---

[128] Père Dehon described himself as "alone" in the Nkol-Nkoumou mission in 1936. ACSSp. 2J1.11a2 R.P. Biechy, Rapport sur la Mission de Nkol-Nkoumou, 1926; also ACSSp. 2J1.11a2 R.P. Biechy, Rapports, Missions de Etudi, Omvan, Medzek, Bikop, Mbalmayo, Obut, Oveng, 1936.

[129] ACSSp. 2J1.11a2 Rapport de la Mission de Nkilzok, 1939. To put this amount in perspective, catechists, who were often salaried, only earned between five and fifteen francs per month.

[130] Foster, *Faith in Empire: Religion, Politics, and Colonial Rule in French Senegal, 1880–1940*, 174–5.

[131] Jean-Henri Tiandong, "Cameroun: Croix-Bleue Camerounaise, la Lutte Contre l'Alcoolisme la Réglementation," *Actes et Travaux de la Première Conférence Interafricaine Antialcoolique*, organisée sous le patronage de l'Union Internationale Contre l'Alcoolisme et du Haut Comité d'Étude et d'Information sur l'Alcoolisme, par le Comité d'Action Antialcoolique en Côte d'Ivoire à Abidjan du 23 au 30 juillet 1956, 393.

tion synodale, there came to be a more public and synergetic domain where the idea of the Christian man and a Christian society – characterized by education, responsibility, and consciousness of rights and duties – began to take root. Protestant organization meeting minutes reflect that leaders believed that migrants and newcomers to cities were "more vulnerable" than village men, and in need of guidance as well as a moral anchor.[132] African Protestant pastors and catechists expressed a palpable fear akin to that of the French official who quoted Rousseau (*"la civilisation déprave"*), worrying that too much development might have deleterious consequences on African morals.[133] Much like their rural counterparts, African Protestant evangelists assumed considerable jurisdiction over urban missionary fields.

The Protestant Mission celebrated the fact that monogamous marriages were more and more common, and that young couples married at a greater rate conforming to Christian dogma, based on mutual consent and without bridewealth. However, they were unable to safeguard these marriages against divorce and conflict, particularly among urbanite couples. Protestant mission records are rife with parishioners' complaints against spouses and accounts of abuse, abandonment, neglect, and infidelity.[134] These accounts fortified certain pastors and catechists' belief that greater attachment to Christianity through the proliferation of social action groups would allow for the flourishing of enduring marital relations and stabilize the monogamous family, still considered in its early stages among much of the populace.[135] The Baptist churches in Douala termed their strategy for continually seeking new recruits and actively evangelizing in poorer areas *Komabe madiba ponda na ponda*, or "pouring water over and over," which summarized pastors' beliefs that steady and unremitting social outreach would discourage prostitution, illegitimate births, and drinking.[136] Mark Hunter has chronicled how urban areas reworked male sexuality in colonial and postcolonial Kwa-Zulu Natal, fashioning an alternative urban

[132] French Protestant mission leader Jean-René Brutsch believed that religious faith was stronger in rural areas than urban areas and that rural–urban migration caused a loss of faith communities and weakened moral values. Brutsch, "A Glance at Missions in Cameroon," 306.
[133] Jones, *The Life of Rowland Hill Evans of Cameroun*, 200–1.
[134] ANC 2AC 7708 Raphael Zali, Gongou Adoh divorce, 1940; SMEP/DEFAP 52.066 B.132 Suggestions pour les cultes de femmes: être chrétienne au Cameroun, être chrétienne dans sa famille, Douala 1956; SMEP/DEFAP EEC FB divers 2/2 L'enquete sur la mortalité infantile (100 foyers catéchistes ou pasteurs) étude Jean-René Brutsch, 1948 Douala.
[135] Station de Douala, Rapport Général de la Mission du Cameroun, 1943, *Journal des Missions Évangéliques*, 1944, 97–8; SMEP/DEFAP EEC FB 1/2 Consécration de deux pasteurs à Douala, 7 nov. 1945.
[136] SMEP/DEFAP EEC FB 1/2, Rapport au Synode Général de Douala, Janvier 1958.

masculinity as a result of exposure to "immoral" influences that embraced criminality and subversion, while simultaneously forging a counter-culture that defined manhood through marriage, home life, and restrained visions of sexual dominance.[137] In interwar Cameroon, African Protestant social activists rejected "modern" attachments to masculine status such as multiple sex partners, and forged ideals based on longstanding cultural conceptions of masculine responsibility, headship, and control as they related to formally recognized marriage and founding a household with children. French Protestant congregations in big cities –particularly in Douala – strongly supported the development of male urbanite magnanimity as a character trait that would promote social conscience. Religious associations would actually leverage the deleterious social environment to stimulate Christian men's sense of moral superiority and incentivize them to take on leadership positions both in their households and in their communities.[138]

Thus, while urbanization and rural–urban migration presented new opportunities to sin and fall from grace, these same temptations allowed for the greater circulation of evangelical messages, larger and more diverse church attendance, public prayer, and the expansion of socio-religious organizations. The highly public dimension of Christianity led to new forms of sociability where gender mixing, cooperative engagement in catechism, and congregation-led charitable outreach contributed to the formation of an ethnically and economically diverse public with a gradually unified set of ambitions for public and private life.

Temperance, Moral Concerns, and Mutual Aid

Managing Christian communities was harder in big cities, even when armed with a powerful message. The most widespread Protestant-based socio-religious collective in Cameroon was the *Croix Bleue*, a temperance society devoted to eliminating alcohol use and dependence among African men for the benefit of African marriages and families, which was sponsored by the Evangelical and Baptist Churches of the French Protestant Mission. Founded in 1876 in Bern by Louis-Lucien Rochat, a pastor with the Swiss Reformed Church, the *Croix Bleue* was brought to Cameroon by Pastor Pierre Galland as

---

[137] Mark Hunter, "Cultural Politics and Masculinities: Multiple-Partners in Historical Perspective in KwaZulu-Natal," *Culture, Health & Sexuality* 7, no. 4 (August 2005): 389–403.
[138] "Le Droit de l'Homme et la Femme," *Bulletin de la Société des Missions Évangeliques de Paris*, Société des Missions Évangéliques de Paris, Paris: Eglise Loi de Dieu, 1928.

a branch of the *Société Française de Tempérance de la Croix-Bleue*.[139] Known as *Mbas'a Blu* in Duala, it quickly gained ground in Cameroon as a brotherhood that aimed to contribute to the "history of communities doing good" (*mwemba ma myango ma bwam*) among Christians primarily in metropolitan areas like Douala and the Yabassi region.[140]

Like the Catholic *confréries*, *Croix Bleue* chapters (*Mwemba ma Mbas'a Blu*) were led by young Africans eager to assume leadership of associations with reformist inclinations. Protestant Pastors Gotliep Soppo and Ebonji led the *Croix Bleue* in expanding their presence in coastal Cameroon during the interwar years, and believed that marriage practices had changed with urbanization in large part because of men's exposure to alcohol, bars, and nightlife – temptations that were practically non-existent in rural areas or villages. They believed that alcohol's effects on men's morals resulted in prostitution and men's isolation from family life, which the *Croix Bleue* had a duty to remedy through "creating unanimity in the anti-alcoholic struggle."[141]

Pastors Soppo and Ebonji believed men could be reformed by granting them greater responsibilities in the Church community. Thus, *Croix Bleue* members could participate as *adhérents*, *confirmants*, *membres actifs*, or *membres correspondants*. Each form of membership signified a different level of inclusion in the association and the Protestant Church, and designated the member's responsibilities at their level in the hierarchy. All *adhérents* and *confirmants* were expected to distribute pamphlets, gather alcoholics or at-risk men for meetings and church services, and exhort young, sober, devout men to "shame drunk men who fall in the street and have children laughing

---

[139] For more on the history of the *Croix Bleue* in Europe, see Sophie Rossier, *La Flamme Sous La Cendre* (Geneva: Coédition Ouvertures et la Croix-Bleue, 2007); Henri Daulte, *Le Livre Du Jubilé 1877–1927. Histoire Des Cinquante Premières Années De La Croix-Bleue* (Lausanne: Agence de la Croix-Bleue, 1927). See also Hans Schaffner, *Im Dienst an Menschen Und Völkern: Das Blaue Kreuz, Ein Missions- Und Liebeswerl von Weltweiter Bedeutung* (Bern: Blaukreuzverlag, 1958). The *Croix Bleu Camerounaise* is currently active in seven out of the ten provinces of Cameroon. It receives financial subvention and support from the government, as well as NGO and religious organizations. It hosts conferences, seminars, and round tables, and works in youth education to fight alcoholism – Cameroon's national alcohol consumption is one of the highest on the African continent with an estimated 2 million liters consumed annually. Karine Koum'enioc, "Cameroun : Les Autorités En Difficulté Avec Les Débits de Boisson," *Journal Du Cameroun*, September 15, 2009.

[140] SMEP/DEFAP EEC FB 2/2, "Statut de la Société de Tempérance de la Croix-Bleue des églises chrétiennes du Cameroun à Yabassi," 1930.

[141] SMEP/DEFAP EEC FB 2/2, "Statut de la Société de Tempérance de la Croix-Bleue des églises chrétiennes du Cameroun à Yabassi," 1930.

at them" and "correct the sins of their fathers."[142] Others were assigned various duties maintaining and repairing churches and chapels and recruiting new members to the organization.

The *Croix Bleue* was explicitly concerned with alcohol's deleterious effect on African marriages and natality. Chapter leaders broadcasted alcohol's contribution to divorce, venereal disease, infertility, impotence (and by extension, the low birth rate), adultery, prostitution, and "the demoralization of the sexual purpose" in sermons and prayers. *Croix Bleue* pamphlets promised "joy and life of the heart" and "a peaceful home, happy children, and a smiling wife" to those who committed to abiding by the group's strict abstinent policies and joined the ranks as a temperance reformer in their communities.[143] Crucially, members touted alcohol use as a form of moral indiscipline that threatened not only personal reputation and behavior, but also the degeneration of African culture and population. Africans allied with the *Croix* Bleue assumed their role as "warriors against alcoholism" in order to "defend against the sadness of the progressive weakening of our beautiful and strong race."[144] By creating cohorts of affiliation and emphasizing collective success and failure through either Christian adherence or faithlessness, Soppo and Ebonji sought to make Protestants and *Croix Bleue* members a moral unit, dedicated to creating and maintaining a particular social order with shared values. This communal unanimity proved very effective, particularly in generating ethical discourses that emphasized monogamous, enduring marriage and loving approaches to family-building as natural corollaries to sobriety.

The *Croix Bleue* was active in peri-urban and rural areas as well. Jean-Henri Tiandong, a pastor in the Evangelical Church who would become president of the *Croix Bleue du Cameroun* in 1956, worked as a catechist and *Croix Bleue* organizer in the village of Nyokon-Ndikinimeki in the Mbam region during the interwar years, and organized catechist visits to isolated villages where he observed increasing alcohol consumption and its effect on village life.[145] Oil palm grew prolifically in Mbam, and during his tenure in the area, Tiandong witnessed the growth of palm wine consumption in work camps, villages, and large cities alike. Before concessionary exploitation, palm wine had been harvested in limited quantities by collecting small amounts of sap from a living tree. Large casks of palm wine would only become available when an

---

[142] SMEP 63.050 3.220, *Mam m'anambe enyin ya melu ma: kalate II, ajo alcool* (Ebolowa: Halsey Memorial Press, 1953); SMEP 11.133 B70, *Statuts et Règelements de la Société Camerounaise d'Abstinence "La Croix Bleue,"* 1953.

[143] SMEP/DEFAP EEC FB 2/2 "Mieka ma Mwemba ma Mbas'a Blu: ma Miemba ma Bonkakristo ma Kamerun," 1930.

[144] SMEP/DEFAP EEC FB 2/2 "Guerre à l'alcoolisme," 1937.

[145] Tiandong, *L'autobiographie Du Pasteur Jean-Henri Tiandong de l'E.E.C.*, 36–40.

entire palm would be felled and all the sap would be collected at once, which occurred only at celebrations or feast days. As regular oil palm harvesting and concessionary logging expanded during the 1920s and 1930s, African laborers felled trees by the thousands, giving them access to much greater quantities of palm sap than ever before.[146]

Government records corroborate Christian activists' concerns over growing alcohol consumption in the Cameroon territory. In 1922, the administration sought to collect greater revenues from liquor distribution and thus legislated the requirement of licenses to sell alcohol and criminalized all local means of alcohol brewing, limiting rural dwellers' access to palm sap from which to make palm wine in the hopes of encouraging consumption of imported European alcohols.[147] However, it was considerably more difficult to tax and regulate the local beer and palm wine trade than the sale and purchase of imported beers and liquors, and thus local alcohol remained more widely popular and lucrative as an underground business, particularly in towns and cities.[148] In the 1920s and 1930s, rural dwellers with a surfeit of palm wine from felled palms began establishing *buvettes*, or *ad hoc* bars, in tents or sheds in forest villages, worksites, and migrant corridors, which sold the wine and eventually sold imported beers, wines, and liquors. By 1939, the administration's concern over indigenous alcoholism compelled officials to *increase* rather than decrease the number of liquor licenses issued to Africans in Douala in order to expand government surveillance of drinking establishments and their clients.[149]

Tiandong blamed the new *buvette* culture as well as the transformation of practices in felling palms for serious increases in alcoholism. He preached to rural communities that he had seen "entire villages emptied because of alcohol-related social degeneration," which included domestic abuse, low fertility, and family abandonment.[150] Tiandong also preached that "fifty percent

---

[146] ANOM AGEFOM 799/1857, Commerce Forestiere, 1917–1918; Compagnies Forestiere et Sangha-Cubangui, 1918; ANOM AGEFOM 151/5, Décret sur les fôrets, 9 juillet 1925, exploitations forestières, 1923–1936.

[147] *Rapport Annuel du Gouvernement Français*, 1921, 11; *Journal Officiel du Cameroun*, July 17, 1922.

[148] Lynn Schler, "Looking through a Glass of Beer: Alcohol in the Cultural Spaces of Colonial Douala, 1910–1945," *International Journal of African Historical Studies* 35, no. 2–3 (2002): 315–34.

[149] ANC APA 11680/B, Alcool Affaires diverses 1927–1944, le Délégué du Haut Commissaire de la République à Monsieur le Haut Commissaire de la République, 16 August 1939.

[150] A 1950 official French report on the village of Ndikinimeki confirmed that "high migration rates" had caused Ndikinimeki and the surrounding region in Bafia to have "lost a third of their population" to "alcoholism and diseases like sleeping sickness," ANOM FM SJ 1, Rapport sur Bafia, Justice de Paix à Competence Etendue, 18 juillet 1950.

of divorces are due to alcoholism as well as the majority of incidences of incest, which psychiatrists today call 'Saturday night incest' because of its link with the lack of self-control men exhibit on days of rest." He continued, "In villages and cities ... family fathers pass their evenings in bars, leaving their wives and children to suffer ... some acquire humiliating nicknames like 'barrel' or 'all-gone' ... These men are sinful, dirty, and degraded."[151]

Tiandong was also influenced by the Presbyterian Church in Mbam, whose pastors preached "To be Christian is to be sober," and tapped into Nyokon villagers' local pride, stating that the inhabitants were "not to behave like the Bassa" of the big towns of Edea, Sakbayemé, and Yabassi, who were "perpetually inebriated." While Tiandong knew that rural people were not paragons of self-discipline and moral superiority, he developed within the *Croix Bleue* a code of "traditional values" of work, restraint, piety, and modesty, which he claimed were embodied by those who embraced Christianity as a means of recapturing the moderation and stability of pre-industrial life.[152] Through *Croix Bleue* meetings, narratives of "preserving" African men, women, and youth from depravity circulated throughout rural and urban spaces. Young men and women proved most adherent to abstemious policies and attended services the most regularly, giving hope to ministers and priests that the next generation could be "preserved" or "guarded" in their pure, devout, earnest forms.[153]

As the *Croix Bleue* grew from 500 African Protestant *adhérents* in 1934 to a membership of over 3000 by 1950, its members developed a rhetoric of discipline, linking abstinence with family stability and moral righteousness, and casting out members for infractions.[154] The Protestant Church would also forbid members who had fallen from the good graces of the community to participate in *Croix Bleue* events and outreach. Exacting discipline and the policing of behavior fostered an aggressively prohibitionist attitude toward alcohol consumption, production, and distribution among many members, which

---

[151] Jean-Henri Tiandong, "Cameroun: Croix-Bleue Camerounaise, la Lutte Contre l'Alcoolisme la Réglementation," *Actes et Travaux de la Première Conférence Interafricaine Antialcoolique*, organisée sous le patronage de l'Union Internationale Contre l'Alcoolisme et du Haut Comité d'Étude et d'Information sur l'Alcoolisme, par le Comité d'Action Antialcoolique en Côte d'Ivoire à Abidjan du 23 au 30 juillet 1956, 389.

[152] SMEP/DEFAP 63.050 3.220, *Mam m'anambe enyin ya melu ma: kalate II, ajo alcool* (Ebolowa, Halsey Memorial Press, 1953).

[153] Jean-Henri Tiandong, "Cameroun: Croix-Bleue Camerounaise, la Lutte Contre l'Alcoolisme la Réglementation," *Actes et Travaux de la Première Conférence Interafricaine Antialcoolique,* organisée sous le patronage de l'Union Internationale Contre l'Alcoolisme et du Haut Comité d'Étude et d'Information sur l'Alcoolisme, par le Comité d'Action Antialcoolique en Côte d'Ivoire à Abidjan du 23 au 30 juillet 1956, 393.

[154] SMEP/DEFAP, Rapport à la conference des missionnaires de 1934; Rapport de Charles Boury à la conference des missionnaires de 1950.

extended to beliefs regarding the legality of polygamy, divorce (for Christian monogamists), abortion, and other taboo acts.[155] In the postwar period, the *Croix Bleue* would become one of the strongest proponents for the institution of vice laws in the post-independence period and for the renewal of African society through rigid legislation and community covenants.

Conclusion

As indigenous religious leaders gained in number and interpreted the emancipating discourses of Christianity to an increasingly literate, mobile, and worldly public, most foreign missionaries were relegated to the margins of pastoral work while Africans devoted themselves to activism and intercession on behalf of believers in distress. The result of widespread and participatory African-led Christian evangelism was that during the second decade of French rule, religious marriage reformers consciously took aim at individuals and influences that compelled their fellow believers to deny their religious obligations. Thus, African catechists, pastors, and priests were the principal interlocutors through which conceptions and objectives for marriage and family life were understood, granting them a privileged position in the dramatic transitions taking place in African societies. The following chapter details some notable exceptions to this, and in particular, the case of Père François Pichon, who, throughout the 1930s, devoted himself to the challenging work of visiting small villages and isolated settlements, recording conversion experiences, and documenting the horrific violence perpetrated against men, women, and children by the colonial regime. Throughout the 1930s, Pichon walked the long roads and railways alongside catechists and confraternal members and created an archive of slavery and abuse of African populations in worksites to provide evidence to support his emancipation and rescue strategies for the most brutally exploited.[156]

While Christian activists struggled to ensure that African couples were not strained or separated by forced labor, village dislocation, or integration into a chief's household, the French administration worked on an antipodean aim, perpetuating an authority structure that they believed would be able to discipline the rural social order.[157] However, occasionally, colonial officials

---

[155] Texte No. 6, Lettre du Secrétaire Général de la Fédération des Eglises et Missions Evangéliques du Cameroun et de l'Afrique Equatoriale au sujet de la polygamie, Fédération des Églises et Missions Évangéliques du Cameroun et de l'Afrique Equatoriale, Secrétariat Général Yaoundé le 26 Août 1952.

[156] Pichon's work is examined in detail in Laburthe-Tolra, *Vers La Lumiere? Ou, Le Désir d'Ariel: A Propos Des Beti Du Cameroun: Sociologie de La Conversion*.

[157] ACSSp. 2J1.7b4, Rapport du Conférence, Mgr. René Graffin, Docteur Louis-Paul Aujoulat, Conference Jan 19, 1946, Les milieux sociaux du Cameroun. See also Louis

questioned chiefs and their motives and wavered from supporting "traditional leaders" when they became worried that chiefs "destroy the clan community, on which much of social life is based."[158]

By the mid-1930s, African Christians were strong enough in number that they did not have to battle chiefs alone. In response to this confrontation, chiefs accused many of their critics of the crime of "degrading the prestige" of chiefdom and custom.[159] Without a sense of eminence and communal reverence, African communities would collapse, they warned.[160] African Christians countered that that it was the chiefs, themselves, who had eroded the prestige of their office, and that political authority was not the same as moral authority. Competition over marriage practices was therefore not only a rivalry for wives, status, and wealth, it was also a vigorous dispute about rights and ethics. Through religious engagement and pious activism, African Christian men learned and then claimed their new "rights" to wives, marriage, and families. They also learned their role as vectors for the rights and dignity of women, whose liberation and full humanity were yet incomplete.

The following two chapters reveal that male Christian leaders' devotional acts became more aggressive during the 1930s because they determined that religious transformation would require more authoritative and energetic male leaders who could influence social morals and exercise criticism more vigorously. Overall, these chapters demonstrate that in addition to sustaining ministerial vocations and implanting Christianity more deeply in everyday life through preaching, catechism, and performing pious works like bride redemption, church construction, and advocating temperance, the close interdependencies between African clergymen and catechists allowed for forceful agendas regarding marriage, the family, and women's guardianship to emerge. Together, these indigenous ministers developed a conceptual arsenal that attracted those who deplored the strife that spread from villages into cities, where the dispossessed sought escape from the impositions of *prestation* and extortion. This arsenal had three main positions of attack: the authoritarian rule of administration chiefs; the patriarchal oligopoly on marriage; and the moral deterioration of African society and African women in particular.

Ngongo, *Histoire des forces religieuses au Cameroun: de la première guerre mondiale à l'Indépendance* (Paris: Karthala, 1982), 80–100.

[158] ACSSp. 2J1.7b4, Rapport du Conférence, Mgr. René Graffin, Docteur Louis-Paul Aujoulat, Conference Jan 19, 1946, Les milieux sociaux du Cameroun.
[159] J.M. Carret, "La Crise Des Villages," *L'Effort Camerounais*, January 5, 1958, 118 edition.
[160] Carret.

CHAPTER 7

African Agents of the Church and State: Male Violence and Productivity

Confrontation and Command

In spring and summer 1930, chiefs and police recruiting laborers for the Mbalmayo–Ngulmekong and Abong Mbang–Doumé roads became increasingly desperate. As men fled to cities or ventured deep into forests with confraternal brothers, recruiters rounded up the remaining women and girls – often with babies tied to their backs – and forced them to march thirty or forty kilometers to worksites to remove earth and rock.[1] Père François Pichon witnessed Chief Tsama Okoa whipping his recruits mercilessly, and heard accounts from villagers that Chief Frédéric Foe, along with his police, raided villages in the middle of the night where he stripped his female captives naked and chained them together at the neck and wrist to drag them to construction zones.[2] When villagers returned home after several weeks – which they were only permitted to do in order to collect food – they shared accounts of their experiences with their spiritual leaders and warned their neighbors to hide themselves or find money for the *rachat*.[3] In April 1930, Père Pichon personally saw chiefs gather work gangs comprised exclusively of women and children for work on the Adjap–Bénébalot road.[4] With help from the local priest, the women of the Minlaba Mission, who were often recruited to work in the nearby Adjap worksites, wrote to Bishop Vogt to complain they were starved on the road under the pretext that as they were women, they could forage or harvest food wherever they were. They also related that they were beaten for refusing rotten food, denied Sunday rest, and that Angba, a catechist's wife, was beaten by a

[1] ACSSp. 2J1.10.12 lettre de Vogt, 6 mai 1930 au Gouverneur; Lettre de Bertaut à Mgr. Vogt, 29 avril 1930; ANC 1AC 3523 travaux forcés femmes enfants, Banebalot, 11 avril 1930.
[2] ACSSp. 2J1.10.12 lettre de Vogt, 6 mai 1930 au Gouverneur.
[3] ACSSp. 2J1.10.12, Lettre de Mgr Vogt au Gov., 14 avril 1930.
[4] ACSSp. 2J1.10.12 Rapport des Pères Pichon et Mader de la Mission Catholique de Milaba au sujet des travaux imposés aux enfants et aux femmes par les services administratifs, 8 juin 1930.

chief for opposing a small girl's recruitment.⁵ The women of Minlaba also protested abuses they saw of other workers: wardens and police knocking out an elderly man's teeth with matraques, workers coughing up blood, and demands to fetch palm wine for guards.⁶

Governor Marchand was the most resolute in his denial of such incidents. In 1930, he responded to Mgr. Vogt's criticisms regarding forced labor: "My administration does not have to justify itself to certain unqualified observers."⁷ In another letter, Marchand responded that missionaries' testimonies of women's *prestation* were "flagrant inexactitudes." "Native administrative auxiliaries," he clarified, "have a strict and formal duty to recruit no woman, girl, or child, for roadwork."⁸ Administration officials were more candid in their correspondence with one another, however. French inspector Guibert acknowledged that "natives are molested and hurt by the violence of guards on patrol" and "natives will flee in droves ... we must have more control by agents of authority."⁹

Although it was unlikely the result of missionary pressure, chiefs and the local *commandement indigène* did adjust their strategies for recruiting women. In April 1931, the Catholic mission in Abong Mbang intercepted a letter bound for the French head of subdivision from an overseer in the Compagnie Forestière Sangha Oubangui, which maintained work camps in Mampang and Abong Mbang, which stated:

> Do not accept laborers who have more than one wife and leave the women in households with many wives because they need to perform work on the farms. Taking women from large farms will cause a depletion of food production. Foodstuffs need a community around them to make them grow. Only those with one wife, who will not contribute much to this work, can be recruited.¹⁰

Père Pichon's outrage at this plan was matched by that of local Christian husbands. For years, Christians in southern Cameroon had felt unfairly persecuted

---

⁵ ACSSp. 2J1.10.12 Père Pichon, l'Esclavage au Cameroun sous le régime de la puissance mandataire, 9 mars 1930.

⁶ ACSSp. 2J1.10.12, Père Pichon, Arbitraire des Agents de la Force Publique, Minlaba, 15 juin 1930; ACSSp. 2J1.10.12 Père Pichon, l'Esclavage au Cameroun sous le régime de la puissance mandataire, 9 mars 1930.

⁷ ACSSp. 2J1.10.12 lettre de Gov. Marchand à Mgr. Vogt, "femmes mortes," 1930.

⁸ ACSSp. 2J1.10.12 Rapport des Pères Pichon et Mader de la Mission Catholique de Milaba au sujet des travaux imposés aux enfants et aux femmes par les services administratifs, 8 juin 1930.

⁹ ANOM AGEFOM 989/3424 Guibert à le chef de circ. de Ngaoundéré, 26 jul. 1932.

¹⁰ ACSSp. 2J1.10.12, Père François Pichon, Doumé, 1930–31, Lettre de M. Soret, Compagnie Forestière Sangha Oubanghi (CFSO), Mampang à le chef de subdivision de Doumé, M. Cazal, avril 1931.

by forced labor, not only for the punishing toil and risks of hunger, disease, and assaults, but also because their monogamous households suffered more greatly from the lack of a wife than polygamous ones. One chief complained in a 1929 Council of Notables session, "Christian men refuse to allow their wives to clean the village of unhygienic elements and weed and sweep the forest paths ... they believe that pagans' wives should do the work because they are more numerous and less needed at home!"[11] After local Christians in Minlaba heard of the concessionary companies' request that the *commandement indigène* target only small households, many men took their wives to the mission to hide in the *sixa* schools.[12]

As authorities who gave a gathering command, both African chiefs and Christian leaders were uniquely positioned to assume control over productive or prestigious elements. It was in chiefs' interests to support administrative and concessionary strategies to concentrate female workers on large farms – which they typically operated and controlled – and use the small family workforces to staff the more grueling work on the roads and railways. By 1932, however, even some French officials noted that in busy circuit points like Sangmélima, "this system of chiefs' polygamy ... has indicated incontestably gruesome repercussions on natality, hygiene, and morals. The woman slave and victim of polygamous organization lives in primitive, degrading, and quasi-animal conditions."[13] This kind of flagrant abuse and iniquity, however, served the missions by stimulating righteously indignant assemblies who organized philanthropic outreach to prevent or resist it. In response to Christians' criticisms' of and interferences in government-sanctioned endeavors, though, officials in the administration rallied around one another. One regional official wrote, "We must engage in incessant surveillance ... chiefs must be reinforced by the *commandement indigène* by a variety of measures."[14]

Christian mutual assistance and volitional work emerged during the 1930s as a profoundly productive, and indeed, destabilizing movement in the Cameroon territory. The power and influence of religious authority in the territory forced the colonial government to confront the failures and uncomfortable inconsistencies of their civilizing mission, which fueled their distrust of indigenous and European spiritual leaders but also occasionally allowed for

---

[11] AFFPOL 2190/1 Conseil de Notables de la Circonscription d'Ebolowa, scéance du 19 nov. 1929.
[12] ACSSp. 2J1.10.12, "La polygamie," Journal du Père François Pichon, Doumé, 1930–31; AFFPOL 2192/6 Missions religieuses, gardiennage du Sixa, 1949–1954.
[13] ANOM AGEFOM 989/3424 Rapport de Guibert, Sangmélima, Ebolowa, 7 jul. 1932.
[14] ANOM TP Série 1 420/11 Rapport annuel adressée par le gouvernement français au conseil de la Société Des Nations sur l'administration sous mandat du territoire du Cameroun pour l'année 1931.

moments where certain officials considered alternative possibilities of rule. Mr. Trebos, the French head of the Bafia subdivision, decried the "twisted religious influence" of the missions, but also asked to his colleagues whether catechists like Jacques Nkouma, David Dapp, and Lucien Mbouma "could perhaps teach children to love France?"[15] In general, though, for African Christians in Cameroon, administrative strategies to curtail, criminalize, or constrain their work and devotionalism were largely unsuccessful and also strengthened their resolve to resist what they perceived as threats to the critical work of their community and its institutions.

Controlling Individual and Collective Action

The accelerated evolution of African-led pastoral organizing in Cameroon's Catholic and Protestant communities was startling to both denominational leaders and the colonial government. Mgrs. Mario Zanin and Carlo Salotti, Secretary General and President, respectively, of the Sacred Congregation of the Propaganda Fide in Rome, noted the rapid development of Christians in Africa and advised the French overseas ministry not to hamper the expansion of seminaries and indigenous priests in their colonies, mentioning that accounts of the African faithful's "tender eagerness brings tears to our eyes."[16] Cameroon's Catholic missions' letters to Rome since the early 1920s vividly described African church communities' reverence of the Holy Body and Blood, exuberant celebrations of feast days like Christmas, Ascension, Assumption, and All Saints' Day, and eager commitments to pious confraternities.[17] The French territorial administration in Cameroon, however, was neither swayed by officials in Rome nor by local French missionaries, and opposed and suppressed worship and religious organizing in unprecedented ways, beginning in the last years of the 1920s and continued to do so until the end of French rule.

The participatory dimension of Christian piety deeply disturbed French officials whose mission was to continually improve production and performance in the traditional sectors of the colonial economy such as infrastructure

---

[15] ANC 1AC 3523 Extrait du Rapport de Tournée: Mr. Trebos, chef de subdivision de Bafia, 8 june–1 juillet 1930, Inspection de la Mission protestante de Nitoukou.

[16] ANOM COL 1 AFFPOL 29 Mgr. Mario Zanin, Mgr. Carlo Salotti, Agence Internationale de Presse Fides, Rome, 4 dec. 1930, "Un appel en faveur de l'oeuvre de Saint Pierre Apôtre."

[17] ACSSp. 2J1.2b2 Rapport sur la Mission Catholique de Ngowayang, Paris, 27 avril 1920; ANOM COL 1 AFFPOL 29 Congrégation du Saint Esprit, "Campagne apostolique 1925–1926; ACSSp. 2J1.2b2 Mgr. Vogt, Division du Vicariat de Cameroun, 12 sept. 1927; ACSSp. 2J1.10.12 Rapport: l'oeuvre des Catéchistes indigènes au Vicariat apostolique du Cameroun, 1929.

and exports. As the flocks gathered to demonstrate their affiliation with the faith through sweat and servitude, the administration and its associated chiefs lost their ability to staff their own enterprises. As a result, the last years of the 1920s and the 1930s were periods of exceptional animosity between the Catholic and Protestant religious establishment and the French government in Cameroon. As French officials sought to expand export production and support the growth of concessionary operations in the southern forests, they came to view both the organizational management of Christian "workforces" and the activism of Christian ministers and confraternal organizations as dangerously political.

Perceiving Christians as enemies of rural productivity in the economic and infrastructural domains, the colonial government routinely dismissed the possibilities of African religious devotion, individual piety, or even theistic conviction, believing African Christians to be nothing more than rebels. In 1932, police commissioner de Calbiac wrote to Père Van Bulck:

> Christianization in Cameroon is superficial ... If the priests truly knew the natives, particularly the Ewondo, one of the most perverted and debased races in Africa, they would understand that. The crowds at the mission at Mvolyé are but trickery and misleading ... In other towns, similar hordes of Africans saying their confessions in the afternoons cannot possibly generate any real results.[18]

In addressing the upcoming consecration of the first African Catholic priests, de Calbiac also added,

> The missionary priests are forming a native clergy far too rapidly – this is already apparent now – and it cannot produce any serious results for the Church. As soon as we have native priests, the sacraments will be for sale and confession will have lost its meaning.[19]

Other French officials accused Pastor Douala Itondo of being a "suspect" for composing a Douala-German dictionary and "possess[ing] an intelligence above his background."[20] French officials were equally mistrustful of European Protestant and Catholic missionaries, accusing Baptists of being "Germanophile," Catholics of acting like "dominant, violent, fanatic, and

---

[18] ACSSp. 2J1.10.7 Père Van Bulck, S.J. avec Mr. de Calbiac, commissaire de police à Yaoundé, 17 mai 1932.
[19] ACSSp. 2J1.10.7 Père Van Bulck, S.J. avec Mr. de Calbiac, commissaire de police à Yaoundé, 17 mai 1932.
[20] ANC 2AC 9285 Mission Protestante, Pasteur Helmlinger; ANOM AGEFOM 799/1856 Notes de Bureau des Affaires Politiques, Question des Transfuges, lettres confidentielles, Labouret, 11 mai 1932, Truitard, 7 septembre 1932.

ultra-fundamentalist monks," and American Presbyterians of running a "citadel" mission that was "contrary to rapprochement with France."[21]

Administrative distrust and cynicism regarding African piety in Cameroon was part of a broader political strategy to delegitimize the missions and particularly their indigenous leaders by portraying them as agitators and usurpers, and to divert attention away from the corrupt and manipulative methods of government-allied chiefs, whose power they continued to uphold despite growing evidence of their own serious malfeasance. The failure of African chiefs to mold moral communities and preserve the integrity of African relational structures and hierarchies and their increasing dependence on violence to procure labor was all the more demoralizing for an administration that had to witness the astonishing diligence of African laborers who were loyal to Protestant and Catholic missions. In the same year as administrative officials discovered that Chief Zé Mendouga tortured his villagers to make them pay their taxes and devised midnight roundups of laborers who were then forced to march unclothed to worksites (which reduced the rate of escapes), they also acknowledged that at the Catholic mission in Ndikinimeki, "all who come to confess ... work without a salary. The work is hard ... All are unsalaried. In return, the catechist Martin Batikalak feeds the catechumens and the students.[22]

Trying to Halt the Spread of Christianity

Governor Marchand's antagonism toward missionary work had been evident since the early 1920s, when he dismissively informed all heads of mission that "teachings on agriculture" would be "more useful than teachings about monogamy" and that he expected "no less than total submission" from African catechists to the administrative directives of chiefs.[23] Like his successor (who had also served as commissioner before him), Paul Bonnecarrère, Marchand

---

[21] French letters specifically questioned the national loyalty of Alsatian Protestant Pastor Helmlinger. ANC 2AC 9285 Mission Protestante Pasteur Helmlinger; ANC APA 10560/A Lettres du Gouverneur Théodore Paul Marchand à Mr. l'Administrateur à Ebolowa, 1931; ACSSp. 2J1.10.7 "Les ecoles de fiancées dans les missions du Cameroun"; Monseigneur F. Vogt, "Palabres Avec l'Administration, 1930"; Congrégation du Saint-Esprit, "L'Administration Mandatée a-t-Elle Ce Droit? Etude Sur La Politique Française Au Sujet Des Missions," *Kolnische Volkszeitung*, July 14, 1930. ANC APA 10170 Rapport sur les missions, 1945; ANC 1AC 3523 Mission Presbytérienne Américaine, 1950.

[22] ANC 1AC 3523 Mission Catholique de Yaoundé Rapport 18 juin 1930; ANC 1AC 3523 Extrait du Rapport de Tournée: Mr. Trebos, chef de subdivision de Bafia, 8 june–1 juillet 1930, Inspection de la Mission Catholique de Ndikinimeki.

[23] ACSSp. 2J1.2b2 lettre de Gov. Marchand à Mgr. Vogt, 4 novembre 1923.

strongly felt that Christianity divided the "natural solidarity and cohesion of the native milieu."[24] Until 1927, however, officials showed little concern for the missions' negotiation of forest concessions with community leaders nor for their use of local materials such as wood, palm, and rock. Since African laborers did nearly all the physical labor for church construction and mission expansion, they harvested timber and local materials from what they believed was within their dominion.[25] The administration halted their own *laissez-faire* approach in the last years of the 1920s and determinedly pursued a policy of restricting all harvest and forest material removal for the purpose of sharply curtailing mission-based construction work.

In autumn 1927, foreign mission leaders began receiving letters stating that they "did not have the right to fell trees without government permission."[26] The ensuing *arrêté* of 3 October 1927 stipulated that whenever trees were cut, the missions were to record the number of trees used, the geographic location and dimensions of the felled area, the diameter of the trunks, and the cubic volume of the yield, as well as paint the mission's initials on the tree stumps.[27] For not respecting these precise requirements, Pères Johasekt, Richard, Brangers, Ritter, and Graffin were called before the tribunal in Yaoundé and condemned to pay fines in 1929 and 1930.[28] In 1931, Père Mader and Père Meyer were accused of "forestry crimes" and sentenced to fines and imprisonment.[29] This particular criminal prosecution appears to have been a procedural ruse, however, intended to punish Mader and Meyer for their extensive complaints to the League of Nations regarding the administrations' use of forced labor in the region around Medzek.[30]

The 1927 regulations regarding the missions' use of forest resources were only the beginning of administrative restrictions. In 1930, regional officials began denying missions land grant rights to prevent the construction of

---

[24] ACSSp. 2J1.2b2 lettre de Gov. Marchand à Mgr. Vogt, 4 novembre 1923.

[25] Mgr. Athanase Bala related to me that his father, a catechist and teacher in the Nlong mission, was an expert tree cutter and knew which trees to fell that would be best used for construction and which to leave in the forest. Oral interview with Mgr. Athanase Bala, CSSp., Bishop emeritus of Bafia, Cameroon, July 8, 2015, Séminaire des Missions, Congrégation du Saint-Esprit, Chevilly Larue, France.

[26] 1AC 3523 Bois de charpente, missions catholiques, 1927; ACSSp. 2J1.10.12 lettre de Yves Nicole, Yaoundé, à la Mission de Mvolyé, 17 sept. 1927.

[27] 1AC 3523 Droit d'exploitation des bois au Cameroun; lettre de Mgr. Graffin, 30 October 1930, "coupé sans autorisation."

[28] ANOM AGEFOM 989/3419 lettre de Marchand, 23 jul. 1930; ACSSp. 2J1.10.12 Mission de Yaoundé, Brangers, Ritter, Graffin au Tribunal, 29 oct. 1930; see also Ngongo, *Histoire des forces religieuses au Cameroun*, 60–1.

[29] ACSSp. 2J1.10.12 Père Mader et Père Leon Meyer, 22 jan. 1931.

[30] ACSSp. 2J1.10.12 persecution des missionaires, 22 mars 1931.

churches and restricted all official mission construction projects larger than 4 hectares in size, enforced through the *arrêté* of 24 April 1930, which allowed only "gradual" projects in primary mission posts and outlawed nearly all work in "secondary posts," which the administration knew were typically manned by African catechists.[31] Marchand and Bonnecarrère rejected Catholic, French Protestant, and American Presbyterian missions' requests to build in Obout, Mvolyé, Nkilzok, Omvan, Bafia, Dschang, Ebolowa, and the Douala region, and instructed their regional officials to countermand all mission construction work in their jurisdictions.[32] In July 1930, Maurice Bertaut, an official in southern Cameroon, dutifully reported to Marchand:

> The missions provide refuge to those who wish to avoid their obligations ... the negro does this: he refuses to fulfill his ten days of *prestation* or work in the public worksites, but he will work for the priest for as long as the "father" deems necessary for no pay. A *chef de circonscription* mentioned that Père Johasket had made a brick kiln and said in a letter dated 6 June 1930, "the great majority of natives, men, women, and children of Meban who were all Catholic were all working for free at the kiln for a month. Women and children dug for clay and men laid tile. I dismissed all the workers and forbade them to return and left a guard at the mission kiln to prevent all work from being restarted. I told them to leave the buildings and materials where they lay.[33]

Less compliant regional officials who approved any mission requests for additional hectarage were harshly reprimanded.[34] When hindering missionary construction did not inhibit catechists' steering of laborers away from the worksites, French officials simply arrested and imprisoned more catechists. In 1930, the head of the Mbalmayo subdivision arrested Zacharie Mbida and Gabriel Owono for working on their own catechist huts, and Benoit Mvog Manga was arrested and sentenced to one year in prison for taking women from the worksites and bringing them to the mission.[35]

In addition to passing regulations limiting timber harvesting, mission construction, and catechist activity, Marchand also began ordering the destruction of "Christian villages," defined as groups of huts occupied by small religious collectives that had sprung up across southern Cameroon to

---

[31] ACSSp. 2J1.10.12 lettre de Gov. Marchand, 28 avril 1930, Omvan.

[32] ANOM AGEFOM 989/3419 lettre de Marchand à le Dir. des Missions Protestantes Russillon, 9 dec. 1930; lettre de Marchand à chef de Bafia, 18 jan. 1931; lettre de Marchand à chef de Yabassi, 30 jul. 1930; ACSSp. 2J1.10.12 Lettre de Marin chef de circ. d'Ebolowa, 4 nov. 1930.

[33] ANC APA 11822/B lettre de Maurice Bertaut, 7 juillet 1930.

[34] ANOM AGEFOM 989/3419 lettre de Marchand à chef de circ. de Bafia, 18 jan. 1931.

[35] ACSSp. 2J1.10.12 Mémoire du Père Pichon, Minlaba, 1930.

accommodate devout communities.[36] Although they were condemned by the territorial administration, Catholic priests had been advocating "new independent villages away from the pagan milieu" since the early 1920s, believing that catechumens and followers would mutually reinforce each other's observance.[37] Pastor Farelly ministered to the Baptist villages outside Douala and in Ndiki-Somo, and preached to them about their preeminent responsibility to "guarantee the organization of Christian society ... and ensure the good of the next generation."[38] In 1930, Marchand issued the *arrêté* of 24 April ordering the razing of *groupement chrétiens* and the "reconstruction of homesteads and huts in the main villages."[39] Bonnecarrère later extended this policy, claiming that limiting mission posts was necessary to "decongest" areas with competition for cultivatable land, and that relocating villages along the rivers would "prevent dense groupings."[40] For roughly the next ten years, French and African evangelists fought to rebuild Christian villages where they had once stood and urged their adherents in villages like Omvam, Bikolo, Badzoué, Ndzem, and Ndzime to continue to "set themselves apart" in any way they could.[41] Heated allegations about violations of duty, responsibility, and law ran through nearly all communications between heads of mission and administrative officials during the 1920s and 1930s as animosities deepened.[42]

More than any other mission activity, pious volunteer work drew the most administrative attention. Writing in a panicked tone in 1932 after arresting local

---

[36] ANC APA 10384, catéchistes condamnés, dec. 1930; ACSSp. 2J1.2b2, Père François Pichon, "200 village chrétiens," 12 mai 1924. See also Reverend Père Augustin Berger, "Dix Années de Travail En Afrique ... Au Cameroun," in *Dix Années de Travail Catéchétique Dans Le Monde Au Service de La Formation Religieuse de l'Enfant*, B.I.C.E. Études et Documents (Paris: Éditions Fleurus, 1960), 32.

[37] ACSSp. 2J1.2b2 Rapport, Mission Catholique de Ngowayang, avril 1920; Vogt rapport du 12 Sept. 1927.

[38] Farelly, *Chronique Du Pays Banen (Au Cameroun)*, 51. See also Maurice Farelly, *Les Actes des apôtres* (Paris: Delachaux & Niestlé, 1958).

[39] Arrêté du 24 avril 1930, circulaire confidential, Gov. Marchand. See also ACSSp. 2J1.10.12, Journal du Père François Pichon, Doumé, 1930–31, non-numerated pages.

[40] ANOM AGEFOM 989/3419 lettre de Comm. Bonnecarrère à Mgr. Bouque, M'Banga, 1932. This excuse is particularly disingenuous, as French officials were continually fighting against disassociated and dispersed groupings.

[41] ACSSp. 2J1.2b2 lettres de Père Pichon, Villages chrétiens, circonscription d'Abong-Mbang, 1930; Rapport de Père Pichon à Doumé, octobre 1931; Comité d'Action Catholique, "L'Etonnante Progression Des Catholiques Au Cameroun," *Vers l'Avenir*, janvier 1939, no. 9 edition..

[42] ACSSp. 2J1.10.12, Journal du Père François Pichon, Doumé, 1930–31, non-numerated pages; "catéchistes, peines de l'indigénat", Cornarie, Chef de circ de Yaoundé, 1 jan. 1931.

catechists, the French police commissioner of Yaoundé de Calbiac accused the administration of being "far too lenient" in their approach to "religious militants." Writing in dark, underlined text, de Calbiac wrote, "Native labor must be organized by chiefs ... We must respect custom or all control over the elders, chiefs, polygamists, fathers, etc. is lost!"[43] A 1933 *circulaire* reprised this sentiment, stating: "The catechists must not be allowed to meddle in administrative affairs, nor can they be allowed to diminish the authority of chiefs."[44] French officials in rural posts frequently complained that not only did catechists recruit laborers away from chiefs, they explicitly sought to reduce their prestige and authority through the act of erecting structures. A 1930 government report on Catholic missions in the Yaoundé area stated: "The 500 catechists in the subdivision of Yaoundé recruit many laborers from among those who wish to be initiated into the religion ... Catechists push volunteers to build houses more beautiful than the chiefs'."[45] Administrator Bertault targeted one missionary in particular for encouraging catechists' unbridled authority, stating "Pere Johasekt in Mvog-Nyenge in Akonolinga is the worst example of this."[46]

In a corresponding example in western Cameroon, tensions between Christians and the *fo* or chief in the town of Bayangam were particularly strained when a Protestant church was built in 1935 in fine materials such as brick and tin (rather than thatch and palm), which the *fo* took as an affront.[47] In soliciting unified community support for the construction endeavor, church disciples had, as Dominique Malaquais describes, "usurped a prerogative" previously reserved for Bayangam's chief, the *fo* Kom Waindja and other elites.[48] In 1930, Officer Tresos, the head of the Bafia subdivision, reported on "the enormous influence of catechists in the Banen region," which meant that the Protestant and Catholic missions in Ndikinimeki had more laborers than any farm or road construction zone, even though these men "worked without a salary."[49] Arrests and punishments, such as the year-long prison sentence

---

[43] ACSSp. 2J1.10.7 Père Van Bulck, S.J. avec Mr. de Calbiac, commissaire de police à Yaoundé, 17 mai 1932.

[44] ANC APA 11016/G circulaire no. 78 sur la réglementation sur les cultes, 16 septembre 1933.

[45] 1AC 3523 Rapport de M. Berthault, Mission Catholique de Yaoundé Rapport 18 juin 1930.

[46] 1AC 3523 Rapport de M. Berthault, Mission Catholique de Yaoundé Rapport 18 juin 1930.

[47] Dominique Malaquais, "Building in the Name of God: Architecture, Resistance, and the Christian Faith in the Bamileke Highlands of Western Cameroon," *African Studies Review* 42, no. 1 (April 1999): 67.

[48] Malaquais, 67.

[49] ANC 1AC 3523 Extrait du Rapport de Tournée: M. Tresos, chef de subdivision de Bafia, 8 juin–1 juillet 1930.

of the catechist Benoit Assamba who recruited twelve young men away from work on the Akonolinga road, or the 100-franc fine for a catechist in Kribi for cutting down palms in the Meyok district without government permission, or even Chief Okoa's forcible recruitment of catechumens from the Mbalmayo Catholic mission to work on the Mbalmayo–Ngulmekong road, did not diminish the interest of devoted volunteers.[50]

The proliferation of unregulated and untaxed spaces of worship and the African spiritual leaders who led the rites continued to resist stringent oversight. In response, Governor Bonncarrère passed the Decree of 28 March 1933 policing religious domains and restricting the construction of all ecclesiastical structures such as churches, cathedrals, temples, as well as auxiliary outposts like bush chapels, *sixa* schools, catechist huts, and other informal religious spaces.[51] According to Article 9 of the *arrêté* promulgating the decree, the principal impetus for the law was "to maintain control over the catechists."[52] Earlier decrees such as Governor Marchand's Decree of 30 August 1930 had attempted to regulate the construction of catechist posts by requiring permits and fees "to reduce immoderate proselytism," but they had little effect.[53] The only result had been a confrontation between representatives of the Congregation of the Holy Ghost and the French government at the October 1930 session of the Mandates Commission at the League of Nations in Geneva, in which the Spiritans claimed the colonial administration in Cameroon violated the Act of London by persecuting Catholic religious workers.[54]

> In this session, the French representative Roger Franceschi had retaliated stating, The Catholic catechist is ... predisposed to Christian villagers, who, under his influence, deny all other forms of authority other than that of the mission. In doing so, he contributes to the disintegration of the family as well as the native commanders and does much to bring about what will soon be a crisis whose consequences we can certainly ascertain.[55]

After the League sided with the Catholic missions against the French mandate administration in that session, Bonnecarrère and Marchand only scaled

---

[50] ACSSp. 2J2.1a Journal de la Mission Saint Joseph de Kribi, 14 mai 1930; ACSSp. 2J1.2b2 lettre de Mgr. Vogt à Gov. Marchand, 6 mai 1930; ANC 1AC 3523 Rapport sur la Mission Catholique de Minlaba.
[51] ANC 1AC 3523 Décret du 28 mars 1933; arrêté du 28 décembre 1933.
[52] ANC 1AC 3523 Article 9, arrêté du 31 mai 1933.
[53] ANC APA 10560/A, lettre du Gouverneur Marchand, 29 août 1930.
[54] UNOG, League of Nations Documents and Serial Publications Reel: C.P.M. – 17, October 1930, the 21st session of the Mandates Commission in Geneva.
[55] Roger Franceschi, Addresse a la Société des Nations, UNOG, League of Nations Documents and Serial Publications Reel: C.P.M. – 17.

up their repressive stances. In the early 1930s, district overseers launched a number of directives aimed at increasing police enforcement of African pastors and priests – as they had tried to do with catechists – by regulating the migrations, ministries, and zones of influence of individual clergymen.[56] In the same period, the French administration continued to suppress religious proselytism and social activism by restricting church and chapel construction and the extent to which Africans could build in the name of God, all of which had the unintended effect of producing a sense of shared resistance to an organized system of godless injustice.

Although the years 1932 and 1933 had had seen requests from the Spiritan and Sacred Heart missions to build dozens of new churches in the Yaoundé and Douala vicariates, and from the Baptist, Evangelical, and Presbyterian congregations to expand temple construction in southern Cameroon, no government approvals were ever made.[57] Nevertheless, followers and congregants continued to build less policed spaces such as *sixa* schools and catechist huts. As these spaces functioned as spiritual gathering places as well as clandestine meeting spaces, Cameroon's governors sought "more strictly applied decrees."[58]

French Pastor Charles Boury protested the decrees limiting religious structures by arguing that Africans' dedication to building houses of worship was proof of their "collaboration with France's civilizing work."[59] His colleague, Pastor Maurice Farelly used more combative language, writing in a letter at the end of 1933: "These spaces represent the holy places of indigenous communities ... they are not simply buildings."[60] In the following year, Farelly continued his campaign of resistance to administrative oversight, pleading,

> The ecclesiastical organization of our work is such that our native pastors do not have responsibility over one church, but rather have commitments to a number of churches and edifices in which they preach and work...They share the work of the sacraments amongst each other as part of their pastoral activities...and use all manner of buildings to administer the sacraments. Please understand our need for our edifices.[61]

---

[56] ANC APA 10674/B APA 10674/B lettres de Farelly, 1 février 1934, Douala; ANC APA 10674/B lettres à Mgr. Bouque de Chef de Region de Mungo à Nkongsamba Repiquet, 27 avril 1936.

[57] ANC APA 11016/G Lettre de Mgr. Vogt, 7 mars 1935; circulaire no. 78 sur la réglementation sur les cultes, 16 septembre 1933.

[58] ANC APA 11016/G Note sur les ecoles de fiancées, signé Bonnecarrère, 16 septembre 1933.

[59] ANC APA 11016/G letter de Pasteur Boury sur le Décret du 28 mars 1933.

[60] ANC APA 10674/B lettre de Pasteur Farelly à le Délégué à Douala, 7 décembre 1933.

[61] ANC APA 10674/B lettre de Pasteur Farelly à le commissaire à Douala, 1 février 1934.

These missives and many others, including furious letters from Spiritan priests and letters of disapproval from the rectors of the Norwegian Lutheran Mission and the Fraternal Lutheran Church, met with stern warnings to obey French law.[62] The *arrêté* of 28 December 1933 specifically ordered the policing of Yaoundé and Douala's principal Catholic communities and the largest Evangelical and Baptist congregations of the Douala and western regions.[63]

Recording Cruelties and Documenting Abuse

Catholic and Protestant clergymen are notable in this period for their impassioned defense of African dignity and for leaving some of the only records of Africans' torture, dehumanization, and deaths in worksites during the interwar decades. Catholic Spiritan missionaries' eyewitness accounts include workers' agony while being whipped with *chicottes* or while removing rocks with their bare hands to create docks along the Nlimi and Nyong Rivers, beatings of the old and infirm by the *force publique*, children and breastfeeding women bent under baskets of rock and earth, thefts of food and clothing, forced marches lasting several days, chain gangs, and laborers' eventual expiration on the side of the road.[64] Protestant pastors also filed official records of cruelties throughout the 1930s and early 1940s, including, "pregnant women and breastfeeding mothers subject to forced labor," "intensive recruitment of laborers, especially when recruitment is left to the discretion of chiefs," and "roundups resulting in grave abuses and great dangers."[65] These and other accounts of horrors are powerful testaments of the consequences of colonial rule.

Attending to and burying the corpses along the roads and railways was a grim task, as was providing compassionate assistance for the families of dead workers (Mgr. Vogt observed, "the catechists regulate their way of praying to help the villagers' vexation"), but Christian leaders performed these and other works of mercy and encouraged everyday believers to perform radical philanthropic acts as demonstrations of Christian character, which, they argued, would "liberate the mental slavery" caused by the injustice of forced labor.[66] Christian leaders encouraged husbands to replace their wives when women

---

[62] ANC APA 11016/M Missions Norvegiennes; ANC APA 11016/H Mission Lutherienne Fraternelle (Yagoua), plan de la police des cultes, 1936.

[63] Arrêté du 28 décembre 1933 portant ouverture d'edefices au culte publique.

[64] These accounts are found throughout Spiritan archive records, most notably in ACSSp. 2J1.10.12, which details the 1930s.

[65] AFFPOL 2190/2 Fédération des Missions Protestantes du Cameroun et de l'Afrique Equatoriale lettre au Gov. Marchand, 12 juin 1931; Fed. des Missions Prot. du Cam., Voeux présentés au gouverneur du Cameroun M. Caras, 19 août 1943.

[66] ACSSp. 2J1.10.12 Mgr. Vogt, Femmes Mortes aux chantiers de la route, 1930.

were recruited to the worksites, proselytizing that it was "the answer to being summoned by Christ."[67] Priests' and catechists' records of deaths along the roads such as that of Sekomo, who died after four months of work on the road between Mbalayo and Ngoulmekong, or Mondani, wife of Tsungi Ngolavina, who died in 1928 on the road from Nemeli to Akono after two uninterrupted months of work, or Baba Mangé and several others who died on the Eseka–Douala line in 1929 of malnutrition, give the historian a sense of the precise spaces of domination and brutalization in Cameroon, which made possible the transit and transactions of goods and materials that funded the bustling economic and religious activities shaping the territory.[68] Citing the role of infrastructure in promoting human suffering, Père Pichon wrote in 1930:

> Our work has disastrous consequences for the life of the tribes. The young emigrate to other colonies ... work we demand gives chiefs deplorable power – nocturnal arrests and kidnappings, chain gangs, men tied together at the neck ... And all this to create five thousand kilometers of road.[69]

Pichon's counterpart in the Protestant Mission, Pastor Marcel Brun, likewise criticized,

> As soon as a boy reaches fourteen years of age ... he falls under the blow of forced recruitment for public works and is obligated to pay taxes ... forced recruitment of laborers authorized by the obligatory labor contribution laws valid in the colony has created an African proletariat that is, in reality, living in a state of slavery.[70]

As a relief effort, French priests and pastors began organizing to pay catechists' taxes and assist young people with fines to release them from jail for evading roadwork conscription.[71]

In addition to brutal and dehumanizing infrastructure work, the timing and organization of regional agricultural work also shaped the local *terroir*. In Christian villages, which were settled without administrative authorization, locals planted cocoa, rather than food crops, because they believed its profitability would inhibit regional police from razing or confiscating it, as it

---

[67] ACSSp. 2J1.10.12 Mgr. Vogt, Femmes Mortes aux chantiers de la route, 1930.
[68] ACSSp. 2J1.10.12 Mgr. Vogt, Femmes Mortes aux chantiers de la route, 1930.
[69] ANOM AGEFOM 355/170 BIS, Lettre du Pere Pichon, directeur de la mission de Minlaba, à Mr. le Chef de Circonscription de Yaoundé, Mr. Bertaut, 10 mai 1930.
[70] ANOM AFFPOL 2190/2 Marcel Brun, Mission Française au Cameroun, questions d'enseignement, 1944.
[71] ACSSp. 2J1.10.13 lettre de Mgr. Graffin, 5 avril 1935.

provided revenues when harvest taxes were due.[72] In 1932 in Sangmélima, the regional inspector noted, "Another radical thing is happening here: the destruction of food agriculture. Each time the natives separate from their chiefs, they plant cocoa where they will want to live, knowing that we will not destroy them."[73] Regions that first experienced significant economic growth and population diversification were also some of the first to invest in crops that could not be eaten. In Edea, Eseka, Mbalmayo, and Ebolowa, cocoa and palm oil not only fetched high prices, they could also not be seized to feed laborers in the worksites. Farther south and east such as in Minlaba, rice and groundnut harvests were commonly taken without pay by regional guards to keep workers from starving.[74] The sooner a population came into contact with roadwork recruiters, the *commandement indigène*, or concessionary companies reliant on railroads, the more quickly those with access to land and labor turned to cash crops with only small areas for growing food. In areas where energies were devoted to edible produce, "hunger reigned."[75]

Africans in this period were highly aware of the terrible bargain they struck with regard to their contributions to roads and railways. An African notable, Eyono Nkoulou from Ambam – a region south of Ebolowa near the Gabon border – lamented in 1929 that his villages were poorer than those in Ebolowa because Ambam did not have a major road connecting it to any transit points. Abessolo Nlem, the chief of Djoum, which was likewise very far south and isolated from major thoroughfares until the mid-1930s, complained,

> the natives of Djoum are Bulu just like those in Sangmélima and Ebolowa and there is no reason they should not benefit from the same advantages. For three years the chiefs and inhabitants of Djoum have asked for roads to Ebolowa or Sangmélima and have not received them. But our men are recruited to work

---

[72] ANOM AFFPOL 2190/2 Marcel Brun, Mission Française au Cameroun, Église Évangélique, 1944.

[73] ANOM AGEFOM 989/3430 Rapport de Tournée de 3 au 21 août 1932 Sangmélima, circ. d'Ebolowa.

[74] ACSSp. 2J1.10.12 Père Pichon, "Une escroquerie administrative" 1927.

[75] ACSSp. 2J1.10.12 Père Pichon, "Une escroquerie administrative" 1927. Chiefs were also more likely to grow cocoa or palm oil on large plantations, avoiding the possibility that their harvests would be requisitioned to feed workers. Of the six chiefs of major southern axis points who received honors from the administration for agricultural productivity, only one grew foodstuffs of millet, groundnuts, and rice, while the other five grew cocoa exclusively. See also "Ordre du mérite indigène," *La Gazette du Cameroun*, no. 47, 15 nov. 1928.

on roads that lead elsewhere. I am ashamed to tell my people when they return from work that there is no road here.[76]

In 1933, an agricultural overseer in Batouri heard entreaties from Baya leaders that the local populations' extensive cultivation of sesame and honeybees merited the construction of new roads and railway stations in the region.[77] Although construction work spelled death and deprivation for hundreds of workers across southern Cameroon every year, it also signaled existing or anticipated wealth, which everyday people actively pursued, most often through selling their harvests or migrating to transit centers.[78] While Eyono Nkoulou might well have known the human cost of a new road, he rationalized: "the natives of Ambam can soon become as rich as those in Ebolowa and no longer be treated as 'bushmen'."[79]

Decentralized Operations of Conflict

As the French administration and foreign missionary leaders clashed openly in meetings of the League of Nations in Europe and in police offices and tribunal courtrooms in Cameroon, African evangelists and chiefs paralleled their struggle and engaged in a mode of violent organizing that included conventional physical brutality but also marshaled symbolic power. Both parties – decentralized Christian leaders and administration-backed political elites – deployed coercive powers that constituted *force,* but which had unpredictable dynamics.

In an attempt to curb the instability engendered by catechists' abductions and encouragements to leave worksites, chiefs in the Yaoundé, Bafia, Nanga Eboko, and Akonolinga subdivisions began proposing new methods to control and police their territories beginning in 1926.[80] Chief Hubert Nanga was particularly beset by escapes of workers from his farms and roads, and offered to work with neighboring chiefs to "ensure that road work is conducted in the subdivision [of Nanga Eboko] at the same time as in the adjoining subdivision ... so as to ensure that labor recruitment will be required no matter where the

---

[76] ANOM AFFPOL 2190/1 Conseil de Notables de la Circ. d'Ebolowa, scéance de 18 nov. 1929, 94.

[77] ANOM AGEFOM 989/3430 Vauzelle, travaux agricoles, tournée du 4 au 17 jan. 1933, Batouri.

[78] In 1930, the head of circonscription of Ebolowa stated plainly, "the natives chase lucre ... on the Ebolowa–Lolodorf road." ACSSp. 2J1.10.12 lettre de M. Marlin, chef de circ. d'Ebolowa, 4 nov. 1930.

[79] ANOM AFFPOL 2190/1 Conseil de Notables de la Circ. d'Ebolowa, scéance de 18 nov. 1929, 94.

[80] These were part of the Nyong et Sanaga and M'bam regions. See map of regions.

population flees."[81] Chief Machia contributed a similar proposition in Bafia asserting, "We shall have multiple worksites in contiguous *circonscriptions.*"[82] Fixing territorial demarcations and reducing worksite desertion also required chiefs to expand their own cadre of enforcers who were exclusively loyal to them and could surpass the powers of the *commandement indigène.*[83] The administration supported chiefs' work to "grow their prestige," and noted in 1932 that the *commandement indigène* was often insufficient for maintaining worksite constancy.[84]

The roads that required the most constant maintenance as a result of rains, heavy usage, and forest regrowth were numerous and, through the 1930s, stretched farther and farther east and south. The Ebolowa–Sangmélima road was extended to Vimeli near Yaoundé and then farther east to Batouri, as well as west to Kribi; the Ambam road was extended south to Gabon; and eventually, the roads surrounding the Yaoundé region stretched south to Djoum as that region's farmers' cocoa harvests grew in the 1930s (see map).[85] As road and railway worksites spread across the territory, so did violent recruitment practices. Illness, particularly sleeping sickness, followed as a result.[86] Chiefs and their police routinely ignored official regulations that restricted *prestation* work on Sundays, which infuriated catechists and missionaries. What caused even more outrage was that chiefs began using religious services as an efficient location for recruitment.[87] In Doumé in 1931, a catechist was arrested while protesting guards who arrived to forcibly round up worshippers "at the precise moment when the catechist sounded the drum call."[88] Pastor Marcel Brun castigated local officials: "We have seen chiefs come and recruit labor during a Sunday service! After that, no one assembled when the church bell

---

[81] ANOM AGEFOM 799/1855, Hubert Nanga, chef superieur des Yokaba, Nanga Eboko, quoted in the proceedings of the Conseil de Notables: Procès Verbal de la séance du 16 février 1926.

[82] ANOM AGEFOM 799/1855, Machia, chef superieur des Bafia-Bapé, quoted in the proceedings of the Conseil de Notables: Procès Verbal de la séance du 16 février 1926.

[83] ANC APA 11828/H, *Rapport sur les Cheffries*, 1933; ANC APA 11626 Inspection de la Région du Mbam, Rapport Annuel 1949, 21, ANOM AGEFOM 799/1855, Zogo Fouda, Hubert Nanga, et Machia, *Conseil de Notables: Procès Verbal de la séance du 16 février 1926*; see also Kaptue, *Cameroun: Travail et Main-d'Oeuvre Sous Le Régime Français, 1916–1952*, 100–5.

[84] ANOM AGEFOM 989/3424 Guibert, Yokadouma, 13 août 1932.

[85] ANOM AGEFOM 989/3430 Cameroun travaux agricoles, 4–7 jan. 1933.

[86] Ordre du mérite indigène," *La Gazette du Cameroun*, no. 47, 15 nov. 1928; ACSSp. 2J1.10.12 Père Pichon, "Une escroquerie administrative," 1927.

[87] ACSSp. 2J1.10.12 Rapport sur Chef Ndomie, 7 feb 1931; Rapport sur catéchumen Giyé, 11 may 1931.

[88] ACSSp. 2J1.10.12 Père François Pichon, "La polygamie," Doumé, 1930–31.

rang for fear of being taken."[89] Catechists in Lomié who objected to Sunday labor recruitment were beaten by soldiers who then rounded up female mission volunteers to work the chief's coffee farm.[90] In the years between 1930 and 1935, more catechists were arrested by chiefs' police for crimes including insubordination, fraud, kidnapping, drunkenness, theft, and "sequestration of young girls" as a result of frequent skirmishes.[91]

During 1932 and ensuing years, control over labor in southern Cameroon became particularly pronounced. With the global economy in crisis, prices dropped for many of Cameroon's commodities, which prompted farmers to expand their fields and increase harvests to maintain their incomes.[92] The administration noted larger harvests of bananas, palm oil, timber, cocoa, coffee, peanut, sesame, and rubber across the southern regions, and argued that restricting religious edifices was necessary to accommodate expanding farmlands.[93] Officer Guibert even noted "disequilibrium" and "social malaise" related to labor recruitment in Yokadouma in the far southeast region, and further added that "the native family dissociates more and more from our influences."[94]

Increased arrests and persecution did little to dissuade Christian leaders from continuing their interventionist work. Catechists abducted or paid bridewealth for chiefs' wives who were married before the legal age and organized

---

[89] ANOM AFFPOL 2190/2 Pasteur Marcel Brun, Mission Française au Cameroun, lettre 1944.

[90] ACSSp. 2J1.10.12 Journal du Père François Pichon, Doumé, 1930–31.

[91] ANOM AGEFOM 989/3424 Guibert à chef de circ. de Nagoundéré, 26 jul. 1932; ACSSp. 2J1.10.12 "la persecution des missionnaires au Cameroun," 22 mars 1931; Journal du Père François Pichon, 18 juin 1931, 7 feb, 1931; lettre de Vogt au gouverneur, 6 mai 1930; ACSSp. 2J1.10.12, Père François Pichon, Doumé, Journal du Cameroun, "La polygamie," 1931; ACSSp. 2J1.11a2 District de Yaoundé, notes sur le personnel, 1939; AFFPOL 2190/2 Fédération des Missions Protestantes du Cameroun et de l'Afrique Equatoriale lettre au Gov. Marchand, 12 juin 1931; Fed. des Missions Prot. du Cam., Voeux présentés au gouverneur du Cameroun M. Caras, 19 août 1943.

[92] ANOM AGEFOM 989/3423 Affaires Economiques 1932; ANOM AGEFOM 989/3430 Cameroun administration 1927–1933, Vauzelle, travaux agricoles, Tournée du 4 au 17 jan. 1933, Batouri.

[93] ANOM AGEFOM 989/3423 Affaires Economiques 1932, Bonnecarrère, Circulaire no. 70 à messieurs les chefs de circonscriptions; ANOM TP Série 1 420/11 Rapport à la Société des Nations 1935, Services des Travaux Publics Chemins de Fer, Portes et Rades; ACSSp. 2J1.10.12 lettre de M. Marlin, chef de la circonscription d'Ebolowa, 4 nov 1930 a Yaoundé. While it is unlikely that there was direct competition between missions and local farms for land and space, the administration used this excuse to defend against attacks that it was discriminating against religious establishments.

[94] AGEFOM 989/3424 Justice 1927–1933, Guibert à le chef de circ. de Yokadouma, 13 août 1932.

new marriages with local Christians throughout the 1930s. They also frequently reimbursed bridewealth for any woman who arrived at the mission claiming to have been married according to her father or elders' arrangement, rather than her own free will. In response to these gestures, the administration threatened to imprison missionaries and catechists for "slavery," as evangelists' payments constituted a modified form of "*la traite des noirs*."[95]

Court Battles

A case that stirred the sentiments of Bangangté chiefs was the trial between Pétro Nsangou, a prominent Bamoun elder, and his erstwhile betrothed, Ngoutano, who refused to marry him despite her father's insistence. In this case, Ngoutano sought release from her arranged marriage in the *Justice de Paix* in Foumban even though Pétro had been paying bridewealth throughout her childhood in order to secure her hand in marriage, which amounted to over 2000 francs, tools, clothing, wine, and kola nuts.[96] When European priests and an African catechist from Foumban heard of Ngoutano's case, they defended her rejection of her father's and Pétro Nsangou's arrangement during her trial, and argued that the men had broken the law by "transacting a forced marriage with a child," which was a crime according to the marriage law of 1922.[97] Another witness from the Catholic mission demanded the court absolve Ngoutano of any liability for the bridewealth repayment, as she had not contracted the marriage herself, and was therefore a victim of attempted slavery.[98] Her father told the court that he had long since spent, eaten, or utilized the gifts, and since he was unable to repay Pétro, his daughter's marriage would have to endure. It is likely that Njimountapmbemo believed that as Ngoutano would be unable to repay her own bridewealth, she would be obliged to accept the marriage, thus resolving the issue. The African judge, Garba Mfofie sided with Nsangou and Njimountapmbemo, declaring that Ngoutano was to remain married unless she could repay the bridewealth, as the outstanding debt could not be discharged as it had been her own decision to renounce her elder's proposal. Judge Mfofie was open to dissolving the marriage, however, conditional on repayment of the bridewealth.

---

[95] ACSSp. 2J1.10.12 chef de subdiv. d'Akonolinga au R.P. Faussier, Medzek, 12 juin 1930.
[96] ANOM Fonds Ministerielles (hereafter FM) Services Judiciares (hereafter SJ) 1 Region Bamoun, Subdivision de Foumban, Convention No. 57, Pétro Nsangou, village Foyet contre Ngoutano village de Nkounga.
[97] ANOM FM SJ 1, Rapport: Foumban, Justice de Paix de Compétence Étendue.
[98] ANOM FM SJ 1, Rapport: Foumban, Justice de Paix de Compétence Étendue.

Shockingly for Njimountapmbemo, Ngoutano assumed the debt and promised to repay her father within one month. Although the court record makes no mention of any direct assistance offered to Ngoutano, the Catholic mission in Foumban upheld a policy of assisting young women in divorce cases, particularly in cases of pre-pubescent marriage, polygamy, and arranged marriage, and also occasionally paid bridewealth to families in restitution for the rescued women's freedom.[99] Likewise, locals in the region were aware of the *Confréries des Cinq Plaies de Jésus* and their interventions on behalf of indebted divorcées. It is likely Ngoutano received some form of aid in order to liberate herself, as she freed herself within one month, despite the general trend of women having to work for months or years on their own to repay their bridewealth.

The chiefs in Bangangté made their displeasure known regarding this and other cases of undutiful daughters to the French administration, demanding that French judges not uphold cases where women sought to dissolve marriages without the consideration of all parties involved. The chiefs also decried missionary interferences in family matters in general. Their letters were several of hundreds received by local officials and high-level administrators in interwar Cameroon, written by African chiefs and family fathers expressing outrage at their daughters' defiance, and more critically, their inability to stem the rising influence of catechists, who were often younger, more educated and well-traveled men, who summoned villagers to religious meetings, preached in towns, distributed literature and news, and solicited wives and daughters to enter the *sixa*, baptize their children, and devote themselves to religious pursuits.[100]

While chiefs in western Cameroon expressed strong animosity for Christian missions, they were also aware that the French administration was an unreliable ally. Although the mandate government in the interwar period was suspicious of missionary activism, French judges and officials tolerated some missionary engagement in matters of local justice and criminal trials. In some courts in southern Cameroon, local missions pressured the administration to demonstrate greater clemency toward converted Catholics who were found guilty of crimes. French judges overturned several judgments of customary tribunals where African judges had handed down harsh decisions to converted

---

[99] ACSSp. 2J1.7a7 Ad Lucem: Milieux sociaux africains, Cameroun fev–mars 1946, no. 7; ACSSp. 2J1.7b4, "Journée d'Etude: Les Jeunes Face au Mariage." Nkongsamba, 5 june 1955.

[100] ANC APA 10634 / A Inspection de la Région de Haut Nyong, 19 juillet à 6 août 1948, Inspecteur M. Faucherand, Subdivision de Messamenta; ANOM AGEFOM 355/170bis, Plainte officielle No. 551 du 27 juin 1930, Akonolinga, Père Faussier; ACSSp. 2J1.10.10, Lettre de Pere Faussier à Medzek, 27 juin 1930.

Christians in the *tribunaux indigènes*. Additionally, some convicted murderers who were sentenced to death had their punishments commuted to life in prison after local missionaries pleaded that the condemned "lived in conformity with Catholicism" and had repudiated their polygamous marriages.[101]

Most infuriatingly for many chiefs, French judges could occasionally be sympathetic to Africans in cases where they had committed crimes against their chief, particularly when chiefs were suspected of disrupting local marriages. In the case of Youtou, who was condemned to death for murdering his chief, the tribunal in Douala wavered in issuing the standard death penalty because it was found that Youtou had only murdered Chief Batangaken because Batangaken had kidnapped Youtou's wives after Youtou had shirked a labor demand. Batangaken had seized Youtou's wives as compensation for his noncompliance, and in doing so had deprived Youtou of critical agricultural production. In this particular case, the French judge expressed concern that chiefs were dangerous provocateurs and their mercenary nature was provoking the murderous impulses of their subjects. Though there is no record of a missionary or catechist pleading for mercy on his behalf, the French judge commuted Youtou's sentence from death to life in prison.[102]

Authority over Women

The construction of masculine authority within male Christian coalitions was heavily dependent on women. In many ways, access to women was the object of men's relations within Christian publics, and many theological discussions probed the tensions between duty and individual liberty, love and loyalty, freedom and subordination. Perhaps more than any other promise, the Christian missions' confirmation of an individual man's sexual *right* lay at the heart of religious negotiations in southern Cameroon. In the religious domain, this right was not – at least in theory – about political power, but rather the power to form a family and an independent household. However, in practice, access to wives became the epicenter of religious politics in southern Cameroon. This is not surprising considering that, as Carole Pateman has revealed, access to women is the central site of the social contract in all "modern" political foundations.[103] Thus, Christian men's and Christian organizations' endeavors to ease and mediate sexual possession ultimately produced political strife. While

---

[101] ANOM AGEFOM 2688/3 Cameroun Affaires Judiciaires, 1938–1939, Recours en grâce de Né Boukar; Recours en grâce de Né Mongo Megné.
[102] ANOM AGEFOM 2688/3 Cameroun Affaires Judiciaires, recours en grâce du Né Youtou.
[103] Carole Pateman, *The Sexual Contract* (Stanford: Stanford University Press, 1988).

Christian organizations refigured male power as benevolent and cooperative, and worked to instill parallel relations in both extended and individualized families, hierarchical, competitive, and coercive dimensions remained in both. Curiously, it was the French colonial administration that recognized the centrality of women in local expressions of political power and assertively curtailed – to the extent possible – Christian men's appropriations of French-allied chiefs' wives and female clients.

On October 30, 1930, Père Dumas and his colleague, the catechist Sylvestre Olinga, were charged with "corruption of a minor, kidnapping of women and children, and forced labor" for recruiting African women to the *sixa* in Nden.[104] In December 1930, the tribunal of first degree of Yaoundé condemned the catechist Michel Bene Bewono to six months' imprisonment for "forcible recruitment to the *sixa*." In that same month, Simon Ondoua was arrested for breaking a fellow Bikop Mission *confrère* out of a jail, where he had been sentenced for committing the same crime.[105] In 1930, the administration in Yaoundé charged the Spiritan leader Mgr. Vogt and his colleagues Père Kapner and Père Germain with "trafficking, forced arbitrary detainment, kidnapping, and slavery"[106] for their work in coordinating local women's "rescues" from chiefs' farms. The administration charged these priests and their colleagues in pious confraternities with "crimes against African women and families." In addition to arresting and censuring Christian leaders, the central administration often repeated that it could not uphold any interventionist methods of reforming African marriage, as they "ran counter to the religious neutrality of state law."[107]

After years of facing arrests of his catechists, evangelists, and confraternal organizers, Bishop René Graffin attempted to smooth relations with the administration through contrite and cooperative letters in the early 1930s. Graffin attested that he would compromise on the interventionist strategies of the previous years that led to women's removal from their homes, and maintained there would be no more protracted confrontations at the League of Nations over religious rights.[108] Humanitarian zeal in rural missions, however, could not be so easily contained by the ecclesiastical leadership. Lower-ranked

---

[104] Monseigneur François-Xavier Vogt, *Palabres Avec l'Administration*, 1930, quoted in Roger Dussercle, *Du Kilimandjaro Au Cameroun* (Paris: La Colombe, 1954), 54.
[105] ANC APA 10384 Catéchistes condamnés, décembre 1930.
[106] ANC APA 10332/B Lettre du Chef Supérieur Belinga Ndizé à Nkulmekong au Père Stoll.
[107] UNOG, League of Nations Documents and Serial Publications Reel: C.P.M. – 17.
[108] ACSSp. 2J1.10.7 Letter Mgr. René Graffin, Mvolyé to Mr. le Gouverneur, Yaoundé, 16 October 1933; UNOG, League of Nations Documents and Serial Publications Reel: C.P.M. – 17, 21st session of the Mandates Commission of the League of Nations in Geneva in October 1930.

French priests battled their ecclesiastical superiors to retain interventionist practices and refused to yield to the administration. In 1931, Father de Maupeou wrote to the Spiritan superior general, "I am reproached for being combative, even aggressive. Then you should never have given me a Christian education or taught me principles that I was never to apply!"[109]

Arrests and police pressure also did little to constrain rescues of women in polygamous marriages or unmarried girls' *sixa* recruitment by catechists. Throughout the 1930s, French missionaries, as well as African catechists and lay marriage reformers continued to shield young girls in residency at the *sixa* from early marriages, partnered *sixa* recruits with unmarried Christian men (defending them from being "bought or sold" by polygamists or fathers demanding bridewealth), and insisted that *sixa* women who had been betrothed with bridewealth remain in residence until its full remittance, motivating husbands to pay quickly so that no children would be born outside of formal wedlock.[110] Catechists and their confraternal partners notoriously proselytized near chiefs' and wealthy men's farms, baptizing and encouraging their wives to renounce their marriages and begin a new life of piety with a Christian man.[111] These resolute but risky strategies often ended tragically. In June 1930, when four catechists were arrested and taken to prison for teaching at the Medzek mission *sixa* school, a group of African guards of the French police raped the remaining *sixa* residents.[112] On March 10, 1932, Gabriel Edanga, a man whose unhappy wife had fled to the *sixa* in the village of Mfumasi, murdered Père Henri de Maupeou, a French priest who attempted to prevent him from dragging his wife back to his homestead at knifepoint.[113]

Père de Maupeou had made himself a public enemy of many local husbands as well as the French administration for his passionate defense of *sixa* recruitment and his physical confrontations with those who interfered in mission work with local women. In 1931, after brawling with one groom over a disagreement regarding when his bride would be released from the *sixa*, French

---

[109] ACSSp. 2J1.10.7 Letter du Père Henri de Maupeou au Supérieur Générale, 7 September 1931, Omvan.

[110] ANC APA 10634/A Circulaire à tous les Circonscriptions, du Commissaire à Yaoundé, 1931. See also Rapport d'Inspection, Inspection de la Région de Haut Nyong, du 19 Juillet au 6 Aout 1948, par l'Inspecteur des Affaires Administratives, M. Faucherand, Subdivision de Lomie.

[111] Note du gouverneur: catechistes condamnés, décembre 1930, APA 10384, ANC. See also Le Roy, *Un Martyr de La Morale Chrétienne, Le Père Henri de Maupeou de La Congrégation Du Saint-Esprit, Missionnaire Au Cameroun.*

[112] ACSSp. 2J1.10.10 Lettre de Père Faussier, Medzek, 27 juin 1930; ANOM AGEFOM 355/170bis Mission Catholique de Medzek, 11 juin 1931.

[113] Le Roy, *Un Martyr de La Morale Chrétienne, Le Père Henri de Maupeou de La Congrégation Du Saint-Esprit, Missionnaire Au Cameroun.*

officer de Calbiac began sending a series of strongly worded letters to Père de Maupeou and his colleague, Père Van Bulck, regarding the issue of consent. Calbiac's criticism centered on the central issue of the "consent of *proprietor*," which he and other French officials demanded in order for a woman to be baptized, recruited to be educated at the *sixa*, or married to a Christian man. Claiming to speak "on behalf of the entire administration," Calbiac wrote,

> If the woman, under the pretext of converting to Christianity leaves her legitimate husband, even though he is polygamous, if he has paid the bridewealth, then this woman belongs to him and the administration is obligated to return her to her husband, as she left without his consent ... The priests of the mission cannot rule over the woman against the wishes of the polygamous man.[114]

Calbiac's letters to mission leaders, as well as those of his compatriots, attest to government vexation over the displacement of patriarchal structures from the political elite toward a new, popular category of common male interest.

Arguing that the woman had not consented to the original marriage and that "the girl exercised her rights over her person and presented herself and committed her full will to the *sixa* in front of the priest with an administrator as witness,"[115] Maupeou forcefully challenged the administration's determinants of guardianship, denying parental and conjugal authority over women and rhetorically declaring women's complete autonomy. However, he and other mission leaders, catechists, and confraternal members affiliates simultaneously granted overarching license to African Christian men to decide the fate of their female congregants and catechumens in the sphere of marriage.

Seeking to reinforce manufactured political hierarchies, even as they faced increasing resistance from local populations, Governor Bonncarrère included an article in the Decree of March 28, 1933 policing religious domains that required women to seek "permission of her guardian" before entering the *sixa* and stipulated she notify the *chef de région* of her intention 48 hours before she presented herself to the mission.[116] Later that year, the administration also issued the Guibet Order of October 7, 1933, which required that each *sixa* student carry an identification card listing her name, children's names, and "names of parents and family, whose parental rights are to be respected" as well as a statement of other family ties, the identification of her fiancé or husband (if existent), and the woman's age, race, village, origins, and name

---

[114] ACSSp. 2J1.10.7 Père Van Bulck, S.J. avec Mr. de Calbiac, commissaire de police à Yaoundé, 17 mai 1932.

[115] ACSSp. 2J1.10.7 Père Van Bulck, S.J. avec Mr. de Calbiac, commissaire de police à Yaoundé, 17 mai 1932.

[116] Article 27, Decret du 28 Mars 1933, signé Bonnecarrère, Cameroun 1933.

of her chief and superior chief.[117] In 1934, the administration passed laws further regulating catechists, which demanded that they carry new permits and consent forms from various regional authorities, including police chiefs and administration engineers in charge of roadwork and labor recruitment in addition to their obligatory identification card, which had been mandated since 1925.[118]

As in previous years, missionaries and catechists continued to staunchly defend their own rights to proselytize and the rights of African men and women to participate in Christian rites and sacraments, denying that women owed obedience to an elder "proprietor."[119] Mission records between 1925 and 1939 reveal that over the course of these decades, confraternal organizing expanded rapidly as marriage reform assumed more creative and aggressive strategies such as dramatic liberations of women and girls, like the seven young wives rescued from husbands who were keeping them from catechism and the emancipation of Nga Ndi, "sold as a girl and married against her will to the Christian, Englebert Effa," who was delivered to the *sixa* by catechists in Doumé and given refuge by Father Pichon.[120] Although Nga Ndi had sought out catechism and baptism at the Catholic mission in Doumé and asked her husband's permission to enter the *sixa* in 1929, Effa refused to grant her liberty to leave his farm. By 1930, Pichon and the catechists agreed to intervene to save her from "concibunage," as the Church did not recognize the marriage, and Nga Ndi left her husband to live in the mission. Effa claimed he was authorized by customary law to retain his wife and relentlessly fought Pichon and the catechists, first by lodging a complaint in the circonscription of Doumé charging "disorder caused by the mission" and "wife sequestration," and later by accusing his wife of abandonment. Pichon rightly agued that as Effa had married Nga Ndi when she was "a girl," the marriage contravened Governor Carde's 1922 marriage law outlawing pre-pubescent marriage. When Pichon lost the case – the Doumé court ruled in late 1931 that the marriage was valid and catechists had no right to interfere in lawful marriage – he told the court Effa was destined for "eternal hellfire." In response, Effa told Pichon, "I will pray that you die."[121]

---

[117] ANOM FM SJ 2 Ordre d'Inspecteur Guibet (Order Guibet), 7 October 1933.
[118] ANOM FM SJ 2 Act de 26 mai 1934, Cameroun.
[119] ACSSp. 2J1.10.7 Père Van Bulck, S.J. avec Mr. de Calbiac, commissaire de police à Yaoundé, 17 mai 1932.
[120] ACSSp. 2J1.2b2 Rapport du R. Père Fr. Pichon, Doumé, octobre 1931,"Mariages des fillettes"; ACSSp. 2J1.10.12, Père François Pichon, Doumé, Journal du Cameroun, "La polygamie," 1931.
[121] ACSSp. 2J1.2b2 Cameroun: Rapport du R. Pere Fr. Pichon in Doumé, Oct. 1931.

After being strongly censured by the administration following the trial, Pichon wrote in his journal that he was "honored" to have been "so condemned by the government."[122] After the Effa case, Pichon affirmed his work and convictions as well as lent encouragement to the missions' evangelists by preaching "Jesus Christ tells us to drown sin and scandal and have no mercy on those who cause them!," and "I must say, 'I, Christian, have the Word of brother Jesus Christ, the supreme judge, who will apply His sentence.' The judge of the French republic is neutral, secular, and Freemason ... and will burn."[123] African catechists and French priests collaborated especially well in the production of pious outrage, and wrote angry letters and sermons denouncing heads of circonscription, the police, and the governor as "inspired by Satan."[124] By lauding their affiliated catechists, defending their virtue, and portraying them in sermons and writings as bearing the cross of Christian duty, French priests imparted on them a strong sense of leadership and righteousness.

Conclusion

The severe restriction of religiously inspired work by Christian leaders during the 1930s decidedly confirms that the French mandate administration in Cameroon sought untransformed continuity rather than complex, unpredictable change, putting to rest any arguments about French officials' conviction in a "civilizing mission" in the territory. Widespread religious activities from masses and services, confessions, baptisms, and holy matrimony, and engagement with the social activism of pious brotherhoods led to profound and irreversible changes in social relations between Africans and in the relationship between African Christians and the colonial government. However, the administration continued to point out evidence of African criminality or social practices that resisted reform or substitution to justify their claim that African piety was superficial and that African Christians were "untransformed," which, officials concluded, conveyed they were simply acting unlawfully and immorally when defying the colonial government.[125]

While the French government resented disruptions to productivity and public works, they also feared any evolutions or forms of regulation that

---

[122] ACSSp. 2J1.10.12 Lettre de Mgr. Vogt, 5 août 1930; Père François Pichon, Doumé, "La polygamie," 1931.

[123] ACSSp. 2J1.10.12, Père François Pichon, Doumé, Journal du Cameroun, "La condemnation," 1931, 17.

[124] ACSSp. 2J1.10.12 Lettre de Mgr. Vogt 5 août 1930; Père François Pichon, Doumé, "La polygamie," 1931.

[125] ACSSp. 2J2 1A Journal de la Mission d'Ambam, notes de Père Delisle sur le Chef de subdivision d'Ambam, 24 janvier 1948.

were beyond their control.[126] In an angry letter to the Presbyterian mission, Marchand wrote, "We wish to develop native society within its proper framework. The *arrêté* of 30 April 1930 defends native society and allows it to progress in conformity with its own pace."[127] Later, a French official candidly compared the political and religious work in the territory, noting, "The missions do not seek to maintain the African in his customary cadre."[128] The missions responded that "custom" was simply a forbearance of progress, and that there was no predetermined "pace" of social transformation. Pastor Allégret testified in early in 1921, "We are ... working to do more than shape polite, devout Africans who speak French well. We are working to transform. ... The administration is both doubtful of our work and is jealous of us."[129] The "transformative" work of the missions was unpredictable, which was largely thrilling for foreign religious workers and terrifying for French governors.[130] Foreign missionary leaders also acknowledged that they, themselves, could not control the innovations and entrepreneurship of their ecclesiastical subordinates. Pastor Marcel Brun revealed that he was in fact awed by the sincerity and intentionality of Africans' conversion, lauding that Africans "pray abundantly ... referring to Jesus and to Biblical images and inspirations in their own language and with their own references ... which emerge from the same *milieu*, the same conditions of life ... as all their other thoughts."[131] Missionary psychologizing aside, it is clear that as local leaders innovated more revolutionary religious agendas, foreign missionaries, by and large, recognized their actions as expressions of devotion that yielded claims for justice and protection – both cosmically and in the world of lived experience. However, Christian leaders' acts were perceived by the administration as the claims of plaintiffs, insurrectionists, or miscreants.

---

[126] ANC APA 11016/G, Circulaire no. 78 application de la réglementation sur les cultes, du 16 sept. 1933; Louis-Paul Ngongo, *Histoire des forces religieuses au Cameroun* (Paris: Karthala, 1982), 60–1.
[127] ANOM AGEFOM 989/3419 lettre de Marchand à la Mission Américaine Presbytérienne, 17 jan. 1931.
[128] ANOM AFFPOL 2192/6 Missions religieuses au Cameroun, 1949–1954.
[129] SMEP/DEFAP Fonds Allégret: Cameroun 1920–1923, lettre Allégret au J. Bianquis, Douala, 30 avril 1921.
[130] ACSSp. 2J1.10.12 Vogt writes a scared letter on 5 août 1930.
[131] ANOM AFFPOL 2190/2 "Questions d'enseignement, Mission Française au Cameroun," Pasteur Marcel Brun, 1944.

CHAPTER 8

Ethical Masculinity: The Church and the Patriarchal Order

Introduction

On February 12, 1930 Albert Tonye married Agnès Albertine Ngonsémél in the Catholic church of Eseka in southern Cameroon. Agnès was Albert's first wife and, according to Tonye's account, they were both devout Catholics and had entered into the marriage according to their own free will. Tonye's father, Chief Makasso Malipem of the village of Songlipem, had sent Tonye at the age of ten to the Catholic mission at N'Gowayang to be educated and baptized. Between 1927 and 1929, Tonye had trained to be part of the colonial government and was appointed as an *écrivain auxiliare*, or secretarial assistant, in the regions surrounding Eseka and Sangmélima. In their first few years together, Agnès and Albert had several children, and Agnès managed their home in Eseka. In 1932, however, Albert fell out of favor with the colonial service, who revoked his position in Eseka and transferred him to Ouesso in the French colony of Moyen Congo. This kind of professional banishment was made worse by the fact that the colonial service refused to also transfer Agnès and the couple's children to Ouesso, a situation Albert described in his letters as "stranding" him "in a foreign land without any affection or family comfort."[1]

Throughout the next six years, Albert Tonye's career disappointment and marital separation grew into a political predicament for the French colonial administration and a delicate matter of religious diplomacy for the French Catholic Church in Cameroon. Beginning in 1932 and extending through 1938, Tonye began writing a series of letters – several dozen in total – to district officers in Eseka, to Pierre Aubert, the Governor of Cameroon, to Léon Solomiac, the Governor-General of French Equatorial Africa, to Bishops Mathurin le Mailloux and François-Xavier Vogt, and to Pope Pius XI in Rome, arguing that he had been married in the eyes of God and French law, and that the administration was violating a sacred bond in effectively terminating his marriage without his consent by separating him from his wife. For the next six years,

[1] ACSSp. 2J1.10.10 l'Affaire Tonye.

Tonye condemned the French government, slandered his wife, aggravated his extended family, and tried to outsmart the Catholic clerical elite in his quest to reunite his family as well as expand his household by taking a second wife to replace Agnès in her absence. Albert Tonye was twenty-two at the time of his marriage and twenty-four when he was terminated from his position in Eseka. Although he was educated, baptized, and salaried, Tonye discovered that he had little real power even, as we will see – over his own wife. He remained dependent on his father, a chief, to work on his behalf, and was at the mercy of a host of foreign elites in piecing his family back together. The letters from Tonye's case offer insight into the process by which many African men sought to control their family lives while religious and political initiatives to manage family life often counteracted their exertions.

Between 1932 and 1938, the wheels of bureaucracy moved slowly while Tonye pressured Eseka district officials and the administration in Yaoundé to reconsider their refusal to transfer Agnès and the children. During this period, Tonye demanded not only that his wife and children be immediately reunited with him in Ouesso, he also insisted to the bishops in Cameroon and the Pope in Rome that he be given permission to take a second wife precisely so that he "would not be without a wife like a pagan, destined for hell after death."[2] Tonye wrote to the Pope in a mixture of French and Latin, citing passages from Genesis and the Psalms, and arguing that a second wife was a right of a Christian man who desired many children. Tonye also explained that his polygamous intentions were righteous, since marrying a new wife could "save her from a life of unmarried prostitution ... and give her the blessings of a large family."[3] According to Tonye, not only were all unmarried women potential prostitutes, but his own wife in his absence was also a prostitute by nature of being separated from her husband, and she required official transfer to Ouesso in order to be saved from her sinfulness. Colorful imagery of women's sexual degradation and exploitation outside of recognized marriage ran throughout Tonye's entreaties for his wife's transfer as well as his demands for permission to marry multiple wives. Tonye's language directly parallels many clergymen and catechists' sermons in this period, which referred to African women as "prostitutes" and "concubines" unless they had been lawfully married in the Christian faith.

Tonye's March 1938 letter to Pope Pius XI made reference to the Holy See's 1930 papal encyclical *Casti Connubii*, which he used to buttress his argument

---

[2] ACSSp. 2J1.10.10 Lettre de Albert Tonye à Ouesso à Msgr. Mathurin le Mailloux à Douala, 10 mars 1938.

[3] ACSSp. 2J1.10.10 Lettre de Albert Tonye à Ouesso à Msgr. Mathurin le Mailloux à Douala, 10 mars 1938.

that as he was a loving husband, he deserved an obedient and present wife. Tonye argued, "The man is the leader of his wife as Christ is the leader of the Church. The man is Lord over her body and the woman must submit all before her husband, as the Church submits before Christ ... I must lead my wives to salvation. I will save these women from prostitution and give them a status as my legitimate wife to be equal before Christ."[4] This and other letters reveal a refracted Christian marriage ideology – adapted to personal convictions and desires – that espoused the redeeming character of not only Christian marriage, but also the Christian husband, who became the moral center through which the African woman could realize her human dignity. The Catholic Church's promotion of female obedience – an attribute emphasized in *Casti Connubii* – met with significant support among African Catholics in Cameroon, and offenses like disobedience and sexual infidelity assumed new legal and moral significance in areas with large Christian publics.[5] Tonye's language affirmed his belief in his right to married life as well as his responsibilities "as a good Christian ... to do [his] part to reform African households as the representatives of Christ on earth instructed."[6] His letters also reveal his frustration with his powerlessness in his professional life and political status, and his determination to affirm his control over the one aspect of his existence that he believed his Christian faith upheld – his marriage.

By December 1937, Tonye's demands had reached the upper echelons of power in the French administration when Governor Solomiac authorized the budget conferring funds to relocate Agnès and the children to Ouesso. All might have ended there, but Agnès decided to complicate matters. Perhaps she had heard that her husband accused her of prostitution in his absence and was upset with Albert, or possibly she had found another companion during her nearly six years of isolation from her husband, or maybe she simply did not wish to leave Eseka. Whatever her motivation, Agnès refused to travel to Ouesso. In letters to French officials, Agnès demanded that she be given an official French escort to chaperone her from Eseka to Yaoundé and from there to Ouesso, or, alternatively stated that she would not budge from Eseka unless Albert, himself came from Ouesso to claim her.

Agnès' stubbornness enraged Albert and made his letters to Rome and the offices of the bishops in Cameroon even more ardent, entreating them: "I need a new wife. I am not a bad Christian."[7] When asking permission to marry a

---

[4] ACSSp. 2J1.10.10 Lettre de Albert Tonye à Ouesso au Pape Pie XI à Rome, 19 mars 1938.
[5] Pius XI. Casti Connubii. Encyclical letter on Christian marriage, December 31, 1930.
[6] ACSSp. 2J1.10.10 Lettre de Albert Tonye à Ouesso à Msgr. François-Xavier Vogt à Yaoundé, 9 March 1938.
[7] ACSSp. 2J1.10.10 Lettres de Albert Tonye 1938.

second wife in the Church, he wrote, "I am pleading respectfully on my knees for your paternal benediction."[8] The bishops discussed Tonye's case among each other, but did not divert from their standard refusal to grant divorce in the case of a marriage between two Catholics or permit marriage to a second wife. While the Catholic Church and its missions strongly encouraged divorce for polygamists and women married to polygamist husbands (arguing that these were "not truly marriages"[9]), those who had received the marriage sacrament were forbidden to divorce or remarry. Throughout his exchanges, Tonye demonstrated what Cameroonian theologian Jean-Marc Ela explains as the deep reverence for the apostolic leadership among African Christian communities in Cameroon and their strong desire to conform to the teachings of the Church while fulfilling what they believed to be their earthly requirements.[10]

This complex and emotional drama came to an end in autumn 1938, when Agnès Albertine Ngonsémél-Tonye was escorted by the French administration to the station to board a train to Brazzaville, where she departed with her two youngest children to meet Albert. The record does not reveal what – or who – made Agnès change her mind, but like Albert she might not have had complete control over her fate. Certain facts allow the historian to speculate about her motives and pressures, however. Agnès and her children had been living with Tonye's father, Chief Makasso, in his home in the village of Songlipem in Albert's absence, and perhaps felt pressure over time to follow Albert to Ouesso, particularly as both Albert and Makasso so ardently demanded administrative approval for her transfer.[11] Agnès also frequently appealed to the administration for money to support her children – something Albert requested for her as well. Although the record makes no mention of this, Agnès might have run out of money entirely, or Chief Makasso might have reminded Agnès that if she refused to rejoin Albert and remain separated from him, she would have to repay her bridewealth. Like the majority of women in Cameroon who sought to end their marriages – particularly with men who were away for long periods of time in worksites or cities – Agnès may have discovered that salaried positions for women were very rare, and while brideservice obligations were hard on a husband seeking a wife, they were even more onerous on a wife seeking to leave her husband. Legal mandates to repay bridewealth often indebted women for years, despite the fact that bridewealth was paid

---

[8] ACSSp. 2J1.10.10 Lettre de Albert Tonye à Ouesso au Pape Pie XI à Rome, 19 mars 1938.
[9] ACSSp 2J1.10.7 lettres de 1923: lettre sur la polygamie à Msgr. Vogt du 12 mai 1923.
[10] Ela, *Ma Foi d'Africain*, 55–60.
[11] ACSSp. 2J1.10.10 Lettre de Albert Tonye à Brazzaville au chef de la subdivision d'Eseka, 30 avril 1937; Lettre du Commissaire de la République Française au Cameroun Aubert à Yaoundé à le Gouverneur Général de l'A.E.F. à Brazzaville, 26 janvier 1938.

to their fathers and male guardians. Although we do not know the complete extent of how Agnès and Tonye's predicament was resolved and what choices were made against what alternatives, we know that African women's abilities to enter into theological debates, exchange political favors, and negotiate their marital and sexual lives according to their own interests were more limited than that of men. The archival record ends with Agnès boarding a train to reunite with her husband.

As Agnès Albertine Ngonsémél's case demonstrates, while a Christian marriage theoretically held out the promise of a woman's spiritual as well as social equity, husbands like Albert Tonye could deploy religious belief to turn their wives into subjects of paternalistic discipline. Rather than becoming "an equal partner of the head of the family"[12] as missionaries promised, African women could be condemned to social subordination as Christian marriage became a male domain of power in which lawfulness and righteousness were open to interpretation by increasingly educated and assertive African Christian men. As Christian marriage conventions gained widespread acceptance, African Christian leaders began to consider a woman's alliances outside of monogamous marriage illicit, and encouraged women to abandon their lives of "prostitution and concubinage" in order to enter the licit sphere of Christian marriage or a life of Christian devotion as a nun.[13]

During the interwar years, African Christian men sought new positions as teachers and reformers, and masculinized social responsibility by liberating women from undesirable marriages, recruiting them for the *sixa* and other women's schools, initiating followers into new evangelical and interventionist collectives, and collectively organizing to stamp out bride price, polygamy, alcoholism, and other social ills. This chapter illustrates that the Christian Churches and their affiliated social and charitable organizations simultaneously fostered two interdependent cultures in the second decade of the interwar years: a restrictive culture that prized attachment to the conjugal domain, where the sole, freely chosen wife was expected to fulfill duties in the realms of spirituality, reproductivity, labor, and family; and a culture of compassionate assistance that emphasized forms of Christian social service among men, which changed possibilities for their leadership in society as well as the home. Religious discourse was complemented by public social discourse with very similar prescriptions. Between 1934 and 1938, when women's education and participation in church life was expanding in Cameroon, the West African journal *L'Education africaine* (the former *Bulletin de l'enseignement de l'AOF*)

---

[12] ACSSp. 2J1.7b4 Louis Paul Aujoulat, Ad Lucem, et Père Pierre Bonneau, *L'Action Catholique au Cameroun*, 1940.

[13] ACSSp. 2J1.10.13 Lettre de Mgr. Graffin au Gov. 27 déc. 1934.

published a series of articles on women's education by African graduates of the prestigious Ecole William Ponty in Senegal, which circulated in Cameroon through the Spiritan missions.[14] The articles' authors, including Papa Gueye Fall from Senegal, Ouezzin Coulibaly from Haute Volta, and Cyrille Aguessy from Dahomey, were eager to express their pragmatic and politically acute vision for elevating women's position in Africa. Coulibaly argued that men like him and his contemporaries at the Ecole Ponty, "have much trouble finding spouses who conform to our aspirations." He wrote, "We suffer more from a lack of educated women than from a lack of *évoluée* women ... perhaps this is because young intellectuals postpone marriage."[15] In his response to Coulibaly, Cyrille Aguessy claimed that it was women's responsibility to ensure that "intimate family life parallels our level of status and reputation."[16] All of the articles in *L'Education africaine* by the Ponty graduates emphasized the necessity of women's education and their emancipation from field labor, forced marriage, and custom "so that they acquire proper formation to be our spouses."[17] This rhetoric mirrored much of the discourse on women's advancement in Cameroon, which, as it developed, resembled less an exchange about women's autonomy than a discussion about how to train proper companionate wives who were exclusively loyal to their husbands.

Religious initiatives targeted men and women separately, and also had distinct agendas for couples or individuals. Crucially, gendered messages and approaches resulted in building Christian institutions that were intently conservative, despite their liberal and emancipating dimensions. While messages of conjugal love and companionate marriage promoted freedom from the tyranny of practices like polygamy, wife exchange, and child marriage and upheld principles of mutual respect, dignity, and rights between man and wife, it also sought to fundamentally define power in gendered terms. Stringent sexual and corporeal discipline over women, with an emphasis on motherhood and parentage as essential markers of individual dignity and of societal improvement,

---

[14] ACSSp. 2J1.10.7, articles de presse, polygamie.
[15] Daniel Ouezzin Coulibaly, "Sur l'éducation Des Femmes Africaines," *L'Education Africaine* 99–100 (1938): 33–6.
[16] Cyrille Aguessy, "Sur l'éducation Des Femmes Africaines," *L'Education Africaine*, no. 101 (1938): 65–8.
[17] Papa Guèye Fall, "L'enseignement Des Filles Au Sénégal et Dans Le Circonscription de Dakar," *L'Education Africaine* 87 (1934): 191–3; Coulibaly, "Sur l'éducation Des Femmes Africaines." See also Jean-Hervé Jézéquel, "Les Enseignants Comme Élite Politique En AOF (1930–1945): Des 'Meneurs de Galopins' Dans l'arène Politique (Teachers as a Political Elite in French West Africa (1930–1945))," *Cahiers d'Études Africaines* 45, no. 178 (January 1, 2005): 519–43; Jean-Hervé Jézéquel, "L'organisation Des Cadres de l'enseignement En Afrique Occidentale Française (1903–Fin Des Années 1930)," *Genèses* 4, no. 69, Spécial: "La parole est aux indigènes" (2007): 4–25.

laid the groundwork for the solidification of the public and private spheres as respectively masculine and feminine in the late interwar years. In spreading the "good news" of marriage reform throughout southern Cameroon, Catholic and Protestant communities reshaped male and female identity along with conformist mentalities regarding Christian family relations.

The Christian Churches' clerical and lay leaderships emphasized the proliferation of sin, greed, violence, and debt, which they blamed on African chiefs and agents of the French administration, but also attributed to everyday people's lack of faith. Christian confraternities capitalized on the growing numbers of mobile, devout single men who either faced penury and spouselessness or wedded indebtedness to enlist them in various campaigns to transform marriage practices such as bridewealth and widow inheritance in their societies. Men like François Bineng, a lay church volunteer who claimed to make only fifty francs per year, and Tam David, a tailor in a mission hospital, eagerly joined their voices to such condemnations, demanding, "How can we be at peace, solid and firm in our morals, and energetic in our efforts if we find ourselves infinitely poorer than others?"[18] African and European Christian leaders underscored bridewealth, polygamy, and other familiar forms of family-building as principally as violations of African *men's* rights as they indebted and exploited junior men and consigned poorer men to "forced bachelorhood."[19]

Moreover, polygamy was framed not only as immoral and unjust "wife hoarding" by wealthy men and chiefs, it was also positioned as a fundamentally *insecure* way of managing one's authority and access to a woman. According to most pre-Christian practices of household management in southern Cameroon's societies, a wife circulated freely between her father's, brothers', and husband's homes and farms, and women in polygamous marriages could rely on her fellow wives to maintain household production if she assisted her parents or relatives. In contrast, a woman in a Christian marriage was *bound* to her marriage according to the doctrines circulating in interwar Cameroon. She was forbidden by canon law to divorce and was exhorted by catechists and missionaries to remain loyal to her husband above all other male authority figures, particularly with regard to her labor and sexual reproductive capacities.[20] Africans read *Casti Connubii* and knew the rules, and also cleverly leveraged their own interference in polygamous marriages to present

---

[18] ANOM AFFPOL 2190/2 lettre de François Bineng, 1936; letter de Tam David, 1936.
[19] ACSSp 2J1.10.7, Notes sur la polygamie et questions connexes (à Yaoundé et environs) 1938, transmis et annoté par Mgr. Vogt.
[20] Protestant leaders in particular widely publicized statistics that claimed monogamous unions engendered greater numbers of children than polygamous ones and emphasized the piteousness of the single man in their prayers. Farelly, *Chronique Du Pays Banen (Au Cameroun)*, 173.

monogamous, Christian marriage as a protected, legitimate realm, in which there would be no threat of outside interference.[21]

Charity to Redeem Sinful Women

In January 1931, Elisabeth Tabi, a Catholic woman living in Yaoundé, sued her husband, Nicolas Belibi, for divorce after having separated from him six months prior. In the months leading to her decision to divorce, Elisabeth refused Nicolas' entreaties to return home and remained at her parents' house, which was several days' journey from Yaoundé, which enraged him. As his revenge, Nicolas, with the help of Captain Mahé, an African policeman in Yaoundé, registered Elisabeth as a "prostitute" in the official city prostitution roster, which subjected Elisabeth to searches and inquiries by the police.[22] Because Elisabeth and Nicolas had been married in the Catholic Church, the mission in Yaoundé informed Nicolas that divorce was impossible and that he was forbidden to demand bridewealth restitution from Elisabeth in the event that she did follow through with the breach. Although it was religiously forbidden, Elisabeth nevertheless obtained the divorce she sought in civil court, and Nicolas, who Mahé described as "not exactly expecting the gates of paradise to be opened before him," hounded Elisabeth for the bridewealth debt of 1000 francs.[23]

Indebted and suspected of prostitution, Elisabeth Tabi enrolled in the Ecole des Infirmières in Yaoundé with the help of the city police commissary and studied to become a nurse. Within a year, she had repaid her bridewealth debt, which the Yaoundé mission insisted that Nicolas either return or donate to the church to absolve his sin.[24] While the Yaoundé mission tried to reconcile the couple through meetings, Elisabeth proved intractably committed to her life as a nurse and expressed no interest in reuniting with Nicolas.

Growing antipathy to women's "proneness to adultery" and "women's litigiousness in seeking divorce" was equally evident among French officials and devoutly Christian men in Cameroon.[25] Although Nicolas Belibi resolutely

---

[21] Président Louis Marin et le Groupe parlementaire des missions, "La reglementation des marriages entre indigènes en Afrique Occidental Francaise et Afrique Equatoriale Francaise," Session du 16 juin 1939, *Journal Officiel du Cameroun*, 1939.

[22] ACSSp. 2J1.10.7, Cas Belibi-Tabi.

[23] ACSSp. 2J1.10.7, 17 janvier 1931, lettre de Mahé à Commissaire de Police de Calbiac.

[24] ACSSp. 2J1.10.7, Cas Belibi-Tabi.

[25] ANC APA 10634/A, Circulaire à toutes Circonscriptions du Commissaire à Yaoundé, 1931; Circulaire de 26 Mai 1934. The trend in maligning African females was not limited to Cameroon. African communities in Congo and Gabon faced the judgment of administrators who de-emphasized environmental factors and colonial labor practices

ignored mission entreaties to not seek bridewealth repayment, he was fiercely opposed to his wife's decision to divorce him, and had contacted the Yaoundé mission to enlist their support in criticizing her separation from him. Catholic Missions were increasingly concerned about the decreasing number of religious marriages in the territory, and began to make pronouncements on women's responsibility to "uphold marriage." The head mission in Yaoundé estimated that between 1930 and 1934, Cameroon's Catholics increased by over 30,000 to include an estimated 162,000 baptized Catholics by the autumn of 1934.[26] However, Church leaders worried that despite this achievement, the number of Catholic marriages had fallen to 1944 in 1934 while in 1930, priests officiated 3364 weddings.[27] Dovetailing foreign missionary concerns over women's behavior, the *indigénat* in Cameroon also criminalized adultery and conjugal abandonment for both men and women starting in the 1920s, but by the 1930s, its enforcement was largely left to local chiefs, who could be swayed by bribes, or, as some administrative reports found, who forced women to work on their farms as a penalty for marital infractions.[28]

The seemingly ambivalent position of Christianity in both restricting and emancipating their members could have drastically gendered effects. Historian of the Catholic Church in Cameroon Luc Ndjodo describes how a woman's extramarital sexual relations were commonplace occurrences in Beti society in pre-Christian times, particularly with regard to pre-marital sex and customs like *mvia* and *mgba*, where wives could be shared sexually with a husband's clients. However, a woman's sexual practices took on taboo dimensions with

---

in analyzing low birth rate dilemmas, and attributed population decrease and social decline that accompanied the flagging economy to "the disorganization of the native family," which was typically blamed on high divorce rates and women's sexual promiscuity. Belgian officials and missionaries in the Congo and Kenya also attributed demographic decline to the conjugal–sexual practices of African societies, particularly polygyny and the reproductive health practices of African women. For examples, see Nancy Rose Hunt, "Noise Over Camouflaged Polygamy: Colonial Morality Taxation, and a Woman-Naming Crisis in Belgian Africa", *Journal of African History* 32 (1991): 471–94; Nancy Rose Hunt, *A Colonial Lexicon: Birth Ritual, Medicalization, and Mobility in the Congo* (Durham, NC: Duke University Press, 1999); Lynn Thomas, "Imperial Concerns and 'Women's Affairs': State Efforts to Regulate Clitoridectomy and Eradicate Abortion in Meru, Kenya, c. 1910–1950," *Journal of African History* 39 (1998): 121–45; Lynn Thomas, *Politics of the Womb: Women, Reproduction, and the State in Kenya* (Berkeley, CA: University of California Press, 2003).

[26] ACSSp. 2J1.11a2 Prospectus status missionis nomen Yaoundé, 8 oct. 1934.
[27] ACSSp. 2J1.11a2 Prospectus status missionis nomen Yaoundé, 8 oct. 1934.
[28] ANOM SJ 2, Rapport du Haut Nyong sur l'article 337 du Code Penal Indigène, Rapport II: Application des Mesures relatives a la Suppression de la "justice penal indigene" 1946–1947.

the rise in Christian conversions.[29] Wife repudiation, lawsuits, violence, and public humiliation for sexual infidelity became commonplace by the 1930s and in this decade, discussions of women's sexual inconstancy and treachery were widespread. Pastor Maurice Farelly recalled the punishment that Bahok, the chief of the Nitoukou, meted out to his wife for betraying him, which included binding her and burying her in a colony of driver ants who "devoured her flesh."[30]

Missions also considered women a special category of catechumens or novice Christians, to be educated and reformed to lead honorable lives. Presbyterian catechist Solomon Enyumu Avebe wrote to the head mission,

> The missionary women have endured the trouble of teaching our wives. They have taught them to respect their marriage, to care for our children and to do the work of women ... Now many women begin to know things. They even know something of sewing and of the wearing of clothes, and of reading and writing. Above all, the women are beginning to respect marriage and to be obedient wives.

Demands for laws and codes that shamed women and sought to instill notions of the dishonor and disgrace of extramarital sexual encounters circulated in newspapers and sermons throughout Protestant and Catholic churches in Cameroon. The rhetoric surrounding "filles mères" and the outrage at "illegitimate" children signaled a cultural transition away from longstanding normative ideas regarding sexuality and flexible parentage governed through bridewealth exchange toward a conservative Christian interpretation of proper sexual relations and child filiation through blood and sacramental bond.[31] Moreover, adultery was punished as disobedience and treachery, and characterized as a crime against God.[32] Corporal punishment and excommunication for female adulterers was not uncommon in devoutly Christian villages in communities throughout Cameroon.[33]

Shifts in Church Organizing

Rising inequality and more punishing debt structures further entrenched Christian men's commitment to governing their wives' loyalty and

---

[29] Ndjodo, *Le Mariage Chrétien Chez Les Beti*, 30–2.
[30] Farelly, *Chronique Du Pays Banen (Au Cameroun)*, 57.
[31] This contrasts with Rachel Jean-Baptiste's examination of the phenomenon of the sexual economy that emerged within married life in colonial Gabon. Jean-Baptiste, *Conjugal Rights*, 23–43.
[32] Ndjodo, *Le Mariage Chrétien Chez Les Beti*, 50–1.
[33] Ndjodo, 53.

contributions to the marital home. Even among men with access to land and labor with which to grow cash crops, considerable wealth was often necessary for securing a wife, and, occasionally, as this chapter reveals, for maintaining custody of children. While bridewealth service or debt had been part of the social structure and cultural tradition of African societies throughout Cameroon prior to exposure to Christianity, new pressures related to novel kinds of indebtedness, bridewealth conspiracies and speculation, and economic uncertainty arising therefrom provoked popular hostilities against the wealthiest and most powerful and motivated collective action in Christian communities.

It is arguable that in this period, public suspicion toward modern, secular power grew considerably and morphed into local epistemologies in which power in the visible world is considered to be derived from and remains connected to (often nefarious) power in the invisible world of the supernatural.[34] Many Cameroonian societies' "deep mistrust of any form of power" as Geschiere phrases it, likely assumed greater prominence in the interwar decades, during which repression and forced dislocation in rural areas coincided with the rise of exploitive and even – as one of my sources put it, "depraved" – local individuals who sought personal advantage within this system.[35]

Persuasive religious arguments about the "freedom to marry," "the liberty of widows," "the natural rights of the Christian man," and "a woman's true guardian," served as self-empowering idioms for African laymen and priests interested in reforming marriage. Bold philanthropic efforts paid off in a certain sense. The Omvan Mission boasted that they performed 108 Catholic weddings in 1937 as a result of "benevolent works."[36] The Douala vicariate married 1510 couples, or 17% of their 89,356 baptized adherents, and the Yaoundé vicariate performed 4721 marriages from a population of 192,909 registered Catholics in that same year. Bishop Graffin acknowledged that such unions were a marked increase from the average of roughly 3000 weddings performed per year during the late 1920s, and is especially revealing of local marriage activism and personal devotion when one considers that between

---

[34] Stephen Ellis and Gerrie ter Haar, *Worlds of Power: Religious Thought and Political Practice in Africa* (New York: Oxford University Press, 2004); Stephen Ellis and Gerrie ter Haar, "Religion and Politics: Taking African Epistemologies Seriously," *Journal of Modern African Studies* 45, no. 3 (2007): 201; Geschiere, *The Modernity of Witchcraft*, 95.

[35] Geschiere, *The Modernity of Witchcraft*, 95. Oral interview with Mgr. Athanase Bala, CSSp., Bishop emeritus of Bafia, Cameroon, July 8, 2015, Séminaire des Missions, Congrégation du Saint-Esprit, Chevilly Larue, France. Mgr. Bala discussed the "depraved" forces who exploited the piety and innocence of villagers.

[36] Criaud, *La Geste Des Spiritans: Histoire de l'Eglise Au Cameroun 1916–1990*, 155.

1927 and 1937, the Catholic Church only added eighteen ordained priests to its ranks in Cameroon (but expanded the ranks of catechists by roughly 1400).[37]

Despite these apparent victories for Christian marriage, catechists' dramatic intrusions targeted all who disobeyed religious law, especially African women. While catechists sought to dismantle a wide array of non-Christian marriages and households as part of broader efforts to resist indebtedness and spouselessness among Christian men and unite believers in holy matrimony, they also practiced a politics of virtue whereby they assumed authority over everyday followers and penalized behaviors contrary to the Commandments. Small farmer, prosperous landowner, family father, devout daughter, penniless laborer, pregnant mother, each had his or her own vantage point with which he or she perceived relations of power or domination, which, as Thomas Piketty reminds us, "shape each person's judgment of what is and is not just."[38] As this chapter demonstrates, as marriage became a symbol of virtuous behavior for the faithful at the same time as it became more firmly implanted as an economic stratagem for the enterprising, the claims and demands of those desiring marriage were subject to growing counterclaims and interference.

The Cost of Marriage

In 1939, the administration reflected on the previous decade of social reform and reported that despite "opening opportunities for men's employment as teachers, nurses, import-export clerks, and agents in Mungo, Noun, N'Tem, and Nyong et Sanaga" African men's desires to marry could not be realized because of "the demands of the cocoa and coffee planters."[39] Some African men's newfound means of accumulating wealth and their greater mobility spurred new fields of competition. Throughout southern Cameroon, traders, cash crop producers, dockworkers, road laborers, importer-exporters, smugglers, plantation owners, and others engaged with new currencies, jockeyed for political opportunities, and struggled against the market to gain status and position.[40] The American Presbyterian Mission commented, "as greater num-

---

[37] ACSSp. 2J1.10.7 Lettre de Mgr. Rene Graffin Vicaire apostolique à le Commissaire de la République au Cameroun, Mvolyé, 24 août 1937; ACSSp. 2J1.8.a1 Rapport "L'Effort Catholique Français au Cameroun, les Peres du Saint-Esprit: Vicariats apostoliques de Yaoundé et Douala." See also "Disparition Progressive de La Famille Regulière Dans Le Sud-Cameroun," *L'Effort Camerounais*, October 6, 1957.

[38] Thomas Piketty, *Capital in the Twenty-First Century* (Cambridge, MA: Harvard University Press, 2014), 2.

[39] Inspecteur des Colonies Lucas Rapport 10 décembre 1938, APA 11196/C, ANC.

[40] Catherine Coquery-Vidrovitch discusses how women in Cameroon were particularly enticed by the economic incentives of cocoa cash-cropping in the early years of its

bers of African men became office boys, interpreters, teachers, carpenters, mechanics, and 'motor boys' ... they developed a craze for fine clothes, bicycles, phonographs, lamps, watches, flashlights ... and a thousand and one things only money could buy."[41] Lynn Schler has documented how the monetary economy had a deeply transformative effect on Africans' lives in Cameroon, linking ownership of certain goods with membership in newly formed communities and thus tying consumption to identity.[42] Schler has argued that the monetary economy was more influential in urban spaces, but interviews with African women conducted by Jeanne-Françoise Vincent between 1967 and 1971 unearth memories of the interwar period, when the "spirit of profit" also swept through the countryside. Vincent's interviews reveal that African men in remote villages also became imbued with the "spirit of individualism" and the lure of wealth as commerce increasingly connected rural regions with ports, cities, and small trading towns. Christian missions recorded the changing attitudes of men who circulated between rural villages, cities, and towns, who were becoming increasingly worldly, wealthy, and open to all forms of transaction.

Bridewealth was one fundamental aspect of the economy that colonial capitalist expansion could not but influence. Across Cameroon in the 1920s and 1930s, women's families increasingly demanded cash as well as goats, hogs, bulls, tools, alcohol, tobacco, palm wine, cloth, utensils, and luxury items like metals, guns, imported liquor, ivory, even fine clothes, bicycles, and cars. In Douala, *état civil* records from 1930 reveal that brides' fathers were demanding 1500 to 3000 francs for their daughters, and further in the interior in Yabassi, they received 800 to 2000 francs.[43] Among the Banen in the central Cameroon city of Bafia, marriage records reveal that average bride price in 1936 was 1500 francs, which rose to 110,000 francs in 1956.[44] In the southern forests, Beti,

---

proliferation in Cameroon, only later to be overtaken by men in their control over cocoa production. Catherine Coquery-Vidrovitch, *Les Africaines. Histoire Des Femmes d'Afrique Noire Du XIXe Au XXe Siècle* (Paris: Desjonquères, 1994), 99–110.

[41] Lois Johnson McNeill, *The Great Ngee: The Story of a Jungle Doctor* (Philadelphia: Commission on Ecumenical Mission and Relations of the United Presbyterian Church in the United States of America, 1959), 163.

[42] Lynn Schler, "Bridewealth, Guns and Other Status Symbols: Immigration and Consumption in Colonial Douala," *Journal of African Cultural Studies* 16, no. 2 (December 1, 2003): 213–34.

[43] Owono Nkoudou, "Le Problème Du Mariage Dotal Au Cameroun Français"; Bureau, "Ethno-Sociologie Religieuse Des Duala et Apparentés"; Manga Bekombo, "Conflits d'autorité Au Sein de La Société Familiale Chez Les Duala Du Sud-Cameroun," *Cahiers d'Études Africaines* 4 (1963): 317–29.

[44] Idelette Dugast, *Monographie de la tribu des Ndiki (Banen du Cameroun): Vie sociale et familiale* (Paris: Institut d'ethnologie, 1959), 256–7.

Bulu, and Bassa farmers incorporated greater amounts of currency into bridewealth exchange as they adopted cocoa.[45] By 1950, Douala and Yaoundé *état civil* registries recorded bride prices of between 80,000 and 200,000 francs.[46] Unable to provide their fathers-in-law full recompense for their daughters, a growing number of grooms were obliged to remain companionless even while maintaining prolonged bridewealth payment contracts.[47] Catholic mission stations throughout Cameroon arguably contradicted their own prohibitions and provoked bridewealth inflation by occasionally reimbursing the bridewealth for female converts seeking divorce from polygamous husbands and by paying bridewealth to the families of women who took vows as nuns.[48] Decrees in 1927, 1933, and 1934 reflect the administration's awareness of the evolving bridewealth economy, and the 1933 decree specifically stated that marriages "where bridewealth is excessively demanded by the father" be discouraged.[49]

The bridewealth economy and the economy at large directly influenced the contrapuntal effects of expanding polygamy practices among some African men and the Christian marriage agenda of the increasingly African-led churches. Recall the experience of Matthias Bakatal from the opening pages of this book, the Catholic man who was whipped in a church entryway for marrying a second wife. While we do not know Bakatal's precise reasons, we can make some informed guesses considering what is known about village life in the Nlong region of southern Cameroon in 1927. Most men in earlier decades

---

[45] See Jane I. Guyer, ed., *Money Matters: Instability, Values and Social Payments in the Modern History of West African Communities* (Portsmouth, NH: Heinemann, 1994); Jane I. Guyer, *Marginal Gains: Monetary Transactions in Atlantic Africa* (Chicago: University of Chicago Press, 2004).

[46] Zoa, "La Dot Dans Les Territoires d'Afrique." ACSSp. 2J1.15b3 Pere Paul Bernier "Avers et revers d'une chrétienté."

[47] Jacques Binet, *Budgets familiaux des planteurs de cacao au Cameroun* (Paris: Office de la Recherche Scientifique et Technique Outre-Mer, 1956), 82; Marie-Paule Bochet de Thé, "La Femme Dans La Dynamique de La Société Bëti, 1887–1966" (Thèse de 3e cycle, Univeristé de la Sorbonne (Paris V), 1970), 269; Owono Nkoudou, "Le Problème Du Mariage Dotal Au Cameroun Français," 53; Guyer, "Beti Widow Inheritance and Marriage Law: A Social History," 206.

[48] Dzou, "Christianisation des Beti du centre Cameroun 1922–1955," 105; Dussercle, *Du Kilimandjaro Au Cameroun. Mgr. F.X. Vogt (1870–1943)*, 119–20, and 155; Père François Pichon, "Les Causes de La Crise de Natalité Au Cameroun," *Marchés Coloniaux Du Monde*, March 26, 1949, Informations d'Outre-Mer edition; Le Roy, *Un Martyr de La Morale Chrétienne, Le Père Henri de Maupeou de La Congrégation Du Saint-Esprit, Missionnaire Au Cameroun.*

[49] ANOM SJ 2 decret du 14 septembre 1933; arrêté du 26 Mai 1934 concernant le reglementation du mariage indigène; ANC APA 10634/A Circulaire à tous les Circonscriptions, du Commissaire à Yaoundé, 1931; Circulaire du 26 May 1934 à tous les Circonscriptions, arrêté concernant le reglementation du mariage indigène.

typically married a second wife in order to expand their household production, advance their status, or secure kinship or political ties. However, Nlong in 1927 was a region in which the market for cash crops was rapidly expanding. Here, and in neighboring regions, a wife assumed new significance. Economic growth made women's labor contributions all the more critical to a family business and thus complicated Christian marriage reform in interwar Cameroon.

In many families in the southern forests and western highlands, the desire for progeny grew relative to the demand for field labor for cash crop production, and a wife or daughter – or an inherited widow – was a critical production partner. Gareth Austin and Jean Allman have illustrated how the labor required for the spread of cocoa in West African societies necessitated the (frequently non-remunerated) contributions of African wives.[50] Societies like the Bulu and Beti in southern Cameroon generally maintained monogamous, sedentary, cocoa-farming households but vigorously controlled offspring and their labor.[51] While scholars such as Philippe Darge have documented that among the Bamileke in western Cameroon, the demands of coffee cultivation required a considerable amount of labor in addition to the immediate family,[52] in the cocoa and palm oil-producing regions of southern Cameroon, family fathers increasingly relied on their daughters for seasonal labor. As a result, fathers postponed their daughters' marriages, demanded higher bride price payments for their marriages, or insisted they leave their conjugal home and return to their family home during seasonal harvests – creating considerable antagonism between husbands and their fathers-in-law. Unfortunately, these antagonisms often played out in litigation against the female spouse.[53] Administrators in Mbalmayo complained that lawsuits against women for abandonment of conjugal domicile were often due to conflicts over a wife's harvest-time labor contribution.[54] In regions with high labor demands – par-

---

[50] Gareth Austin, *Labour, Land, and Capital in Ghana: From Slavery to Free Labour in Asante, 1807–1956* (Rochester, NY: University of Rochester Press, 2005); Jean Allman, "Making Mothers: Missionaries, Medical Officers and Women's Work in Colonial Asante, 1924–1945," *History Workshop Journal* 38, no. 1 (September 21, 1994): 26.

[51] Guyer, "Beti Widow Inheritance and Marriage Law: A Social History"; Jane I. Guyer, "Female Farming and the Evolution of Food Production Patterns Amongst the Beti of South-Central Cameroon," *Africa: Journal of the International African Institute* 50, no. 4 (1980): 341–56.

[52] Philippe Darge, "Le Cafe Au Cameroun" (Ecole Nationale de la France d'Outre-Mer, 1958).

[53] Thomas Mongo, "La Dot ce Mal d'Afrique," *l'Effort Camerounais*, no. 213, 6 septembre 1959; Iwiye Kalalobe, "Au Cameroun, à quelle famille appartient une femme mariée?," *L'Effort Camerounais*, no. 208, octobre 1959.

[54] ANOM AGEFOM 989/3430 Circonscription d'Abong Mbang Bulletin Agricole, 1927–1933. Letters from the 1940s also refer to the 1930s as a critical period of marital

ticularly in the southern forest zones along the transport lines that crossed Akonolinga, Yaoundé, Doumé, Akono, and other commercially production centers – marital dissolution was commonplace.[55] This launched a flurry of letters between district officials and African chiefs and fathers over "moral concerns" for women "escaping work everywhere."[56] Husbands in monogamous marriages were particularly passionate in their pleas to the courts, stating that their wives "betrayed" them by assisting their fathers instead of working on their own farms.[57] Widows were likewise forcefully pursued in the courts for failing to appear during a harvest at the homestead of their late husband's kin.[58] Accusations of denying labor contributions were more common than accusations of adultery in cases where women were charged with conjugal abandonment, particularly between the late 1920s and throughout the 1930s.

Therefore, it can be inferred that some men – even some baptized Catholics such as Matthias Bakatal – took a second wife to either replace a wife who had been called to harvest her father's field, or perhaps to assist the first wife with farm work, or simply to expand his farm's productivity in a time of high prices. Christian men like Simon Mbem from the town of Bafia labored in small enterprises, and claimed to need five wives to help oversee production in different villages. In 1936, Mbem found work as a transporter with a trucking agency that serviced the region's cocoa farms and used his salary to acquire more wives whose agriculture he transported and sold.[59] Perhaps because he was reproachful of his sinfulness or jealous of his success, a local man framed Simon Mbem for the crime of theft, for which Mbem was tried and imprisoned until several witnesses appeared to reveal the resentful scheme against him.[60]

Mission records note that a great many Africans found the economic changes occurring in their communities destabilizing, marginalizing, and

---

conflicts with regard to harvest contributions. See ACSSp. 2J1.15.b2, Chef du subdivision de Mbalmayo H. Chaussivert, lettre du 22 juin 1944; Chef de Region de Nyong et Sanaga, letter du 26 juin 1944.

[55] ACSSp. 2J1.10.12 Mémoire du Père Pichon, Minlaba, 1930; ANC APA 10634/A Charles Faucherand, Rapport d'Inspection de la Région de Haut Nyong, du 19 juillet au 6 aôut 1948.

[56] ANOM AGEFOM 989/3424 (Justice 1927–1933), Lettre 1 nov 1928, Gov. Générale de AOF Brazzaville; *La Gazette du Cameroun*, no. 39, jan.–mars 1927; see also ACSSp. 2J1.15.b2, lettre de convocation no. 205, Mbalmayo, 20 juin 1944.

[57] ANOM FM SJ 2, Rapport du Nyong et Sanaga; Rapport II: Application des mesures relatives à la suppression de la "justice penal indigène," la période critique (1946–1947). See also Guyer, "Beti Widow Inheritance and Marriage Law: A Social History," 197–9.

[58] ACSSp. 2J1.15.b2 Mbalmayo, 14 october 1944, Chef de Subdivison de Mbalmayo Henri Chaussivert au Père Mader à la Mission Catholique d'Obout: la veuve de M'Bazoa Ngoa.

[59] ANOM FM SJ 1, Bafia, Justice de Paix, Lettre de Madame Ndem Simon, 12 juillet 1950.

[60] ANOM FM SJ 1, Général de la justice, Bafia.

immoral. Not all Africans became wealthier – or as wealthy as some – and income and marital disparities caused considerable tension and grievances. French agricultural production reports to the League mention that a class of wealthy African planters and palm oil refiners reaped considerably more financial benefits from the robust economy, which they used to control access to labor as well as wives.[61] The administration neglected to include in the report to the Permanent Mandates Commission its policy of endorsing the labor recruitment practices of wealthy African producers, which allowed them to forcibly remove young men from villages and towns to work on their farms.[62]

The Mbam region, where Simon Mbem visited his many wives, was connected by major thoroughfares leading to Yaoundé to the south and Nkongsamba and Douala to the west. Regions such as these were purchase and exchange hubs for palm oil and cocoa, where currency circulated as much as the ever more ambitious populace. The market economy did not overshadow, but rather fueled the marital economy. A small palm oil producer in the town of Somo could only carry thirty kilos of oil to sell in Yabassi on his own, and so depended greatly on his wife to carry another twenty alongside him. Having a second wife meant that the five day walk to the market was more profitable.[63] Procuring a wife without assuming considerable bridewealth debt, however, was a challenge for most men – even those seeking a bride from a Christian family.

Bridewealth inflation marked the late 1920s through the 1930s, ensnaring men in long-term commitments to share their wealth.[64] In burgeoning market towns like Edea, Bafia, Nkongsamba, and Ebolowa, fathers sought to expand their businesses with investment procured from their daughters' bridewealth. Brothers paid their own marriage debts by collecting their sisters' bridewealth. French officials noted that even some administration chiefs paid for their own marriages by collecting their sisters' bridewealth.[65] Geschiere has chronicled

---

[61] ANOM AGEFOM 151/5 Agriculture en Cameroun, 1923–1936, Rapport Angelini, 1933. Palm oil cash cropping and refining was one of the most lucrative enterprises. Cameroon exported 140,000 tons per year of palm oil between 1944 and 1948: Guernier and Briat, *Cameroun, Togo, Encyclopédie de l'Afrique Française*, 203–5.
[62] ANOM AGEFOM 151/5 Autorisation de recrutement, 14 décembre 1935 de Jules Repiquet.
[63] Farelly, *Chronique Du Pays Banen (Au Cameroun)*, 27.
[64] Owono Nkoudou, "Le Problème Du Mariage Dotal Au Cameroun Français," 53–4; Jacques Binet, *Budgets familiaux des planteurs de cacao au Cameroun* (Paris: Office de la Recherche Scientifique et Technique Outre-Mer, 1956), 82–3; Marie-Paule Bochet de Thé, "La Femme Dans La Dynamique de La Société Bëti, 1887–1966" (Univeristé de la Sorbonne (Paris V), 1970), 269–70.
[65] AFFPOL 2190/1 Rapport annuel du gouvernement français sur l'administration sous mandat des territoires du Cameroun pour l'année 1923, 76.

how generational conflicts arose in the interwar period between fathers and sons over who would receive and disburse the bridewealth of a female family member. Sons still largely remained dependent on their sisters' bride prices to fund their own marriages, but as bridewealth was paid more and more in currency, the older generation spent the payments for bridewealth on themselves.[66] As Geschiere notes, in earlier times, when payments were made in prestige goods like livestock, iron, and tools, these could be more effectively redistributed to the younger generation.[67] Elders' ability to capture the profits of marriage was aggressively challenged, particularly as younger men could express resentment at their dispossession in religious meetings taking place on a near daily basis and strategize ways to circumvent them.

Across the Cameroon territory, fortunes grew among certain families and lineages, making the marriage market fiercely competitive. District reports detail that chiefs faced resistance when collecting taxes from men fulfilling brideservice, and chiefs, themselves, could be voracious when extracting livestock, gifts, and payments from their villagers to help pay their sons' bridewealth.[68] Iwiye Kalalobe, a Duala intellectual and journalist, wrote that as a result of capitalism, African men ceased their discipline over "conjugal conduct" and replaced it with a discipline of "commercial conduct," which deformed their approach to family-building and promoted marriage and bridewealth exchange as necessary transactions to create wealth in a new, more competitive economy.[69]

Bridewealth Inflation and Investment

New pressures on household production considerably impacted the institution of bridewealth. Between the early 1920s and mid-1930s, Christian mission workers and French officials noted that bridewealth had transformed from a standard practice, "negotiated in phases of contraction and endless discussion to bridge two families," to one of manipulation and extortion between fathers

---

[66] While French officials were predisposed to reduce bridewealth to "slavery," Governor Marchand did discern a subtle shift in the bridewealth "scheme" in 1928, noting that "exploitation" had become more severe as fathers used bridewealth to fund personal ventures, rather than distribute the wealth to allow their dependants to acquire wives. ANOM AGEFOM 989/3424 (Justice 1927–1933) Gov. Marchand à Yaoundé, Circulaire à toutes les circonscriptions, 18 octobre 1928.

[67] Geschiere, *Village Communities and the State*, 409.

[68] ANOM AGEFOM 989/3424 Cameroun Justice legislation civile 1927–1933, Lettre à Monsieur le Gouverneur, 14 novembre 1928.

[69] Iwiye Kalalobe, "Au Cameroun, à Quelle Famille Appartient Une Femme Mariée?," *L'Effort Camerounais*, October 1949, 208 edition.

and junior men.[70] During the 1920s, Catholic mission workers negotiated with baptized men regarding their allowances to live with the women whose bridewealth they were still in the process of paying.[71] To varying extents, bridewealth was paid over the long term in many societies, which complicated the question of when to hold the official church ceremony, which would grant the husband full rights over his wife and children according to religious law, but not necessarily local understandings of guardianship.

Among Beti societies, for instance, bridewealth was not only defined by the conferral of goods and/or services to the father, guardian, or male kin of the bride over time (often over several years) in exchange for the recognition of a marriage alliance with a daughter, it was also the foundation of the entire economic system on which spousal rights and child guardianship was recognized.[72] Conventionally, as long as the bridewealth remained unfulfilled, the bride did not fully "belong" to her fiancé, nor did the fiancé have rights to custody over any children born between them, and the bride's father could retain her in his house and employ her labor and that of her offspring.[73] Other societies in Cameroon also had this understanding or slight variances on this approach. Among the coastal Duala, all marriage was legitimized through *bémà*, or bridewealth, without which all labor and progeny produced by the woman was retained by her family of origin.[74] Joshua Dibundu, one of the first Duala pastors ordained in 1883 by the London Baptist Mission, was compelled to insist on marriage without *bémà*, and consequently, in accordance with Duala custom, the pastor's children were regarded as belonging not to him but to his wife's family.[75] It was also common practice across many African societies in Cameroon to allow residence and movement between households while bridewealth continued to be serviced if payments were agreed upon by both parties. A fiancée and any children she bore could live in and move freely between her fiancé's home and her paternal home, and the wife and children could perform labor in any of those spaces.[76] When Christian doc-

---

[70] ANOM AFFPOL 3349/8, La Situation Politique de la femme africaine, Decrets du 1939–1951; ANC 2AC 552, La dot et la femme africaine.

[71] ACSSp. 2J1.2b2 Lettre du Mgr. Vogt à Gouverneur Marchand, 3 September 1924.

[72] Ndjodo, *Le Mariage Chrétien Chez Les Beti*; Guyer, "The Value of Beti Bridewealth."

[73] Essomba Fouda, *Le Mariage Chrétien Au Cameroun: Une Réalité Anthropologique, Civile et Sacramentelle*, 35–43.

[74] The *bémà* was also a cornerstone of the neighboring Batanga and Malimba peoples, who speak Tanga and Limba, languages very closely related to Duala, with many mutually intelligible words, including "*bémà*." Bureau, "Ethno-Sociologie Religieuse Des Duala et Apparentés," 160–5.

[75] Brutsch, "A Glance at Missions in Cameroon," 309.

[76] Jean-Pierre Ombolo, *Essai Sur L'histoire, Les Clans et Les Regroupements Claniques Des Eton Du Cameroun* (Yaoundé: Presses Universitaires de Yaoundé, 1986), 426–33;

trines formally established custody's dependency on receiving the sacrament of marriage, local grooms and fiancés strategically weighed the benefits and assurances of being a member of a particular community.

However, French colonial law utterly complicated the choice between a local or "customary" understanding of marriage and guardianship and a Christian one. In the 1930s, Governor Bonncarrère's laws recognized claims to marriage and custody only with bridewealth's "full remittance," which would be recorded in an *état civil* registration center.[77] In 1935, Bonnecarrère's edit proclaimed, "The children born to the wife before marriage are the custody of the wife's paternal family."[78] As the mandate progressed, civil laws entrenched the dependency of marital and custodial "belonging" on bridewealth's full payment, which served fathers (elders), rather than young men seeking marriage.[79]

Local reactions to these contradictory policies were varied. In some cases, family fathers would register their daughter's marriage in the *état civil* after the groom's first bridewealth payment, but would only allow a church, or sacramental marriage to take place after the entire sum had been paid.[80] However, in 1937, Mgr. Graffin wrote to officials in Yaoundé that women's guardians were "afraid of signing away their daughters' hand...without receiving one hundred percent of the *dot* payments." "This procedure," wrote Graffin, "is enormously burdensome ... but the risk of losing a daughter is too great."[81] African Catholic men were disturbed when missionaries and catechists regarded their wives as "concubines" as a result of their "unofficial" marriage status in the church (i.e. they had not received the marriage sacrament), but they had rendered

---

Isidore Tabi, *La Theologie Des Rites Beti: Essai D'explication Religieuse Des Rites Beti et Ses Implications Socio-Culturelles* (Yaoundé, Cameroon: Éditions St. Paul, 1991), 21–63; Ngoa, "Le Mariage chez les Ewondo: Étude sociologique"; Bureau, "Ethno-Sociologie Religieuse Des Duala et Apparentés"; Marlene Dobkin, "Colonialism and the Legal Status of Women in Francophonic Africa," *Cahiers d'Études Africaines* 8, no. 31 (1968), 390–405; Edwin Ardener, *Coastal Bantu of the Cameroons: The Kpe-Mboko, Duala Limba, and Tanga-Yasa Groups of the British and French Trusteeship Territories of the Cameroons (Western Africa, Part XI)* (London: International African Institute, 1956), 65–7; Pierre Alexandre and Jacques Binet, *Le Groupe Dit Pahouin (Fang-Boulou-Beti)* (Paris: Presses Universitaires de France, 1958), 64–6.

[77] ANC APA 11016/G lettre de Mgr. Graffin, Mvolyé, 30 avril 1937; Gov. Bonncarrère Circulaire no. 107 de 20 juin 1937.

[78] Loi du mariage 1935, Governor Auguste Bonnecarrère.

[79] Jeanne-Françoise Vincent, *Femmes Beti Entre Deux Mondes: Entretiens Dans La Forêt Du Cameroun* (Paris: Karthala, 2001), 23–6.

[80] Lettre de Mgr Rene Graffin Vicaire apostolique à Mr. le Commissaire de la République au Cameroun, Mvolyé, 24 août 1937; Ordres d'Inspectur Guibet, 7 oct. 1933; Lettre de Mvolyé, 16 oct. 1933, à Mr. le Gouverneur à Yaoundé, 2J1.10.7, ACSSp.

[81] Lettre de Graffin de Mvolyé, 30 avril 1937, APA 11016/G, ANC.

some, if not all, of the bridewealth.[82] Pastor Farelly also noticed increased anxiety among young Protestant grooms in the mid-1930s, writing, "Men borrow to begin making bridewealth payments in order to marry ... And so the man owes his lender and his father-in-law who both demand payments ... Creditors hound their debtors and old debts are brutally restituted."[83]

In some villages during the 1930s, fathers found a way to monetize the statutory enforcement of child custody by increasing the bridewealth debt after a daughter birthed a child, as she had proven her fertility and made herself more valuable. This lucrative expropriation prolonged brideservice, coining the Beti adage, *nkoe meveg wa dzidzie* ("the bridewealth basket is never full").[84] This innovation was addressed in several administrative decrees, including the Mandel Decree of 15 June 1939, which pronounced the strictest punishments for "extortive" fathers who pursued "excessive" and "sustained" bride price. Despite this, the French administration never overturned the 1935 law making legally recognized custody dependent on full bridewealth remittance, and thus the law remained unamended and regularly exploited.[85]

French officials noted another procedural corollary of Bonnecarrère's 1935 law in the late 1930s, when reports disclosed that in southern Cameroon, women were "resold" to different spouses once their fertility had been proven with the birth of a child. In this scheme, which the administration termed "bridewealth speculation," a father would contract a marriage with his daughter by declaring a specific bridewealth sum in the *état civil*. Then, following the birth of a child from that union, the woman's father would request a divorce from her original husband and contract another marriage with a man willing to pay a higher bridewealth for a fertile mother and her child.[86] The father would then nullify the first marriage agreement by repaying the original bridewealth

---

[82] Témoignages sur la dot, enregistré à la Journée d'Etudes, Les Jeunes Face au Mariage, Nkongsamba, 5 juin 1955, 2J1.7b4, ACSSp.

[83] Farelly, *Chronique Du Pays Banen (Au Cameroun)*, 28–9.

[84] Lettre de Charles Atangana à Mvolyé, 23 mars 1932, 2J1.10.7, ACSSp.

[85] Jugement Enoncé des faits; Article 11 du décret du 19 novembre 1947; Procureur publique, Cour d'appel, chef du service judiciare, No. 408/PAC/1, "La réforme de justice africaine," Douala, 29 Jan. 1949, APA 10634/A, ANC. Rapport sur le Conférence Africaine de Brazzaville de 1944, les mandates sur le mariage indigène en AEF; Circulaire no. 751, Direction des Affaires Politiques, Décret sur les modalités du mariage en AOF, AEF, Cameroun, et Togo, 19 Septembre 1951, F. Luchaire, AFFPOL 3349/8, ANOM.

[86] Many pieces of evidence, both missionary and administrative, are used to illustrate this general picture of bridewealth speculation. Certain practices varied among families, but the general practice of encouraging divorce from a first husband to form a more advantageous alliance with a second husband due to the proven fertility and strength of the bride is demonstrated to have increased in the 1930s and 1940s as reports of such behavior emanated from regions across southern, central, and coastal Cameroon. See

to the first husband and collect the higher sum from the second. Bridewealth speculation was not only limited to daughters, but could also involve inherited widows. Writing in 1935, French administrator Maurice Bertaut was dismayed to find out that a Bulu man who inherited a wife after his brother's death was eager to "sell her again to the highest bidder."[87] Savvy manipulation of civil and customary legal recognitions of bridewealth as proprietorship allowed fathers and elder kin to profit from a daughter, niece, or inherited widow's social value and emboldened wealthy men seeking a wife to acquire a bounty of a wife and progeny simultaneously. This practice was so commonly observed that the administration in Yaoundé specifically banned it in 1939 with a law against "the commerce of girls … through commercial speculation on the marriage market."[88] French attorney Robert Blin excoriated African family fathers in his 1939 report, accusing them of "speculative profiteering, slavery, and prostitution," and advised that the act be punishable by up to two years in prison and 6000 francs fine.[89]

Divorce and Remarriage as Economic Opportunities

In 1930, the French administration expressed alarm over the particular acceleration of Christian conversion in the western highlands in Cameroon, where catechists were disrupting clan and family hierarchies and political leaders.[90] In a series of angry letters to administration and mission officials, Bangangté clan leaders articulated that they could not manage discipline among village men and expressed considerable anger over the recruitment of local women to the Protestant *internat* in Bangangté and the Catholic *sixa* schools in Foumban.[91] Reports from Bamiléké customary courts also revealed high numbers of lawsuits against women for abandonment of conjugal domicile, which

---

Dossier APA 10634/A and Dossier 2AC 552, ANC as well as "La Situation Politique de la femme africaine, Decrets du 1939–1951," AFFPOL 3349/8, ANOM.

[87] Maurice Bertaut, *Le Droit Coutoumier Des Boulous* (Paris: Domat-Montchrestien, 1935), 172. See also Jane I. Guyer, *The Economic Position of Beti Widows: Past and Present*, African Studies Center Report (Boston, MA: Boston University, African Studies Center, 1979).

[88] Loi du 3 mars 1939.

[89] Lettre à Mr. Blin, procureur de la République près le Tribunal Supérieur, Chef du Service Judiciaire, du Tribunal de première instance, 1939, APA 10634/A, ANC.

[90] ANOM AGEFOM 355/170bis Justice Indigene avant 1946, Liberté de conscience, Pays Bamiléké 1930.

[91] ANOM AGEFOM 355/170bis, Affaire de Bangangté entre le chef de Bangang et les ressortissants de la mission protestante, jugement 52 Co. octobre 1924; affaire entre le chef de Bangoua et la mission protestante, jugement no. 48 Co. septembre 1924; affaire du chef de Bana avec la mission protestante, jugement no. 2 Co. janvier 1925.

officials blamed on missionary interference in local marriages as well as labor conflicts.[92] In a case in Dschang in 1929, Ngohoua, a local father, was put on trial for murdering his daughter because she had left her husband. In court, he testified that he had killed her "so that she would not inspire others."[93] Much was at stake in his daughter's marriage, including a hefty bridewealth that he could not afford to repay her abandoned husband. Ngohoua was given a death sentence so that his fate would also serve as a warning to others who wished to interfere in their children's marriages.[94] Despite upholding capital punishment even after Ngohoua's appeal in the court in Douala, French officials were deeply troubled by such family strife. Administrators expressed growing anxiety about the effects of Christian "radicalism," and believed that interfering too greatly in polygamy, arranged marriage, or other customs affirming paternal privilege existentially threatened the delicate power structures of the western highlands.[95]

In western Cameroon, Protestant missionary evangelism was predominantly carried out by Bamoun and Bamileke farmers, tradesmen, and administration auxiliaries, as well as a growing number of unemployed students and migrants who had been educated at mission schools.[96] Many young

---

[92] ANOM FM SJ 2, Bamiléké tribunaux coutoumiers, 1940.

[93] ANOM Cameroun Affaires Judiciaires, 2688/3 Ministère des Colonies François Piétri, Rapport au Président de la République Française, 12 décembre 1930, Recours en grâce du Né Ngohoua, condamné à mort, Cameroun, 23 août 1929.

[94] ANOM Cameroun Affaires Judiciaires, 2688/3 Chambre d'Homologation Douala, 30 novembre 1929.

[95] In western Cameroon, coffee farms that were first established around the Chemin de Fer du Nord in the early 1920s soon expanded in the high plateaus of the Bamileke and Bamoun regions, but remained tightly regulated by the French administration. Favoring the investments of their European settlers, district officials limited the number of coffee licenses issued to Africans as well as the land area an African coffee planter could cultivate. This guaranteed that there would be abundant field labor for white coffee farms and less competition among growers. It also meant that a small, connected cadre of Africans in the western highlands of Cameroon acquired the rights to participate in lucrative coffee growing and trading, which many translated into wealth in the form of wives and control over low-wage workers. The territorial administration estimated that 4 million coffee plants had been planted in the Mungo region in 1939 by African planters. By 1947, there were 6 million coffee plants cultivated by African farmers in Mungo, Dschang, and Foumban. Guernier and Briat, *Cameroun, Togo, Encyclopédie de l'Afrique Française*, 202–3. See also ANOM FM SJ 1, Convention entre Indigènes No. 101, Décret du 29 Septembre 1920, Région Bamiléké; Affaire du Kamaha, Chef du village de Badokassang; Affaire du Gaston Ngandjui, Chef des Bafang; ANOM FM SJ 1, AEF Cameroun Rapport de l'Avocat General Rolland sur la situation judiciaire, 1950, Rapport sur le Justice de Paix à Competence Etendue à Foumbam.

[96] SMEP/DEFAP EEC FB 1/2 Notes sur l'histoire de l'Église au Cameroun, Jean René Brutsch, 1946.

Christians in western Cameroon, not unlike their counterparts farther south, were typically mobile and literate, and whether salaried or unemployed saw themselves as junior laborers who resented or openly challenged elites like politicians, elders, and administration-backed chiefs. In most of western and coastal Cameroon, Protestants considerably outnumbered Catholics.[97] In 1930, government records indicate that there were a total of 2727 Protestants in the *Pays Bamoun* in contrast to only 209 Catholics. However, the Apostolic Prefect of Dschang and African catechists in the nearby Mission of Bafang grew the number of baptized Catholics in the region from several hundred in 1930 to 16,000 by 1959.[98]

The Protestant and Catholic churches both gained a great number of young men and women by promising to "facilitate their marriages" and shield their marital choices from interference from their elders.[99] Catholic missionaries and catechists contextualized Christianity by instructing their adherents to follow the declaration of the Council of Trent – which confirmed that the essence of marriage was the mutual consent of two spouses – in an attempt to translate the faith into a struggle against inveterate senior men whose sanction for marriage was required.[100] African and European Catholic leaders in the Bamileke region reinforced their calls for reform by sponsoring the renovation of village and housing construction to replace previous patterns of the extended family compound or clusters of buildings around a chief's estate with freestanding homes of monogamous families centered on the village church.[101] By the end of the interwar period, the administration expressed concern over the "spirit of independence" and unbridled reformist zeal of catechists and young Christians in the region.[102] One French official accused young Christian men of "bullying" chiefs and demoralizing their elders.[103] African pastors stated the

---

[97] See Slageren, *Origines de l'Eglise Evangélique du Caméroun*, 231–45.
[98] ACSSp. 2J1.9b3 Terrorisme à Bafang Catholique, 1959. In 1950, the French Protestant Mission lamented the progression of Catholicism in the Bamiléké region, blaming the dearth of missionaries. In that year, there was one European protestant missionary and seventy Catholic missionaries in the *Pays Bamiléké* and the *Pays Bamoun*. See Rapport de la 28eme Conférence des Missionaires du Cameroun, *Journal des Missions Evangéliques*, 1950, 343.
[99] ANOM FM SJ 1, Rapport sur le Justice de Paix à Competence Etendue à Foumban, 19–20 July 1950; ANOM AGEFOM 355/170bis, Liberté de conscience, Pays Bamiléké 1930.
[100] ACSSp. 2J1.7b4 Conference Jan 19, 1946, Les milieux sociaux du Cameroun.
[101] Malaquais, "Building in the Name of God: Architecture, Resistance, and the Christian Faith in the Bamileke Highlands of Western Cameroon," 68.
[102] ANOM AGEFOM 355/170bis, Justice Indigène avant 1946.
[103] ANOM AGEFOM 355/170bis, Liberté de conscience, Pays Bamiléké 1930.

opposite, however, decrying African Christians' persecution at the hands of the Bamoun sultan and Bamileke chiefs.[104]

In 1935, the Apostolic Prefect of Dschang informed the French administration that it intended to make significant progress in the Bamileke population, which it estimated to be between 20,000 and 30,000 souls, by encouraging Bamileke and Bamoun catechists to travel deeper into rural areas and find new young people to join the Catholic Church as marriage reformers.[105] The Protestant mission similarly avowed that African pastors would "convert their Dschang and Bana brothers," who would then deliver the entire region to Christianity. Although the administration doubted the missions' ability to entrench themselves in a region where Islam was widely embraced, it nonetheless gave stern warnings that the proliferation of unrestricted Christianity could disrupt the rural order and thus threaten France's administrative and economic objectives in the region.[106]

Despite this, the French Protestant Mission maintained a large congregation by educating boys at the local Ecole Normale and training catechists and pastors at the nearby Ecole Biblique in Foumban and the Ecole de Theologie in Ndoungué. Bamoun and Bamileke Christians also occupied all the catechist posts in the Bamileke synodal region of the Protestant Church. The French administration assented to missionary pressure to exempt catechists from porterage and labor *prestation*, giving them the same privileges as African chiefs.[107] Catechists would capitalize on their privilege and cite their educational commitments and evangelical commissions to extricate themselves from customary responsibilities as well as family obligations and everyday chores, and consequently inflamed the sensibilities of elders and chiefs. However, it was the catechists' interferences in the lives of young women and the marriage negotiations of family leaders that led them to be pursued in the tribunal of Bangangté for fraud, arbitrary sequestration, and violation of domicile.[108]

Despite the increasingly high cost of bridewealth and stringent laws requiring bridewealth repayment, women in Cameroon increasingly took advantage

---

[104] SMEP/DEFAP EEC FB 2/2, Allocution prononcée par Benjamin Ngu, 28 avril 1959; Allocution de Charles Kassi, 1954.

[105] Paul Bocque, Eveque de Nkongsamba, *La Politique et les Chrétiens en Afrique Noire*, Publication d'Action Catholique, Imprimerie St. Paul, Mvolyé, Yaoundé, 1955.

[106] ANOM AGEFOM 355/170bis, Liberté de conscience, Pays Bamiléké 1930.

[107] Arrêté du février 1933, *Journal Officiel du Cameroun*, no. 306, 15 février 1933, 92–3. See also Myazhiom, *Sociétés et Rivalités religieuses au Cameroun sous domination Française (1916–1958)*, 139.

[108] ANOM AGEFOM 355/170bis, Liberté de conscience, Pays Bamiléké 1930; ANOM FM SJ 1, Région Bamiléké, Subdivision de Bafang, Tribunal Coutoumier, Affaire de Terrain, 17 mai 1950.

of the 1922 and 1926 divorce decrees to extricate themselves from their marriages throughout the 1920s and 1930s. In 1924, African customary courts heard 14,750 cases across Cameroon, the vast majority of which concerned marriage and family cases.[109] By 1930, each regional court in the southern regions of Akonolinga, Mbalmayo, and Yaoundé were hearing over 4000 cases concerning divorce or custody disputes.[110] By 1935, this number increased to 5000 in each region.[111] Women also brought a great number of family cases before the French tribunals of first and second degree – often citing that they wished to marry another man other than their first or chosen husband, and, in some cases, stated directly that they were encouraged to do so by a Christian mission.[112] French government reports from the 1920s and 1930s were highly critical of African females, arguing that word-of-mouth transmission of divorce laws motivated women to "copy the legal acts of her sisters."[113] The administration also criticized what they termed as "women's proneness to adultery," and blamed the low birthrate on "women's litigiousness in seeking divorce."[114] The administration frequently assigned culpability in marriage dissolution to females but also chastised chiefs for their inability to control women's immorality and exert authority over them.[115]

In rural areas, bridewealth paid in the form of palm wine and foodstuffs was often consumed immediately. Currency and livestock received by a father often went to help pay for his son's bridewealth. How could a woman seeking divorce or an inherited widow repay goods that had already been consumed or exchanged? Prior to French rule, most longstanding African divorce traditions in the territory maintained that the wife's father pay restitution to the husband in case of divorce.[116] Fathers of divorcées would negotiate repayments

[109] Rapport Annuel du Gouvernement Français sur l'administration sous mandat des Territoires du Cameroun, Pour l'année 1924.
[110] ACSSp. 2J1.10.12 Chef du subdiv. d'Akonolinga au R.P. Faussier, Mission de Medzek, 12 juin 1930.
[111] ANOM AFFPOL 2190/1 Conseil de Notables de la Circonscription d'Ebolowa, scéance de 19 nov. 1929, Rapport annuel du gouvernement français sur l'administration du Cameroun pour l'année 1929, 95.
[112] Extrait de Rapport d'Inspection de la Région du Haut-Nyong, 19 Juillet au 6 Aout, 1948; SMEP/DEFAP EEC FB 2/2 Allocutions Benjamin Ngu, 28 avril 1959; Paul Maffire, 7 mai 1959.
[113] ANC APA 10560/A Rapport du circonscription de l'Ebolowa, 1931.
[114] ANC APA 10634/A, Circulaire à toutes Circonscriptions du Commissaire à Yaoundé, 1931; Circulaire de 26 Mai 1934.
[115] ANOM SJ 2 Rapport II: Application des mesures relatives à la suppression de la "justice penal indigene". La period critique: (1946–1947): Une Colonisation provisoire.
[116] Essomba Fouda, *Le Mariage Chrétien Au Cameroun : Une Réalité Anthropologique, Civile et Sacramentelle*, 40–5.

or exchanges to former husbands, and new marriages could be arranged subsequently. However, French law codified bridewealth in ways that shifted the burden of reimbursement to women, rather than those who negotiated their marriages, since both the 1928 and the 1934 versions of the territory's marriage law explicitly mentioned that women seeking divorce were liable for bridewealth repayment.[117] Missionaries noted that many African fathers and male guardians throughout Cameroon went along with the letter of these laws, and renounced their personal obligation to repay bridewealth in case of a divorce that was initiated by their daughter, even though they had been the recipients of the payment.[118] In an interview with Idelette Dugast in 1959, a Banen chief revealed that he told his daughters at the time of their marriages: "I warn you, once I have eaten the price of your marriage, I cannot be like the goats and regurgitate in my mouth what I have just swallowed."[119]

Seizing an opportunity to both capitalize on rising divorce suits and, per government orders, dissuade women from abandoning their marriages, African chiefs in southern Cameroon began confiscating labor as payment from indebted divorcées. Reports from the late 1920s through the 1950s speak to the widespread phenomenon of chiefs "operating the courts like a private business,"[120] and "using the tribunal as a credit agency ... where divorced women become employees of the chief's plantation where they work off their bridewealth debt to their former husbands.",[121] In 1928, André Raynaud, a French jurist who later became head of the Bafang subdivision noticed that chiefs in Ebolowa were nimbly capitalizing on divorce lawsuits by even marrying indebted women and using their labor to slowly repay their former husbands. Raynaud suggested employing anti-slavery laws in order to explicitly combat this practice, which he argued resembled "polygamy, bigamy ... and excessive marriage."[122] Between 1938 and 1942, local farmers and other chiefs from the Akok region lodged complaints against Chief Manga Etua for his "confiscation of wives through divorce judgments."[123] The case finally drew the administration's attention after one chief concluded that Etua's scheme was a

---

[117] ANC APA 10634/A Rapport d'Inspection de la Région de Haut Nyong, du 19 Juillet au 6 Aout 1948.
[118] ANC APA 10384 Les missions et la dot, 1930.
[119] Dugast, *Monographie de la tribu des Ndiki (Banen du Cameroun)*, 257.
[120] ANC 2AC 552/2, Plainte No. 4/TR/DJ.
[121] ANOM SJ 2 Rapport du Nyong et Sanaga, and Rapport II: Application des mesures relatives à la suppression de la "justice penal indigene". La period critique: (1946–1947); Extrait de Rapport d'Inspection de la Région du Haut-Nyong, 19 Juillet au 6 Aout, 1948.
[122] ANOM AGEFOM 989/3424 Lettre de Administrateur Raynaud à Monsieur le Gouverneur, APA, récu le 14 Novembre 1928.
[123] ANC 2AC/2043 Villages, Akok, 1935–1945.

socio-economic threat as it caused "shiftlessness, abandonment of worksites, and rural flight" among the men of the region.[124] Therefore, the social field was wide open for those who could preserve or restore a sense of moral authority, instructing and challenging everyday people to distinguish between what was just from what was merely legal, or commonplace.[125]

I discussed this phenomenon with two men – Samuel Mzeanj and Otto Biba – in Yaoundé whose roots were in the Littoral and Nyong-et-Sanaga regions and whose families in rural Cameroon still remembered acts of bridewealth extortion and Christian interventionist countermeasures such as the ones mentioned in court records.[126] I did not determine these informants' ages, but both were older than middle age and had several adult children. A self-described Bamileke transplant to Yaoundé, Samuel Mzeanj (known as Papa Sam), explained that among his community, it was believed that a woman held two essential "spaces" within her body – the *ventre* and the *bas-ventre*, or the belly and the womb. The *ventre*, or belly, belonged to her husband, and he had to feed it and keep her healthy and satisfied. The *bas-ventre*, or womb, on the other hand, always belonged to her father. What a daughter's womb produced was cherished kin, as well as a claim and an asset. "The *bas-ventre* is part of the family of origin of the woman," Mzeanj insisted. "It is not only the endowment of the man and wife." When I responded that children inevitably make up an integral part of the conjugal family since they are the children of the husband and wife, Mzeanj replied, "Yes. The child is the child of the couple. But there is the question if *patrimoine* (heritage). The *bas-ventre* is part of a woman's father's heritage and thus it belongs to the woman's father."[127] Samuel Mzeanj believed that bridewealth extortion was bad for young husbands, but a man's right to govern his grandchildren was inalienable.

When I discussed these perhaps controversial ideas with Otto Biba, he heartily defended the *ventre–bas-ventre* contrast, and stated that a woman's head (or mind) was also highly prized in families. However, this also belonged

---

[124] ANC APA 10784/C Rapport Semestriel Abong-Mbang, Situation Politique, 22 Janvier 1932; ANC 2AC/2043, Lettre Personnelle du Thomas Nyangon Nnanga, 27 avril 1942, Chef du Groupement à Ekowong, Subdivision de Ebolowa à l'Administrateur–Chef de la Subdivision de l'Ebolowa.

[125] Organizing chiefdom was more than a duty of officialdom to create order out of chaos and tribal "purity" out of tribal "patchwork," as Mahmood Mamdani has argued. Alongside codifying custom and transforming agglomerations of people into distinct "tribes," the process of assigning centralized political leadership was fundamentally about forging rational, legible hierarchies at the domestic, community, and "tribal" levels. See Mamdani, *Citizen and Subject*, 81.

[126] Samuel Mzeanj (Papa Sam) and Otto Biba, oral interview, September 2, 2007, Bastos neighborhood, Yaoundé.

[127] Samuel Mzeanj, oral interview, September 2, 2007, Bastos neighborhood, Yaoundé.

to the father, he claimed, and fathers expected their daughters to share their opinions, traditions, and stances on issues. "The head belongs to the father," Biba stated, "because he must manage conflict in his family. His own wife will disagree with him, and his relatives and in-laws will too. But his children must be his allies, his trusted defenders."[128] Biba and Mzeanj were two of the most loquacious informants on the issue of family belonging and alliance, and revealed to me the philosophy of "family coherence." Both men professed to be Christian, and did not believe Christianity stood in conflict with notions of "family coherence" and expectations for cross-generational bonds and obligations. When I asked if they could remember much of the resistance of young couples to their fathers' bridewealth demands and their exploitation of their daughters' fertility in the decades before independence, they said they certainly could, and explained that the colonial period was one in which there were myriad struggles over "family coherence," which was why there was "no social peace."[129]

A Religious Solution to Marital Corruption

Religious workers identified African junior men's need to attain masculine status and worked to implant consent, monogamy, complementarity, and costlessness in marriage as its manifestations. Catechists, clergymen, and missionaries criticized that "customary" or non-Christian marriage was too easily exploited for private profit. Adult Christian men were thus charged with finding a solution to inequity caused by a competitive economy. Protestant catechist Jean Mwambo attested that he became a catechist in 1932 "when I realized that God reserved for me a great and heavy task to accomplish: to be the spiritual guide of my poor brothers."[130]

A monogamous, consensual, indissoluble marriage union and a fertile, conjugally centered household became not only demonstrations of Christian virtue, but also evidence of one's participation in the building of a new heritage

---

[128] Otto Biba. Biba's reflections echoed the Bulu community ideals transcribed by George Horner during the 1950s and early 1960s. Horner recorded that among the Bulu, a woman could serve as the *mone ka* or intermediary between villages in instances where she had no son. When a woman served as a *mone ka* (also referred to as *monekal*) she typically spoke for the interests of her father. See Horner, "The Allocation of Power and Responsibility in Bulu Society: A Test of the Usefulness of a Methodology Developed by Marion Levy Jr. in 'The Structure of Society,'" 413.

[129] Samuel Mzeanj and Otto Biba, oral interview, September 2, 2007, Bastos neighborhood, Yaoundé.

[130] SMEP/DEFAP EEC FB 2/2, Allocution de Jean Mwambo à l'occasion de sa consécration pastorale à Bagam, 31 octobre 1954.

from which to draw moral strength.[131] African ministers and teachers conceptually intertwined Christianity with masculine rights and emphasized conjugal love and family stability defended by pious authorities rather than customary routines that were susceptible to the manipulations of self-interested elites. Father John the Baptist Zamcho related to me during an interview that Christian communities assuredly influenced people to hesitate to divorce once married in the church. As the church anchored so much community life and marriage was the mortar that maintained connections between church and lineage members, both of these entities came to have a vested interest in sanctified unions. Once church membership was entrenched in both the couple and their lineage, uncoupling (after being married by a priest) became a serious taboo.[132]

Part of what dissuaded many Christian couples from divorcing was a renewed focus on reproduction, paternal custody, and family leadership. Historian of marriage among Cameroon's societies Luc Ndjodo asserts that within all forms of marriage in southern Cameroon, romantic love was not as essential as the responsibility to reproduce. The exigency to make progeny was felt by men in both monogamous and polygamous marriages in the territory and was at the root of related goals of expanding social status, wealth, and community standing.[133] African catechists and priests like Léon Messi and Jean-Pierre Ombolo agree that the romantic basis of marriage was celebrated and preferred among Beti societies, but that fertility and reproduction were the ultimate ambitions of all marriages.[134] As the desire for successors and greater control over them grew, monogamy increased in popularity among African Christians as a family ideal.[135] Christian leaders like Léon Messi and Albert Ndongmo emphasized that polygamy was not essential for producing many children, and more importantly, it threatened men's authority over their wives and children. Moreover, catechists argued that young monogamous men

---

[131] In discussing the formation of a new, modern Ijesha identity among Nigerians, J.D.Y. Peel makes the claim that adoption of new practices and identities presupposes a history that goes beyond the invention of a "mere 'mythical charter' conjured solely out of contemporary interest." Peel asserts that temporal continuity and the mobilization of memory are required to have a "history active in the present," even if the engagement, idioms, and practices are profoundly novel. See J.D.Y. Peel, *Ijeshas and Nigerians: The Incorporation of a Yoruba Kingdom, 1890s–1970s* (Cambridge: Cambridge University Press, 1983), 261–2.

[132] Oral interview, John the Baptist Zamcho Anyeh, S.J., May 25, 2014, Maison Jesuite, Mvolyé, Cameroon.

[133] Ndjodo, *Le Mariage Chrétien Chez Les Beti*, 9–12.

[134] Ombolo, *Sexe et Société En Afrique Noire: L'Anthropologie Sexuelle Beti: Essai Analytique, Critique et Comparatif*, 228–30.

[135] Ela, "Le Droit à La Différence Ou l'enjeu Des Églises Locales En Afrique Noire."

should refuse to pay bridewealth, as it was an even greater threat to a young husband's authority since it indebted him and based recognition of rights to his children on a series of payments to his wife's patri-kin.[136] With these arguments, African Christian men began to view the monogamous, church-sanctioned family as a domain of domestic sovereignty, where a husband would have undisputed rights over his wife and children, free bridewealth obligations or from the interferences of women with religious justifications for divorce.

Marriage Activism in Southern Cameroon

In southern Cameroon, the issue of widow inheritance became a particular focus of catechist intervention and confraternal organizing, despite the fact that the French administration never passed any laws against the practice, per the insistence of many chiefs on the Councils of Notables.[137] Mission records in southern Cameroon point to a trend of Christian men persuading young widows to marry them, as their situation could potentially provide the possibility of marrying without paying bridewealth if there was no expectation that the woman be inherited by her late husband's kin.[138] More often than not, the widows' erstwhile inheritors perceived these men as inveiglers, seducing women away from their rightful place in their inheritors' homesteads. Catechists in the Obouti-Mbalmayo mission engaged in "prolonged battles" to defend local men who married widows and prevented their late husbands' kin from acquiring them.[139] In 1928, the widow Mengha Mbili married Megouo, a Christian man who attended the Obouti-Mbalmayo Catholic church, rather than be inherited by Nga Zamba, her husband's brother. Between 1928 and 1933, Megouo and the mission's catechists hid Mengha Mbili, advocated for Megouo in court, fought with Nga Zamba, and gathered supporters to fortify the couple's claim "to marry freely."[140] The zealousness of local Christians in nullifying Nga Zamba's claim to Mbili and the authority they gave themselves to supplant all local established practices of widow inheritance astonished French officials in Mbalmayo, who received a number of letters both from disavowed inheritors regarding women's "escape of domicile," and from catechists and missionaries demanding "jurisprudence that reflects ... consent,

---

[136] Abbé Albert Ndongmo, "Au Cameroun: Trois sortes de Polygames," *La Croix*, 26 juin 1962.

[137] ANOM AGEFOM 799/1855 Chef Atamengue, Chef Zogo Fouda, Conseil de Notables: Procès Verbal de la séance du 16 février 1926.

[138] ACSSp. 2J1.15.b2 loi du mariage 1934 considérations; lettre de Père Mader, Obout, 14 oct. 1944.

[139] ACSSp. 2J1.15.b2 Mission d'Obouti-M'balmayo, catéchistes.

[140] ACSSp. 2J1.15.b2 Veuve Mengha Mbili, 1928–1933.

validity, and freedom of widows."[141] When brought before the tribunals, however, widows and their chosen companions did not gain their legal right to marry without reimbursing the traditional beneficiary. Only through secretive arrangements or by going into hiding – often arranged by catechists and other religious leaders – could a widowed woman enter into holy matrimony with a man of her choosing without reimbursing her bridewealth.

Catechist and confraternal members' work with unmarried men was intensive, but apparently effective. African men who participated in confraternal organizing demonstrated the strongest desire to marry within the Church, and as a group significantly increased participation in marriage sacraments. In 1935 and 1936, the Kribi mission attributed their increased numbers of weddings to their confraternal members' interventions. During those same years tithing was generous enough that nearly all Kribi catechists were fully salaried, which reinforced their sense that their efforts were being rewarded. This fact also appears to hve encouraged more catechist recruits, who contributed to what the mission record referred to as "progress in supervising village participation" in communions, baptisms, and feast days.[142] Members of the *Confrérie de Saint Jospeh* (*Ekoan Joseph*) in the Ewondo region policed each other's marriage transactions to guarantee that members neither paid nor received bridewealth. Professing a desire to be "examples," *Ekoan Joseph* leaders called themselves "good men" and organized retreats and confessions to monitor behavior among one another and their fellow faithful.[143] The Bassa catechists and the *Confrérie de la Sainte Vierge* of the Nlong Mission assembled locals for confessions and did not hesitate to inform on their fellow believers who they considered in need of repentence.[144] Religious men did not only impose surveillance on their fellow men, they also policed women and even their own wives. Embittered expressions such as *okukut mininga* (Ewondo for "stupid wife" and *akukut bininga*, or "stupid wives") circulated in church meetings referring to women who desired a marriage with bridewealth or who sought divorce from a Christian man.[145]

Christian leaders were not alone in their efforts to circumscribe women's freedoms in interwar Cameroon. The later decades of French rule saw the

---

[141] Reglementation des mariages entre indigènes en Afrique Occidentale Française, *Journal Officiel du Cameroun*, 16 juin 1939; ACSSp. 2J1.15.b2 loi du domicile, 1934; lettre du Chef de subdivision de Mbalmayo, 20 juillet 1938; Chef de Région de Nyong et Sanaga, Femmes et travail, 1944.

[142] ACSSp. 2J2.1a Mission Saint Joseph de Kribi, Journal de 1936, Journal de 1935.

[143] ACSSp. 2J1.2b2 Vicariate du Cameroun 1927, Confrérie de Saint Joseph; ACSSp. 2J2.1a Confrérie de Saint Joseph, 4 mars 1934.

[144] ACSSp. 2J2.1a Mission Saint Joseph de Kribi, Journal de 3 mars 1929.

[145] ACSSp. 2J1.15.a7 Ewondos Catholiques.

narrowing of African women's access to legal divorce as the administration along with several missionary societies compelled chiefs to limit a woman's means of extricating herself from wedlock, particularly in the case of a Christian marriage.[146] During the 1940s, women seeking divorce were increasingly accused of adultery, "abandonment of conjugal domicile," and "kidnapping" of children, which could carry high fines and penalties, even if they were granted a divorce. Encouraged by resentful former spouses as well as an anxious political administration, courts also increasingly sought reimbursement of the bride price from divorced women. Former husbands also took ex-wives to court for default on bride price debt, all of which eliminated many women's avenues for divorce.

Pierre Mbogo, a Catholic leader in Douala and its environs in the interwar and postwar periods, recorded that many youth were migrating to cities a result of pressure from their parents to find salaried work so they could pay bridewealth and contribute to the financial security of their villages.[147] Mbogo's interviews with Douala-area Catholics and catechumens reveal a transition in the conventional wisdom on marriage and conjugal life as a result of social networks and brotherhoods. As men developed networks in cities, they tended to depend more on their salaried labor and religious and professional connections as means of coordinating marriage alliances, rather than their lineages or village elders. Many young Catholics communicated to Mbogo that they felt divided from their elders on this issue, as their elders continued to seek to build connections through their juniors' marriage arrangements.[148] However, young, urban men also related to Mbogo that while their elders were marginalized from marriage decisions, they still expected young men to service them with customary tributes and bridewealth to be shared among the extended family. The contradictory pressures of individualization through migration/professionalization and mandatory wealth redistribution among elders, wives, and in-laws prompted many men to seek out social groups sponsored by the numerous missions and churches in southern Cameroon, where they could

---

[146] For histories of divorce lawsuits in Francophone African colonies and their social consequences, see Richard Roberts, "Representation, Structure and Agency: Divorce in the French Soudan during the Early Twentieth Century," *The Journal of African History* 40, no. 3 (1999): 389–410; additionally, for concerns in British Africa, see Judith Byfield, "Women, Marriage, Divorce, and the Emerging Colonial State in Abeokuta (Nigeria), 1892–1904," *Canadian Journal of African Studies* 30 (1996): 32–51.

[147] ACSSp. 2J1.13b1, JOC Camerounaise, Compte-Rendu de la journée-d'études, 31 octobre 1954.

[148] ACSSp. 2J1.13b1, Pierre Mbogo, Secretariat Territorial, equipe federale de Douala de la Jeunesse Ouvrière Chrétienne.

work to appease their elders and fulfill their lineage obligations while pursuing more companionate marriages of their own choosing.

As indigenous religious advocates continued their material and symbolic construction of the Churches to which they pledged allegiance, they consciously calculated that the public's receptivity to their creeds would depend on their ability to mold systems of collective engagement and mutual aid that would remedy economic and legal problems, as well as evoke a sense of the familiar. Destabilizing forms of economic and political competition demanded Africans innovate new responses, but as colonial rule evolved in the second decade of French presence, catechists instructed that their followers blend charity, personal obligation, and justice-seeking in their engagements with their spouses, families, and lineages in ways that signaled approval of confrontation and conflict, but also echoed communal traditions of social action.

Conclusion

Père Louis Barde, a French Jesuit priest, reflected upon his visit to Cameroon in 1934 that the "stunning devotion" of Christians in Cameroon – which he reported to constitute 352,366 souls – was a "peaceful revolution," but that French missionaries had little control over its evolution. It was the responsibility of "2500 black catechists … to lead distinct, parallel actions with a civilizing aim."[149] Indeed, thousands of Catholic and Protestant catechists and clergymen, as well as other consecrated members and lay associations continued to craft reformative and restorative policies in the years leading up to and following World War II. As the war drew European missionaries, government officials, doctors, and other colonial agents back to the metropole by the end of the 1930s, Africans took up positions of greater official authority in most major religious, administrative, industrial, and scientific institutions.[150] However, their influence and leadership had been established during the interwar years, particularly in the intimate social cells of rural and urban life.

---

[149] Barde, *Au Cameroun Avec M. Wilbois, Les Graves Problèmes de La Polygamie et de l'instruction*, 9–11. Barde's estimation of the Catholic population likely included the number of catechumens and those in mission schools as well as baptized believers.

[150] For analysis of the revolutionary and anti-colonialist corollaries of this transition, see Eric T. Jennings, *Vichy in the Tropics: Petain's National Revolution in Madagascar, Guadeloupe, and Indochina, 1940–44* (Stanford: Stanford University Press, 2001).

CHAPTER 9

The Significance of African Christian Communities Beyond Cameroon

Christian Responsibility Beyond the Home Front

Pious brotherhoods had organized spiritually motivated men (and some women) during the interwar decades, but during the late 1930s, the emergence of *cercles* (aid societies) sponsored by French-funded Catholic Action allowed for an even greater degree of professional organizing for Catholics in Cameroon. The goals of the *cercles* were initially straightforward, and mirrored those of *confréries*: spread Christianity in towns and villages, organize social life and rituals around the liturgical calendar, and mobilize the apostolate to address challenges to family life, social stability, and marriage alliances.[1] As Catholic Action expanded its focus from missions to clinics, hospitals, and orphanages, it helped link them to the *cercles* it financed, and transformed these aid societies into professional organizations.[2] These new professional cadres with a religious identity lent new meanings to Christian membership and constructed new possibilities for reformist and social action. Perhaps most importantly, *cercles*, along with *confréries*, became large and influential enough to attract not only financial investment from Catholic Action, but also from parishes and organizations in France, which allowed for more communication between French and African Christians, and imparted a sense of inclusion in a wider community of believers than simply the one demarcated by the local church or missionary society.[3]

The main Catholic organization that worked to link African and French dioceses was the *Association des Ligeurs Universitaires et Missionnaires (Ad*

---

[1] ACCSp. 2J1.7b4, Louis Paul Aujoulat, Ad Lucem, Pierre Bonneau, "*L'Action Catholique au Cameroun,*" 1940.
[2] Guillaume Lachenal and Bertrand Taithe, "Une Généalogie Missionnaire et Coloniale de l'Humanitaire: Le Cas Aujoulat Au Cameroun, 1935–1973," *Le Mouvement Sociale*, no. 227 (2009): 45–63.
[3] "Formation *Ad Lucem*," *Journal officiel du Cameroun*, 15 février 1948, 67; "Personnel médical Africain des établissements de santé," *Journal officiel du Cameroun*, 15 mai 1948, 90.

Lucem), which, along with Catholic Action, sponsored social outreach paired with technical training for African Christians.[4] *Ad Lucem*'s directors in France, Abbé Robert Prévost and Cardinal Achille Liénart, Bishop of Lille, were trade union sympathizers who had been active in the Worker-Priest Movement as a means of reconnecting a disaffected and despiritualized industrial class with the Catholic Church.[5] *Ad Lucem* also had spiritual and social connections with the broader *Action Catholique*, or Catholic Action movement, which likewise had a base in Lille and was deeply committed to deepening the spiritual foundations of France's civilizing responsibility within the nation as well as throughout the world as part of securing souls against the menace of communism.[6] *Ad Lucem*'s interest in French Africa was not merely a pious venture, but also a political one, aimed at safeguarding the religious loyalties of the African Christian population and ensuring that leftist, anti-colonialist, and Marxist influences did not captivate the hearts and minds of those who would soon end their political subordination.[7]

At the 1932 *Ad Lucem* national congress, Louis-Paul Aujoulat, a French doctor born in Algeria, a devout Catholic, and a *colon* settler in Cameroon, joined with Bishop René Graffin, who attended as the coadjutor of François-Xavier Vogt, Bishop of Yaoundé, to sponsor *Ad Lucem* and Catholic Action endeavors in Cameroon. Pierre Bonneau, a young French priest who had led the Catholic mission at Mvolyé since 1930, was nominated to lead *Ad Lucem* in the territory alongside Aujoulat, and both men desired that these

[4] *Ad Lucem* was born in 1931 out of the Ligue Universitare Catholique et Missionnaire (LUCEM) and the Ligue Missionnaire des Étudiants de France (LMEF), which were founded by French priests in collaboration with students at the Catholic University of Lille as a plan to encourage graduates to evangelize in universities and youth groups as well as pursue careers in medicine, social work, and philanthropy in France's overseas territories. Jean-Pierre Ribaut, "Le Cardinal Liénart et Ad Lucem (Journée d'étude Du 25 Septembre 1993 à l'Université Catholique de Lille)," *Mélanges de Sciences Religieuses* 54, no. 3 (1997): 37–56; Jules Monchanin, Edouard Duperray, and Jacques Gadille, *Théologie et Spiritualité Missionnaires* (Paris: Editions Beauchesne, 1985), 18.

[5] See Guillaume Cuchet, "Nouvelles Perspectives Historiographiques Sur Les Prêtres-Ouvriers (1943–1954)," *Vingtième Siècle. Revue d'histoire* 87, no. 3 (September 2005): 179–87; Ribaut, "Le Cardinal Liénart et Ad Lucem (Journée d'étude Du 25 Septembre 1993 à l'Université Catholique de Lille)"; Charles Suaud and Nathalie Viet-Depaule, *Prêtres et Ouvriers: Une Double Fidélité Mise à l'épreuve, 1944–1969* (Paris: Karthala, 2004).

[6] Françoise Jacquin, "Naissance Du Laïcat Missionnaire: L'exemple d'Ad Lucem (1930–1939)," in *Diffusion et Acculturation Du Christianisme (XIXe–XXe s.) Vingt-Cinq Ans de Recherches Missiologiques Par Le CREDIC* (Paris: Karthala, 2005), 397.

[7] For more on Catholic organizing efforts in anti-communism, see Giuliana Chamedes, "Pius XII, Rights Talk and the Dawn of the Religious Cold War," in *Religion and Human Rights*, ed. David Pendas (New York: Routledge, forthcoming).

organizations become vehicles for socio-religious transformation that would "finally eradicate ... the polygamy, fetishism, and paganism that still exists..."[8] Beginning in 1935, with a critical subvention from Cameroon's Governor Jules Repiquet, Catholic Action and *Ad Lucem* established the *Cercle Catholique de Mvolyé* and the *Cercle de Jeunesse Catholique d'Efok*, and soon followed with other social and professional organizations that staffed nursing, educational, and social work enterprises.[9] After World War II, Christian social organization continued to grow across rural, small-town, and urban Cameroon through the introduction of scout and youth groups, which were also launched by Protestant churches.[10] Christian mobilizations for increased human and capital investment in social service traced preexisting regional family and lineage networks and depended on preexisting socio-religious associations such as *confrérie* and *Croix Bleue* chapters. With expansions in mobilized religious work came questions about the social and moral foundations of African society in Cameroon and its relevance to questions about national independence and the true meaning of "national liberation."[11] The organizational foundation for collective action that had been put in place during the interwar period soon responded to new political questions and new stimuli emanating from Eastern and Western Europe, neighboring territories of west and central Africa, and locally from the hotbeds of union organization and anti-colonial nationalism in Douala and Yaoundé.[12]

---

[8] ACCSp. 2J1.7b4, Louis Paul Aujoulat, Ad Lucem, Pierre Bonneau, "*L'Action Catholique au Cameroun*," 1940.

[9] Lachenal and Taithe, "Une Généalogie Missionnaire et Coloniale de l'Humanitaire: Le Cas Aujoulat Au Cameroun, 1935–1973." See also Jean Paul Messina and Jaap Van Slageren, *Histoire Du Christianisme Au Cameroun: Des Origines à Nos Jours : Approche Oecuménique* (Paris: Karthala, 2005), 170–80; Frédéric Turpin, "Le Mouvement Républicain Populaire et l'avenir de l'Algérie (1947–1962)," *Revue d'histoire Diplomatique* 2 (1999): 171–203.

[10] SMEP/DEFAP EEC FB 2/2 Scoutisme, 1940–1943, Fédération des Mouvements de Jeunesse du Cameroun (FEMOJEUCA); Juilienne Ngoumou, "A Propos d'une Assemblée Dite "des Organisations de Jeunesse,'" *Essor Des Jeunes*, juin–juillet 1962.

[11] Jean Zoa, "Les Chrétiens et La Communauté Nationale," *Nova et Vetera* 1 (1960): 12–14; Jean Zoa, *Pour un nationalisme chrétien au Cameroun* (Yaoundé: Imprimerie Saint-Paul, 1957).

[12] See also Charlotte Walker-Said, "Christian Social Movements in Cameroon at the End of Empire: Transnational Solidarities and the Communion of the World Church," in *Relocating World Christianity: Interdisciplinary Studies in Universal and Local Expressions of Christianity*, ed. Joel Cabrita, David Maxwell, and Emma Wild-Wood (Boston. MA: Brill, 2017).

Toward Formal Recognition of Church Authority

Paul Etoga, who would become the first Cameroonian auxiliary bishop of Yaoundé in 1955, became the seniormost African Catholic Action leader in the years following the war; his career provides a glimpse of how African Christian leaders broadened the scope of religious organizing from the realms of the domestic sphere and local social and political life to include questions surrounding emancipation from colonialism and the future of the African Church in the world. Etoga had begun his ministry in the parishes near his home in Nlong and in Yangben in the early 1930s, and was ordained in 1939. Like Mpeke and Aoué, Etoga had been a catechist and developed a considerable following of family members, catechumens, and parishioners prior to his official ordination, balancing his relationships and duties to his lineage with those of the Church.[13] His investiture strengthened his momentum in mobilizing local communities to activism, and joined them with French and trans-regional African Catholic leaders and groups looking to expand education and health programs in postwar Cameroon.[14] Etoga's success in recruiting and mobilizing large followings of Catholic social workers and volunteers drove the momentum to have him nominated as bishop, where he became a critical interlocutor between international political and religious leaders and African Catholics.[15] Etoga was part of the clerical leadership that facilitated a richly communitarian spirituality that was also developing an increasing awareness of global issues, which would force believers to consider the role of their faith in their personal and family lives, and soon in their lives as citizens of an independent nation-state.

Bishop Etoga and many of his contemporaries who filled high ecclesiastical positions in Cameroon and throughout Africa in the era of decolonization are often believed to signal the shift from "Western Christianity" to "World Christianity."[16] As missionary leaders and European bishops formally handed power to African Christians, and local congregations became formally part of a national "Churches," many observers expressed alternatively hope or anxiety that Christianity would remain an incorporative, universalist community, or

---

[13] ACSSp. 2J1.7a7 Dossier Etoga, auxiliaire de Yaoundé.
[14] Charlotte Walker-Said, "Science and Charity: Rival Catholic Visions for Humanitarian Practice at The End of Empire," *French Politics, Culture & Society* 33, no. 2 (Summer 2015): 33–54.
[15] ACSSp. 2J1.7a7 Dossier Etoga, auxiliaire de Yaoundé.
[16] The best review of this shift is found in Joel Cabrita and David Maxwell, "Relocating World Christianity," in *Relocating World Christianity, Interdisciplinary Studies in Universal and Local Expressions of the Christian Faith*, ed. Joel Cabrita, David Maxwell, and Emma Wild-Wood (Boston, MA: Brill, 2017), 1–47.

that particular and regional expressions of Christianity would localize it to the extent that would limit cross-cultural continuities.[17] However, much more than symbolizing a historic shift or even a transfer of ecclesiastical power, the emergence of formally autonomous African Catholic and Protestant Churches really demonstrated an amplification of African control over their religious communities. When Pastor Jean Keller, head of the Paris Evangelical Missionary Society, returned to France at the start of World War II, he attested that his own leadership in Cameroon was nonessential and that all European missionaries were "mere witnesses and seed-sowers."[18] Having cultivated followers and even managed, disciplined, and supervised congregations, catechumen cohorts, and coadjutors for over half a century, and incorporated the tenets of the faith into the structures of everyday life, African Christians in Cameroon had decentralized institutional power from white overseers and were the true implementers of the Christian Churches' visions of a world mission.

In a pastoral letter in 1959, Mgr. Thomas Mongo, the first African bishop of Douala, made reference to Cameroon's imminent national independence, writing, "It is in the womb of the household where nations' destinies are written."[19] As someone who had implanted Christianity in Cameroon's families at the village level, Mongo also understood the significance of the household as a "womb" of religious destiny. As Osborn reminds us to collapse the supposed divisions between the "public" and "private" spheres in Africa, it is equally important to blur the boundaries between the supposed "religious" and "secular" worlds of human experience. Between the two World Wars, southern Cameroon's households, families, and marriages were "wombs" in which profane and the sacred – visible and invisible – forces were believed to act. They were also, as American Presbyterian missionary Ebenezer Jones remarked in

---

[17] Cabrita and Maxwell.
[18] Jean Keller, "Missions d'A.O.F," *Monde Non Chrétien*, Société des Missions Evangéliques, Paris, 1951, 1–3.
[19] Mongo made reference to Pope Pius XI in this letter, and this statement seems to be a paraphrasing of Pope Pius XI *Quas Primas* ("... the unity and stability of the family undermined; society in a word, shaken to its foundations and on the way to ruin. We firmly hope, however, that the feast of the Kingship of Christ, which in future will be yearly observed, may hasten the return of society to our loving Savior."... para. 24); as well as *Casti Connubii*: "For experience has taught that unassailable stability in matrimony is a fruitful source of virtuous life and of habits of integrity. Where this order of things obtains, the happiness and well being of the nation is safely guarded; what the families and individuals are, so also is the State, for a body is determined by its parts. Wherefore, both for the private good of husband, wife and children, as likewise for the public good of human society, they indeed deserve well who strenuously defend the inviolable stability of matrimony" (para. 37). For reference, see Encyclical *Quas Primas* of *Pius XI*, 11 December 1925; Encyclical *Casti Connubii* of *Pius XI*, 31 December 1932.

1934, "laboratories of Christian service."[20] The metaphors of "womb" and "laboratory" are especially useful when considering the enigmatic, unknowable, or experimental dimensions of marriage, family life, and reproduction, and how these dimensions shape and are shaped by larger entities like a colonized territory or a nation-state.[21] In Cameroon, Christians often attended first and foremost to the spiritual needs of their families, and even innovated familial composition and leadership to better serve their members as well as the ideals contained within the faith. This history presents an alternative reading to histories of the family in empire, which have primarily focused on Europeans' policing of racial boundaries and the sexual distinctions between colonizer and colonized, or colonialists' re-creation of the moral-sexual "native."[22]

This book has undertaken to explore how Africans linked individual sin to the workings of an oppressive colonial state and their methods of critiquing, reforming, and, indeed, policing each others' behaviors in an effort to ward off the hierarchical, exploitive, and unequal consequences of colonial power. Investigating religion and authority in colonial spaces has often centered on the question of missionary influence, and has investigated foreign missionaries as agents of cultural change or as opponents to the violence of colonial extraction and decentralization.[23] While demonstrating the intellectual and spiritual claims of European and American missionaries acting in French Cameroon, this book has also aimed to reveal that the struggles over the composition of everyday life as well as the conflicts that arose with colonial power were organized principally by African evangelists and everyday believers. While Catholic

[20] Ebenezer Edwin Jones, *The Life of Rowland Hill Evans of Cameroun: A Narrative of Service in the West Africa Mission, Presbyterian Church, U.S.A., 1909–1932* (Columbus, OH: F.J. Heer Print. Co., 1932), 170.

[21] Lynn Thomas's analysis of the "womb" as an arena in which all manner of moral, social, and political concerns intersect as a matter of course in daily life is deeply resonant here. Lynn M. Thomas, *Politics of the Womb: Women, Reproduction, and the State in Kenya*, 1 edition (Berkeley, CA: University of California Press, 2003).

[22] Ann Laura Stoler, *Carnal Knowledge and Imperial Power: Race and the Intimate in Colonial Rule* (Berkeley, CA: University of California Press, 2002); Emmanuelle Saada, *Empire's Children: Race, Filiation, and Citizenship in the French Colonies* (Chicago: University of Chicago Press, 2012).

[23] Jean Comaroff and John L. Comaroff, *Of Revelation and Revolution, Volume 1: Christianity, Colonialism, and Consciousness in South Africa* (Chicago: University of Chicago Press, 1991); John L. Comaroff and Jean Comaroff, *Of Revelation and Revolution, Volume 2: The Dialectics of Modernity on a South African Frontier*, 1 edition (Chicago: University of Chicago Press, 1997); Meredith McKittrick, *To Dwell Secure: Generation, Christianity and Colonialism in Ovamboland, Northern Namibia*, Social History of Africa Series (Portsmouth, NH: Heinemann, 2002); Elizabeth Foster, *Faith in Empire: Religion, Politics, and Colonial Rule in French Senegal, 1880–1940* (Stanford: Stanford University Press, 2013).

and Protestant missionaries in Cameroon demonstrated a greater commitment to a "civilizing mission" than the colonial administration, both of these forces could not match the influence of self-directed African reformers, not least because these local agents inhabited the veins of rural and urban life and had an intimacy with the adversities and ordeals wrought by the "colonial encounter." Frederick Cooper has argued, "Power in colonial societies was more arterial rather than capillary – concentrated spatially and socially, not very nourishing beyond such domains and in need of a pump to push it from place to place."[24] As we know from Chapter 6, foreign missionaries were also sparsely concentrated and depended on various "pumps" like motorcycles, catechist assistants, or sharp orders from their overseer to coax them to navigate the walks of several days in the humid climate or the riverine villages in the interior.[25] There is perhaps no greater analogy for a "capillary" of social life in the equatorial rainforest zone – particularly in southern Cameroon – than the lineage. Christian doctrines, rituals, and routines in southern Cameroon were transmitted through and maintained within lineages and were used to craft responses to the destabilizing energies of village reorganization, forced labor, unequal accumulation, taxation, and exploitation. Lineage heads had typically been male before colonial domination, and as lineage relations and religious practices shifted, males who captured the power of Christian knowledge and spiritual authority often secured new positions of lineage leadership or endeavored to found their own families. While the colonial state believed that controlling the means of violence, securing elite political loyalty, and maintaining economic productivity were to be achieved through formal institutions of rule, African Christian leaders understood that the true political resource – and the source of spiritual catharsis, supernatural intervention, and economic opportunity – was the family.[26]

Throughout the interwar period, African communities implanted Christianity in their own societies, and alongside this process, renovated the rules, processes, and indeed, boundaries of the licit in the domains of marriage, sexuality, and family-building. This process was both the result of and gave rise to highly perceptive and capable African Christian leaders with

---

[24] Frederick Cooper, "Conflict and Connection: Rethinking Colonial African History," *The American Historical Review* 99, no. 5 (1994): 1533.

[25] ACSSp. 2J1.11a2 R.P. Biechy, Résidence de Saint Thérèse de l'enfant Jésus de Samba, 1936.

[26] This argument supports Emily Osborn's claim that West Africa's political history has largely neglected how the domestic sphere acted as a political regime. See Emily Lynn Osborn, *Our New Husbands Are Here: Households, Gender, and Politics in a West African State from the Slave Trade to Colonial Rule* (Athens, OH: Ohio University Press, 2011), 1–2.

forceful spiritual and social agendas. As they circulated religious instruction, constructed churches where new social agglomerations could meet and exchange ideas, and popularized new moral, marital, and sexual codes among their brethren, they slowly built indigenous, autonomous Churches. Perhaps because of its fundamental and yet complex and shrouded nature, the family remained the nucleus of religious and social life in Cameroon's southern forests, much as it remains the foundation of a "global" religion like Christianity.[27]

The history of how Africans built Christian Churches using the organizing capacities, resilience, and reciprocities of the lineages (i.e. the "capillaries") in a period of colonial domination also allows for a reconsideration of the focus on "resistance," "collaboration," or "accommodation" within studies of colonialism. This study has, to borrow from Frederick Cooper, sought to present "a multi-sided engagement with forces inside and outside the community" in order to move beyond questions of how or why Africans "confronted" colonial subordination and reveal their paramount priorities, which they continued to pursue despite the hindrances put in their path.

Formally Acceding to Church Leadership

In 1939, foreign missionaries were once again summoned to war in Europe, leaving African religious leaders in Cameroon to manage ecclesiastical affairs.[28] In contrast to 1914, by the start of World War II, Catholic and Protestant missions had become rooted and fortified by strong religious institutions, with indigenized clergies and expanded catechist ranks leading affiliated schools, social work organizations, confraternities, piety associations, and a host of other institutional outlets. By the outbreak of war, roughly 300,000 Catholics networked through 258 religious associations and 2200 villages with a Catholic affiliation to organize religious life.[29] Fourteen African priests managed the

[27] Following the Synods on the Family held in 2014 and 2015, Pope Francis issued a post-synodal apostolic exhortation addressing the pastoral care of families in *Amoris laetitia*, or "On Love in the Family." The introduction to *Amoris laetitia* begins with Pope Francis recalling the Synods' examination of the circumstances of families and calls for "a broader vision and a renewed awareness of the importance of marriage and the family." Francis I, *Amoris laetitia* [Post-Synodal Apostolic Exhortation of the Holy Father Francis on Love in the Family]. Vatican City: Libreria Editrice Vaticana, Vatican website, http://w2.vatican.va/content/dam/francesco/pdf/apost_exhortations/documents/papa-francesco_esortazione-ap_20160319_amoris-laetitia_en.pdf [accessed February 4, 2018].

[28] ACSSp. 2J1.8a1 Rapport de Abbé Krummenacker, Le District de Douala pendant la guerre, 1944.

[29] ACSSp. 2J1.7a7 Union Missionnaire du Clergé, July 1948. Official statistics of the number of Catholics in Cameroon vary. In May 1937, the Douala Vicariate announced

vicariate of Douala, and fifteen indigenous priests and eighteen African friars coordinated the larger vicariate of Yaoundé between 1939 and 1945 alongside the few French priests who had remained following Colonel Philippe Leclerc's August 1940 declaration that Cameroon was be part of Free France and there was hope for local resistance.[30] Before Pères Gaschy and Déhon left the Nlong Mission for the front in September 1938, they told their congregation that they were off to defend Christianity against the "paganism of the leader of Germany."[31] Abbé Theodore Tsala and the African friars who assumed leadership of the mission reported that over the next several months, the sight of airplanes in the sky and persistent rumors that German soldiers would arrive to avenge their defeat in Cameroon prompted locals to more scrupulously observe the Commandments and receive the sacraments.[32]

Likewise, Protestant Churches overseen by the Paris Evangelical Mission had been managed by indigenous leaders for decades, and at the start of the war, thirty-five African pastors and several thousand catechists managed their 800 churches and temples and 120,000 worshippers, many of whom were fourth-generation Protestants.[33] The Paris Evangelical Mission continued to officially oversee the Evangelical and the Baptist Churches, whose congregations were mixed in coastal and western Cameroon, as the two Churches worked together and overlapped in their schools, clinics, and missionary activities. While the denominations were interdependent, the Evangelical Church was more active in Foumban, Ndoungué, and Bafoussam, and the Baptists more so in coastal regions, Douala, and the Somo region. By 1946, both the Evangelical and Baptist Synodal Commissions, which decided the composition of the indigenous personnel, salaries, consecrations of pastors, and the celebration of feast days and ceremonies, were headed by Pastors Douala

---

in *Le Cameroun Catholique* that it had recorded 230,000 Catholics and 140,000 catechumens in Cameroon; in May 1939, *Le Cameroun Catholique* announced there were "350,000 Catholics in Cameroon." Statistics continued to vary across mission and vicariate records into the 1950s. "Statistiques de la Mission de Douala," *Le Cameroun Catholique*, 1 mai 1937; "350,000 Catholiques au Cameroun!," *Le Cameroun Catholique*, 12 mai 1939. More estimates that roughly match these numbers can be found in Bengt Sundkler and Christopher Steed, *A History of the Church in Africa* (Cambridge: Cambridge University Press, 2000), 756, and Pere Louis Barde, *Au Cameroun Avec M. Wilbois, Les Graves Problèmes de La Polygamie et de l'instruction* (Paris: Maison Mère des Peres du Saint-Esprit, 1934), 9–11.

[30] ANC APA APA 11016/D liste Catholique, 1941; ACSSp. 2J1.8.a1 District de Douala pendant la guerre.

[31] ACSSp. 2J2.1a Mission de Nlong 1938–1956, 1 octobre 1938, mobilisation générale.

[32] ACSSp. 2J2.1a Mission de Nlong 1938–1956, 10 septembre 1939.

[33] Maurice Farelly, "Les Eglises Indigènes," *Journal des Missions Évangéliques*, 1946, 7–16.

Itondo, Thomas Ekolo, Paul Jocky and regional evangelists. In 1946, Pastor Farrelly of the Paris Evangelical Mission conceded that French missionaries were no longer influential in managing evangelical affairs: "Our native workers are in general sufficient for the operation of the Church."[34]

While the Americans of the Presbyterian Mission were less disrupted than French missionaries at the start of the war, they too were vastly outnumbered and outperformed by indigenous ministers. On the whole, the American Presbyterian Mission estimated roughly 100,000 baptized adherents and counted fifty African pastors, over one hundred African teachers in their 42 primary schools, and 800 catechists.[35] Reports APM leaders were required to submit to French authorities declared that together, African and American ministers had "succeeded in the penetration of religiosity into everyday life."[36]

While some foreign missionaries expressed concern over whether African clergymen were sufficiently subordinate to the institution of the Church, they largely endorsed indigenous clerics' defiance of the French colonial administration. Indeed, foreign missionary leaders were often well pleased and even awed by the commitment African Christian men demonstrated, even at the risk of persecution. French pastor Maurice Farelly referred to catechists as an "army" and the "last defense" against the evil and injustice of colonial policies, and commended Africans who "discussed their rights and claimed their salaries as dignified men and children of God."[37] Likewise, French priests like Henri de Maupeou and François Pichon supported dozens of ministers, catechists, and acolytes who engaged in disruptive acts like inciting widows to abscond to the missions and beseeching forcibly recruited laborers to throw off their chains and refuse to work.[38] Mgr. Vogt was also passionately devoted to promoting an African clergy and expanding African membership in Catholic religious orders, but was most ardent in his defense of African men and women who protested the "harshness of civil laws" and the "tortures" of chiefs and police by recruiting new members to seek refuge in church sanctuaries.[39]

---

[34] Farelly, 14.
[35] ANC 1AC 3523 Rapport sur le Mission Presbytérienne Américaine 1950; ANC APA 11016/D liste de pasteurs, 1941.
[36] ANC 1AC 3523 Rapport sur le Mission Presbytérienne Américaine 1950.
[37] Maurice Farelly, *Chronique Du Pays Banen (Au Cameroun)* (Paris: Société des missions évangéliques, 1948), 150.
[38] ANC APA 1AC 3523 Rapport des Pères Pichon et Mader, Mission Catholique de Minlaba, 11 avril 1930; ACSSp. 2J1.10.7 Rapports de police 1932.
[39] ANC 1AC 3523 Mission Catholique de Yaoundé Rapport 18 juin 1930; ACSSp. 2J1.10.3 "Vogt et les fondateurs de la congregation des filles de marie de Yaoundé."

Conversions to Christianity continued after the war. By 1949, the Catholic community of Cameroon counted 1.3 million baptized believers, catechumens, and students in Catholic schools.[40] At the Easter Congress of 1949, the Protestant churches celebrated their 130,000 believers and extended ranks of ministers, evangelists, teachers, and students.[41] In both Churches, African social reformers and activists constituted the ranks of the clerical and lay leadership. While there were some contemplative spiritual devotees, by and large, devout Africans with who did evangelical work forcefully ingrained a Christian culture that acknowledged the matrimonial rights of individual men, sought the loyalty and companionship of virtuous women, and championed the rights and obligations of members of social communities, including monogamous families, lineages, and communities.

Overall, Africans throughout southern Cameroon built the Christian Churches by blurring the lines between the "public" and the "private" in the organization of everyday life. Incremental changes throughout the interwar period are visible in church registries, court records, oral testimonies, and print media, where many young Africans manifested and expressed their desires to marry according to new principles and create new modes of family dependency and reciprocity, which had serious implications for the capacities of political leaders and the execution of colonial projects. Transformations in expectations and claims on which the notions of "family," and "rights" were based led large numbers of Africans to reconstitute their households and marriages, as well as their obligations to wider kin networks, which translated into dramatic changes in formulations of masculinity, male authority, and gendered power.[42] Over time, as Christian conversion expanded and administrative policies brought about other forms of economic and political change, an increasing share of social relations within communities was governed by standards that were derived from Christian belief.

In the years leading up to the outbreak of World War II, African Christians in Cameroon were considerably disrupting notions of a traditional periphery and a reform-minded metropole. By then, the full effect of Christian marriage renovation policies had become apparent and had rendered Cameroon a field of competitive activism between local agents – many of whom the French administration had little authority to restrain. Throughout its tenure

---

[40] Sundkler and Steed, *A History of the Church in Africa*, 756.
[41] Jean-Rene Brutsch, "Impressions d'un premier séjour au Cameroun," *Journal des Missions Évangéliques*, 1950.
[42] For further analysis of marriage "rights" and property claims in Africa, see Martin Chanock, "A Peculiar Sharpness: An Essay on Property in the History of Customary Law in Colonial Africa," *Journal of African History*, no. 32 (1991): 65–88.

in governing the League of Nations mandate of Cameroon, the French administration was reluctant to acknowledge Africans' strategic actions and their personal faith, misreading much as subversion or manipulation. This left the Christian Churches and their indigenous leaderships in a much better position to influence the general population, as the history of the last decade of French rule in Cameroon reveals.[43]

Although French administrative measures envisioned harmonious development, they also ignored many local implications of inequality and social competition – the most common manifestations of which were polygamy, forced marriages, or marriages with high bride price. Overall, actions taken by religious organizations against local malevolence and wrongdoing – rather than French overrule – sharpened perceptions of social and economic relationships at the local level and considered the future in an intimate way. The legacies of the interwar period of Christian inspiration and institution-building include complex and divided expressions of nationalism and anti-colonialism in the 1950s as well as a post-independence era marked by a robust Christianity that continues to evolve and assume new political resonance in the era of authoritarian rule.

Conclusion: Christian Marriage and Social Transformation

Within the history of Cameroon's populations who experienced Christian conversion, holy matrimony was recognized as a sacred event in the turbulent decades of French mandate rule.[44] Frère Philippe reflected that although his

---

[43] Although the last decade of French rule was marked by anti-colonial nationalism and the influence of communism, African Church leaders were able to nimbly and clearly articulate a pro-nationalist but anti-communist message in unique ways. See Kengne Pokam, *Les Églises Chrétiennes Face à La Montée Du Nationalisme Camerounais* (Paris: L'Harmattan, 1987); Martin Atangana, *The End of French Rule in Cameroon* (Lanham, MD: University Press of America, 2010).

[44] The extensive historiography on Christian marriage and the transformation of indigenous marriage practices in Cameroon over the twentieth century – written largely by Cameroonian scholars – attests to the centrality of marriage and the history of African marriage rites and forms in the cultures of Cameroon. See Antoine Essomba Fouda, *Le Mariage Chrétien Au Cameroun : Une Réalité Anthropologique, Civile et Sacramentelle* (Paris: L'Harmattan, 2010); Manga Bekombo, "La Femme, Le Mariage et La Compensation Matrimoniale En Pays Dwala," *L'Ethnographie* 62–3 (69 1968): 179–88; Jacques Binet, "Le Mariage et l'évolution de La Société Sud-Camerounaise," *L'Afrique Française. Bulletin Mensuel Du Comité de l'Afrique Française, Du Comité Du Maroc et Du Comité Algérie-Tunisie-Maroc* 62, no. 6 (1953): 40–2; Jean-Marie Vianney Balegamire A. Koko, *Mariage Africain et Mariage Chrétien* (Paris: L'Harmattan, 2003); Michel Legrain, *L'Eglise catholique et le mariage en Occident et en Afrique (Tome II):*

aunt had performed many pious acts in her lifetime, she always claimed "to be married religiously is to possess a true Christian spirit."[45] For Anne Nguimeya, the revered and holy status accorded to marriage was considered a pathway to a life of righteousness and a way of knowing God. This book has endeavored to reveal how spiritual inspiration and political subordination reinforced the practice of Christian marriage. The obligations and requirements for marriage in the Catholic or Protestant Churches changed the nature of interpersonal ties and dislodged preexisting kinship and spiritual commitments, but they also shaped new forms of affiliation. These bonds were accomplished through the celebration of liturgical, sacramental, and festival rites as well as through social activism that critiqued immoral marriage practices and the powerful human and economic forces that promoted them, and cultivated communal unanimity on the advantages of sanctified monogamous unions.

The cooperative and contending forces of both spiritual submission and free will among African societies are well described by Ruth Marshall, who asserts that these have existed in African religious process as the fruit of an ongoing struggle occurring within a complex web of contradictory, parallel, and juxtaposed forces, at once arising from outside and inside both the society and the self.[46] Frère Philippe revealed to me during our discussions that in addition to being drawn to Christian theology like many in her village, Anne Nguimeya decided even before her own formal conversion and complete knowledge of doctrine that Christian marriage as holy act of devotion as much as a commitment shaped everyday life. For Anne, and, as this book has hopefully demonstrated, many other Africans in Cameroon, religious mystery and political ambiguity reinforced the practice of Christian marriage as a way of illuminating Christianity's meaning in their lives.

L'ébranlement de l'édifice matrimonial (Paris: L'Harmattan, 2009); Luc Ndjodo, *Le Mariage Chrétien Chez Les Beti* (Douala: Yonga & Partners, 1997); Henri Ngoa, "Le Mariage chez les Ewondo: Étude sociologique" (Sorbonne, 1968); J.R. Owono Nkoudou, "Le Problème Du Mariage Dotal Au Cameroun Français," *Études Camerounaises* 39–40 (March 1953): 41–83.

[45] Oral interview, Fr. Philippe Azeufack, S.J., Résidence St. François Xavier, Yaoundé Cameroon, May 30, 2014.

[46] Ruth Marshall, *Political Spiritualities: The Pentecostal Revolution in Nigeria*, 1 edition (Chicago and London: University of Chicago Press, 2009), 45.

Bibliography

I. Archival Sources

Cameroon

Archives Nationales du Cameroun, Yaoundé
Archives de l'Hotel de Ville de Douala, Douala

France

Archives Nationales d'Outre-Mer, Aix-en-Provence
Archives de la Congrégation du Saint-Esprit, Chevilly-Larue
Archives de la Société des Missions Evangéliques de Paris, Bibliothèque du Défap, Paris
Archives Militaires, Fonds du Service historique de la Défense, Paris

II. Published Primary and Secondary Sources

"214 Mariages Chrétiens." *Le Cameroun Catholique*. mai 1937.
Abessolo, Eugénie. "L'épiscopat de Monseigneur Paul Etoga : 1955–1987." *Mémoire de DIPES II En Histoire* ENS, 2000.
Abwa, Daniel. "The French Administrative System in the Lamidate of Ngaoundéré." In *Introduction to the History of Cameroon: Nineteenth and Twentieth Centuries*, edited by Martin Njeuma, 137–69. London: Macmillan, 1989.
Acollas, Emile. *Nécessité de Refondre l'ensemble de Nos Codes et Notamment Le Code Napoléon Au Point de Vue de l'idée Démocratique*. Paris, 1866.
Ada, F. Owono. *De La Mission de l'Église Catholique Camerounaise: Origine, Formation et Rôle Des Prêtres Noirs*. Yaoundé: ENS, 1981.
Aguessy, Cyrille. "Sur l'éducation Des Femmes Africaines." *L'Education Africaine*, no. 101 (1938): 65–68.
Aït-Aarab, Mohamed. *Mongo Beti. Un écrivain engagé*. Paris: Karthala, 2013.
Akamba, Robert. *One mvom: psaumes cantiques et autres chants liturgiques pour la prière du peuple chrétien du groupe linguistique Fang, Bulu, Beti (Cameroun, Gabon et Guinée equatoriale)*. Yaoundé: Imprimé au Centre d'edition et de production de manuels et d'auxiliaires de l'enseignement, 1971.
Akoa-Mongo, Francois. *Le Pasteur François Akoa Abômô: l'homme et l'oeuvre*. Bloomington, IN: Xlibris Corp, 2011.
Alega Mbele, Séverin. "Entretien Avec Le Père Olivier Paulin Awoumou, Curé de Mvolyé et Membre de La Société de l'Apostolat Catholique." *Cameroon-Info*. May 21, 2001. http://www.cameroon-info.net/stories/0,6908,@,mvolye-a-cent-ans-un-siecle-d-histoire.html.

Alexandre, Pierre, and Jacques Binet. *Le Groupe Dit Pahouin (Fang-Boulou-Beti)*. Paris: Presses Universitaires de France, 1958.

Allman, Jean. "Making Mothers: Missionaries, Medical Officers and Women's Work in Colonial Asante, 1924–1945." *History Workshop Journal* 38, no. 1 (September 21, 1994): 23–47.

———. "Rounding up Spinsters: Gender Chaos and Unmarried Women in Colonial Asante." *The Journal of African History* 37, no. 02 (1996): 195–214.

Allman, Jean Marie, and Victoria B. Tashjian. *I Will Not Eat Stone: A Women's History of Colonial Asante*. Portsmouth, NH and Oxford: Heinemann; James Currey, 2000.

Amadiume, Ifi. *Male Daughters, Female Husbands: Gender and Sex in an African Society*. London and Atlantic Highlands, NJ: Zed Books, 1987.

Anya-Noa, Lucien. *Pierre Mebe: Hymne a Hospitalite Beti*. Yaoundé, Cameroon: Abba Ekan/Centre culturel beti, 2003.

Ardener, Edwin. *Coastal Bantu of the Cameroons: The Kpe-Mboko, Duala Limba, and Tanga-Yasa Groups of the British and French Trusteeship Territories of the Cameroons (Western Africa, Part XI)*. London: International African Institute, 1956.

———. *Divorce and Fertility: An African Study*. Oxford: Published for the Nigerian Institute of Social and Economic Research by Oxford University Press, 1962.

Argenti, Nicolas. *The Intestines of the State: Youth, Violence, and Belated Histories in the Cameroon Grassfields*. Chicago: University of Chicago Press, 2007.

———. "Things of the Ground: Children's Medicine, Motherhood and Memory in the Cameroon Grassfields." *Africa: Journal of the International African Institute* 81, no. 2 (2011): 269–94.

Asad, Talal. *Formations of the Secular: Christianity, Islam, Modernity*. Stanford: Stanford University Press, 2003.

Atangana, Martin. *The End of French Rule in Cameroon*. Lanham, MD: University Press of America, 2010.

Atangana, Martin-René. *French Investment in Colonial Cameroon: The FIDES Era (1946–1957)*. New York: Peter Lang, 2009.

Austen, Ralph A., and Jonathan Derrick. *Middlemen of the Cameroons Rivers: The Duala and Their Hinterland, c.1600–c.1960*. Cambridge: Cambridge University Press, 1999.

Austin, Gareth. *Labour, Land, and Capital in Ghana: From Slavery to Free Labour in Asante, 1807–1956*. Rochester, NY: University of Rochester Press, 2005.

Aymerich, Joseph G. *La Conquête Du Cameroun*. Paris: Payot, 1931.

Azeufack, S.J., Philippe. *Mgr. André Wouking: Artisan de Paix*. Yaoundé, Cameroon: Presses Universitaires de Yaoundé, 2010.

Azombo, Soter. "Séquence et Signification Des Cérémonies d'initiation So." Thèse pour le doctorat d'Etat, Université de Paris I, 1970.

Bahoken, Jean Calvin, and Engelbert Atangana. *Cultural Policy in the United Republic of Cameroon*. Paris: The Unesco Press, 1976.

Barde, Pere Louis. *Au Cameroun Avec M. Wilbois, Les Graves Problèmes de La Polygamie et de l'instruction*. Paris: Maison Mère des Peres du Saint-Esprit, 1934.

Bayart, Jean-François. "Civil Society in Africa." In *Political Domination in Africa: Reflections on the Limits of Power*, edited by Patrick Chabal, 109–25. Cambridge: Cambridge University Press, 1986.

———. "Les Eglises Chrétiennes et La Politique Du Ventre: Le Partage Du gâteau Ecclésial in L'argent de Dieu." *Politique Africaine*, no. 35 (1989): 3–26.

———. "Les Rapports Entre Les Églises et l'État Du Cameroun de 1958 à 1971." *Revue Française d'Etudes Politiques Africaines* 80 (1972): 79–104.

———. *L'Etat Au Cameroun*. Paris: Presses de la fondation nationale de science politique, 1985.

———. *The State in Africa: The Politics of the Belly*. London and New York: Longman Group, 1993.

Bayon, Goustan Le. *Les prêtres du Sacre-Cœur et la naissance de l'Eglise au Cameroun: Kumbo, Foumban, Nkongsamba, Bafoussam*. Yaoundé, Cameroon: Procure des Missions S.C.J., 1986.

Bediako, Kwame. *Jesus in African Culture*. Accra: Asempa Publishers, 1990.

Bekombo, Manga. "Conflits d'autorité Au Sein de La Société Familiale Chez Les Duala Du Sud-Cameroun." *Cahiers d'Études Africaines* 4, no. 14 (1963): 317–29.

———. "La Femme, Le Mariage et La Compensation Matrimoniale En Pays Dwala." *L'Ethnographie* 62–3 (69 1968): 179–88.

Bender, Carl Jacob. *Der Weltkrieg Und Die Christlichen Missionen in Kamerun*. Cassel: Oncken, 1921.

Berger, Reverend Père Augustin. "Dix Années de Travail En Afrique ... Au Cameroun." In *Dix Années de Travail Catéchétique Dans Le Monde Au Service de La Formation Religieuse de l'Enfant*, 30–41. B.I.C.E. Études et Documents. Paris: Éditions Fleurus, 1960.

Bergeret, Yvette. *Banganté: Un Internat de Jeunes Filles Au Cameroun*. Paris, 1949.

Berliner, Paul. *The Soul of Mbira: Music and Traditions of the Shona People of Zimbabwe*. Chicago: University of Chicago Press, 1993.

Bernault, Florence. *Démocraties Ambigües En Afrique Centrale, Congo-Brazzaville, Gabon: 1940–1965*. Paris: Karthala, 1996.

Berry, Sara. *Chiefs Know Their Boundaries: Essays on Property, Power, and the Past in Asante, 1896–1996*. Portsmouth, NH and Oxford: Heinemann; James Currey, 2000.

Berry, Sara S. *No Condition Is Permanent: The Social Dynamics of Agrarian Change in Sub-Saharan Africa*. 1 edition. Madison, WI: University of Wisconsin Press, 1993.

Bertaut, Maurice. *Le Droit Coutoumier Des Boulous*. Paris: Domat-Montchrestien, 1935.

Beti, Mongo. *Le pauvre Christ de Bomba*. Paris: Presence africaine, 1976.

———. *Mission Terminée*. Paris: Buchet/Chastel, 1957. https://www.decitre.fr/livres/mission-terminee-9782283018002.html.

Betz, Rudolf. "Die Trommelsprache Der Duala." In *Mitteilungen von Forschungsreisenden Und Gelehrten Aus Den Deutschen Schutzgebieten*, edited by Alexander Danckelmann, 11:1–86. Berlin: Mittler, 1898.

Bilongo, Barnabé. *Les Pahouins Du Sud-Cameroun : Inventaires Bibliographiques, Connaissance Des Fang, Ntoumou, Muaé, Boulou, Beti (Menguissa, Eton, Muëlë, Bënë et Ewondo) et Du Groupe Dit Sanaga*. Yaoundé, Cameroon: Imprimerie Saint-Paul, 1974.

Binet, Jacques. *Budgets familiaux des planteurs de cacao au Cameroun*. Paris: Office de la Recherche Scientifique et Technique Outre-Mer, 1956.

———. *Le Mariage En Afrique Noire*. Foi Vivante: Série Vie Des Missions. Paris: Les Éditions du Cerf, 1959.

———. "Le Mariage et l'évolution de La Société Sud-Camerounaise." *L'Afrique Française. Bulletin Mensuel Du Comité de l'Afrique Française, Du Comité Du Maroc et Du Comité Algérie-Tunisie-Maroc* 62, no. 6 (1953): 40–42.

Bjornson, Richard. *The African Quest for Freedom and Identity: Cameroonian Writing and the National Experience*. Bloomington, IN: Indiana University Press, 1991.

Blanchard, Emmanuel, Quentin Deluermoz, and Joël Glassman. "La Professionnalisation Policière En Situation Coloniale : Détour Conceptuel et Explorations Historiographiques." *Crime, Histoire & Sociétés* 15 (2011): 33–53.

Blanchard, Emmanuel, and Joël Glassman. "Le Maintien de l'ordre Dans l'empire Français : Une Historiographie Émergent." In *Maintenir l'ordre Colonial. Afrique et Madagascar, XIXe–XXe Siècles*, edited by Jean-Pierre Bat and Nicolas Courtin, 11–41. Histoire. Rennes: Presses Universitaires de Rennes, 2012.

Bouchaud, R.P. "Cameroun: Eglise et Communisme." *Spiritains: Missions Des Peres Du St. Esprit* 31, no. 1 (March 1958).

Boulaga, F. Eboussi. *Christianity Without Fetishes: An African Critique and Recapture of Christianity*. 1st edition. Maryknoll, NY: Orbis Books, 1984.

Bowes, Kim. *Private Worship, Public Values, and Religious Change in Late Antiquity*. 1 edition. Cambridge and New York: Cambridge University Press, 2008.

Brasseur, Paule. "L'Église Catholique et La Décolonisation En Afrique Noire." In *Les Chemins de La Décolonisation de l'Empire Colonial Français, 1936–1956: Colloque Organisé Les 4 et 5 Octobre 1984*, edited by Charles-Robert Ageron, 55–68. Paris: Editions du Centre National de la Recherche Scientifique (CNRS), 1986.

Brown, Peter. *Through the Eye of a Needle: Wealth, the Fall of Rome, and the Making of Christianity in the West, 350–550 AD*. Princeton, NJ: Princeton University Press, 2014.

Brutsch, Jean René. "Les Relations de Parenté Chez Les Duala." *Bulletin de La Société Des Études Camerounaises* III (1950): 216–17.

Brutsch, Jean-Rene. "A Glance at Missions in Cameroon." *International Review of Missions* 39, no. 155 (July 1950): 302–10.

Buell, Raymond Leslie. *The Native Problem in Africa*. Vol. II. New York: Macmillan Company, 1928.

Bureau, René. *Anthropologie, Religions Africaines et Christianisme*. Paris: Karthala, 2002.

———. "Ethno-Sociologie Religieuse Des Duala et Apparentés." *Recherches et Etudes Camerounaises* 1&2, no. 8 (1962): 1–369.

———. "Sociologie Religieuse." *Mission d'Aujourd'hui: Bulletin Mensuel Des Oeuvres Catholiques*, October 15, 1958.

Burnham, Philip. "'Regroupement' and Mobile Societies: Two Cameroon Cases." *Journal of African History* 15, no. 4 (1975): 577–94.

Burnham, Philip, Elisabeth Copet-Rougier, and Philip Noss. "Gbaya et Mkako: Contribution Ethno-Linguistique à l'Histoire de l'Est-Cameroun." *Paideuma* 32 (1986): 87–128.

Burrill, Emily S. *States of Marriage: Gender, Justice, and Rights in Colonial Mali*. New African Histories. Athens, OH: Ohio University Press, 2015.

Cabrita, Joel. *Text and Authority in the South African Nazaretha Church*. Cambridge: Cambridge University Press, 2014.

Cabrita, Joel, and Maxwell, David. "Relocating World Christianity." In *Relocating World Christianity: Interdisciplinary Studies in Universal and Local Expressions of the Christian Faith*, edited by Joel Cabrita, David Maxwell, and Emma Wild-Wood, 1–47. Boston, MA: Brill, 2017.

Cabrita, Joel, David Maxwell, and Emma Wild-Wood. *Relocating World Christianity: Interdisciplinary Studies in Universal and Local Expressions of the Christian Faith*. Boston, MA: Brill, 2017.

Cador, Grégoire. *L'héritage de Simon Mpeke: prêtre de Jésus et frère universel*. Paris: Lethielleux: Desclée de Brouwer, 2009.

Calvès, Anne-Emmanuèle, and Dominique Meekers. "The Advantages of Having Many Children for Women in Formal and Informal Unions in Cameroon." *Journal of Comparative Family Studies* 30, no. 4 (1999): 617–39.

Camus, Albert. *The Rebel: An Essay on Man in Revolt*. First Vintage Interntional Edition. New York: Random House, 1991.

Cannadine, David. *Ornamentalism: How the British Saw Their Empire*. Oxford: Oxford University Press, 2001.

Carret, J.M. "La Crise Des Villages." *L'Effort Camerounais*, January 5, 1958, 118 edition.

Catholic Church. *The Catechism of the Council of Trent*. Translated by John A. McHugh and Charles J. Callan. Reprint edition. Rockford, IL: Tan Books and Publishers, 1992.

Chamedes, Giuliana. "Pius XII, Rights Talk and the Dawn of the Religious Cold War." In *Religion and Human Rights*, edited by David Pendas. New York: Routledge, forthcoming.

Chanock, Martin. "A Peculiar Sharpness: An Essay on Property in the History of Customary Law in Colonial Africa." *Journal of African History*, no. 32 (1991): 65–88.

———. *Law, Custom and Social Order: The Colonial Experience in Malawi and Zambia*. Cambridge and New York: Cambridge University Press, 1985.

Chatterjee, Partha. *The Nation and Its Fragments: Colonial and Postcolonial Histories*. Princeton, NJ: Princeton University Press, 1993.

Chauvenet, Fernand de. *Tchad, 1916–1918: Carnets de Route d'un Officier de Cavalerie*. Collection Racines Du Présent. Paris: L'Harmattan, 1999.

Choupo, Michel. "Mariage sans Dot." *Essor Des Jeunes*, javier 1962, no. 23 edition.

Clarence-Smith, W. Gervase. "Plantation versus Smallholder Production of Cocoa: The Legacy of the German Period in Cameroon." In *Pathways to Accumulation in Cameroon*, edited by Peter Geschiere and Piet Konings, 187–216. Paris: Karthala, 1993.

Clarke, John. *Memoir of Joseph Merrick, Missionary to Africa*. London: Benjamin L. Green, 1850.

Clignet, Remi. "L'Influence Du Concept de Cohorte Sur La Démographie Des Pays En Voie de Développement: Le Cas Du Cameroun de l'Ouest." *Population*, no. 4–5 (1983): 707–32.

Coger, Dalvan M. "An Early Missionary Enterprise: The Baptists at Fernando Po, 1840–1860." *American Baptist Quarterly* 9, no. 3 (1990): 158–66.

Cohen, William B. *Robert Delavignette and the French Empire: Selected Writings.* Chicago: University of Chicago Press, 1977.

Cole, Jennifer. *Love in Africa.* Chicago: University of Chicago Press, 2009.

Comaroff, Jean, and John Comaroff. "Home-Made Hegemony: Modernity, Domesticity, and Colonialism in South Africa." In *African Encounters with Domesticity*, edited by Karen Tranberg Hansen, 37–74. New Brunswick, NJ: Rutgers University Press, 1992.

Comaroff, Jean, and John L. Comaroff. *Of Revelation and Revolution, Volume 1: Christianity, Colonialism, and Consciousness in South Africa.* Chicago: University of Chicago Press, 1991.

Comaroff, John L., and Jean Comaroff. *Of Revelation and Revolution, Volume 2: The Dialectics of Modernity on a South African Frontier.* 1 edition. Chicago: University of Chicago Press, 1997.

Comité d'Action Catholique. "L'Etonnante Progression Des Catholiques Au Cameroun." *Vers l'Avenir*, janvier 1939, no. 9 edition.

Congrégation du Saint-Esprit. "L'Administration Mandatée a-t-Elle Ce Droit? Etude Sur La Politique Française Au Sujet Des Missions." *Kolnische Volkszeitung*, July 14, 1930.

Conklin, Alice. *A Mission to Civilize: The Republican Idea of Empire in France and West Africa, 1895–1930.* 1 edition. Stanford: Stanford University Press, 2000.

———. "Colonialism and Human Rifhts, A Contradiction in Terms? The Case of France and West Africa, 1895–1914." *The American Historical Review* 103, no. 2 (1998): 419–42.

Constantin, François, and Christian Coulon. *Religion et Transition Démocratique En Afrique.* Paris: Karthala, 1997.

Cooper, Barbara. *Marriage in Maradi: Gender and Culture in a Hausa Society in Niger, 1900–1989.* Portsmouth, NH and Oxford: Heinemann, 1997.

Cooper, Frederick. *Africa since 1940: The Past of the Present.* Cambridge and New York: Cambridge University Press, 2002.

———. *Decolonization and African Society: The Labor Question in French and British Africa.* Cambridge: Cambridge University Press, 1996.

Copet-Rougier, Elisabeth. "Du Clan a La Chefferie Dans l'est Du Cameroun." *Africa: Journal of the International African Institute* 57, no. 3 (1987): 345–63.

———. "Étude de La Transformation Du Mariage Chez Les Mkako Du Cameroun." In *Transformations of African Marriage*, edited by David Nyamwaya and David J. Parkin, 75–91. Manchester and Wolfeboro, NH: Manchester University Press, for the International African Institute, 1987.

———. "Parenté et Rapports de Productions Chez Les Mkako." *L'Ethnographie* 121, no. 79 (1979): 7–39.

Coquery-Vidrovitch, Catherine. *Les Africaines. Histoire Des Femmes d'Afrique Noire Du XIXe Au XXe Siècle.* Paris: Desjonquères, 1994.

Corbin, Alain. *Village Bells: Sound & Meaning in the 19th-Century French Countryside.* New York: Columbia University Press, 1998.

Costedoat, René. *L'effort Français Au Cameroun, Le Mandat Français et La Réorganisation Des Territoires Du Cameroun.* Paris: Editions Larose, 1930.

Costen, Melva Wilson. "The Lord's Feast." *The Presbyterian Survey*, May 1995, 11–12.

Coulibaly, Daniel Ouezzin. "Sur l'éducation Des Femmes Africaines." *L'Education Africaine* 99–100 (1938): 33–36.
Cozzens, Lucia Hammond. "'Why I Left the Things of the Fathers': An Interview with Ndile Nsom, Native Judge." *The Drum Call* 3, no. 3 (October 1924): 20–24.
Criaud, Jean. "Etienne Nkodo, de 1911 à 1983: Le Premier Spiritain Camerounais." *Mémoire Spiritaine* deuxième semestre, no. 8 (1998): 50–73.
———. *La Geste Des Spiritains: Histoire de l'Eglise Au Cameroun 1916–1990*. Yaoundé: Imprimerie Saint-Paul, 1990.
Cuchet, Guillaume. "Nouvelles Perspectives Historiographiques Sur Les Prêtres-Ouvriers (1943–1954)." *Vingtième Siècle. Revue d'histoire* 87, no. 3 (September 2005): 179–87.
Dager, William M. "A Great Frontier Church." *Assembly Herald* 20 (September 1914): 511–14.
Darge, Philippe. "Le Cafe Au Cameroun." Mémoire, Ecole Nationale de la France d'Outre-Mer, 1958.
Daughton, J.P. *An Empire Divided: Religion, Republicanism, and the Making of French Colonialism, 1880–1914*. Oxford: Oxford University Press, 2008.
Daulte, Henri. *Le Livre Du Jubilé 1877–1927. Histoire Des Cinquante Premières Années de La Croix-Bleue*. Lausanne: Agence de la Croix-Bleue, 1927.
Deane, Shirley. *Talking Drums: From a Village in Cameroon*. London: John Murray, 1985.
Dekar, Paul R. "Alfred Saker and the Baptists in Cameroon." *Foundations* 14, no. 4 (1971): 325–43.
Dekar, Paul Richard. "Crossing Religious Frontiers: Christianity and the Transformation of Bulu Society, 1892–1925." Ph.D. Dissertation, University of Chicago, 1978.
Delange, Jacqueline. "La Discussion Parlementaire Sur Le Code Du Travail En Afrique Noire." *Présence Africaine*, no. 13 (1952): 377–400.
Delavignette, Robert Louis. *Les Paysans Noirs*. Paris: Éditions Stock, 1931.
———. *Service Africain*. Paris: Gallimard, 1946.
Diaw, Mariteuw Chimère, and Phil René Oyono. "Dynamiques et Représentation Des Espaces Forestiers Au Sud-Cameroun: Pour Une Relecture Sociale Des Paysages." *Bulletin Arbres, Forêts et Communautés Rurales* 15, no. 16 (1998): 36–43.
"Disparition Progressive de La Famille Regulière Dans Le Sud-Cameroun." *L'Effort Camerounais*. October 6, 1957.
Djoumessi Dongmo, Odette, and Antoine Nguimzang. *Djoumessi Mathias, 1900–1966: Un Exemple de Chef Traditionnel Chrétien*. Yaoundé, Cameroon: Éditions SOPECAM, 1991.
Dugast, Idelette. *Monographie de La Tribu Des Ndiki (Banen Du Cameroun)*. Travaux et Mémoires de l'Institut d'ethnologie 58. Paris: Institut d'ethnologie, 1955.
———. *Monographie de la tribu des Ndiki (Banen du Cameroun): Vie sociale et familiale*. Paris: Institut d'ethnologie, 1959.
Dupré, Georges. *Un Ordre et Sa Destruction*. Paris: ORSTOM, 1982.
Durkheim, Emile. "La Famille Conjugale." In *Textes 3: Fonctions Sociales et Institutions*, edited by Victor Karady. Paris: Les Editions du Minuit, 1975.
———. "La Prohibition de l'inceste et Ses Origines." *L'année Sociologique* 1 (1896–1897): 1–70.
Dussercle, Roger. *Du Kilimandjaro Au Cameroun*. Paris: La Colombe, 1954.

Dzou, Antoine Ondoa. "Christianisation des Beti du centre Cameroun 1922–1955: essai d'interprétation." Thèse d'université, Lyon III, 1994.

Eboussi Boulaga, Fabien. "Pour Une Catholicité Africaine." In *Civilisation Noire et Eglise Catholique*, edited by Société africaine de Culture, 331–70. Paris: Editions Présence Africaine, 1978.

Eboussi-Boulaga, Fabien. "Le Bantou problématique." *Présence Africaine* 66, no. 1 (1968): 5–40.

Eckert, Andreas. "African Rural Entrepreneurs and Labor in the Cameroon Littoral." *Journal of African History*, no. 40 (1999): 109–26.

———. "Cocoa Farming in Cameroon, c.1914–1960." In *Cocoa Pioneer Fronts since 1800: The Role of Planters, Smallholders, and Merchants*, edited by W. Gervase Clarence-Smith, 137–53. New York: St. Martin's Press, 1996.

Église Evangeliste du Cameroun. *Mjuopshe Po-Kristo: Cantiques Bamilekes*. Nkongsamba: Église Evangeliste du Cameroun, 1976.

Ekollo, Thomas. *Mémoires d'un Pasteur Camerounais (1920–1996)*. Paris: Karthala, 2003.

Ela, Jean-Marc. "Le Droit à La Différence Ou l'enjeu Des Églises Locales En Afrique Noire." In *Civilisation Noire et Eglise Catholique*, edited by Société africaine de Culture, 204–17. Paris: Editions Présence Africaine, 1978.

———. "L'Eglise, Le Monde Noir et Le Concile." In *Personnalité Africaine et Catholicisme*, edited by Meinrad P. Hebga, 59–83. Paris: Présence africaine, 1963.

———. *Ma Foi d'Africain*. Paris: Karthala, 1985.

Elbourne, Elizabeth. *Blood Ground: Colonialism, Missions, and the Contest for Christianity in the Cape Colony and Britain, 1799–1853*. Montreal: McGill-Queen's University Press, 2008.

Ellis, Stephen, and Gerrie ter Haar. "Religion and Politics: Taking African Epistemologies Seriously." *Journal of Modern African Studies* 45, no. 3 (2007): 385–401.

———. *Worlds of Power: Religious Thought and Political Practice in Africa*. New York: Oxford University Press, 2004.

Essomba Akamse, Soeur Thérèse-Michèle. "Hommes et Femmes Pour Construire Ensemble l'Église En Afrique." In *Spiritualité et Libération En Afrique*, edited by Engelbert Mveng, 79–83. Paris: L'Harmattan, 1987.

Essomba Fouda, Antoine. *Le Mariage Chrétien Au Cameroun : Une Réalité Anthropologique, Civile et Sacramentelle*. Paris: L'Harmattan, 2010.

Essono, Aloyse Kisito Patrice. *L'annonce de l'Evangile Au Cameroun: L'oeuvre Missionnaire Des Pallottins de 1890 à 1916 et de 1964 à 2010*. Paris: Karthala, 2013.

Essousse, Erik. *La Liberté de La Presse Écrite Au Cameroun: Ombres et Lumières*. Paris: L'Harmattan, 2008.

Etaba, Roger Onomo. *Histoire de l'Eglise Catholique Du Cameroun de Grégoire XVI à Jean-Paul II*. Paris: L'Harmattan, 2007.

———. "Maximum Illud, de Benoît XV, et l'œuvre Missionnaire Au Cameroun (1890–1935) : Entre Anticipations, Applications et Contradictions." *Présence Africaine* 2, no. 172 (2005): 125–45.

Etoga, Paul, and Edmond Dillinger. *Paul Etoga: Mon Autogiobraphie*. Friedrichsthal: CV-Afrika-Hilfe, 1995.

Eyezo'o, Salvador. "La Partition Du Vicariat Apostolique Du Cameroun." In *Histoire et Missions Chrétiennes N-007. A La Rencontre de l'Asie – La Société Des Missions*

Etrangères de Paris (1658–2008), edited by Catherine Marin, 130–49. Paris: Karthala, 2008.

———. "La partition du vicariat apostolique du Cameroun." *Histoire, monde et cultures religieuses* n°7, no. 3 (September 1, 2008): 121–46.

Eze, Léopold-François. "Le Commandement Indigène de La Région Du Nyong et Sanaga, Sud-Cameroun, de 1916 à 1945." Thèse (Doctorat en Histoire), Université de Paris I, 1975.

Eze, L.F. "Le Commandement Indigène de La Région Du Nyong et Sanaga (Sud-Cameroun) Du 1916 à 1945." Thèse du 3e cycle, Université de Paris I, 1974.

Fabre, Frédéric. *Protestantisme et colonisation: l'évolution du discours de la mission protestante française au XXe siècle*. Paris: Karthala, 2011.

Fall, Papa Guèye. "L'enseignement Des Filles Au Sénégal et Dans Le Circonscription de Dakar." *L'Education Africaine* 87 (1934): 191–93.

Farelly, Maurice. *Chronique Du Pays Banen (Au Cameroun)*. Paris: Société des missions évangéliques, 1948.

———. *Les Actes des apôtres*. Paris: Delachaux & Niestlé, 1958.

———. "Les Eglises Indigènes Au Cameroun." *Journal Des Missions Évangéliques* (1946): 7–16.

Feldman-Savelsberg, Pamela. "Cooking Inside: Kinship and Gender in Bangangte Idioms of Marriage and Procreation." *American Ethnologist* 22, no. 3 (1995): 483–502.

———. *Plundered Kitchens, Empty Wombs*. Ann Arbor, MI: University of Michigan Press, 1999.

Festa, Lynn. *Sentimental Figures of Empire in Eighteenth-Century Britain and France*. Baltimore, MD: Johns Hopkins University Press, 2006.

Fields, Karen Elise. *Revival and Rebellion in Colonial Central Africa*. Princeton, NJ: Princeton University Press, 1985.

Findlay, Eileen J. Suárez. *Imposing Decency: The Politics of Sexuality and Race in Puerto Rico, 1870–1920*. Durham, NC: Duke University Press, 2000.

Fisiy, Cyprian. *Palm Tree Justice in the Bertoua Court of Appeal: The Witchcraft Cases*. In African Studies Centre, Leiden, Working Paper No. 12. Leiden, Netherlands, 1990.

Ford, Edward A. "Reconstruction in West Africa." *Missionary Review of the World* 43 (February 1920): 122–24.

Foster, Elizabeth. *Faith in Empire: Religion, Politics, and Colonial Rule in French Senegal, 1880–1940*. Stanford: Stanford University Press, 2013.

Foucault, Michel. *Discipline and Punish: The Birth of the Prison*. London: Vintage Books, 1977.

Fouellefak Kana–Dongmo, Célestine Colette. "Acteurs locaux de l'implantation du catholicisme dans le pays Bamiléké au Cameroun." *Chrétiens et sociétés. XVIe–XXIe siècles*, no. 13 (December 31, 2006).

Fouillée, Alfred. *Les Éléments Sociologiques de La Morale*. Paris: Félix Alcan, 1905.

———. *Tempérament et Caractère Selon Les Individus, Les Sexes, et Les Races*. Paris: Félix Alcan, 1895.

Gardinier, David E. *Cameroon: United Nations Challenge to French Policy*. Oxford: Oxford University Press, 1963.

Geary, Christraud M. *On Legal Change in Cameroon: Women, Marriage, and Bridewealth*. Boston, MA: African Studies Center, Boston University, 1986.

"Germans Interned in Spanish Guinea." *The Sacred Heart Review* 55, no. 9 (February 12, 1916): 3.

Geschiere, Peter. "Chiefs and Colonial Rule in Cameroon: Inventing Chieftaincy, French and British Style." *Africa: Journal of the International African Institute* 63, no. 2 (1993): 151–75.

———. "Funerals and Belonging: Different Patterns in South Cameroon." *African Studies Review* 48, no. 2 (2005): 45–64.

———. "Slavery and Kinship among the Maka (Cameroon, Eastern Province)." *Paideuma* 41 (1995): 207–25.

———. *The Modernity of Witchcraft: Politics and the Occult in Postcolonial Africa*. Charlottesville, VA: University of Virginia Press, 1997.

———. *Village Communities and the State: Changing Relations among the Maka of South-Eastern Cameroon since the Colonial Conquest*. London and Boston, MA: Kegan Paul International, 1982.

———. *Witchcraft, Intimacy, and Trust: Africa in Comparison*. Chicago and London: University of Chicago Press, 2013.

Geschiere, Peter, and Cyprian Fisiy. "Domesticating Personal Violence: Witchcraft, Courts and Confessions in Cameroon." *Africa: Journal of the International African Institute* 64, no. 3 (1994): 323–41.

Girardet, Raoul. *L'idée Coloniale En France de 1871 à 1962*. Paris: La Table Ronde, 1972.

Glaser, Clive. "Managing the Sexuality of Urban Youth: Johannesburg, 1920s–1960s." *The International Journal of African Historical Studies* 38, no. 2 (2005): 301–27.

Gouellain, René. *Douala: Ville et Histoire*. Enquête réalisée dans le cadre de l'ORSTOM. Publié avec le concours du CNRS. Paris: Institut d'ethnologie, Musée de l'Homme, 1975.

Gray, Christopher J. *Colonial Rule and Crisis in Equatorial Africa: Southern Gabon, c. 1850–1940*. Rochester, NY: University of Rochester Press, 2002.

Grob, Francis. *Témoins Camerounais de l'Evangile (Les Origines de L'Eglise Evangélique)*. Yaoundé, Cameroon: Editions CLE, 1967.

Guernier, Eugène, and René Briat. *Cameroun, Togo, Encyclopédie de l'Afrique Française*. Paris: Éditions de l'Union Française, 1951.

Guilday, Peter. "The Sacred Congregation de Propaganda Fide (1622–1922)." *The Catholic Historical Review* 6, no. 4 (January 1, 1921): 478–94.

Guimera, L.M. *Ni Dos Ni Ventre: Religion, Magie et Sorcellerie Evuzok*. Paris: Société d'Ethnographie, 1981.

Guyer, Jane I. "Beti Widow Inheritance and Marriage Law: A Social History." In *Widows in African Societies: Choices and Constraints*, edited by Betty Potash, 193–219. Stanford: Stanford University Press, 1978.

Guyer, Jane I. "Family and Farm in Southern Cameroon." [Boston, MA]: Boston University, African Studies Center, 1984.

Guyer, Jane I. "Female Farming and the Evolution of Food Production Patterns Amongst the Beti of South-Central Cameroon." *Africa: Journal of the International African Institute* 50, no. 4 (1980): 341–56.

———. "Head Tax, Social Structure and Rural Incomes in Cameroun, 1922–37." *Cahiers d'Etudes Africaines* XX, no. 3 (1980): 305–29.

———. "Indigenous Currencies and the History of Marriage Payments: A Case Study from Cameroon." *Cahiers d'Etudes Africaines* 26, no. 104 (1986): 577–610.

———. *Marginal Gains: Monetary Transactions in Atlantic Africa*. Chicago: University of Chicago Press, 2004.

———, ed. *Money Matters: Instability, Values and Social Payments in the Modern History of West African Communities*. Portsmouth, NH: Heinemann, 1994.

———. *The Provident Societies in the Rural Economy of Yaoundé, 1945–1960*. Working Paper No. 37, African Studies Center, Boston University, 1980.

———. "Traditions of Invention in Equatorial Africa." *African Studies Review* 39, no. 3 (1996): 1–28.

———. "Wealth in People and Self-Realization in Equatorial Africa." *Man* 28 (1993): 243–65.

Guyer, Jane I., and Samuel M. Eno Belinga. "Wealth in People as Wealth in Knowledge: Accumulation and Composition in Equatorial Africa." *Journal of African History* 36 (1995): 91–120.

Halsey, Abram Woodruff. *A Visit to the West Africa Mission of the Presbyterian Church in the U.S.A.* Philadelphia: Board of foreign missions of the Presbyterian church in the U.S.A., 1912.

Harrison, Victoria S. "The Pragmatics of Defining Religion in a Multi-Cultural World." *International Journal for Philosophy of Religion* 59, no. 3 (2006): 133–52.

Hastings, Adrian. *The Construction of Nationhood: Ethnicity, Religion and Nationalism*. Cambridge: Cambridge University Press, 1997.

Hebga, Meinrad P. *Personnalité africaine et catholicisme*. Paris: Présence africaine, 1963.

Hoffman, Danny. *The War Machines: Young Men and Violence in Sierra Leone and Liberia*. Durham, NC: Duke University Press, 2011.

Horner, George R. "The Allocation of Power and Responsibility in Bulu Society: A Test of the Usefulness of a Methodology Developed by Marion Levy Jr. in 'The Structure of Society.'" *Cahiers d'Études Africaines* 4, no. 15 (1964): 400–34.

Horton, Robin. "On the Rationality of Conversion. Part I." *Africa: Journal of the International African Institute* 45, no. 3 (1975): 219–35.

Hunter, Mark. "Cultural Politics and Masculinities: Multiple-Partners in Historical Perspective in KwaZulu-Natal." *Culture, Health & Sexuality* 7, no. 4 (August 2005): 389–403.

Institut catholique de Paris, Soeur Marie-Andre du Sacré Coeur, and Joseph Wilbois. *La femme noire dans la société africaine: conférences données à l'Institut Catholique de Paris 1938–1939*. Paris: Bibliothèque de l'Union Missionaire du Clergé, 1940.

Ittmann, Johannes. *Krokodil und Löffel die Geschichte zweier Kameruner Missionsschüler*. Stuttgart: Evang. Missionsverlag, 1928.

Ittmann, Johannes, and Friedrich Edbing. "Religiöse Gesänge Aus Dem Nördlichen Waldland von Kamerun." In *Afrika Und Übersee, Sprachen Und Kulturen*, edited by Seminar für Afrikanische Sprachen der Universität Hamburg, 169–77. Berlin: Reimer, 1954.

Jacquin, Françoise. "Naissance Du Laïcat Missionnaire: L'exemple d'Ad Lucem (1930–1939)." In *Diffusion et Acculturation Du Christianisme (XIXe–XXe s.) Vingt-Cinq Ans de Recherches Missiologiques Par Le CREDIC*, 395–405. Paris: Karthala, 2005.

Jean-Baptiste, Rachel. *Conjugal Rights: Marriage, Sexuality, and Urban Life in Colonial Libreville, Gabon*. Athens, OH: Ohio University Press, 2014.

Jennings, Eric T. *Vichy in the Tropics: Petain's National Revolution in Madagascar, Guadeloupe, and Indochina, 1940–44*. Stanford: Stanford University Press, 2001.

Jézéquel, Jean-Hervé. "Les Enseignants Comme Élite Politique En AOF (1930–1945): Des 'Meneurs de Galopins' Dans l'arène Politique (Teachers as a Political Elite in French West Africa (1930–1945))." *Cahiers d'Études Africaines* 45, no. 178 (January 1, 2005): 519–43.

———. "L'organisation Des Cadres de l'enseignement En Afrique Occidentale Française (1903–Fin Des Années 1930)." *Genèses* 4, no. 69, Spécial: "La parole est aux indigènes" (2007): 4–25.

Johnson-Hanks, Jennifer. *Uncertain Honor: Modern Motherhood in an African Crisis*. Chicago: University of Chicago Press, 2006.

Jones, Ebenezer Edwin. *The Life of Rowland Hill Evans of Cameroun: A Narrative of Service in the West Africa Mission, Presbyterian Church, U.S.A., 1909–1932*. Columbus, OH: F.J. Heer Print. Co., 1932.

Joseph, Richard A. *Radical Nationalism in Cameroon: Social Origins of the U.P.C. Rebellion*. Oxford: Oxford University Press, 1977.

Kalalobe, Iwiye. "Au Cameroun, à Quelle Famille Appartient Une Femme Mariée?" *L'Effort Camerounais*. October 1949, 208 edition.

Kalaora, Bernard. "Le Mysticisme Technique de Joseph Wilbois." In *Les chantiers de la paix sociale: 1900–1940*, edited by Yves Cohen and Rémi Baudouï, 185–94. Paris: ENS Editions, 1995.

Kaptue, Léon. *Cameroun: Travail et Main-d'Oeuvre Sous Le Régime Français, 1916–1952*. Paris: L'Harmattan, 1986.

Keller, Jean. "Missions d'A.O.F." *Monde Non Chrétien*, Société des Missions Evangéliques, Paris, 1951, 1–3.

Kemner, Wilhelm. *Kamerun*. Berlin: Freiheits-Verlag, 1937.

Kendemeh, Emmanuel. "Mvolye Basilica – The Pope's Church." *Cameroon Tribune*, December 6, 2006.

Kibénél Ngo Billong, Soeur Gertude Thérèse. *Noces de Grâce de La Congrégation Des Soeurs Servantes de Marie de Douala: 70 Ans d'existence*. Douala: Congrégation des Soeurs Servantes de Marie de Douala, 2009.

Kisembo, Benezeri, Laurenti Magesa, and Aylward Shorter. *African Christian Marriage*. London: Chapman, 1977.

Klinken, Adriaan S. van. "Imitation as Transformation of the Male Self: How an Apocryphal Saint Reshapes Zambian Catholic Men." *Cahiers d'Études Africaines* 53, no. 209/210 (2013): 119–42.

Koch, Henri. *Magie et Chasse Dans La Forêt Camerounaise*. Paris: Berger-Levrault, 1968.

Koko, Jean-Marie Vianney Balegamire A. *Mariage Africain et Mariage Chrétien*. Paris: L'Harmattan, 2003.

Koselleck, Reinhart. *Critique and Crisis: Enlightenment and the Pathogenesis of Modern Society*. Oxford: Berg Publishers, 1988.

Koum'enioc, Karine. "Cameroun : Les Autorités En Difficulté Avec Les Débits de Boisson." *Journal Du Cameroun*, September 15, 2009.

Kuate, SCJ, Joseph. *Théologie de Deux Pasteurs de l'Eglise Camerounaise: Mgr. Jean Zoa et Mgr. Albert Ndongmo*. Yaoundé: Presses de l'Université Catholique d'Afrique Centrale (PUCAC), 2012.

Kujumdzieva, Svetlana. "The Byzantine–Slavic Sanctus: Its Liturgical Context through the Centuries." *Studia Musicologica Academiae Scientiarum Hungaricae* 39, no. 2/4 (1998): 223–32.

"La Dot et l'Eglise Au Cameroun." *Revue de L'Alliance Sainte Jeanne D'Arc*, 1934, 12–15.

Laade, Wolfgang. "Reviewed Work: Psalmodie Bassa and Missa Bassa. Directed by Abbé Aloys Lihan, Duala, Camerouns." *Ethnomusicology* 12, no. 2 (May 1968): 307–8.

Labouret, Henri. *À La Recherche d'une Politique Indigène Dans l'ouest Africain*. Paris: Editions du Comité de l'Afrique Française, 1931.

———. *Paysans D'Afrique Occidentale*. Paris: Gallimard, 1941.

Laburthe-Tolra, Philippe. "Charles Atangana." In *Les Africains*, edited by Charles André Julien, 109–41. Paris: Jaguar, 1977.

———. *Initiations et Sociétés Secrètes Au Cameroun: Les Mystères de La Nuit : Essai Sur La Religion Beti, Volume 1*. Paris: Karthala, 1985.

———. "Intentions missionnaires et perception africaine : quelques données camerounaises." *Civilisations. Revue internationale d'anthropologie et de sciences humaines* 41, no. 1/2 (1993): 239–55.

———. "La Mission Catholique Allemande Du Cameroun (1890–1916) et La Missologie." In *Diffusion et Acculturation Du Christianisme (XIXe–XXe s.) Vingt-Cinq Ans de Recherches Missiologiques Par Le CREDIC*, edited by Jean Comby, 227–49. Paris: Karthala, 2005.

———. *Les Seigneurs de La Forêt: Essai Sur Le Passé Historique, l'organisation Sociale et Les Norms Éthiques Des Anciens Béti Du Cameroun*. Paris: Publications de la Sorbonne, 1981.

———. "Minlaaba." Ph.D., Atelier de l'Université de Lille III, 1977.

———. *Minlaaba: Histoire et Société Traditionnelle Chez Les Bëti Du Sud-Cameroun*. 3 vols. Paris: Librairie Honoré Champion, 1977.

———. *Vers La Lumiere? Ou, Le Désir d'Ariel: A Propos Des Beti Du Cameroun: Sociologie de La Conversion*. Paris: Karthala, 1999.

Lachenal, Guillaume, and Bertrand Taithe. "Une Généalogie Missionnaire et Coloniale de l'Humanitaire: Le Cas Aujoulat Au Cameroun, 1935–1973." *Le Mouvement Sociale*, no. 227 (2009): 45–63.

Landau, Paul Stuart. *The Realm of the Word: Language, Gender, and Christianity in a Southern African Kingdom*. Portsmouth, NH: Heinemann, 1995.

Le Roy, Alexandre. *Un Martyr de La Morale Chrétienne: Le Père Henri de Maupeou de La Congrégation Du Saint-Esprit, Missionnaire Au Cameroun*. Paris: Editions Dillen/Maison Mère des Pères du Saint-Esprit, 1936.

Le Vine, Victor T. *The Cameroons from Mandate to Independence*. Berkeley, CA: University of California Press, 1964.

Legrain, Michel. *L'Eglise catholique et le mariage en Occident et en Afrique (Tome II): L'ébranlement de l'édifice matrimonial*. Paris: L'Harmattan, 2009.

Lembezat, Bertrand. *Le Cameroun*. Paris: Editions Maritimes et Coloniales, 1954.

Leplaideur, Alain. "Vie et survie domestique en zone forestière camerounaise : la reproduction simple est-elle assurée." In *Le Risque en agriculture*, edited by Michel Eldin and Pierre Milleville, 277–90. Paris: Editions de l'ORSTOM, 1989.

Lindsay, Lisa A. "'No Need... to Think of Home'? Masculinity and Domestic Life on the Nigerian Railway, c. 1940–61." *The Journal of African History* 39, no. 3 (1998): 439–66.

———. *Working with Gender: Wage Labor and Social Change in Southwestern Nigeria*. Portsmouth, NH: Heinemann, 2003.

Livingston, Julie. *Debility and the Moral Imagination in Botswana*. Bloomington, IN: Indiana University Press, 2005.

Locoh, Thérèse. "Evolution of the Family in Africa." In *The State of African Demography*, edited by Étienne Van de Walle, Patrick O. Ohadike, and Mpembele Sala-Diakanda, 47–65. Paris: International Union for the Scientific Study of Population, 1988.

Mainet, Guy. *Douala: Croissance et Servitudes*. Paris: L'Harmattan, 1985.

Mala, William Armand. "Knowledge Systems and Adaptive Collaborative Management of Natural Resources in Southern Cameroon." Ph.D. Dissertation, Stellenbosch University, 2009.

Malaquais, Dominique. "Building in the Name of God: Architecture, Resistance, and the Christian Faith in the Bamileke Highlands of Western Cameroon." *African Studies Review* 42, no. 1 (April 1999): 49–78.

Malkki, Liisa. *Purity and Exile: Violence, Memory, and National Cosmology among Hutu Refugees in Tanzania*. Chicago: University of Chicago Press, 1995.

Mallo, Eugène. *Sermons de chez nous: sermons pour les temps de l'Eglise*. Yaoundé: Editions CLE, 1965.

Mamdani, Mahmood. *Citizen and Subject: Contemporary Africa and the Legacy of Late Colonialism*. Princeton, NJ: Princeton University Press, 1996.

Mann, Gregory. *Native Sons: West African Veterans and France in the Twentieth Century*. Durham, NC: Duke University Press, 2006.

Mann, Kristin. *Marrying Well: Marriage, Status, and Social Change among the Educated Elite in Colonial Lagos*. Cambridge: Cambridge University Press, 1985.

Manning, Patrick. *Francophone Sub-Saharan Africa 1880–1985*. Cambridge and New York: Cambridge University Press, 1988.

Marie-André du Sacré Coeur, Soeur. "La Loi d'airain Du Mariage Dotal Au Cameroun Français." *Études* 267 (1950): 3–21.

Marshall, Ruth. *Political Spiritualities: The Pentecostal Revolution in Nigeria*. 1 edition. Chicago and London: University of Chicago Press, 2009.

Matip, Marie-Claire. *Ngonda*. Paris: Bibliothèque du Jeune Africain, 1958.

Mazower, Mark. *Governing the World: The History of an Idea, 1815 to the Present*. New York: Penguin, 2012.

Mbembe, Achille. "Domaines de La Nuit et Autorité Onirique Dans Les Maquis Du Sud-Cameroun (1955–1958)." *Journal of African History* 31 (1986): 37–72.

———. *La Naissance Du Maquis Dans Le Sud-Cameroun, 1920–1960: Histoire Des Usages de La Raison En Colonie*. Paris: Karthala, 1996.

Mbozo'o, Samuel Efoua. "La Naissance Du Clergé et Des Congrégations Religieuses Autochtones Au Cameroun 1919–1939." Mémoire d'histoire sous la direction du professeur Gadille Jacques, Lyon III, 1978.

McClintock, Anne. "Family Feuds: Gender, Nationalism and the Family." *Feminist Review*, no. 44 (July 1, 1993): 61–80.
McCullers, Molly. "'We Do It so That We Will Be Men': Masculinity Politics in Colonial Namibia, 1915–49." *The Journal of African History* 52, no. 1 (2011): 43–62.
McNeill, Lois Johnson. *The Great Ngee: The Story of a Jungle Doctor*. Philadelphia: Commission on Ecumenical Mission and Relations of the United Presbyterian Church in the United States of America, 1959.
Médard, Jean-François. "Les Eglises Protestantes Au Cameroun, Entre Tradition Authoritaire et Ethnicité." In *Religion et Transition Démocratique En Afrique*, edited by François Constantin and Christian Coulon, 189–220. Paris: Karthala, 1997.
Medou, Jean Louis Ndjemba. *Nnanga Kon*. Yaoundé: Edition Sopecam, 1989.
Meka Oyo, Gabriel. "Onyol'a Bosangi Ba Mundi: Jenene La Kwankwan La Mundi Mi Duala / 'La Dot.'" *Jumwele La Bana Ba Kamerun*. avril -27 avril 1935 1935, 18 edition.
Merry, Sally Engle. *Colonizing Hawai'i*. Princeton, NJ: Princeton University Press, 1999.
Messina, Jean Paul. *Le Centenaire de La Conversion Andre Mbangue: Le Premier Chrétien Catholique Camerounais*. Yaoundé: publisher not known, 1988.
Messina, Jean Paul, and Jaap Van Slageren. *Histoire Du Christianisme Au Cameroun: Des Origines à Nos Jours : Approche Oecuménique*. Paris: Karthala, 2005.
Messina, Jean-Paul. "Contribution Des Camerounais à l'expansion de l'Église Catholique Le Cas Des Populations Du Sud-Cameroun, 1890–1961." Thèse de 3e cycle, Université de Yaoundé, 1988.
———. *Des témoins camerounais de l'evangile: Andre Kwa Mbange*. Yaoundé, Cameroun: Presses de l'UCAC, 2001.
Messina, Jean-Paul, Owono Mimboé, and Bernardin Gantin. *Jean Zoa, Prêtre, Archevêque de Yaoundé: 1922–1998*. Paris: Karthala, 2000.
Miller, Maureen C. "Masculinity, Reform, and Clerical Culture: Narratives of Episcopal Holiness in the Gregorian Era." *Church History* 72, no. 1 (2003): 25–52.
Minter, William. *Apartheid's Contras: An Inquiry Into the Roots of War in Angola and Mozambique*. William Minter, 1994.
Mission Protestante Française. *Nwa'ni Nescane Nwa'ni Neji'te Nescan Ntsub Bamileke (Livre de Lecture En Langue Bamileke à l'usage Des Écoles de La Mission Protestante Francaise Au Cameroun)*. Third edition. Paris: Société des Missions Evangeliques, 1952.
"Missions Catholiques Au Cameroun." *L'Eveil Du Cameroun*, no. 374 (août 1939).
Moberly, F.J. *Togoland and the Cameroons 1914–1916*. London: Imperial War Museum, 1931.
Monchanin, Jules, Edouard Duperray, and Jacques Gadille. *Théologie et Spiritualité Missionnaires*. Paris: Editions Beauchesne, 1985.
Monga, Yvette. "The Emergence of Duala Cocoa Planters under German Rule in Cameroon: A Case Study of Entrepreneurship." In *Cocoa Pioneer Fronts Since 1800: The Role of Smallholders, Planters, and Merchants*, edited by William G. Clarence-Smith, 119–36. Basingstoke: Palgrave Macmillan, 1996.
Mongo Beti. *Le roi miraculé; chronique des Essazam, roman*. Paris: Buchet/Chastel, Correa, 1958.

Mouiche, Ibrahim. *Autorités traditionnelles et démocratisation au Cameroun: entre centralité de l'Etat et logiques de terroir*. Munster: LIT Verlag Münster, 2005.

———. "Mutations Socio-Politiques et Replis Identitaires En Afrique: Le Cas Du Cameroun." *African Journal of Political Science / Revue Africaine de Science Politique* 1, no. 2 (December 1, 1996): 176–201.

Mveng, Engelbert. *Album Du Centenaire: 1890–1990: L'Eglise Catholique Au Cameroun, 100 Ans d'évangélisation*. Yaoundé: Conférence Episcopale National du Cameroun, 1990.

———. *Histoire Des Églises Chrétiennes Au Cameroun: Les Origines*. Yaoundé, Cameroon: Saint-Paul Mvolyé, 1990.

———. *Histoire du Cameroun*. Paris: Présence africaine, 1963.

———. *L'Art d'Afrique Noire: Liturgie Cosmique et Langage Religieux*. Paris: Mame, 1964.

Mviena, Pierre. *Univers Culturel et Religieux Du Peuple Beti*. Yaoundé: Imprimerie Saint-Paul, 1970.

Myazhiom, Aggée Célestin Lomo. *Sociétés et Rivalités religieuses au Cameroun sous domination Française (1916–1958)*. Paris: L'Harmattan, 2001.

Ndjeng, Philippe Nken. *L'idée nationale dans le Cameroun francophone: 1920–1960*. Paris: L'Harmattan, 2012.

Ndjodo, Luc. *Le Mariage Chrétien Chez Les Beti*. Douala: Yonga & Partners, 1997.

Neeley, Paul. "Drummed Transactions: Calling the Church in Cameroon." *Anthropological Linguistics* 38, no. 4 (December 1, 1996): 683–717.

Nekes, Hermann. "Vierzig Jahre Im Dienste Der Kamerunmission. Zum Tode Des Schwarzen Lehrers Andreas Mbange." *Stern Der Heiden* 39, no. 12 (1932): 317–23.

Newell, Stephanie. *The Forger's Tale: The Search for Odeziaku*. 1 edition. Athens, OH: Ohio University Press, 2006.

Ngando, Blaise Alfred. *La France Au Cameroun: 1916–1939: Colonialisme Ou Mission Civilisatrice?* Paris: L'Harmattan, 2002.

Ngoa, Henri. "Le Mariage chez les Ewondo: Étude sociologique." Ph.D., Sorbonne, 1968.

Ngoa, Moise Ateba. "Histoire de La Traduction et de l'interpretation En Pays Beti: De La Période Coloniale à Nos Jours." In *Perspectives on Translation and Interpretation in Cameroon*, edited by Emmanuel Nges Chia, Joseph Che Suh, and Alexandre Ndeffo Tene. Bamenda, Cameroon: Langaa RPCIG and African Books Collective, 2009.

Ngoh, Victor Julius. *History of Cameroon since 1800*. Limbé, Cameroon: Presbook, 1996.

Ngongo, Louis-Paul. *Histoire des forces religieuses au Cameroun*. Paris: Karthala, 1982.

———. "Pouvoir Politique Occidental Dans Les Structures de l'Église En Afrique." In *Civilisation Noire et Eglise Catholique*, edited by Société africaine de Culture, 37–56. Paris: Editions Présence Africaine, 1978.

Ngoumou, Juilienne. "A Propos d'une Assemblée Dite 'des Organisations de Jeunesse.'" *Essor Des Jeunes*, juin–juillet 1962.

Nguini, Marcel. "La Valeur Politique & Sociale de La Tutelle Française Au Cameroun." Thèse pour le doctorat, L'Université d'Aix-Marseille, 1956.

Nicod, Henri. *Une École de Catéchistes Au Cameroun*. Paris: Société des Missions Evangeliques, 1930.

Nicol, Yves. "Cameroun-1959." *Marchés Tropicaux* 21 (November 1959): 2564–65.

———. *La Tribu Des Bakoko: Étude Monographique d'Économie Coloniale. Un Stade d'Évolution d'une Tribu Noire Au Cameroun*. Paris: Larose, 1929.

Njele, Judith. "Les Débuts Du Christianisme et Son Évolution En Pays Bamoun Au Cameroun." Thèse de doctorat, Université Panthéon-Sorbonne, 2005.

Njimoluh, Hamidou Komidor. *Les Fonctions Politiques de l'école Au Cameroun: 1916–1976*. Paris: L'Harmattan, 2010.

Njougla, Frédéric. "Dieu Dans La Pensée Originale Des Camerounais: Première Partie." *L'Effort Camerounais*. October 25, 1959.

Nolte, Insa. "New Histories of Marriage and Politics in Africa." *Gender & History* 29, no. 3 (2017): 742–48.

Nord, Philip. *The Republican Moment: Struggles for Democracy in Nineteenth-Century France*. Cambridge, MA: Harvard University Press, 1998.

Ombolo, Jean-Pierre. *Essai Sur l'histoire, Les Clans et Les Regroupements Claniques Des Eton Du Cameroun*. Yaoundé: Presses Universitaires de Yaoundé, 1986.

———. *Etre Beti, Un Art Africain d'etre Un Homme et de Vivre En Societe?: Essai d'analyse de l'esprit d'une Population : Une Etude Ethno-Historique (Collection Societes)*. Yaoundé: Presses Universitaires de Yaoundé, 2000.

———. "Les Eton Du Cameroun." Yaoundé, Cameroon: Université de Yaoundé, 1978.

———. *Sexe et Société En Afrique Noire: L'Anthropologie Sexuelle Beti: Essai Analytique, Critique et Comparatif*. Paris: L'Harmattan, 1990.

Onambélé, Marie-José Simone. *Oncle Maternel-Neveu: Une Relation Privilégiée Chez Les Éwondo*. Paris: L'Harmattan, 2010.

Orosz, Kenneth J. "The 'Affaire Des Sixas' and Catholic Education of Women in French Colonial Cameroon, 1915–1939." *French Colonial History* 1 (2002): 33–49.

———. "The 'Catechist War' in Inter-War French Cameroon." In *God's Empire: French Missionaries and the Modern World*, edited by Owen White and J.P. Daughton. Oxford: Oxford University Press, 2012.

Osborn, Emily Lynn. *Our New Husbands Are Here: Households, Gender, and Politics in a West African State from the Slave Trade to Colonial Rule*. Athens, OH: Ohio University Press, 2011.

Owono, Jacques Fulbert. *Pauvreté ou paupérisation en Afrique: une étude exegético-ethique de la pauvreté chez les Beti-Fang du Cameroun*. Bamberg, Germany: University of Bamberg Press, 2011.

Owono, Joseph. *Tante Bella: Roman d'aujourd'hui et de Demain*. Yaoundé: Librairie "Au Messager," 1959.

Owono Nkoudou, J.R. "Le Problème Du Mariage Dotal Au Cameroun Français." *Études Camerounaises* 39–40 (March 1953): 41–83.

Pasquier, Roger. *La jeunesse ouvrière chrétienne en Afrique noire (1930–1950)*. Paris: Karthala, 2013.

Pateman, Carole. *The Sexual Contract*. Stanford: Stanford University Press, 1988.

Pauvert, J.C., and J.L. Lancrey-Javal. *Le Groupement d'Evodoula (Cameroun): Étude Socio-Économique*. Rapports Du Conseil Supérieur Des Recherches Sociologiques Outre-Mer. ORSTOM, 1957.

Peel, J.D.Y. *Ijeshas and Nigerians: The Incorporation of a Yoruba Kingdom, 1890s-1970s*. Cambridge: Cambridge University Press, 1983.

Peel, J.D.Y. *Religious Encounter and the Making of the Yoruba*. Bloomington, IN: Indiana University Press, 2003.

Penvenne, Jeanne. *African Workers & Colonial Racism: Mozambican Strategies & Struggles in Lourenco Marques, 1877–1962*. Portsmouth, NH and London: Heinemann, 1994.

Père Antoine de Padoue Chonang. "Mgr Dieudonné Watio et Le Culte Des Ancêtres: Notre Tradition Comporte Des Éléments Positifs Qu'il Faut Exploiter." *L'Effort Camerounais*. January 2006.

Père Dubourget. "Mariage sans Dot." *Le Cameroun Catholique*. November 1953.

Perham, Margery. "France in the Cameroons." *The Times (London)*, May 17, 1933.

Perraud, R.P. *L'Église Catholique En Afrique Occidentale et Équatoriale*. La Paquelais: Imprimerie Vanden Brugge, 1986.

Peterson, Derek. "Gambling with God: Rethinking Religion in Colonial Central Kenya." In *The Invention of Religion: Rethinking Belief in Politics and History*, edited by Derek Peterson and Darren Walhof, 37–58. New Brunswick, NJ: Rutgers University Press, 2002.

———. "The Rhetoric of the Word: Bible Translation and Mau Mau in Central Kenya." In *Missions, Nationalism, and the End of Empire*, edited by Brian Stanley, 165–79. Grand Rapids, MI: William B. Eerdmans, 2003.

Peterson, Derek R. *Ethnic Patriotism and the East African Revival*. Cambridge: Cambridge University Press, 2012.

Philippe-Roger, Essama. "Evolution de La Cheffrie Traditionnelle En Pays Bëti." E.P.H.E. 6eme section, 1966.

Piketty, Thomas. *Capital in the Twenty-First Century*. Cambridge, MA: Harvard University Press, 2014.

Pokam, Kengne. *Les Églises Chrétiennes Face à La Montée Du Nationalisme Camerounais*. Paris: L'Harmattan, 1987.

Pougoué, Paul-Gérard. *Ethnicité, identités et citoyenneté en Afrique centrale*. Yaoundé, Cameroon: Presses Universitaires de l'Université catholique d'Afrique Centrale (PUCAC), 2002.

Privat, André. *Coup de coeur pour l'Afrique: 1956–1957*. Geneva: Editions du Pressoir de Montalègre, 1992.

Psalmodies camerounaises psalmes Ewmondo, Bassa, Bamileke. Radiodiffusion du Cameroun. Paris: Unidisc, 1958.

Pury, Roland de. *Les Eglises d'Afrique Entre l'Evangile et La Coutume*. Paris: Collection Présence de la mission, SMEP, 1958.

Quinn, Frederick. "Charles Atangana of Yaounde." *The Journal of African History* 21, no. 04 (1980): 485–95.

———. *In Search of Salt: Changes in Beti (Cameroon) Society, 1880–1960*. New York: Berghahn Books, 2006.

Ranger, Terence. "Missionary Adaptation of African Religious Institutions: The Masasi Case." In *The Historical Study of African Religion*, edited by Terence Ranger and I.N. Kimambo, 221–51. Berkeley: University of California Press, 1972.

Ranger, Terence O. "Religious Movements and Politics in Sub-Saharan Africa." *African Studies Review* 29, no. 2 (1986): 1–69.

Renan, Ernest. *La Réforme Intellectuelle et Morale*. Paris: Michel-Levy frères, 1871.
———. *Souvenirs d'enfance et de Jeunesse*. Paris: Calmann-Lévy, 1883.
Ribaut, Jean-Pierre. "Le Cardinal Liénart et Ad Lucem (Journée d'étude Du 25 Septembre 1993 à l'Université Catholique de Lille)." *Mélanges de Sciences Religieuses* 54, no. 3 (1997): 37–56.
Robbins, Joel. "Continuity Thinking and the Problem of Christian Culture: Belief, Time, and the Anthropology of Christianity." *Current Anthropology* 48, no. 1 (2007): 5–38.
Robcis, Camille. *The Law of Kinship: Anthropology, Psychoanalysis, and the Family in France*. Ithaca, NY: Cornell University Press, 2013.
Robert, Kpwang K. "La Résistance Des Ekang Du Sud-Cameroun Face Aux Chefs Supérieurs Imposés Par l'administration Coloniale Française: De l'avènement Des 'Présidents Claniques' à La Création de l'Efulameoñ (1920–1948)." In *La Cheffrie "Traditionnelle" Dans Les Socitétés de La Grande Zone Forestière Du Sud-Cameroun (1850–2010)*, edited by Kpwang K. Robert, 235–55. Paris et Cameroun: L'Harmattan, 2011.
———. "Les Bulu de La Subdivision de Kribi Face Aux Méthodes Musclées Des Chefs Des Groupements Bulu-Centre (Ebemvok) et Bulu-Sud (Zingui) (1920–1944)." In *La Cheffrie "Traditionnelle" Dans Les Socitétés de La Grande Zone Forestière Du Sud-Cameroun (1850–2010)*, edited by Kpwang K. Robert, 139–69. Paris et Cameroun: L'Harmattan, 2011.
Robert, Kpwang K., and Samah Tondji Walters. "Invention of Tradition: Chieftaincy, Adaptation and Change in the Forest Region of Cameroon." In *La Cheffrie "Traditionnelle" Dans Les Socitétés de La Grande Zone Forestière Du Sud-Cameroun (1850–2010)*, edited by Kpwang K. Robert, 71–84. Paris et Cameroun: L'Harmattan, 2011.
Roberts, Richard. *Litigants and Households: African Disputes and Colonial Courts in the French Soudan, 1895–1912*. Portsmouth, NH: Heinemann, 2005.
Roberts, Richard, and William Worger. "Law, Colonialism, and Conflicts Over Property in Sub-Saharan Africa." *African Economic History* 25 (1997): 1–7.
Robineau, Marcel. "La Lèpre Dans La Circonscription d'Ebolowa." *Bulletins de La Société de Pathologie Exotique et de Sa Filiale de l'Ouest Africain* 16 (1923).
———. "Quelques Remarques Cliniques Sur La Lèpre Observées à Ebolowa (Cameroun)." *Bulletins de La Société de Pathologie Exotique et de Sa Filiale de l'Ouest Africain* 16 (1923).
Robinson, David. *Paths of Accommodation: Muslim Societies and French Colonial Authorities in Senegal and Mauritania, 1880–1920*. 1 edition. Athens, OH and Oxford: Ohio University Press, 2000.
Rodet, Marie. "'Under the Guise of Guardianship and Marriage': Mobilizing Juvenile and Female Labor in the Aftermath of Slavery in Kayes, French Soudan, 1900–1939." In *Trafficking in Slavery's Wake: Law and the Experience of Women and Children in Africa*, edited by Richard L. Roberts and Benjamin Lawrance, 86–100. Athens, OH: Ohio University Press, 2012.
———. "'I Ask for Divorce Because My Husband Does Not Let Me Go Back to My Country of Origin with My Brother': Gender, Family, and the End of Slavery in the Region of Kayes, French Soudan (1890–1920)." In *Sex, Power, and Slavery*, edited by Gwyn

Campbell and Elizabeth Elbourne, 182–202. Athens, OH: Ohio University Press, 2014.

———. "'Le Délit d'abandon de Domicile Conjugal' Ou l'invasion Du Pénal Colonial Dans Les Jugements Des 'Tribunaux Indigènes' Au Soudan Français, 1900–1947." *French Colonial History* 10 (2009): 151–69.

Roitman, Janet. *Fiscal Disobedience: An Anthropology of Economic Regulation in Central Africa*. Princeton, NJ: Princeton University Press, 2004.

Rosny, Eric de. *Les Yeux de Ma Chèvre: Sur Les Pas Des Maîtres de La Nuit En Pays Douala*. Paris: Plon, 1981.

Rossier, Sophie. *La Flamme Sous La Cendre*. Geneva: Coédition Ouvertures et la Croix-Bleue, 2007.

Rush, Ormond. *The Eyes of Faith: The Sense of the Faithful and the Church's Reception of Revelation*. Reprint edition. Washington, DC: The Catholic University of America Press, 2016.

Saada, Emmanuelle. *Empire's Children: Race, Filiation, and Citizenship in the French Colonies*. Chicago: University of Chicago Press, 2012.

Sanneh, Lamin. *Whose Religion Is Christianity?: The Gospel Beyond the West*. Grand Rapids, MI: William B. Eerdmans Publishing, 2003.

Sappia, Caroline, and Olivier Servais. *Mission et engagement politique après 1945: Afrique, Amérique latine, Europe*. Paris: Karthala, 2010.

Sarraut, Albert. *La Mise En Valeur Des Colonies Francaises*. Paris: Payot & Compagnie, 1923.

Schaffner, Hans. *Im Dienst an Menschen Und Völkern: Das Blaue Kreuz, Ein Missions- Und Liebeswerl von Weltweiter Bedeutung*. Bern: Blaukreuzverlag, 1958.

Schler, Lynn. "Ambiguous Spaces: The Struggle Over African Identites and Urban Communities in Colonial Douala, 1914–1945." *Journal of African History* 44, no. 1 (2003): 51–72.

———. "Bridewealth, Guns and Other Status Symbols: Immigration and Consumption in Colonial Douala." *Journal of African Cultural Studies* 16, no. 2 (December 1, 2003): 213–34.

———. "Looking through a Glass of Beer: Alcohol in the Cultural Spaces of Colonial Douala, 1910–1945." *International Journal of African Historical Studies* 35, no. 2–3 (2002): 315–34.

———. *The Strangers of New Bell: Immigration, Public Space and Community in Colonial Douala, Cameroon, 1914–1960*. Pretoria: Unisa Press, University of South Africa, 2008.

Schoenbrun, David L. "Conjuring the Modern in Africa: Durability and Rupture in Histories of Public Healing between the Great Lakes of East Africa." *The American Historical Review* 111, no. 5 (2006): 1403–39.

Schulte-Varendorff, Uwe. *Krieg in Kamerun: Die Deutsche Kolonie Im Ersten Weltkrieg*. 1. Aufl. Schlaglichter Der Kolonialgeschichte, Band 13. Berlin: Ch. Links Verlag, 2011.

Schwarz, Leonard John. *Cocoa in the Cameroons under French Mandate and in Fernando Po*. United States. Bureau of Foreign and Domestic Commerce. Trade Promotion Series, no. 148. Washington, DC: U.S. Govt. Printing Office, 1933.

Singh, Daleep. *Francophone Africa, 1905–2005: A Century of Economic and Social Change*. Delhi: Allied Publishers, 2008.

Skolaster, Hermann. *Die Pallottiner in Kamerun; 25 Jahre Missionsarbeit.* Limburg/Lahn: Kongregation der Pallottiner, 1924.

Slageren, Jaap Van. *Origines de l'Eglise Evangélique du Caméroun.* Leiden: Brill Archive, 1972.

Smith, Etienne. "Merging Ethnic Histories in Senegal: Whose Moral Community?" In *Recasting the Past: History Writing and Political Work in Modern Africa*, edited by Derek Peterson and Giacomo Macola, 213–32. Athens, OH: Ohio University Press, 2009.

Société africaine de culture. "Civilisation noire et Église catholique : colloque d'Abidjan, 12–17 septembre 1977." Paris: Présence africaine, 1978.

Stoler, Ann Laura. *Carnal Knowledge and Imperial Power: Race and the Intimate in Colonial Rule.* Berkeley, CA: University of California Press, 2002.

Suaud, Charles, and Nathalie Viet-Depaule. *Prêtres et Ouvriers: Une Double Fidélité Mise à l'épreuve, 1944–1969.* Paris: Karthala, 2004.

Sundkler, Bengt, and Christopher Steed. *A History of the Church in Africa.* Cambridge: Cambridge University Press, 2000.

Surkis, Judith. *Sexing the Citizen: Morality and Masculinity in France, 1870–1920.* Ithaca, NY: Cornell University Press, 2006.

Tabi, Isidore. "Cameroun Terre Mariale: Les Sanctuaires et Centres de Pélerinage Marial du Cameroun." Manuscript en l'honneur et Souvenir de l'arrivé de S.S. Jean Paul II au Cameroun. Ndonko, Cameroun, 1995.

———. *La Theologie Des Rites Beti: Essai d'explication Religieuse Des Rites Beti et Ses Implications Socio-Culturelles.* Yaoundé, Cameroon: Éditions St. Paul, 1991.

———. *Les Rites Beti Au Christ. Essai de Pastorale Liturgique Sur Quelques Rites de Nos Ancêtres.* Yaoundé: Imprimerie Saint-Paul, 1991.

Tambiah, Stanley J., Mitzi Goheen, Jane I. Guyer, Emilie A. Olson, Charles Piot, Klaas Van Der Veen, and Trudeke Vuyk. "Bridewealth and Dowry Revisited : The Position of Women in Sub-Saharan Africa and North India." *Current Anthropology* 30, no. 4 (1989): 413–35.

Tandafor, Mirabel Azangeh. "Marial Sanctuary in Mvolye Becomes Minor Basilica." *L'Effort Camerounais.* April 30, 2006.

Tardits, Claude. *Contribution à l'étude Des Populations Bamiléké de l'Ouest Cameroun.* L'Homme d'Outre-Mer 4. Paris: Berger-Levrault, 1960.

Tetouom, Abraham. "La polygamie et le Christianisme au pays Bamiléké." Licence de théologie, Faculté libre de théologie protestante, 1966.

Thé, Marie-Paule Bochet de. "La Femme Dans La Dynamique de La Société Bëti, 1887–1966." Thèse de 3e cycle, Univeristé de la Sorbonne (Paris V), 1970.

———. "Rites et associations traditionnelles chez les femmes bëti (sud du Cameroun)." In *Femmes du Cameroun: mères pacifiques, femmes rebelles*, 245–76. Paris: Karthala, 1985.

Thomas, Lynn M. *Politics of the Womb: Women, Reproduction, and the State in Kenya.* 1 edition. Berkeley, CA: University of California Press, 2003.

Through Swamp and Forest: The British Campaigns in Africa. London: Harrison, Jehring, 1917.

Tiandong, Jean-Henri. *L'autobiographie Du Pasteur Jean-Henri Tiandong de l'E.E.C.* Douala: Douala, S.N., 1973.

Tonme, Jean-Claude Shanda. *La France a-t-elle commis un génocide au Cameroun ?: Les Bamiléké accusent*. Paris: L'Harmattan, 2009.

Tracey, Andrew, and Gei Zantzinger. *Mbira: Njari, Simon Mashoko's Traditional and Church Music*. Documentary. International Library of African Music and University Museum, University of Pennsylvania, 1975.

Turpin, Frédéric. "Le Mouvement Républicain Populaire et l'avenir de l'Algérie (1947–1962)." *Revue d'histoire Diplomatique* 2 (1999): 171–203.

"Un Beau Mariage sans Dot." *Laiccam: Bulletin Trimestriel de Liaison Pour La Formation d'un Laicat d'Action Catholique Au Cameroun*, mai 1962.

Van de Velde, Mark L.O. *A Grammar of Eton*. Berlin: Mouton de Gruyter, 2008.

Van Onselen, Charles. *Chibaro: African Mine Labour in Southern Rhodesia, 1900–1933*. London: Pluto Press, 1976.

Van Slageren, Jaap. *Les Origines de l'eglise Évangélique Du Cameroun: Missions Européennes et Christianisme Autochtone*. Leiden: Brill, 1972.

Vandercook, John W. "The French Mandate of Cameroun." *National Geographic Magazine* LIX, no. 2 (1931): 225–60.

Vansina, Jan. *Paths in the Rainforests. Toward a History of Political Tradition in Equatorial Africa*. Madison, WI: University of Wisconsin Press, 1990.

Vicariat de Doumé. "Lumière Vers l'Est." *Le Cameroun Catholique*, June 15, 1950.

Viers, Georges. "Le cacao dans le monde." *Cahiers d'outre-mer* 6, no. 24 (1953): 297–351.

Vincent, Jeanne-Françoise. *Femmes Beti Entre Deux Mondes: Entretiens Dans La Forêt Du Cameroun*. Paris: Karthala, 2001.

Viswanathan, Gauri. *Outside the Fold – Conversion, Modernity, and Belief*. Princeton, NJ: Princeton University Press, 1998.

Von Morgen, Curt. *A Travers Le Cameroun Du Sud Au Nord: Voyages et Explorations Dans l'Arrière Pays de 1889 à 1891*. Translated by Philippe Laburthe-Tolra. Publications de la Sorbonne. Série: Afrique 7. Paris: Serge Fleury, 1982.

Walker, Charlotte. "Legal Revolutions and Evolutions: Law, Chiefs, and Colonial Order in Cameroon, 1914–1955." Ph.D. Dissertation, Yale University, 2009.

———. "The Trafficking and Slavery of Women and Girls: The Criminalization of Marriage, Tradition, and Gender Norms in French Colonial Cameroon, 1914–1945." In *Sex Trafficking, Human Rights, and Social Justice*, edited by Tiantian Zheng, 150–69. New York: Routledge, 2010.

Walker-Said, Charlotte. "Christian Social Movements in Cameroon at the End of Empire: Transnational Solidarities and the Communion of the World Church." In *Relocating World Christianity: Interdisciplinary Studies in Universal and Local Expressions of Christianity*, edited by Joel Cabrita, Emma Wild-Wood, and David Maxwell. Boston, MA: Brill, 2017.

Weber, Hyman L. *Do Missions Pay?: The Story of Dr. J. Bulla Mfum*, 1956.

Wellesz, Egon. "Words and Music in Byzantine Liturgy." *The Musical Quarterly* 33, no. 3 (1947): 297–310.

Wetzer, Heinrich Joseph, Benedikt Welte, and Isidore Goschler. *Dictionnaire Encyclopédique de La Théologie Catholique*. Paris: Gaume Frères et J. Duprey, 1865.

Wheeler, W.R. *The Tribe of God in Africa*. New York: Board of Foreign Missions of the Presbyterian Church in the U.S.A., 1929.

White, Luise. "Separating the Men from the Boys: Constructions of Gender, Sexuality, and Terrorism in Central Kenya, 1939–1959." *International Journal of African Historical Studies* 23, no. 1 (1990): 1–25.

Wilbois, Joseph. *L'Action Sociale En Pays de Missions*. Paris: Payot, 1938.

———. *Le Cameroun: Les Indigènes-Les Colons-Les Missions-l'administration Française*. Paris: Payot, 1934.

Wilson, Kathleen. "Rethinking the Colonial State: Family, Gender, and Governmentality in Eighteenth-Century British Frontiers." *The American Historical Review* 116, no. 5 (December 1, 2011): 1294–1322.

Wirz, Albert. "La 'Rivière Du Cameroun': Commerce Précolonial et Contrôle Du Pouvoir En Société Lignagère." *Revue Française d'Histoire d'Outre-Mer*, no. 60 (1973): 172–95.

Wonyu, Eugene. *Le Chrétien, Les Dons et La Mission Dans l'Eglise Africaine Independente: Réflexions d'un Laïc*. Douala: Eglise Protestante Camerounaise (BP 5421), 1979.

Yetna, Jean-Pierre. "Les Bassa et Mpoo Du Cameroun à La Recherche de l'unité Perdue." *Anthropos* 97, no. 2 (January 1, 2002): 551–52.

Zéba, Claude. "L'Eglise Dit Adieu à l'Abbé Benoît Bell Bayamack." *L'Effort Camerounais*, November 14, 2007.

Zenker, Georg, and Philippe Laburthe-Tolra. *Yaoundé, d'après Zenker (1895): le plan de 1892*. Extrait des Annales de la Faculté des Lettres et Sciences Humaines de Yaoundé. 2. Yaoundé, Cameroon, 1970.

Zoa, Jean. "La Dot Dans Les Territoires d'Afrique." In *Femmes Africaines; Témoignages de Femmes Du Cameroun, Du Congo Belge, Du Congo Français, de La Côte-d'Ivoire, Du Dahomey, Du Ghana, de La Guinéa, de La Haute-Voita, Du Nigéria, Du Togo, Réunies à Lome Par l'Union Mondiale Des Organisations Féminines Catholiques, 1958*, edited by l'Union mondiale des organisations feminines catholiques, 53–71. Paris: Editions du Centurion, 1959.

———. "Les Chrétiens et La Communauté Nationale." *Nova et Vetera* 1 (1960): 12–14.

———. *Pour un nationalisme chrétien au Cameroun*. Yaoundé: Imprimerie Saint-Paul, 1957.

Index

Ad Lucem, 272, 273
adultery, 95, 123, 124, 203, 244, 245, 246, 252, 262, 269
agriculture, 13, 44, 173–9, 214, 223, 252–3
alcohol: consumption, 203, 204, 210, 227, 249, 262; religious prohibitions of, 95, 147, 199, 201–5, 241, 249
Akonolinga, 14, 58, 61, 62, 64, 167, 174, 192, 219, 224, 252, 262
Allégret, Elie, 57, 65, 66, 74, 75, 94, 99, 105, 106, 235
American Presbyterian Church: mission, xxi, 3n7, 21, 22, 24, 60–2, 65, 67, 69, 70, 73, 77, 82, 88, 94, 103, 110, 127, 129, 156, 165, 167, 168, 180, 183, 186, 197, 205, 216, 220, 235, 246, 248, 275, 280; schools, 146; cooperative, 175
Anabaptists, 33, 94
arrests, of catechists, 46, 59, 62, 67, 68, 69, 129, 132, 192, 216, 217, 218, 225, 226, 230, 231; of worksite deserters, 187, 222
Aoué, Jean-Oscar, 180, 195
A Samé, Lotin, 3n6, 56n18
Aujoulat, Louis-Paul, 272
Azeufack, Philippe, 46, 80, 159, 160

Bala, Athanase, 25n84, 89, 160, 215n25,
Bamileke societies, 13, 17n51, 19n61, 39, 55, 56, 83, 124, 125, 155, 160n96, 180, 185, 251, 258–61, 264
Bamoun Protestant Church, 54
Bamoun society, 13, 39, 55, 56, 92, 110, 124, 163, 168, 180, 227, 259, 260, 261,
Banen society, 13, 82, 83, 100, 105, 168, 182n44, 218, 249, 263

Baptist: churches, 22, 26n86, 39, 54n3, 55–7, 62, 77, 153–4, 164–6, 180, 200–1, 220–1, 279; missionaries and catechists, 75, 77, 79, 81, 100, 108, 109, 161, 186, 217
Baptism, 6n17, 11, 25, 26, 54, 59, 84, 86, 92–5, 106, 109, 114, 131, 153, 159, 166, 183, 189, 233, 234, 268
Basel Mission, 21, 55, 56, 57, 103
Bassa society, 13, 15, 39, 55, 56, 70, 82, 83, 85, 93–5, 109, 110, 111, 126n126, 161, 162, 163, 167, 168, 178, 182n44, 185, 186, 191, 205, 250, 268
Beanland, Cavin, 66, 69
Beti, Mongo, 22
Beti societies, 13–26, 38, 48, 68, 75, 79, 80, 82–91, 98, 102n4, 109–24, 147–58, 182–95, 245, 249, 251
Bible: translation of, 7, 56, 182; use and teaching of, 147, 235
Bible readers, 94–6
birth rates, 101, 130, 131, 203, 244n25, 262
Bonneau, Pierre, 272
Bonnecarrère, Paul, 42, 137, 138, 214, 216, 217, 219, 256, 257
Boury, Charles, 220
Brévié, Jules, 134–5
bridewealth: criticism of, 106, 111–12, 127, 148–9, 158, 194, 231, 243; in court cases, 195–6, 244–50; inflation, 26, 102, 118, 121, 250, 253; practice of, 4, 35, 44, 45, 74, 93, 107–8, 115–16, 128, 132–3, 147, 151–4, 254–62, 264–9; regulation of by the colonial government, 134, 137, 138, 142, 232, 240, 263; use

310 INDEX

in Christian conversion, 197, 200, 227–8, 250
Brun, Marcel, 222, 225, 235
Bulu society, 13, 14n42, 15–16, 19n59, 39, 44n144, 61, 79, 82–9, 95, 98, 110–11, 116–121, 129, 147, 155–6, 165–7, 175, 178, 181–5, 190, 223, 250, 251, 258, 265, 285, 291, 295,

Carde, Jules, 101, 103, 130, 134, 135, 137, 233
cash-crop cultivation, 14, 67, 118, 122, 123, 127n133, 133, 138, 173–5, 178, 194, 223, 247–51, 253n61
Casti Connubi, 238, 239, 243, 275n19
catechism, 20, 25, 26, 43, 60, 68, 69, 81, 85, 91, 93, 96, 114, 128, 132, 147, 160, 167, 168, 177, 182, 183, 188, 194, 201, 207, 233,
Catholics, 3, 6, 8, 24, 41–3, 48, 54–60, 64, 77, 81, 94n84, 100, 104, 126n126, 151, 152, 161, 168, 179, 186, 194, 199, 213, 228, 237–52, 260, 269–79
Catholic Action, 271–4
Cameroun Catholique, 111, 43n142
cercles, 271, 273
chiefs: appointment and recruitment of forced labor, 13–15, 18, 30, 42, 43, 45, 61, 63, 64, 71, 101–5, 115–120, 149, 173, 175n10, 176–9, 209–52; criticism of, 27, 31–7, 46, 66–9, 73–82, 96–8, 106, 185–91, 207, 26–69, 280; conversion of, 164, 167; wives, 19, 44n144, 66, 73–82, 107–14, 120–39, 159, 195–7, 252–4 ; prior to French colonialism, 16, 17, 54, 65
child marriage, 111, 118,124, 137, 228, 233
children, as productive resources, 8, 17, 19, 102, 115, 120, 121–4, 143, 147, 153, 154, 155, 201, 203; bridewealth payments for, 106, 107, 112, 120 , 231, 247, 255; conversions of, 91, 99, 114, 149, 156, 157, 160, 162, 166, 212, 228, 246; conversions by, 11, 129; forced labor of, 14, 18, 30, 74, 206, 209, 216, 221, 230; prohibitions on for priests,

25; struggles over, 230, 237, 238, 255, 256, 259, 265–7, 269
commandement indigène, 11, 63, 64, 69, 70, 97, 136, 210, 211, 223, 225
Compagnie forestière Sangha-Oubangui, 29n99, 210
Copet-Rougier, Elisabeth, 116
civilization ideology, 21, 28, 104, 113n59, 114, 142n4, 143, 160n96
civil code, 137n184
cocoa cultivation, 13, 14n42, 30n102, 44, 71, 116, 117, 127n133, 128, 153, 173, 174, 175, 179, 185, 222–6, 248–53
concubinage, 121, 238, 241, 256
confession, 1, 43, 54, 55n9, 57, 58, 68, 87–93, 106, 166, 190, 191, 192–3, 213, 234, 268
confraternal organizations, 44, 45, 112, 187, 190–9, 206, 212, 213, 230–3, 243, 267, 268, 278
confrérie, 45, 187, 190, 191–8, 202, 228, 268, 271, 273
Congregation of the Holy Ghost, 60, 106, 111, 129, 132n163, 141–6, 153, 157, 165n124, 182n44, 219, 220, 221, 242
concessionary system, 14, 18, 27, 29, 30, 34, 69, 70, 71, 117, 118, 203, 204, 211, 213, 215, 223
coffee cultivation, 13, 44n143, 177n81, 173, 174, 226, 248, 251, 259n95
Cooper, Frederick, 277, 278
cotton cultivation, 174
councils of notables, 45n146, 135, 176, 181n43, 211, 267
Council of Trent, 152, 260
courts, 14, 33, 99, 114, 129, 133, 137, 190, 195, 224, 227–33, 244, 252, 258–9, 262–4, 267, 269, 281
Criaud, Jean, 166, 167
Croix Bleue, 201–6, 273
customary law, 31, 35, 113, 135–8, 144, 228, 233, 235, 256, 258, 261, 262, 265, 269, 281.

deacons, 149
deaconesses, 25
Delavignette, Robert, 101, 103

de Maupeou, 168, 231, 232, 280
de Pury, Roland, 145
Din Jacob, Modi, 56
diseases, 65, 72, 73, 203, 204n150, 211
  see also various diseases by name
divorce, 26, 113, 114, 128–34, 137, 138, 150, 151, 200, 203–6, 228, 240, 243–5, 250, 257–8, 262–3, 266–9
Douala: city, ix, 58, 59, 66, 77, 81, 92, 93, 104, 108, 187, 195, 200, 201, 202, 204, 229, 249, 250, 273; region, 12–15, 21, 56, 64, 70, 118, 121, 124, 216, 217, 269; Vicariate, 34, 76, 130, 178, 179, 180, 186, 197, 220–1, 247, 279
Doumé, 13, 14, 58, 59, 67, 69, 92, 168, 173, 180, 225, 233, 252
Douvry, Jules, 54, 59
Drum Call, 110
drumming, 86, 225
Duala society, 39, 41n139, 48, 55–6, 82–6, 97, 110–11, 120, 124, 149, 150, 152–7, 168, 178, 183, 202, 255
Dugast, Idelette, 263

Ebolowa, 13, 14, 44, 61, 62, 64, 69, 73, 75, 92, 116, 122, 129, 130, 147, 165, 173, 175, 178, 180, 185, 191, 192, 216, 223, 224, 225, 253, 263
Eboussi-Boulaga, Fabien, 10
education, 36, 47, 98, 115, 145, 155, 156, 181, 273, 274; religious, 80, 95, 109, 131, 133, 147, 154, 161, 165, 183; women's 241, 242
Elat, 62, 82, 90, 91, 94, 95, 110, 147
Enyegue, Jean-Luc, xii, 37, 89, 164
état civil, 115, 124, 131, 185, 249, 250, 256, 257
Etoga, Paul, 25n84, 60, 160, 161, 189, 274
Eucharist: veneration of, 91,188n73, 190, 192; sacrament of, 6n17, 87, 90, 94n86, 153, 191
Ewondo society, 14, 60, 68, 70, 79, 81n8, 86, 89, 90, 91, 92, 93, 95, 111, 116n77, 117, 125, 126, 156, 168, 178, 186, 191, 193, 197, 213, 268

famine, 8, 70, 74

Farelly, Maurice, 75, 100, 105, 166, 217, 220, 246, 257, 280.
feast days, 106, 175n10, 204, 212, 268, 279
feasting, 68, 190
Fernando Po, 3n6, 53, 54n3, 55, 58, 65, 67
fertility, ix, 20, 102, 120, 203, 257, 265, 266
Fields, Karen, 32, 33
friars, x, 25, 76, 166, 279
forced labor, 8, 15n44, 18n59, 26, 27, 30, 45, 99, 132, 187, 206, 210, 211, 215, 221, 230, 277; rationale for, 5n11, ; *mise en valeur,* 5n11, 42, 45n146, 101, 183n43
Fraternal Lutheran Church, 21, 22, 77, 180, 221
French Equatorial Africa, 7n18, 15n44, 18n58, 20, 22–4, 27, 114, 120n96, 206n155, 237, 277
French mandate administration, 20, 21, 27, 28, 29, 30, 33, 34, 47, 60, 69, 75, 101, 113, 115, 132, 133, 177, 219, 228, 233, 234, 256, 282
French Protestant Mission, *see Paris Evangelical Missionary Society*
Foster, Elizabeth, 8, 9n27, 49n158, 104, 105n19, 143
Fouda, Antoine Essomba, 5
Fouda, Zogo, 114, 116
Fourneau, Lucien, 34, 55, 62, 66, 67, 90, 104

Gbaya society, 9n28, 14, 15, 16, 115
Geschiere, Peter, 10, 16n46, 117, 247, 253, 254
German administration of Cameroon, 3, 6, 19, 21, 28, 53–7, 59, 60–5, 81, 115
Gospels, 57, 91, 189, 195n111, 199
Graffin, René, 143, 165, 166, 178, 180, 215, 230, 247, 256, 272
Grassfields region, 19n61, 79, 80, 81
Gray, Christopher, 23
groundnut cultivation, 13, 173, 174, 179, 223
Guyer, Jane, 120

INDEX

Hoffman, Danny, 35, 91, 92
Horton, Robin, 5

identity cards, 69, 71
imprisonment, 11, 30, 53, 54, 55, 56, 58, 59, 68, 69, 132, 138, 192, 195, 215, 216, 218, 227, 229, 230, 231, 252, 258
Indigénat, 30, 31n104, 45, 68, 102, 245
Infertility, 73, 102, 130, 203 *see also* Fertility
Itondo, Duala, 56, 213, 280
individualism, 31, 46, 90, 119, 142, 148, 160, 163, 164, 185, 213, 230, 249, 269

Jocky, Paul, 26n86, 80, 111, 280
Johnson-Hanks, Jennifer, 17

Keller, Jean, 77, 275
Kribi, 13, 14, 58, 77, 94, 174, 175, 178, 179, 180, 185, 187, 193, 196, 219, 225, 268

labor code, 14, 15n44, 22, 45n146, 71, 73n121, 115, 182n43
Laburthe-Tolra, Philippe, 20, 41n139, 42, 48, 80, 82, 83, 84, 98, 122, 158
Last Supper Service (*Culte de Sainte Cène*), 149, 183
League of Nations, 18, 20, 27, 28n90, 42, 72, 132, 174, 215, 219, 224, 230, 253, 282
Le Mailloux, Mathurin, 96, 179, 237
Le Roy, Alexandre, 77, 131
lineage, as family structure, 8, 15–19, 23, 106–7, 115, 117–120, 141, 152, 156, 184, 187, 278, 281; as religious network, 11, 12, 25, 27, 33, 36, 41, 43, 85, 141, 143, 160, 161–3, 166, 266, 273, 274, 277; and marriage, 7, 49, 154, 155, 158, 254, 269, 270
Livingston, Julie, 10

Mallo, Eugene, 122, 123, 125
Maka society, 9, 14, 15, 16, 17, 58, 115–19, 155
Mamdani, Mahmood, 31, 264n125

Marchand, Theodore Paul, 42, 66, 70–2, 103, 104, 114, 177, 210, 214–19, 235, 254n66
masculinity, 31, 35, 36, 84, 97, 123, 125, 141, 143n8, 148, 150, 152, 201, 229, 237, 243, 266, 281
Mbembe, Achille, 7, 12, 13, 24, 96, 123, 184
Messi, Léon, 150, 166, 266
Messina, Jean-Paul, 37, 85n35
Minlaba mission, 59, 66, 75, 93, 129, 178–80, 192, 209, 210, 211, 223
Mongo, Thomas, 275
monogamy, 113, 114, 119, 120, 127, 152, 153, 156, 214, 265, 266
Moyen Congo, 72, 165, 237
Mpeke, Simon, 107, 180, 182, 189, 194
music: sacred music, 38, 85n34, 86n39; religious song, 9, 79, 84n28, 110, 192; folk song, 117n79, 149
Mveng, Engelbert, ix, 8, 37, 84
Mvondo, Edjoa, 116, 176

Native Baptist Church, 6n17, 21, 24, 55, 56n18
Nkwe, George, 55
Nleb Bekristen, 111, 43n142
Nicol, Yves, 113, 125
nkap, 124, 125
Nord, Philip, 143
Norwegian Lutheran Church, 104, 221
nuns, African, 25, 39, 46, 191, 197, 250

Ombolo, Jean-Pierre, 38, 123n109, 266
Ottou, Pius, 3n6, 59, 90, 129,

Pallottine Mission, 21, 58, 59, 69, 131, 161, 163, 182n44, 193,
palm cultivation, 13, 63, 71, 85, 122, 128, 173–5, 177, 179, 185, 203–4, 210, 219, 223, 226, 251, 253, 262.
Paris Evangelical Missionary Society (SMEP), 6n17, 24, 81, 110, 168, 180, 183, 275, 279–80.
pastors, American and European, 85, 88, 95, 97, 99–100, 144, 145, 166, 201, 217, 220, 221, 222, 225, 235, 246, 257;

African, 25–7, 33, 39, 46, 55, 56, 80, 82, 94, 105, 110, 111, 122, 125, 126, 141, 147–9, 158, 161–8, 180, 183, 186, 200–6, 213, 255, 260–61, 275, 279, 280
Peel, J.D.Y., 27, 32, 266n131
penance, *see Confession, see also Reconciliation*
Permanent Mandates Commission, 20, 113, 253
Peterson, Derek, 10, 11, 33n112, 90
Pichon, François, 64, 143, 206, 209, 201, 222, 233, 234, 280
pidgin, 131
Pius XI, 181, 237, 238
police: French, 18, 36, 62, 67, 69, 178, 213, 218, 220, 222, 231, 233, 234, 280; indigenous auxiliary police, 14, 30, 42, 45n146, 100, 102, 209–10, 225–6, 244
polygamy: criticism of, 34, 37, 88, 101, 102, 103, 106, 112–14, 122, 125, 127, 134, 148, 158, 197, 211, 241, 242, 243, 263, 266, 273; practice of, 35, 119, 130–1, 153, 282; reforms to, 8n24, 128, 129, 133, 147, 150, 206, 228, 250, 259
porterage, 67, 72, 261
priests, African, 25–7, 33, 39, 46, 77, 80, 109, 150, 158, 160–6, 180–2, 197, 205, 206, 212, 230, 248, 266; European, 1, 21, 55, 59, 66, 69, 75, 76, 81, 87, 88–90, 97, 100, 105, 109, 110, 122, 132, 133, 141, 143, 153, 154, 179, 186–9, 191, 193, 196, 199, 209, 216, 217, 220–2, 227, 230–4, 245, 247, 270, 272, 278, 279, 280
Priests of the Sacred Heart of Saint Quentin, 21, 76, 80, 126, 141, 146, 159, 162, 220
prisoners of war, 54, 55, 58
Presbyterian Church elders, 25, 56, 77, 94, 141, 165
Presbyterian Church in the U.S.A., *see American Presbyterian Church*
press: secular and public, 248; confessional, 36, 70, 109–12, 149, 199
prostitution, 112, 200, 202, 203, 238, 239, 241, 244

public works: expansion of, 15, 30, 75, 177, 222, 234, 222, 223, 253 ; labor for, 18n58, 118, 121, 176, 179, 210

railroads, xvi, 13–15, 18, 30, 33, 66–75, 92–6, 109, 115–18, 121, 175, 177, 185–7, 192, 195, 206, 211, 221–5
reconciliation, 1, 89, 93, 159
Repiquet, Jules, 273
reproduction, biological, 11, 20, 73, 123, 153, 266, 276; social, 115
resettlement, 61, 64, 71
rice cultivation, 70, 74, 175, 177, 223
roads, xvi, 13, 15, 61, 64, 66, 67, 70, 72, 74, 75, 92, 94, 96, 117, 118, 121, 175, 178, 179, 185, 186, 209, 218, 219, 222–5, 248
Robineau, Marcel, 73

sacraments, 1, 4, 7, 11, 26, 37, 39, 43, 54, 87, 89, 90, 93, 105, 108, 129, 139, 151, 153, 197, 213, 220, 233, 246, 256, 268, 279, 283
Sacred Congregation of the Propaganda Fide, 63, 130, 179, 212
Sangmélima, 14, 61, 62, 72, 73, 130, 175, 184, 185, 187, 192, 211, 223, 225, 237
Sarraut, Albert, 5n11, 61, 101, 103
Schler, Lynn, 249
seminary, 160, 162, 165, 181
Senegal, 8, 104, 105, 199, 242
sex work, *see prostitution*
sixa, 131–3, 159, 163, 166, 193, 196, 211, 219, 220, 228, 230, 231, 232, 233, 241, 258
sleeping sickness, 72, 73, 187, 204n150, 225
Soeurs Servantes de Marie, 161
Spanish Guinea, *see Fernando Po*
Spiritans, *see* Congregation of the Holy Ghost
St. Ottilien Abbey, 58, 84
Surkis, Judith, 142
Swiss Congregation of the Benedictine Confederation, 165, 181
syphilis, 72, 73, 102, 130–2

taxation, 13, 27, 30, 33, 71, 74, 99, 102, 117, 119, 126, 127, 131, 153, 175, 181, 223, refusal to pay, 35, 64, 67, 69, 138, 185, 187, 204, 214, 222, 254
terroir, 12, 13, 183–7, 222
Tiandong. Jean-Henri, 203–5
Tirailleurs, 57, 63, 64
tobacco cultivation, 13, 71, 116, 174, 175, 177, 249
torture, 214, 221, 280
typhoid, 72

Vansina, Jan, 7n18, 22, 23, 27
Vieter, Heinrich, 58n30, 131, 193
Vogt, François-Xavier, 76, 81, 88, 91, 94, 100, 105, 106, 109, 125, 130, 132, 168, 178, 179, 180, 181, 198, 209, 210, 221, 230, 237, 272, 280

wage labor, 36, 71, 73
work permit, 71, 115
World War I, 1, 5, 20, 21, 27, 28, 29, 54–63, 70, 76, 94, 167
World War II, 6, 25, 31, 270, 273, 274, 275, 278–81

Yaoundé, city ix, xii, 13, 14, 59, 61, 62, 70, 74, 82, 215, 218, 221, 238, 244, 250, 258, 262, 264, 273; region, 21, 62, 64, 65, 68, 74, 173, 114, 166, 224, 225; Vicariate of, 34, 76, 94, 106, 130, 147, 168, 179, 198, 220, 245, 247, 274, 279
Yevol Mutual Aid Society, 175

Zamcho Anyeh, John the Baptist, 67, 81, 266
Zoa, Jean, 129, 147, 151

Previously published titles in the series

Violent Conversion: Brazilian Pentecostalism and Urban Women in Mozambique, Linda Van de Kamp (2016)

Beyond Religious Tolerance: Muslim, Christian and Traditionalist Encounters in an African Town, edited by Insa Nolte, Olukoya Ogen and Rebecca Jones (2017)

Faith, Power and Family: Christianity and Social Change in French Cameroon, Charlotte Walker-Said (2018)

Contesting Catholics: Benedicto Kiwanuka and the Birth of Postcolonial Uganda, Jonathon L. Earle, J. J. Carney (2021)

Islamic Scholarship in Africa: New Directions and Global Contexts, edited by Ousmane Oumar Kane (2021)

From Rebels to Rulers: Writing Legitimacy in the Early Sokoto State, Paul Naylor (2021)

Sacred Queer Stories: Ugandan LGBTQ+ Refugee Lives and the Bible, Adriaan van Klinken, Johanna Stiebert, Sebyala Brian and Fredrick Hudson (2021)

Labour and Christianity in the Mission: African Workers in Tanganyika and Zanzibar, 1864–1926, Michelle Liebst (2021)

The Genocide against the Tutsi, and the Rwandan Churches: Between Grief and Denial, Philippe Denis (2022)

Competing Catholicisms: The Jesuits, the Vatican and the Making of Postcolonial French Africa, Jean Luc Enyegue, SJ (2022)

www.ingramcontent.com/pod-product-compliance
Lightning Source LLC
Chambersburg PA
CBHW051558230426
43668CB00013B/1898